DATE DUE

DEC - 6 2006		
~~University~~		
~~of British Columbia~~		
~~June 14/11~~		

Brodart Co. Cat. # 55 137 001 Printed in USA

GREATER IRAN

GREATER IRAN

A 20th-Century Odyssey

Richard N. Frye

MAZDA PUBLISHERS, Inc. ◆ Costa Mesa, California ◆ 2005

Mazda Publishers, Inc.
Academic Publishers since 1980
P.O. Box 2603, Costa Mesa, California 92628 U.S.A.
www.mazdapub.com

Copyright © 2005 by R.N. Frye
All rights reserved. No parts of this publication may be reproduced or transmitted by any form or by any means without written permission from the publisher except in the case of brief quotations embodied in critical articles and reviews.

Library of Congress Cataloging-in-Publication Data
Frye, Richard Nelson, 1920-
Greater Iran: A Twentieth-Century Odyssey/ Richard N. Frye.
p.cm.
Includes index.
ISBN: 1-56859-177-2
(Hard cover, alk. paper)

1. Frye, Richard Nelson, 1920- 2. Historians—United States—Biography. 3. Middle East—Study and teaching—United States—History—20th century. 4. Middle East—History—20th century. I. Title.
DS61.7F79A3 2004
955'.0072'02—dc22 [B]
2004048892

Motifs used in this book are from a Sasanian crown at Taq-e Bostan and a silver bowl from the Parthian period.

CONTENTS

Acknowledgments ix
Preface xi

CHAPTER 1
The Frontier Mail to Peshawar   1

CHAPTER 2
First Envoy to Afghanistan   16

CHAPTER 3
The Road to Kabul   20

CHAPTER 4
Life in Afghanistan   29

CHAPTER 5
Kabul to Cairo   47

CHAPTER 6
Last Days in Kabul   57

CHAPTER 7
Spying in Istanbul   66

CHAPTER 8
1945 in Washington   78

CHAPTER 9
Pre-War Harvard   82

CHAPTER 10
Post-war Harvard 89

CHAPTER 11
With the Aid of the Qashghais 104

CHAPTER 12
Through the Deserts of Iran 111

CHAPTER 13
Back to Afghanistan 130

CHAPTER 14
Dr. Mossadegh and Irandoost 138

CHAPTER 15
Iranian Studies in the USA 146

CHAPTER 16
Breaking Soviet Ice 152

CHAPTER 17
A Year in Germany 172

CHAPTER 18
An Armenian Guidepost 180

CHAPTER 19
Sturm und Drang 185

CHAPTER 20
A Cultural Stay in the USSR 196

CHAPTER 21
Prelude to Change 207

CHAPTER 22
Hamburg Upheavals 215

CHAPTER 23
Shiraz Successes 223

CHAPTER 24
Fading Hopes 230

CHAPTER 25
Life Changes 239

CHAPTER 26
Japanese Idyll 246

CHAPTER 27
Wives and Children 254

CHAPTER 28
Revolutions in Iran and Afghanistan 262

CHAPTER 29
Free Afghanistan and Beyond 269

CHAPTER 30
Two Trips to Western China 275

CHAPTER 31
Retirement 286

CHAPTER 32
A Tajik Interlude 292

CHAPTER 33
Land of the *Zhigitovka* 301

CHAPTER 34
Conferences Galore 305

CHAPTER 35
My Heart Returns to Iran 313

CHAPTER 36
Incident in Isfahan 317

Postscript 323
Photo Section 325
Appendix 355
Index 365

Acknowledgments

This publication has been supported by the following:
The A. K. Jabbari Trust Fund,
The Iranica Institute, Irvine, California,
Ilex Foundation, Boston, Massachusetts, and
Dr. Don Babai.

Preface

Iran's glory always has been its culture. Persian poetry, music, art and architecture were all formed in a vast area much larger than the contemporary country with its capital Tehran. 'Greater Iran' in the past included much of the Caucasus, Afghanistan and Central Asia, with cultural influences extending to China, India and the Semitic speaking world. My life came to be dedicated to portraying and explaining the role of Greater Iran in the history of civilizations. In August 1953, shortly before the overthrow of Dr. Mossadegh, Prime Minister of Iran, I received the sobriquet, or *laqab* as the Arabs call it, of *Irandoost* 'lover of Iran' from a distinguished Persian author and poet, Ali Akbar Dehkhuda. For me Iran meant all lands and peoples where Iranian languages were and are spoken, and where in the past multi-faceted Iranian cultures existed.

An autobiography is the story of one's life, while memoirs, we are told, are more ambiguous than events in a life, including what one heard or witnessed, sometimes of historic interest, but more often of personal situations in which he or she has participated. A story or anecdote, either true or fictitious, may have been heard or even read by the author, and included in either memoirs or autobiography, or even expanded into a work of literature. In the pages which follow I plead guilty to a mixture of autobiography and memoirs, but a lifetime of writing historical prose, much of it accessible to the lay public, has given me a sense of the sweep of 3000 years of the history of 'Greater Iran', and this enters these pages, as well as some of the actors in the cultural and political history of the Middle East and Central Asia. Our paths crossed throughout the physical and intellectual journeys which I made in these areas for more than half a century which saw the transition of the Middle East, Central Asia and the Caucasus from the Medieval era into the uncertain steps of global politics and culture.

I am glad I experienced the British Raj in India before partition, and the cooperation of Jews and Arabs in Palestine before the rise to power of fanatics and extremists on both sides. The end of incipient democracy in Iran with the fall of Mossadegh, and the second revolution and its aftermath, left deep impressions. I witnessed the upheaval in Tajikistan after the dissolution of the Soviet Union, and conflict in southern Ossetia, around its capital Tskhinvali. But this is also an autobiography, so personal encounters also enter into the picture.

Throughout life certain principles have guided my work as an historian, adherence to facts, and interpretations based on logic, simplicity and common sense. Here primarily my aim is to record events both chronologically and topically in the manner of historical writing. In some cases a considerable amount of detail appears, as, for instance, with regard to travel in the Biyabanak, or central deserts of Iran in the 1950s. Time and again, as I read over my diaries, trip reports , and even some long-ago written articles, incidents came to mind which I had quite forgotten. Therefore, especially for the early years of my work in 'Greater Iran', the records I had made as a childhood habit-the keeping of diaries-knitted together the events that have transpired as I witnessed them.

Once time, personal commitments to family, and my professional life ended diary keeping, I began a practice of writing reports on particular conferences and meetings, some of which were published but most not. These reports, together with old appointment books and calendars, all of which like the proverbial church mouse, I kept in boxes and files, have now come to serve as sources for this chronicle of events as I experienced them, and as they relate to 'Greater Iran.' Occasionally I have felt pressed to move along in this story and skip incidents that particular readers may wish to know more about, such as the establishment of the Center for Middle Eastern Studies at Harvard, the expansion of the Asia Institute, reports on national surveys of Middle Eastern Studies in the USA, or even my relationship with various figures in Iran, Afghanistan and Tajikistan. Such readers may benefit from the materials which I have placed in the archives of Harvard University. Also, since trips and residence abroad occupied much of life, some features of a past world, now being rapidly homogenized and globalized, may be of interest to young readers.

To concentrate and penetrate vertically in a subject, while at the same time spreading one's vistas horizontally, to cover the forest as well as analyzing the tree, was advice I constantly gave students. Whether anyone ultimately could be successful in both, always raised a question as well as a challenge. History remained a dominant interest throughout my life, but I believe also in the reverse of the usual aphorism about history, 'to know the past one must also study the present.' To reside, rather than just travel, in a foreign country gives a completely different perspective to one's understanding of other peoples and their cultures. Too often Americans living in remote lands, while employed by their government or company, do not, or cannot, appreciate the mores and customs of others, either past or present. While residence abroad, as a kind of expatriate, frequently engenders respect for another society, a real test emerges when a person is employed by another government or foreign institution. Then one is subject to all of the frustrations, as well as bounties, to which local folk are exposed. My life, fortunately or not, at times has been spent in service of foreign institutions, such that truthfully I can say in one case that five years as director of the Asia Institute of Pahlavi University in Shiraz, Iran, taught me more about the era of Cyrus and Darius than much reading and study of books.

Above my desk is a sign reading 'keep it complex, stupid,' which may be attributed to lawyers and bankers, but hopefully not to scholars and scientists. Perhaps one may go too far in trying to simplify, or reduce complex matters to simple solutions or clichés, but at least the latter usually are true. If asked to explain the history of world civilizations in one word, it would be 'death.' Of all animals, man alone knows he will die, and this has fashioned his approach to life, and indeed to all existence. Either one follows the 'prehistoric' shamans, who hope to raise the bones of the dead, later amplified to include the body in some religions, or a belief of the voyage of the soul alone to heaven dominates thought. The cognition of death has determined religion, which in turn influenced poetry, music, art and architecture, and all facets of man's time on earth. Another approach to death, the Buddhist extinction of the self, was not favored by people outside of the Orient, even though it makes sense.

In every person's life from the beginning of time, there are three principal events- birth, joining of male and female, or the equivalent, and death. Since no one can control the first and the last, the middle experience is especially important. On the other hand, since such perceptions are universal, only something unusual may be worth recording, unless one is writing poetry or a titillating novel.

Yet every person's experiences are different, or even unique, at least in the telling of them, if not in the events themselves. Perhaps the relating of personal, intimate experiences can interest or even enlighten the reader. But that is left to others, since he who writes can hardly foresee the reactions of those who read his story.

In the end, however, we agree with the words of Ecclesiastes: *vanitas, vanitatum omnia est vanitas.*

CHAPTER 1

The Frontier Mail to Peshawar

THE TRAIN was agonizingly slow as it stopped at every village, or even just a gathering of people by the tracks. But what an exotic landscape of brown, beige and sunset shaded desert or dusty green oases the likes of which I had never seen before. It was August 1942 and the old steam engine pulling wagons of the 'Frontier Mail' resembled those of the nineteenth rather than the twentieth century. Although the monsoons had passed, the air was stifling and to move at all entailed the risk of perspiring profusely. The wagons were different from those in America. Rather than the aisle between two seats, here compartments ran the full width of the wagon, with doors from each that opened to the outside. Any communication between the compartments had to wait until the train stopped since, unlike European railroad cars, there was no corridor. Trains had three classes of wagons; the deluxe, and most expensive, boasted accommodations of a shower in each compartment, as well as other amenities. I had bought a ticket for the middle category which meant it was clean and comfortable, with padded seats rather than the bare wooden benches of the bottom class.

The train stops were long enough to allow one to buy oranges or papaya from vendors, or tea from the train attendant, who passed from compartment to compartment on the platform, offering his large glasses of sugary, milky tea. It was tempting to try the food from the many vendors who thrust their trays through the lowered windows, but I already had been warned against such edibles. This unfamiliar and strange land brought back images from Kipling, Forester and such travelers and residents in India.

Soon we passed alongside a river, a mighty yet muddy stream with small boats passing occasionally by our windows. It was the famed Indus, on its way toward the Indian Ocean. Looking out the windows of the compartment on the opposite side, I could see some traffic on the unpaved road running along the tracks. Donkeys and camels were moving along, pulling two-wheeled carts, traveling at a pace only slightly slower than the train. At that time and place automobiles were a rare sight, and two wheeled carts, in some areas even pulled by oxen, were the normal means of transport. Later, as I made my way into Afghanistan, the carts gave way to load animals—donkeys, mules and camels the normal means of transport over its mountainous terrain.

I was on my way to Afghanistan with a dual purpose, outwardly to teach at the Habibiya School, but secretly to listen to German radio communication with the Japanese, and to report on enemy activities among the Pushtun tribes on the frontier of India. The 'Enemy' as defined then, were the Axis powers, which had retained their diplomatic presence in Kabul because Afghanistan had been allowed to remain a neutral country. Reza Shah, the Iranian ruler had been forced to abdicate when he too insisted on neutrality in the war, because Iran was important for the war effort, and the Axis embassies had been closed in Tehran by the Anglo-Russian invasion in June 1941.

Shortly thereafter, in October 1941, I had been called to Washington to train as an expert on Afghanistan. Such was the lack of informed people about this little known part of the world that even though I had never been outside the USA, my graduate studies about Central Asia, including the Persian and Turkish languages, were enough to prompt an invitation to Washington. As I sat in my compartment, slowly moving northward along the Indus, I wondered what would await me at the end of the line in Peshawar, and later in Kabul.

The British had followed the model of past conquerors of the Indian sub-continent, like the Greeks, Arabs and Central Asian Turks, in establishing their military camps next to existing towns. Thus New Delhi sat beside old Delhi, Lahore had its military cantonment and so did Peshawar, all of which had developed into municipalities of their own. In that part of India, which in 1947 was to become Pakistan, there were many Hindus, and some Sikhs, who seem to have gravitated toward managing most of the hotels, bookstores, groceries, and the like, especially in the cantonments. In post-WW II India, this proved to be a great source of friction.

The long trip began to lose its fascination as one station seemed to repeat the next. Between reading the *History of the Arabs* by my old teacher at Princeton, Philip Hitti, and watching the passing landscape, I daydreamed and dozed. Resting on my seat in the Frontier Mail, thoughts of home, and the fate which had brought me to such a strange place filled my mind. If I had not come here I probably would have been on a ship in the Pacific trying to decipher Japanese radio messages, but the changes of fortune had decreed a different course for my life, one more in keeping with my desires.

By pure chance, when in high school in Danville, Illinois on an autumn afternoon, while walking from school to my father's Colonial movie theater where I worked as a ticket seller in the box office, a book in the window of the sole local book store caught my eye. Below the title, *Tamerlane, the Earth Shaker,* by Harold Lamb, appeared a horseman on his rearing steed with a scimitar in his hand, and a strange pointed helmet on his head. My curiosity was aroused, and without hesitation I stepped into the store and asked the price of the book. In 1932, the first 'official' year of the American depression, one dollar seemed a princely sum for a twelve year old to pay for a book, but I had to have that volume. As it turned out, that book did not simply arouse my interest; it consumed me. Central Asia would be my life's goal, but just how, remained unclear. In any event, academic life, mostly at Harvard University, would be my passion for the rest of my life.

On my return to Harvard in September 1941, for the third year of my graduate work, an atmosphere of tension and foreboding was in the air. The war was going badly for Great Britain and Japan's intentions were unclear. Several fellow students, who had studied Chinese as I had, were approached by a Naval officer asking them to volunteer to enroll in an intensive Japanese language course. "We badly need people who have studied Chinese or Japanese because of future developments," he urged. Although prepared to assume my second lieutenant's commission in the Signal Corps which, would have resulted sequentially from previous ROTC training, instead I also volunteered for the Navy program, and began intensive study of Japanese. A few days later however, a telephone call came from Washington, from Walter L.Wright, my Turkish teacher at a Princeton summer session during 1938. Wright, who headed the Near East Section of the Research and Analysis department, of the new Coordinator of Information (COI), asked me to come to Washington to join a team of Middle Eastern specialists on the staff of William (Wild Bill) Donovan, the Coordinator of Information. Donovan's task was to advise President Franklin D. Roosevelt about specific critical areas of the world. Wright's focus on the Near East meant he was pulling in specialists on the area and he wanted someone on his team to man the 'Afghan desk'. He brushed aside my protestations that I had never been there, and in fact had never left the USA. He simply replied, "At least you are interested in the area and can do research on that part of the world." Of course, I would prefer to work in the area of my interests, but there remained the problem of my having volunteered for the Navy to do Japanese, but a week later Wright secured my transfer from the Navy to the COI, and within a few days I was at a desk in the large hall in the Library of Congress Annex which accommodated not only the Near East but also the Far East, East European, and West European Sections. That made using the Library of Congress resources handy, and these were most of the materials available, for the capital then was not the multi-headed research base that it became as the need to provide information for super-power decision making increased. At that time the Library of Congress holdings in Arabic and Persian were few and far between, whereas the Chinese and Russian holdings were already quite remarkable. My initial task was to compile the first ever bibliography of Afghanistan, a logical place to begin. To the amusement of my fellow experts, my naiveté was revealed when one of the items I included was an article entitled 'How to make an Afghan' that had appeared in *The Ladies Home Journal*. Life in pre-war Washington was leisurely and appeared to me at least, not prompted by any need to hurry. But three months later came Pearl Harbor and December 7 changed everything, just as September 11, 2001 was to do sixty years later. After that, speed and efficiency in the use of personnel became imperative, and the significance of Afghanistan surfaced. German armies were driving towards the Caucasus and Stalingrad, while the Japanese were moving westward in Burma. The Axis powers could not get direct connections from Berlin to Tokyo, so It was assumed that they were communicating by radio through Afghanistan. The Kabul embassies of Japan and the Third Reich became the relay stations for German language radio messages. The tall antenna for the radio, however, was in the Italian embassy, the third partner in the Axis.

The USA at that time had no representative in Afghanistan, and it was decided to send a military attaché as the first official American in the country. More people were needed at this strategic location, however, which as a neutral state, could continue to host German, Italian and Japanese diplomats, who were able to contact Indian dissidents who also had established themselves in the country. When my training in cryptanalysis and knowledge of German and Russian, as well as Chinese, became known to the Secret Intelligence part of COI, they shifted me from Research and Analysis and prepared to ship me off to Kabul. But I got neither diplomatic posting with its comforts and protection nor any other official status; instead I went as a teacher under contract to the Afghan government. Fortunately for the COI the Afghan government had requested teachers from the USA already before December 1941, and this seemed a good way to insert me into the Afghan situation.

After spending several months at a hidden estate in Virginia, training in small firearms and more cryptanalysis, I was ordered to the Brooklyn Navy Yard at the beginning of August 1942 to board a ship headed to Suez. In preparation, the Secret Intelligence people suggested I buy a tuxedo (my first, bought at Woodward and Lothrop department store in DC) and some medical supplies. I packed these, extra socks, tropical clothing, and the PhD thesis I was writing on Narshakhi's *History of Bukhara* into the single trunk I was allowed to take, and boarded the train to New York.

The transport which was to take me to Suez was a small 9,000 ton freighter sailing out of Batavia (now called Jakarta), and manned by Dutch officers and an Indonesian crew. It was packed with about thirty American military personnel and six civilians all of us going east for different purposes. One was Donald Wilber, an acquaintance from Princeton and now bound for Iran. Another was Dan Ingalls a student of India from Harvard, also on his way to Habibiya in Kabul. I never learned whether he too was a COI recruit. Two journalists, Ernst Hauser, bound for Chungking, and Jack Iams heading for Cairo, plus doctor Wiebe, who became the ship's doctor for the voyage, completed the group of civilians. All six of us were crammed together in a small cabin normally assigned to one passenger. Because of the crowding, during most of the trip I felt more comfortable sleeping on deck, underneath a staircase, wrapped in a blanket. After the first flooding of my 'quarters' at dawn, when the dutiful swabbing of the decks took place, however, I learned to scramble down to the cabin to avoid a soaking , much to the grumbling of its occupants awakened too early. Adjusting to this schedule was made easier since we could not have lights at night, and had to calibrate our lives to the setting and rising of the sun. A net with mines extended across New York harbor, held up by large, empty, red oil cans tied together with rope. As our freighter, the Bantam headed out of New York harbor we were preceded by a tug boat. This was necessary because the tugboat had to open a small passage in the net to allow our boat to pass. But after half an hour on the open sea, we returned to the safety of the mine net. We wondered aloud what the purpose of this sally was but received no answer. Several days later, on August 6 we headed out again following a convoy of sixteen ships, escorted by five destroyers, on its way to England. But shortly we again returned to the safety of the harbor and perplexed went to sleep on board again. We supposed these departures were made to foil or avoid German submarines.

The next morning when we awoke we found ourselves alone on the high seas, and out of sight of land. Throughout the day a bomber roared overhead, only a few feet above our tallest mast, searching for the enemy. A call to lifeboats caught us unawares and scrambling for life jackets below deck. The officers, a colonel and a major, in charge of the troops, scolded the civilians and instituted ship's discipline in our lives. Afterwards we had numerous life boat drills. Also, as part of the precautions, we were each assigned to a three hour watch each night, and instructed to search for any lights on the horizon.

My regular companion, with whom I was frequently on night shift, was Jan den Hartog, chief engineer of the Bantam, who had been at sea when the Germans bombed and occupied his home-city of Rotterdam. Stranded in Jakarta, he had fled from the advancing Japanese in Indonesia. Long away from home, he had strong feelings about the Germans, and he refused to speak German, thus denying me the practice I needed. In passable English he vented his anger in the nights when we stood on deck looking for lights and seeing only the stars.

A steady diet of cheese, cold cuts and Dutch gin began to repel us from meals, but fasts did not last long when hunger conquered all. In the south Atlantic flying fish, whales and especially albatrosses, with wing spreads of five or six feet, were our companions. The birds followed the ship to eat the garbage thrown overboard and night and day they were always with us. We wondered how they could fly so far from land, for no one saw them alight on our ship to rest. The constant throbbing of the ship's engines, and the swaying of the small freighter on high seas, remained with us several days after we landed.

The elderly American Dr. Wiebe gave us advice about living in the Orient, but he did not reveal where he was going. In fact each of us had been instructed not to talk about his mission. In consequence, generalities about the nature of man and the universe, and reflections about the course of the war formed the substance of our conversations. Also specific information about one's personal life was avoided, so the sea voyage was unusual in this respect. In the second week the steward opened a cupboard in which were several books in both Dutch and English, and I was able to read Tolstoy's *War and Peace,* which I never would have finished on shore. His depiction of people, whose characters and opinions changed with events, did not suit Wilber or Ingalls, who were rather fixed and convinced of the superiority of their convictions. Ivy league colleges instilled an arrogant outlook on their graduates in those days. After three weeks of increasing boredom, and only once sighting of smoke on the horizon, we arrived in Capetown.

One day in the town was not sufficient to qualify us as tourists, but here some of our passengers left to join a convoy going to India, among them Dan Ingalls. We had to reveal our destinations at that time to decide who should travel to India and who to Suez. Since there were not enough places on the India convoy, four of us civilians elected to remain on the little Bantam. She continued north to Suez with a British convoy. Undismayed at not going to India directly, I was happy to anticipate seeing more of the Middle East on the way to Kabul. At Aden we were surprised to see our Muslim Indonesian sailors dump the accumulated garbage of several days on the heads of the Arabs, who came out to the ship in small boats hawking their handicrafts and souvenirs. The Indonesian sailors explained their rude behavior by saying that the Arabs take advantage of pilgrims coming to Mecca, and the Indonesians were only too eager to repay their co-religionists for the indignities their fellow countrymen suffer on the pilgrimage.

Limericks and jokes more and more became the subjects of conversations. One of the soldiers gave a parody on the four ages of women, like four continents: at twenty unexplored like Australia, at thirty hot like Africa, at forty technical like America and at fifty worn out like Europe. Today one would have to extend the ages considerably.

Toward the end of our voyage, Dr. Wiebe shared with us the poem he had composed to chase away the boredom of a fifty plus days sea journey. I copied it from his notebook into my notes of the trip. Here it is:

> T'was on a bleak and misty day,
> The Dutch ship Bantam stole away
> From Brooklyn's port of embarkation,
> To ports of foreign destination.
>
> From Wilhelmina's Netherlands,
> Came courage, skill and steadfast hands,
> Who would her men and cargo save,
> And guide her through hazards grave.
> Would save her from the vultures high,

Who through the sky like demons fly,
From monsters, who below her deep
Like snakes through salty waters creep.

From raiders, who on waters clear
Approach their target without fear,
And aim destruction to the end,
Where men and blood and waters blend.

The Navy and the Army too,
Assistance gave our good ship's crew,
And added safety and skill,
To power, strength and iron will.

Its passengers were men of fame,
Who from the States, the union, came,
Where men and wealth form victory's tool,
Where people think, where people rule.

Our course by east and south was bound,
With vision clear, perception sound,
Through north Atlantic's foam and spray,
We sailed by night, we sailed by day.

Then to equator's sun we came,
Where Neptune reigned in pomp and fame,
Where albatrosses formed our guests,
The ocean in its' doldrum rests.

Still east by south our course we plied,
Through days, through weeks, through ebb and tide.
Until in winter's icy chill,
Far south of Capetown's fabled hill,

Far south around the Cape of Hope,
We slid through swells of monstrous scope,
Which rolled our ship from side to side,
As t'were a toy that lost its guide.

T'was here we changed our southward motion,
And turned into the Indian Ocean.
East of the Madagascar shore,
We to the tropics steered once more.

Thus on we sailed for fifty days,
Through sun and rain, through mist and haze.
And everyone on board our ship,
Was getting tired of this trip.

By Aden's shark infested waters,
And through the 'tear gate's' steaming gutters,
Then by the Red Sea's shores of sand,
We came to Egypt's far off land.

Here by a ditch once dug by hand,
Two continents divided stand.
Here in the awe of ages past,
Our journey's end was reached at last.

Goodbye, good ship, goodbye to all,
And thanks for favors great and small.
Your captain, crew and food were grand,
But we prefer the solid land.

We sailed past Suez to the Bitter Lakes where, by night, the ship began to unload its cargo of explosives, amid sighs of relief that we had not met any enemy submarines on the trip. But the lights were shut off at 11:00 PM, as Rommel's airplanes approached. Anti-aircraft guns went off all around, but our puny aft gun remained silent. The following morning, the civilians who were left, Dr. Wiebe, Wilber, Iams and I, caught a ride to Cairo, where we needed several days to recover our land legs. There we met a colleague, Lewis V. Thomas, later professor of Turkish at Princeton, who had studied three years of Arabic at the University of Chicago, and was eager to use that knowledge on the patio of Sheapherd's hotel. He patiently explained to the waiter that he wanted a banana split, with ice cream on it, and chocolate sauce on top. The Egyptian waiter acknowledged his understanding with a *hadher*, but when he returned it was with a scotch and soda. Such was the teaching of spoken foreign languages at American universities.

A jeep ride with an American lieutenant across the Sinai desert to Jerusalem at the end of August was a trip not to be recommended for tourists. It took most of a day, but the holy city was a lovely sight after the hot desert. An incident there has remained etched in my memory.

I was invited to attend a conference in the YMCA, across from the King David Hotel, where Arab and Jewish leaders were discussing the future of their country in the singular, after the war ended. Judah Magnes, head of Hebrew University, was the leader of the Jewish delegation, and Husain Nashishibi, of a prominent Arab family in Jerusalem, led the Arabs. One of them, I have forgotten which one, made the suggestion that after the war coins would be minted with the word Israel in Hebrew on one side and Filistin in Arabic on the other. Such moderation, cooperation and reason, however, would not be tolerated by fanatics on both sides. Nashishibi was murdered by his own extremist people and Magnes escaped a similar fate, although his chauffeur was killed, by a member of the Irgun gang led by Menachim Begin. The King David Hotel, together with Count Folke Bernadotte the Swedish envoy to the region, was blown up by the same gang in May 1948. That is how fanatics change history and defeat moderation. Unfortunately they still do.

From Jerusalem to Tel Aviv, which was a German speaking city in those days, and on to Damascus aboard an Egged bus, was an uneventful though long trip. I had obtained a visa for Syria from the Free French consulate in Cairo, but these for Syria or Iraq turned out to be unnecessary since our passports were not examined, and people were friendly everywhere. The twenty-five hour trip across the Syrian desert at the end of summer in a Nairn bus, was hot and jarring. The single food and rest stop came at the oasis of Rutba (south of Palmyra), but long before that stop the road had already petered out into a stony trail. They rooked us at Rutba, where the bedouin in charge of the tea shop charged us the equivalent of sixty cents (a Syrian pound) for a cup of tea that in the US would have cost no more than ten cents at the time. Even though we were in a desert, the mosquitoes made mincemeat on any bare skin of all in the bus. The transport company, founded by an Australian army officer after World War I, offered one air-conditioned vehicle, but as my luck ran, all the seats were already sold on that one. On the other hand, our bus had a motley but entertaining group of passengers: six Jewish auxiliary soldiers, a bedouin sheikh with his wife and black servant, a Free French air force lieutenant, a group of British soldiers, and a Persian merchant named Akbar from Meshhed, the first Persian I had met in the Middle East. One of the Jewish soldiers played gypsy songs on the guitar. Hebrew, German, Arabic and English were the languages that allowed us to communicate. I was delighted to use my language skills, a trait that has remained with me throughout my life.

Baghdad, after the attempted pro-Axis coup of Rashid al-Gailani in the summer of 1941, was tense. Polish soldiers, who had been held in Soviet Central Asian prisons, after the officer class had been killed at the Katyn forest in 1939, had been released at the insistence of the British and had arrived in Baghdad via Tehran, and to my consternation, occupied all the beds in town. No facilities were available, but the YMCA provided floor space for transients like me, provided they attended Bible readings every day at eight in the morning. A stay there of several days gave me my fill of the good book.

To arrange for transport from Baghdad to Kabul, I naturally went to the American Legation, which offered no help at all to a lowly teacher employed by Kabul for I could reveal nothing more to them. The Afghan Legation, however, telephoned Thomas Cook & Sons to put pressure for my travel arrangements, and the travel company thought they could fly me out of Habbaniya airport west of Baghdad, but wartime conditions prevailed, meaning that people were being bumped off flights and transport was hard to come by. Overland transport through Iran was deemed impossible due to the monopoly of all transport to Iran by the military. So after seeing Ctesiphon's impressive arch, the Baghdad museum (then named after Gertrude Bell) with its remains from Nineveh, Seleucia, and Ur, I made arrangements to go south to Basra.

The narrow gauge railroad from Baghdad to Basra, was frequented by a variety of travelers, among them a group of drunken American civilians without tickets who were working at a newly established Douglas air plane factory in Abadan, Iran. These were not the last American civilians I was to meet who behaved badly toward local people while drunk. They almost attacked the conductor, threatening to throw him off the train, so he retreated in fear, rather than making further attempts to collect their fares. In Basra were several acquaintances: Ted Lockhart, assistant Naval attaché, and Jim Gault, his assistant, were both anthropologists, and both from Harvard. Jim was later killed in Yugoslavia. Eventually Lockhart was able to put me on a British Wellington (Whimpy) bomber flying to Karachi.

Whimpies were made of wood with canvas around the fuselage. Together with the other two passengers, both British officers, I sat on the cat-walk, holding onto struts, careful not to put my feet through the canvas. I was not able to see anything. At an altitude of 10,000 feet, it was cold, about 40 degrees Fahrenheit contrasting with the 100 degrees at ground level. About twenty-five minutes after take-off the corporal machine gunner invited me to crawl back into his rear bubble where he pointed out a camp in the desert below, called Dhahran. He remarked, "The Americans think they have found oil there." There was nothing to see, and I was only interested in regaining my precarious seat and praying that no accident would happen. Years later when I returned to eastern Arabia to lecture, the Dhahran Aramco complex had become the largest oil producer in the world.

To my relief, soon we landed. "That was a short trip to Karachi, and it is good to be warm on the ground", was my remark.

"We've had engine trouble and have landed in Sharja," came the reply.

The monotony of three days on an air strip in the oasis of Sharja on the Persian Gulf was broken by the end of Ramadan, the Islamic month of fasting. Bedouin on their camels rode into the port of Sharja for several nights of feasting and celebration. They danced, or rather swayed in two lines facing each other, shooting their rifles in the air. Women were nowhere to be seen. On the last night of the three days of the feast 'Id al-Fitr, the airplane crew and I were invited to the palace of Sultan ben Saqir al-Qasim ruler of Sharja for a feast, with four sheep roasted on spits. The Sultan was an imposing figure in black robes and the traditional Arab headdress of a golden rope band around a white silk shawl which covered his head and shoulders. The wide band, however, was not only decorated with golden rope but also set with pearls, for Sharja was then a center in the Persian Gulf for pearl diving. Out of a bag he drew some black pearls which divers had found near Sharja, but he gave none to us. Instead, to show his esteem for the foreign guests of honor, we each received an eye of a sheep, put in our mouths by the hand of the Sultan himself. The eye tasted like a hard oyster and required strong chewing before the pieces could be swallowed. Small cups of bitter coffee followed the meal, and we were advised to drink three of them, before turning the last cup upside down to signal our satisfaction and the end of festivities.

Sharja, with its adobe houses and bazaar looked like an oasis from the Middle Ages, with camels the only means of transport. No one thought that this medieval oasis in the desert would be completely transformed in the future by oil. My first bargaining in this part of the world was with a tribesman for a curved knife held in a silver scabbard. The Arabic I had studied at home was sufficient to conclude the sale, even though the pronunciation in Sharja resembled that of Egypt, with a hard g- for soft j- (as *masgid* for *masjid* 'mosque').

Finally with the airplane repairs completed, we indeed flew to Karachi, leaving early in the morning and arriving there in the evening. When I was invited to look through the gunner's bubble at the landscape of Baluchistan, it seemed more like a moon panorama of mountain peaks, even more desolate than the Syrian desert, as we viewed it flying along the Arabian Sea coast. At Karachi we walked off the airfield and drove into the city, without any passport control or even interest in our arrival. Karachi then was a sleepy provincial town with none of the overpopulation of post-partition Pakistan days. I stayed the night on a cot at the American Enlisted Men's Club, where someone stole my camera with all the pictures I had taken from Cairo to Sharja. After several days awaiting confirmation of my Afghan visa at their consulate, I was able to go to the station and purchase a train ticket to Peshawar. The Afghans refused to honor my visa issued in Washington, and it took a second visa to obtain the stamp in my passport.

And here I sat, rocking on the train, watching exotic India pass before my eyes. I only exchanged occasional remarks with a taciturn British officer in the same compartment. I found he was going to Lahore, and when I expressed fears of arriving at the end station of Peshawar where one might find primitive living conditions, he smiled and remarked, "Take a cab to Dean's Hotel."

"A cab, a taxi in Peshawar?"

No, it was not an automobile but a *tonga* (called a *godi* by the Afghans), available from the railway station to the hotel in the cantonment. This two wheeled cart pulled by one horse, where the passenger sat, back to the driver, was the sole taxi system in that part of the world. With the age of mechanization, the *tonga* was later transformed into a three wheeled scooter pulling an enclosed passenger compartment, a vehicle that still pollutes the choked streets of Karachi and other Pakistani cities today. The horse pulled "taxi," on the other hand, offered other pungent odors in warm climates.

Somewhat reassured by the words of my terse companion, I returned my gaze to the fields and hills outside the window. Again the food on trays at the stations seemed appetizing, for the various kinds of citrus fruits, as well as mangos, and melons of many sizes and colors, were just as wondrous as the variety of smells which arose from different incenses and burning herbs. Yes India in the time of the Raj was truly an exotic place.

We arrived in Peshawar and my day dreaming came to an end. Forewarned that mud huts were not to be expected, still the luxury of Dean's hotel was a shock. It was a sprawling one storied structure with several large gardens filled with flowers. Every guest was provided with a suite of three rooms, one of which was a large living room furnished with heavy Victorian furniture and ceiling fans above, plus a bathroom. One of the rooms was a dressing room beside the bedroom, a rather formal addition it seemed. In the dining room tables were set with linen cloths and napkins, and behind every guest stood a waiter in white uniform, with a white turban and gloves, who filled your glass every time you drank the ice water. In India life was not difficult for non-Indians before independence. All foreigners, including the Brits, who intended to live in the country, were expected to hire at least three servants- a cook, a sweeper and a bearer- the last a kind of butler to attend to all of one's needs

At a question about possible transportation to Kabul, the Hindu manager of the hotel directed me to the room of the newly appointed US military attaché, Major Gordon Enders.

CHAPTER 2

First Envoy to Afghanistan

HE WAS short, but not fat or even stocky, usually with a cigarette in a long silver holder in the corner of his mouth, possibly copying President Roosevelt. A slight moustache, unlike the short and bushy one of Hitler, gave him an air of distinction, but his face was ruddy from over indulgence in alcohol, and he walked with a conscious look-at-me attitude. If he had been in the British army he surely would have carried a stick under his arm, and as it was, he occasionally did hold a short fly whisk in a similar manner. In short, one could characterize him as flamboyant or cocky, and perhaps he had a right to be somewhat condescending towards others. After all, as he said, he had been an aviator for Chang Kai-Shek out of Chungking, and had endured many perilous missions over China. How he had become a major in the US army and appointed the first military attaché to the non-existent US embassy in Kabul, Afghanistan in 1942 was never revealed. He was the first envoy of any kind to be sent to represent the USA in Kabul in that fateful year of World War II. Previously Kabul had been under the jurisdiction of the Legation at Tehran, but diplomats there had shunned the long and arduous trip overland to visit the eastern realm. Furthermore, the USA had no interests in the country, for it was in the British sphere of influence. Pearl Harbor had changed this, and the far-away and little-known land now attracted the attention of Washington.

After meeting him at Dean's hotel he at once dubbed me 'flied lice,' in reference to my knowledge of Chinese, a language he did not know but knew something about. I had to endure this nickname throughout my time with him. Not that he was mean, or even sarcastic, but he sought to mimic those British officers who were clever at misnaming Indian or other subordinates. When two army privates arrived, several months later to assist him, one he dubbed Arkie and the other Oakie, after their states of origin. Enders himself was born in India, while his father had served as a missionary in the northern part of the country. Gordon had learned Hindustani, at that time the name in English for the eclectic language which later was to be separated into Hindi in India and Urdu in Pakistan, although both names were previously in local use because of difference in alphabets. He easily could have donned a British Indian army uniform, and it would have better suited him than US issued 'fatigues' because his mannerisms were far more colonial British than American. When he was removed from office and returned to the States early in 1944, he left with real regret and we, the ex-pat community, missed such an interesting character. His replacement Major Ernest Fox, a former geology engineer in Afghanistan, was quite the reverse of Enders, orderly, down-to-earth and utterly colorless.

Enders had received information of my coming and was willing to help in transport on the rocky road to Kabul.

"You don't have much luggage, so come with me in my jeep tomorrow, but don't forget to wear something red, just a kerchief around your neck would be fine." Curiosity mixed with scepticism sounded in the question "Why?"

"We are going through tribal territory and the Khyber Pass, where tribesmen do not shoot women who always are distinguished by wearing red in their clothes. The snipers don't differentiate gender in the distance." was his reply. I could not decide if he was joking or simply seeking to impress a neophyte in the East with his intimate knowledge of the people. The wild Pushtuns may well have had such a custom, possibly even in their code of honor called Pushtunwali. According to it, if an enemy came to your encampment one was obliged to be a good host and attend to all needs of the guest. But as soon as he left he was fair game to be killed, for revenge and retribution were features of their code. At this time the Pushtuns were little interested in religion, but much later, under the influence of Muslim missionaries and teachers from Pakistan, they began to succumb to fanatic calls to fight for Islam. In 1942 one would not have believed that the Pushtuns would become fanatic supporters of the Taliban at the end of the century.

The bazaar of Peshawar was a bustling center with caravans and peddlers constantly coming and going. Camels and donkeys were everywhere, the carriers of goods between India and Central Asia. Yet there was no distinctive smell to the bazaar, unlike chilly Kabul where the burning of camel dung lent a pungent, sweetish odor to all the surroundings. At that time Peshawar had a multi-ethnic population, including refugees from the Soviet Union, such as Uzbeks, Tajiks, Kazakhs, and Kyrgyz. Although Pushtu, or Pakhtu, as the local idiom was called, was the common language of the region, in some parts of the city an Indian dialect called Hindko was spoken. This may have been the original local tongue before the Pathans (British usage for Pakhtuns) moved into the lowlands beginning in the sixteenth century.

The local museum was surprisingly good, containing many Buddhist stone and plaster reliefs or heads in the style called Gandharan. In the bazaar a number of such antiquities were for sale, and the second purchase of my trip, after the dagger in Sharja, was a small head of the Buddha in black stone. Since the number of antiquities unearthed by peasants was so large, forgeries were hardly worth the effort, although some masterpieces were made by expert craftsmen, for sale especially to British officers. Peshawar was small in area and relatively quiet, unlike the expanded town of forty years later, when the influx of Afghans from the Soviet invasion transformed the life of the people.

A bookstore in the cantonment, run by a Hindu, Bodh Raj Marjwah, was surprising in the number of rare English language books available relating to that part of the world One's mouth watered at the sight of the complete works of Sir Aurel Stein, such as *Serindia* and *Innermost Asia*, but lack of funds, as well as the weight of the large tomes, prevented any acquisitions. Unlike contemporary large bookstores in the USA, the small shops of Peshawar were ideal places to sit and talk while drinking tea with interesting proprietors. The stalls in the bazaar of the old city, of course, were even more suited for talk, and as sources of information. One could easily get around the town on foot, although the cantonment covered a larger area where a *tonga* was necessary. Empty fields reached from the city to the entrance of the Khyber Pass, later to be filled by refugee camps of Afghans.

Today, or rather before the Soviet invasion, one could drive from Peshawar to Kabul in five hours, but then it took two days over a road which in many places was only a track, for traffic was sparse in the war years. Occasional busses did ply the route, taking a full two days, but breakdowns were common and sometimes the trip was much longer. Fortunately, we were going in an official jeep, otherwise trouble would have been our lot. Even then at the frontier of India a problem arose; no stamp in my passport revealed when and where I had entered the country. The border officials were upset and perplexed; they demanded a lengthy written explanation of my arrival and subsequent travel in India before permission could be granted to leave the country. After some argument they relented and accepted only a summary, but it was really through the intercession of Major Enders that the border officials allowed us to depart into Afghanistan. In spite of the jeep having diplomatic status the wait at the Indian frontier took over an hour, while ordinary travellers on a bus might spend three hours or more in customs and passport control. After the ease of passing through frontiers in the Near East the bureaucracy in this part of Asia was annoying. As I found out, red tape had been reduced elsewhere only because of the war and all would change for the worse later.

I learned that travelers should take with them bedding and food if traveling any distance in the Orient. So the first of several trips between Peshawar and Kabul began.

# CHAPTER 3

The Road to Kabul

THE LANDSCAPE of Afghanistan looks like parts of Arizona, New Mexico or southern Tunisia, mountainous, barren, dry and dusty, or muddy in the rainy season. From Peshawar the road through the Khyber Pass was asphalted, or macadamized as the Brits said, and heavily fortified. Through the Pass, skirting around obstacles in the road, we counted five dragons' teeth or tank traps made of concrete, and many concrete pill boxes or bunkers. Were these constructed in the past when Russian forces in Central Asia and British troops in India were playing 'the great game' of control over Afghanistan? Or were most newly constructed to stop an invasion of Nazi forces from the Caucasus and Central Asia? Landi Kotal, a village in the Indian part of the Pass, was, and still is, a center of smuggling narcotics and firearms, at that time most of the latter home made by Pathan tribesmen. Although Indian policemen and soldiers were in evidence they did little to disturb the local trade, since it was better to keep activities under eye rather than hidden away in one of the countless ravines or valleys in the area. Two roads existed, one for camel and donkey caravans and the other for cars and trucks. But after the Pass there was no more asphalt on the second car road.

After Landi Khana, the Afghan frontier post, the road virtually disappeared, and it seemed we had returned to a distant past. Camels, horses and donkeys were still the major means of transportation, and few automobiles ventured over the difficult stones and ruts. At one place the Afghan mail truck had blown a tire and lay abandoned in the middle of the so-called road. From the frontier onward, however, the road stretched out mainly on level ground, up to the town of Jalalabad, in the province of Nangrahar. Jalalabad was the winter destination of Zahir Shah, ruler of Afghanistan and his court. Here we were able to fill our jerry cans with gasoline, and our canteens with water, both of which would have to last us to Kabul. Peshawar was a bustling metropolis compared to Jalalabad, which had little to commend it to foreigners, or for that matter to locals. Because it lay in the lowlands below the extended Iranian plateau, its winters were mild and Kabulis used it as a winter resort.

Beyond Jalalabad we reached the gardens and cypresses of Nimla where running water, grass and trees explained why poets in this part of the world extolled oases as miniature paradises. We spent the night in a government rest house, said to have been originally the stopping place of the Moghul emperor Akbar, who ruled Afghanistan from his capital at Agra. Here for the first time we slept on the ubiquitous *char-poy* 'four leg' Afghan bed, a light bed frame of thin logs on four legs, over which rope was stretched in a crisscross manner. A thin cotton mattress was spread on the ropes, but I was assured it might be better to avoid a mattress and endure the ropes, since the former frequently was the abode of bed bugs. Fortunately there were no other inhabitants of the mattress, although later in Kabul my infested mattress had to be thrown out of the second story window by Frau Plaut, my Jewish German landlady, to be burned on the street.

For breakfast we were lucky to find eggs, flat bread and tea without sugar, for the war generally had curtailed such luxuries. Waiting for breakfast gave time for conversation. The Major asked me why I was not in the service. "Do you want a detailed account from my first encounter with the military and what happened afterwards?," I asked. "Why not; we have plenty of time now," was the reply.

"In 1935 as a Freshman at the University of Illinois I had to choose from among the required two year ROTC services, infantry, cavalry, signal corps and engineers and I chose the field artillery. In the first year we learned everything about caissons and French 75's used in World War one. But in the second year there was a choice between motorized or horse drawn artillery.

Since the former was unlikely because of my young age (16) and inexperience, it was horses for me. But I had never before had anything to do with a horse, as the commanding officer soon learned when he ordered 'saddle and bridle.'

Everyone went to the stables and proceeded to put a blanket and saddle on his chosen mount except one person who remained standing, to the annoyance of the officer. "What the hell is wrong with you," was his angry question. "I don't know what to do," was the retort. Impatiently he explained. Necessity insured learning how to ride and also how to care for a horse, its brushing and feeding, which stood me in good stead later in Iran.

"During that year I was thrown from a horse several times, and had a horse under me die suddenly in the traces while pulling a caisson. I was riding on the middle pair of a six horse team on maneuvers, but the other horses, lead and wheel, stopped abruptly almost throwing their riders. Horses had not yet become obsolete in the army, but I had enough, and when a call came for volunteers to enlist in a further two year stint in the ROTC in a new program of cryptanalysis under the Signal Corps I signed up. In the summer of 1939 at Camp Custer, near Battle Creek, Michigan, however, as regular Signal Corps cadets we had to climb telephone poles, string wire and service field telephones. A lot of the time, however, was spent in KP (kitchen police) and cleaning both tents and the grounds. Especially irksome was the practice of an officer with white gloves inspecting cleaned dishes, and if a speck of dirt was found on one plate the entire dishware had to be rewashed by hand."

"So you received a second lieutenant's commission in the Signal Corps," asked the Major. "No, I had to wait until twenty-one years of age to get it, and in the meantime I went to graduate school at Harvard." Since Enders was only interested in my military career, that period of my life was skipped, until the fall of 1941, when I returned to classes and found a request from the Navy for volunteers to enter an intensive Japanese language course. After two years of Chinese at Harvard, Japanese *kanji* (Chinese characters) was familiar, and I was persuaded to forgo a commission in the Army's Signal Corps and join the Navy. But concentration on Japanese lasted only a week, for a telephone call from Washington took me there. I outlined how I got from the Navy to Secret Intelligence of the COI, and thus on the road to Kabul. "My trip here was quite an experience, which is another story, but now you know why I am not in the military and how and why I am here."

As we approached the Lataband Pass, many camel and donkey caravans belonging to wild but picturesque nomads, passed us heading south to the plains of India for the coming winter, making the drive an ordeal. They raised clouds of dust, and I had never eaten so much dust as on that trip to Kabul in an open jeep. The kerchiefs we tied around mouth and nose did little to keep out the dust. Fortunately our tires survived the rough terrain, and near the capital we reached the first barrier. During the war foreigners in Kabul were forbidden to leave the city except with rare special governmental permission, and all of the roads had several control points where barriers were manned by soldiers.

In Kabul Enders drove to the caserne, or former barracks, turned over to the Ministry of Education for use by its foreign teachers. The large two story building had mud floors and brick walls. All foreign teachers were housed in this structure. My colleague, Dan Ingalls had reached the city several weeks previously, and had hired his complement of servants- bearer, cook and sweeper- who had helped him set up house with a minimum of furniture. Only the sweeper was an Afghan, for the other two were from India where they had been trained by British officers. For several days I stayed with Dan until I too was able to hire servants and furnish my two rooms with a *charpoy,* a *bukhari* (wood and charcoal burning stove), and a small table with three chairs, plus some dishes and cutlery. On the floor every room required a *farj,* the local word for any floor covering, usually a kind of blanket, called *gilim* in Persian, or just a reed mat. The bathroom had a tin tub, a large pitcher on a stand for washing and a hole in the floor for a toilet. The stove was most inefficient and only sitting directly in front of it could one relieve the nightly chill. The mud walls, however, needed coverings of colored textiles to relieve the drabness.

The rate of exchange at that time was about twelve Afghanis to the dollar, and it seemed expensive to furnish the two rooms of my apartment, each of which required a *farj,* 200 Afghanis for one and 85 for the second. The stove was 85, and furniture- three chairs, desk, bookcase and small chest of drawers- came to 350 Afs. The same amount went for the monthly salary of the bearer, while the cook received 250 and the sweeper, a Hazara, only 40. The cook was quite limited in his repertoire, usually a rice pilau with a sauce on it, and the only dessert he knew how to prepare was creme caramel. It would seem that his training had been very short and elemental.

One day after returning from school, the bearer appeared with the message that the sweeper Mahmud Din had a seizure. On the kitchen floor he was squirming in pain, holding his stomach. The bearer vetoed the suggestion that he go for a doctor, declaring that he needed a certain *mullah* who would act as a magician to put the boy's navel back in place since it was out of line. The *mullah* came and confirmed that indeed his navel was displaced. He ordered a glass of water and some charcoal, plus a small piece of paper and a pen. On the paper he wrote a selection from the Quran, or a charm which I did not see, and washed it off in the water which the boy drank with the charcoal. He then prescribed bread for the boy, to be eaten over a space of six hours. Mahmud recovered as a result of one or all of the prescribed remedies, but always remained sickly, while the bearer and cook from India constantly complained of the cold in Kabul. The altitude, over 6,000 feet, slowed everyone in their tasks, except the sweeper and other inhabitants of Kabul, who had become acclimatized to the elevation.

Within two months the first American consul, Charlie Thayer, arrived from Tehran with a stripped down bus holding furniture and supplies. His servant and cook, a Chinaman called Wang from Manchuria, had been with Thayer as he moved from Berlin to Moscow and then Kuibyshev before being transferred to Kabul. Wang hated every minute he lived in Kabul, but we had a bond in the halting Chinese language which I had studied at the university. With Thayer came a secretary called Bill Eilers, and a consulate was established. One had to bend his head to enter the low doorway into the consulate, a rather embarrassing entry for foreign guests, but this locale was not to last long. It was at a dinner at Thayer's house that Dan and I met the four princes, Wali, who spoke German, and Timur, Qadir and 'Abdallah who were French speakers. They, especially Qadir, proved to be a nuisance, coming to us seeking *limonade*, a euphemism for all alcoholic drinks, strictly forbidden by their uncle, prime minister Hashim Khan who ruled the country with an iron hand on behalf of the young king Zahir Shah. Once Hashim Khan detected alcohol on the breath of Qadir and thrashed him soundly, after which Qadir did not visit foreigners for half a year.

Daily chores left little time to go to Ender's house and listen to German broadcasts on his radio, but in any case there was little of the expected important communications between the Nazis and the Japanese. There were few radios in private possession in Kabul at that time, and one could not buy a radio here or in India. As noted, the tall antenna tower of the Axis powers was in the Italian Embassy, and with the lack of radio activity one wondered if perhaps the Italians already were not as cooperative with their colleagues as the latter expected. When Italy left the war in September 1943 the embassy officials in Kabul did not hesitate a minute to join the Allied representatives in the city, but that came later. The personnel of the Axis embassies in Kabul always were invited to Afghan receptions on dates different from the Allies, and even in the bazaar or on the streets it was rare for enemies to meet. On one occasion, in the darkness of the only cinema in town, a Japanese diplomat was sitting next to me when the lights came on, but we politely bowed and moved away.

Our delay in reaching Kabul left me with the teaching of mathematics instead of English, since Ingalls had preempted all of those classes. Algebra and analytical geometry presented few problems, but when assigned to teach calculus to the twelfth grade I was an utter failure, since I had never studied calculus and was unable to keep ahead of the class. Soon instead of mathematics my teaching load of the standard twenty eight hours a week was changed to several classes of elementary English, which had opened because of the departure of an Indian teacher.

Four foreign language schools existed for boys in Kabul, through the twelfth grade, and there was no college or university in Afghanistan, for the university came later in 1947. The most prestigious was Istiqlal the French school. Nejat was the German language school, and Ghazi and Habibiya were the English language schools, the former mainly with Indian instructors and the latter with two American teachers, Ingalls and myself. The school for girls Malalay was off limits to males, and we did not even know where it was located.

Habibiya 'College' was a two storied building in the center of town, on the *lab-e darya* ,'lip of the (Kabul) River'. In front was the only asphalt covered road in the country, some 500 yards. At least it foiled the dust in the summer and mud in winter, which was the fate of other streets in the capital. The classrooms had mud floors with white plaster walls, while students sat in twos on benches with narrow desks. In the front of the classroom were a table, chair and a small board painted black, on which the teacher was supposed to write with rare pieces of chalk. The only heat in the entire school was a *bukhari* in the office of the principal, whom we always addressed as *mudir seb (sahib),* so between classes the teachers would gather in the office to warm themselves. Everyone wore thick coats, which I didn't have, so a tailor had to make a heavy woolen overcoat which reached to the ankles, and was most uncomfortable in teaching classes. The fabric, British Herringbone, lasted well except where I burned the lower front while leaning over the *bukhari* to warm my hands. Many years later, having reduced its weight by half after dry-cleaning away the dust of Kabul, I was able to pass the coat on to my son Nels who sported it dashingly at the University of Chicago.

Among the teachers was a Muslim Ossete from the north Caucasus who had fled to Turkey after the Russian revolution, and then had found his way to Afghanistan in search of work. Although he never revealed anything about his early life, we had many conversations about world affairs, in both Persian and Russian. Since teachers' salaries were always delayed and barely enough for living expenses, to augment mine I taught English to Turkish children, mostly sons and daughters of army officers who had replaced the Germans as instructors of the Afghan military. Compensation from the COI, though minimal, was deposited in my American account and unavailable in Kabul. But I did use those funds later to complete my education.

The Axis officials were less an object of scrutiny than the anti-British Indians and Afghans, who sought to rouse tribes on the Afghan-Indian frontier, and came to Kabul to seek money and support from the German and Japanese embassies. I found myself a collector of rumors, in which the capital abounded. But for the war effort they were of little if any value, which was a reason for much frustration. My inability to visit other parts of the country because of restrictions during the war, added to my frustration. Even a visit to India was difficult. First one had to obtain written permission from various Afghan authorities to leave the country, then the British Embassy would have to telegraph to Delhi for the visa, and the entire process hardly could have been accomplished in less than a fortnight, usually considerably longer. It was essential to remain on good terms with Major Enders, who after two months received, several vehicles driven by his two enlisted men, Wilkins and Nicholson, who acted as couriers for both the consulate and the military attaché.

The foreign colony of Kabul, other than diplomats, was diverse and larger than one would have expected, since all were employed by the Afghan state in various capacities. They, as well as the Iranian and Egyptian diplomats, kept much to themselves. Of several architects, two, Rudi Stuckert and Albert Engler, were Swiss, and one Zhestovsky was a 'White' Russian. Stuckert was a follower of Rudolf Steiner and his Goethe centered group at Schaffhausen, and Engler came from Wädenswil on the lake of Zürich. Zhestovsky, a good architect, was an excellent draughtsman as well as artist, and his wife was well educated and charming. Engineers seemed to be the domain of Czechs, the most prominent being Bretschneider and his lovely blonde wife, who had a continuous case of malaria, plus Schultze and Zahorski. Jewish Herr Plaut and his wife were from Hannover, where his factory had been seized, but he had been allowed to leave for Kabul, probably because of the Iron Cross he had won in World War I, or so he thought. Another German Jewish refugee Dr. Hans Türk was advising the Afghans about legal matters, but with scant success. The French group was divided between those who supported Vichy, such as the consul, and those who were partisans of the Free French, or the 'Fighting French.' Several wags in Kabul asserted that this name was most appropriate, since the French were constantly fighting among themselves. A half dozen Poles, included a family with two small boys, called Wyczrski, which name I never learned to pronounce correctly.

The foreign community in the capital spent much of their time going to each other's receptions on national holidays, or to private parties. Card playing, especially bridge, was the main source of amusement, although occasionally films were shown by the British or Russian embassies, the two principal foreign representations in the country since long before the war. Americans definitely were newcomers and much beholden to the British for information and help. When the first American ambassador, Cornelius Van Engert, arrived, he turned out to be an ardent Anglophile to the great annoyance of Enders and others.

My time was spent in teaching, talking to fellow teachers and students, and visiting various foreigners, usually by simply knocking on the gate of the mud wall surrounding house and garden for there were few telephones in homes. It was always interesting to stroll through the bazaar, talking to craftsmen and merchants. I developed a strong distaste for arrogant Westerners who vaunted the difference in character between Europeans and Orientals. Decades later when discussion of 'the clash of civilizations' became popular, I always maintained that there was a clash of fanatics rather than cultures or peoples. Perhaps different customs existed, but basically people everywhere were similar in most respects, except those incited by self-seeking fanatics.

My first diplomatic reception, of which there were to be many, was at the Soviet Embassy located at the end of the paved street on the Kabul River. It was to celebrate the October Revolution of the old Russian calendar, on November 7, and it was my first experience of a reception line, where one had to shake hands with over a dozen embassy officials. My study of Russian stood me in good stead with several of the staff, and a desire to visit the Soviet Union had an interesting result later. Life in Kabul was underway.

CHAPTER 4

Life in Afghanistan

WITH the coming of winter it seemed best to leave the barren caserne and rent a house which was evacuated by two Frenchmen departing Kabul. All of their furniture, including skis and a bicycle, were for sale, and the last had a noteworthy feature of a novel tire repair kit. To fix a tear or hole in the tire one would insert a long needle-like gadget on which were stretched rubber bands, enough to fill the hole. The rubber would be shot into the crevice and then vulcanized with matches or a candle. This was to prove a life-saver on future bike trips in the country. The flies of Kabul were remarkable, for they continued to annoy us well into a cold December, hibernating at night to revive as soon as the sun rose. Snow followed a similar pattern in reverse, falling at night and melting in the morning, leaving mud and water on every street.

I would not miss the old gate keeper at the caserne who wore what appeared to be long john underwear for trousers, covered by a tattered coat held together by a rope around his middle. Every morning early he could be heard talking to himself and waking up everyone. Dan thought he was training a captive bird to speak, but others said he was just crazy. In various parts of town, and just outside the caserne, was a loudspeaker where every morning and evening a flutist played the same somewhat mournful tune, similar to Pan in Debussy's *Après midi d'un faune*. Were the days to be as melancholy as the music presaged?

Since Rudi Stuckert left for Akcha in the northern part of the country after his wife had eloped with Chaudan, a Frenchman teaching at Istiqlal school, Albert Engler, who had been living with the Stuckerts, was looking for a new residence. We decided to move together to the new French house.

Since we needed supplies, and I had a vacation approaching, it fell on me to go to India for them, but over two weeks passed before the Indian visa and an Afghan exit visa could be secured. Fortunately Sgt. Wilkins had to go to India, so the ride in an army command car to the frontier was much easier than arrival by jeep. It was dusk when we arrived at the frontier station of Torkham, and because it was forbidden to drive through the Khyber Pass at night, we slept on the floor of the customs house. At dawn we drove to Peshawar and spent the day in buying foodstuffs. Several items were unobtainable locally, so a train trip to Lahore was in order, giving me a chance to see the old city. Here medical supplies, even ski boots, pants, and an electric heater were secured, although the unreliable electric supply in Kabul made the last item a dubious purchase. The Anarkali bazaar of Lahore was fascinating for the small stalls of booksellers where old lithographed books, in Persian but printed in India, could be found. There was a certain prestige then in speaking Persian, although not many local people understood it. The pace of life was leisurely like the train back to Peshawar.

The return trip to Kabul was delayed until noon because the post office had to sort letters for the American Legation, which we were to carry to Kabul. Because of the delay we did not stop on the trip but arrived at the outskirts of the capital past midnight, after a fast and wild ride through the Lataband Pass. The soldiers were asleep at the barrier and could not be awakened, so we pulled up the stakes holding the log barrier and swung it aside to pass. We then replaced the stakes and continued to the city. It should be noted that driving an 'official' vehicle enabled one to pass the Afghan border quickly, otherwise another lengthy procedure would be followed to obtain an exit stamp on one's passport. This especially applied to Indians, who were not well regarded by Afghans, and sometimes had problems.

Every Thursday morning all government employees, including foreigners, were supposed to go to classes to learn Pushtu, the national language of the country, even though the language of Kabul was Persian, in a dialect called Dari by the Afghans.

Many foreigners were excused, but all teachers were expected to attend the classes, since they were exempted from teaching during the hour and a half of instruction in the national tongue. Since the verbal grammatical structure of Pushtu was like Russian with its aspects, and with gender distinctions, hence difficult, few people learned the language, for Persian was so much simpler in all aspects, including pronunciation. Even the royal family and officials of the ruling class, all Pushtuns, could hardly speak their native language, but had adopted the language of the capital. This 'nationalism' of language had grave effects later, and gave rise to a party for Pushtunistan, a movement for union with brethern in Pakistan. This policy was initiated by 'prince' Daud, the favorite nephew of Hashim Khan, the real ruler of the country.

Our house in *shahr-e now*, 'new town,' where most of the foreigners lived, had a bathroom facing south, with a bathtub and a wood fueled hot water heater. There was a garden, surrounded by high mud walls, as around all other houses, providing privacy from passers on the street. Just as suspected, the electric heater did not give enough heat to warm anything, so it was necessary to construct a *sandali,* or *kursi* as it is called in Persia. This was a low table covered with a quilt, under which a brazier of coals, or an electric heater, would be placed, and one or more persons would sit on cushions on the floor with legs and feet under the table. One could be roasting below the waist but with nose and shoulders freezing. With wood so scarce and expensive few non-official foreigners could maintain stoves to heat an entire house, much less a room. Many repairs to the house were needed and workmen, carpenters, electricians, etc. were difficult to find, but gradually order came into our lives. Compared to Afghan houses elsewhere in the capital our home was luxurious.

At the Christmas party at the new American Legation a fascinating newcomer appeared, a blond free lance writer called Nilla Cram Cook. Born to a wealthy family in New York, she had left home after her parents separated and went to Greece where she was married but soon divorced. Afterwards she became a disciple of Gandhi in India, remaining with him eight years. She claimed that the British deported her to the USA for being a Communist. In New York she became a Muslim and founded the

Muslim League of New York, and then set out for the Near East. After a year in Turkey she came to Iran and made a pilgrimage to the shrine of Imam Reza in Meshhed. With an invitation from the Afghan ambassador in Tehran she came overland with him to Kabul, ostensibly to translate a Persian book on famous women in Islam. She claimed to be a journalist, and could be described as vivacious rather than pretty, but a fascinating addition to the foreign colony in the capital.

The Iranian embassy had a reception for Ms. Cook, and the cards of invitation said one was to come dressed in *'habit avec decorations'*. We ascertained that it meant white tie and tails, and I had brought only an ordinary tuxedo, but after some raised eyebrows at the gate, guarded by two lines of soldiers, admission was granted. Such relics of the nineteenth century still held sway in Afghanistan, at least in protocol and official functions. Unfortunately Ms. Cook only remained a month in Kabul and returned to Iran in the company of Afghan diplomats.

Returning one night in January from a movie at the Soviet legation with Charlie Thayer, the jeep he was driving fell into a *jui* at the side of the road, a danger on the unlighted streets. We had to fetch an army tractor to pull us out. The *jui* or *jube* is the ubiquitous ditch on both sides of streets in villages and towns on the Iranian plateau and in Central Asia, in which water is brought to gardens and baths. Drinking water in Kabul, on the other hand, was brought by donkey carts in large barrels from springs, and then carried to houses in leather bags on the shoulders of the water carrier, called *saqao*. It was advisable to boil that water before drinking. Irrigation water for gardens was obtained from a *karez*, called *qanat* in Iran, an underground canal which had been excavated by a series of holes in the ground, connected by a tunnel which usually began at a mountain spring, and which extended sometimes miles to reach a village or town. The construction and cleaning of such underground canals was the domain of special diggers who passed this hazardous profession from father to son. A *jui*, however, was simply a ditch by the side of a road, through which water passed at certain times of the day, regulated by a *mirab*, or official in charge of the distribution of water. For water was precious in a dry land where irrigation of crops was vital.

Thayer had a number of difficulties in maintaining a reputable American presence in Kabul, with few amenities available. Also problems beset him, as they did all of us, because of the general uncleanliness of the surroundings, including food which resulted in stomach ailments. Once at a reception of the Ministry of Foreign Affairs, Charlie had a bout of Kabul tummy. In the toilet there was neither paper nor water in an *aftabeh*, the tin watering can principally used in Persia, but also found in Afghanistan in place of toilet paper. As a result he had to resort to Afghani notes, declaring it the most expensive evacuation he had ever experienced.

The Oriental Secretary of the British Embassy was a Pathan officer, Sir Nawab Khan, who at dinners held in the embassy told many tales of his experiences on the Northwest frontier. It seems that the chiefs or *maliks* of Pathan tribes, although receiving obedience and authority from their tribesmen, nonetheless were subject to the council or *jirga* of sub-chiefs and elders of the tribe, who, having commonly agreed to anything, invariably upheld their decision even against the wishes of the *malik*. These were the people the Allies feared might cause trouble for the war effort.

Four people in Kabul were especially interesting to me because of their knowledge of Afghanistan. One was the French archaeologist, originally from Odessa, Roman Ghirshman, who would later become a leading authority on ancient Iran. He was successor to Josef Hackin who lost his life when his ship back to France was torpedoed in the Indian Ocean. Another was a Russian Orientalist Lucien Dugin, attaché in the French embassy, who had changed his name from Bogdanov, and was a superb calligrapher in Persian, as well as being a Sufi. Then there was Shah Abdullah Badakhshi, an Afghan who was full of information about historic sites in the country. Finally there was Father Caspani, the only Christian cleric in the country with long time residence in the Italian embassy. I heard that he had a copy of a book which I might be able to borrow. This posed a problem since the Italians were enemies, and I had to pretend to need a priest to be able to enter the embassy to talk with him about Afghan history. He also had a small but select library about the archaeology and history of this part of the world, and was willing to lend books, and especially to discuss them with someone who shared his interests. The Afghans did not allow missionaries into the country, but the Soviet ambassador had suggested that Father Caspani should have diplomatic status as an ambassador from God, and the Afghans accepted this subterfuge. Father Caspani was worried that I had committed a grievous sin to come to him on enemy terrain, but on learning otherwise, was delighted to talk about the history of the country.

One day I received a note from Ghirshman with an invitation to meet Sir Aurel Stein, a distinguished aged British archaeologist, who had come to Kabul from Srinagar where he lived. Sir Aurel, originally a Hungarian of Jewish background, had been a British civil servant for many years. Although a distinguished scholar of Central Asia, for years the Afghans had refused him a visa to enter their country. Sir Aurel had never been to Afghanistan, but had travelled extensively in all of its neighbors. The Afghans did not want an Englishman wandering about their country, and had denied him entry until Ghirshman secured a relaxation of their ban. His doctor had advised him against the trip but he wanted to see the Kabul museum. It proved to be his last trip for he caught a bad cold at the museum, and died after a few days at the age of 81. We buried Stein in the foreigner's cemetery on a hill near town.

It was still our winter vacation in February, so I decided to go to India again in the military truck with Sgt. Tommy Nicholson to hire a cook and buy supplies from the store of Gai, who had the largest general store in Peshawar. Since we decided to reach Peshawar in a day, we left at 3:00 AM and arrived at our goal before nightfall, a record for speed. At that time all foreigners had to report both to the Indian CID (Civil Intelligence Division) and the military counterpart as well. The head of the latter was an interesting Major Burns, who had written about coins and antiquities from this part of the world, and was a delightful conversationalist.

I had decided to see something of India and to return to Kabul by way of Quetta and Kandahar, but several tasks had to be finished before returning. I found a cook for a monthly salary of 60 Indian rupees (about $22). He insisted on being paid in Indian rupees, locally called *kaldars,* instead of Afghan money. It was a chore to obtain a passport and Afghan visa for him but it was finally secured, and he received fifty Afghanis for travel expenses to Kabul. He promised to leave for Kabul as soon as he could find a ride, and to report to Engler on his arrival. He swore by the Quran he would do this, but we never saw him again.

The first stop on the train was the archaeological site of Taxila where the *dak* bungalow, or government rest house, was built of stone and was clean like the local museum. It was a treat to find stone after the mud buildings of Afghanistan. Unlike Egypt where swarms of soldiers constantly visited the sights during the war, Taxila was out of the way and appeared desolate, which made the Buddhist remains, including the ruins of monasteries and *stupas*, even more attractive. On the second day, after a long walk to the distant Jaulian and Dharmarajika *stupas*, I saw two strangely attired figures coming down the path. One was on a pony, rarely found in India. After my halting Hindustani was not answered, on a hunch I tried Turkish and got a response. They were Kazakhs who long ago had fled from their native land to Urumqi in Chinese Turkestan, and after ten years there had wandered over the high Himalayan passes to western Tibet and Kashmir. Many had perished on this arduous voyage. In Kashmir the Hindu ruler had refused permission for them to settle, so they had arrived in the Northwest frontier province and, several hundred strong, were encamped in *yurts* about twenty miles from Taxila. Unsure of their welcome in India, they inquired if Afghanistan were a better place to live, and if the Afghans were fighting the English. A negative reply to both questions, however, did not reassure them. They eventually did go to northern Afghanistan, where some joined their fellowmen in the Pamirs.

In a crowded third class train carriage to Lahore, an Indian sergeant questioned my pronunciation of English, and demanded that I leave and go to a first class carriage. He became suspicious, and on my refusal declared me to be a spy. At the stop in Rawalpindi he brought police to question me, but my fellow passengers, in defense, had him removed from the carriage, for which I was thankful. The train to Delhi passed through Lahore, and the passengers joining me were Muslim and Sikh officers, all good conversationalists. At one stop two Hindu soldiers entered our compartment with a Muslim deserter from the army held in chains which halted our talk. On arrival at the suggestion of the officers, I phoned the Imperial Hotel in New Delhi to obtain a room. But the trip in a *tonga* was in vain for all rooms were reserved for Air Corps officers. In fact it was impossible to find lodging in New Delhi, so I returned to the old city and found an Indian hotel owned by a Persian with whom an instant friendship formed. A visit to a dentist was necessary, and by the hotel owner I was well directed. In fear of a primitive and unsterile office, as in Kabul, I was pleasantly surprised to find a British trained Indian dentist who knew his business, and performed a filling with competence. On a *tonga* ride back to New Delhi, at the barrier between the old and new towns, British soldiers admonished me for traveling in the crowded old city which was dangerous and out-of-bounds for British citizens and soldiers.

Delhi in war time was not only filled with soldiers but also journalists and British civil servants, all engaged in the war effort. My contacts mostly with Indians, however, revealed great unrest, little stilled by the war which the local people did not consider their affair. Demonstrations were almost a daily occurrence, but Gandhi's non-violence was having some effect in preventing them from turning into riots. Muslims spoke quite openly about a Muslim state after the war, already calling it Pakistan. Many were adamant that they could not live under Hindu rule.

The train trip back to Lahore was short and pleasant, to be impossible in a few years after the war because of the division of the country. It seemed that agitation was on the whole restricted to young hot heads, for many Muslims and Hindus were friends and worked in cooperation. On the Northwest frontier a Muslim religious movement called the 'red shirts' even opposed any division of the country, but instead followed Gandhi.

The train trip from Lahore to Quetta took twenty hours because the rise in elevation from the Indus plain to the mountains of Baluchistan, slowed our speed. Quetta was a depressing site, for the ravages of the earthquake five years previously were still much in evidence. All buildings had been razed to the ground, and now only one story mud structures with tin roofs could be seen, even though Quetta was the capital of the province of Baluchistan.

A motley array of foreigners were in town, Sikhs, Hindus, Hazaras and Pathans, waiting to travel to Zahedan in Iran on the railroad, built during WW 1. Since accommodations in town were few and crowded I was advised to leave by train for Chaman the next day. Even though the distance was only seventy miles, the train took over seven hours through tunnels and snow. I had taken the precaution of getting a return visa for Afghanistan, but here too the consul in the border town of Chaman insisted that another visa and two photos were necessary. The formalities were ended by two in the afternoon, but the next problem was transportation, for there were no busses between Chaman and Kandahar at that time. Trucks or lorries, however, were fairly frequent and the driver of one, full of tins of kerosene, was glad to carry a foreigner to his home town, some seventy miles away over level ground, for twenty Afghanis.

Any thought that the level terrain would permit a quick journey was soon abandoned, for we stopped for an hour at the customs on the Afghan side of the frontier, another hour for dinner, sitting on the floor of a tea house, eating *pilau* with our right hands, as well as stopping for every person who wanted a ride along the way. This took negotiation about the price, and some who refused to pay were left behind. As usual we had to stop for evening prayers, which the driver and I omitted. But by the time we arrived at the control barrier of Kandahar at nine at night the truck was loaded with passengers, hanging onto whatever they could find for their hands to hold, to keep from falling off.

On the way we passed several camel caravans camped for the night, and each followed the same pattern, probably an inheritance from the distant past. The camels and men stayed inside a circle made of the bales of wool, stacked as inverted Vs, and this procedure was followed even in caravanserais in towns. In the south only educated persons spoke Persian, and the mandated Pushtu classes every Thursday did not help much with communication in the bazaar, or with peasants. Fortunately the Kandaharis, much like Italians, were much more hospitable and understanding of speech difficulties than the people of Kabul. Several students from Kabul made a few days stay in Kandahar most pleasant, while Turkish teachers and military men going to or from Kabul provided an interlude to practice their language.

One day students took me on an all day trip and picnic in the rich and green Arghandab plain to the west of Kandahar. On the way we stopped at the ruins of old Kandahar, destroyed in the eighteenth century by the Persian ruler Nader Shah. Much later British archaeologists were to find remains here dating from the fifth century B.C. The hillsides were terraced and four irrigation ditches, one on top of the other, carried life giving water to the fields which made this area of the country its bread basket. The picnic was a sumptuous meal of various rice and meat dishes, including flat bread baked on the spot.

Most bazaars now are mainly for selling various modern wares, but at that time old traditions still obtained, and roving barbers, clowns, camels and donkeys filled the lanes where schools, mosques, workshops and dwellings made the bazaar the center of the old town with all its services and organizations. Odors of spices, and some not so pleasant, were a constant feature of the bazaars, and on entering them, as well as in narrow lanes, one had to cry out that someone was passing, to avoid having garbage inadvertently land on one's head from projecting windows above. On the street I had my hair cut and had a shave by an Uzbek barber, who used only water and no soap with his long but sharp bladed razor.

The trip from Kandahar to Kabul in a bus was a tribute to the driver and the motor, since we drove in second gear most of the way. As usual departure was three hours late, for time is most relative in this part of the world. Winter is not a recommended time for travel in the mountains of Afghanistan, and the trials of flat tires, snow, and mud in lower valleys, can best be imagined rather than described. We stopped the first night in a decent hotel in the town of Mukur, after which the terrain became mountainous slowing our progress. Even though the bus arrived in Kabul after midnight, the relief at leaving the hard wooden benches compensated for the lateness of the hour.

Not having the servant whom I had hired in Peshawar was a crisis, for it was virtually impossible to find a competent Afghan cook, although the Mongol looking Hazaras were good workers and could be trained. Neither Engler nor I could cook, and we had some miserable meals before we found a local servant who was little better. When a foreigner left Kabul there would be competition for his cook or servant, since experienced domestics were rare in the capital. Most foreigners lived scattered in Shahr-e now, where all legations except the British and Soviet were located. The former was a large compound with gardens and living quarters for personnel several miles to the north of the city, while the Soviet embassy also was a large compound on the bank of the river in town.

Shortly after *noruz* 'new year' on March 21, Engler and I decided to prepare a feast for many foreigners, since the US consul, Charlie Thayer had volunteered a smoked turkey and South African wines he had received by diplomatic pouch. We enlisted the French teacher, Chaudan to cook, and he proved to be a credit to his country. Unfortunately one of the problems of foreigners in Kabul embarassed us. Stuckert arrived from Herat without notice and joined us at the same time as his ex-wife, who had left him for Chaudan. Our new servant brought in the turkey three times before we were ready for it, and it turned out so tough when the main course was served that the knife to cut it was bent out of shape after the first slices. The night ended with rain which not only turned our lane into a morass of mud, which dismayed the guests, but also made a sieve of the flat mud roof, drenching some of the furniture below. Both Engler and I soon tired of house and servant problems, so we resolved to leave the house and separately seek room and board with foreign families.

A move to the apartment of Herr and Frau Plaut only a short distance from the school, turned my attention from the new town to the old and native part of the city, a relief from constant card games and dinners with foreigners. More time to read books borrowed from the ample library of the British Embassy, complemented my interest in local affairs. Plaut had many stories about the country. He had been hired to advise the directors of the dried fruit and juice canning factory in Kandahar, but he found conditions most unsanitary, with workers washing their hands and feet in the same water with which they cleaned the fruit. Recommendations to change conditions were ignored, so he gave up attempts at reform and resigned himself to respect local customs. He, as well as most foreigners, regarded Afghanistan as a place to take refuge from the war, and did not try to improve affairs there in any way.

I wanted to see the countryside, and permission to leave Kabul was not forthcoming, so taking matters into our own hands, Engler and I set out with bicycles going north over the hills to the valley of Koh-e Daman, where an ancient site called Iskandariya had been found and examined by Ghirshman. We left the road before the first control barrier and circled wide to the right so the guards could not see us as we struggled up a narrow pass to the other side. By the time we reached a village called Sarai Khwaja we were too exhausted and hot, however, to search for the nearby ruins. After consuming enormous quantities of green tea we decided to return to the road, but on passing a river we jumped in to cool off. As we approached the barrier we decided to wait until the guards were busy checking the line of trucks, and simply go around them, trusting we would not be stopped. In a cloud of dust we passed the barrier and continued until Kabul. It took several days to recover from this trip, but our desire to venture farther afield was not unwhetted.

In the Polish colony was a young widow Jadwiga Telatyska from Vilna with whom I was able to speak Russian, but she lived with a bachelor Hilinski, so attempts to make amorous advances with Yadya, as I called her, failed. Nonetheless frequent visits to Slavic friends continued, and parties with dancing, bridge and many conversations about the post-war world kept us occupied. Invariably criticism of the United States as a materialistic and uncultured society came from all Europeans, and it was difficult to defend American boorishness abroad. There was much characterization of people as monolithic groups, which seems to have been the fad everywhere, as it was in the USA before the war. For example, the Ossete teacher in school described his Ingush neighbors as thieves, where the women do all the work. His own people were hospitable; the Circassian women were noted for their beauty, and the Chechens were very brave. The quality of the last has been demonstrated in recent times.

School was not without incidents. One day I was ordered to the office of the *mudir* 'principal' and accused of photographing students and reciting Persian poetry in English classes. The charges were true, but other teachers defended me, and forgiveness followed. Another day the students were standing on their desks when I entered. The Pushtu teacher said they had not learned their lessons and needed to be punished. In another school all teachers had been deprived of one month's salary because a student had been found with hashish.

Summer was not only hot but unpleasant because of the *shimal* 'north wind' which blew incessantly raising clouds of dust which settled in one's throat. It was a pleasant surprise when the *mudir* announced that the boys of the twelfth grade, as well as the Afghan teachers and I, were invited to make a trip into the Hindukush mountains to visit Bamiyan and Band-e Amir. The former was the site of many caves and two huge standing Buddhas carved out of the mountain, while Band-e Amir was a lake created by a dam built by Habibullah, the ruler of Afghanistan half a century ago. The Buddhas were destroyed by the Taliban Afghan government in 2001.

Since the bus was crowded I climbed on top and sang with some of the boys until we reached a hotel in Bamiyan after midnight. The next morning we continued to the lake some forty miles to the west on a trail rather than a road, for the trip took over four hours. One pass or *kotal* after another slowed the bus, and frequently all passengers had to descend and help push it, or hold large wooden mallets behind the rear wheels to keep them from sliding backwards. Several times the trail allowed only inches from the edge, where a deep drop persuaded everyone to walk. The earthen dam had been built, and then became calcified because of chemical deposits in the water, which was too cold to spend more than a few minutes in it. The water was deep blue and beautiful in contrast to the barren mountains.

The wind and dust on this trip was much worse than in Kabul, but the nomad women we passed on the way took it in stride, not wearing any veils, whereas some of the boys and I wore handkerchiefs over mouth and nose. We returned to Bamiyan at night exhausted but glad to enjoy a good meal and sleep. The next morning we explored the caves and climbed on the heads of the Buddha statues, after which we returned, reaching Kabul at 3:30 AM.

Each of us had obtained a pass to go to Bamiyan, but for some reason mine was not collected at any of the three barriers on the northern road, which gave me the idea that the same pass could be used again, since I had heard that there were no controls outside of the Kabul region. Stuckert was staying in the hotel in Mazar-e Sharif, and I could bring him cigarettes, coffee and especially several books and magazines. Fortunately the school was closed five days for the national holiday, so I loaded the bicycle on the only bus bound for the north, going to Khanabad. I was surprised that there was no objection to a foreigner buying a ticket. At the first barrier I explained that I would descend from the bus at the top of the Shibar pass and continue by bicycle to Bamiyan, which the pass stated was my goal. My gifts of melons and fruit to other passengers on the bus won their support, and they persuaded the officials at the other barriers that I should be allowed to continue. During the trip the driver and his assistant joked and made songs about the foreigner on the bus, pretending to telephone ahead to Farrokh Khan's tea-house at the top of the pass to prepare food and a bed for their passenger. It was a jovial trip with songs and poetry, but hardly comfortable.

There was no bed free in the tea-house, but a youth was persuaded to give up his *charpoy* for the foreign guest. If there had been any bed bugs during the day, the cold eliminated them at night. At that altitude of over 10,000 feet nights were very cold even in summer, and I shivered all night long. By bike the next morning I reached the ruins of Shahr-e Zohak at the entrance to the Bamiyan valley where I hoped to spend the day and night, but changed plans when the ruins turned out to be not as interesting as I hoped. Also the ordeal of wading across a cold, swiftly flowing river with bicycle and heavy knapsack on my back dampened any spirits of adventure. On descending from the mountain where the ruins were located, some nomads crossed the river and asked for medical aid. Powder for stomach trouble, and iodine for the cuts on the legs of their camels, for which I left to them to handle, seemed to satisfy them. But when they learned I had a jar of atabrine tablets against malaria they forcefully took the entire amount, since malaria was widespread in the land.

Back at the tea-house, after drinking many full teapots, at half past four in the afternoon I foolishly decided to cycle on the road beside the Kunduz River down to the town of Doab some forty miles distant. The tea-house stood at the top of the Shibar pass which divided the watershed between the northern and southern drainages of the Hindukush mts. Although the road led downhill it was rightly called *Dandan-shikan* 'teeth breaker'. It was impossible to remember the number of times punctures came to front and back tires. My pocketful of rubber bands and matches was exhausted and I ended up wheeling the bike the last few miles into Doab late at night. Two Polish engineers were at the rest house with a car bound for Pul-e Khumri, and it was a relief to bind the stricken bike to the back of their car and the next morning to ride in comfort with them.

The town of Pul-e Khumri 'grape (colored) bridge' owed its existence to a dam which transformed the desert into a flourishing plain, and made possible a bazaar and spinning factory. After repairing the bicycle I cycled to the bus 'station' and asked if I could board the Mazar-e Sharif bus soon to arrive. It was then discovered that I had a ticket to Khanabad and no permission to travel to Mazar, and the chief of police threatened to imprison or beat me. The head of the bus service suggested that we telephone Kabul and discover if there had been a mix-up in permission and ticket, since I had been on a bus bound for Khanabad. The holiday or national celebration (*jashn*) in Kabul was in full swing, so no one was at work and so no answer. The bus for Mazar finally arrived and a well dressed Afghan passenger, head of the National Bank in Mazar, who spoke Russian, intervened to help the foreigner. Accepting the explanation that I was bringing medicine and supplies to a sick friend in Mazar, he took responsibility from the relieved chief of police. The bike was loaded on top of the bus and we continued to Tashkurghan, spending the night on the floor of a caravanserai. The next morning the bus arrived at Mazar and a *jawali* 'coolie' carried my knapsack to the hotel where Stuckert was drawing plans for a new villa for the governor (*naib*). He was very surprised and delighted to see me and to receive the supplies.

In the afternoon we attended a conference outside the governor's house, where the head of the local press and information office spoke about the past glories of nearby Balkh. The governor did not appear, but the notables of Mazar sat in two facing rows on chairs, the usual protocol in such matters. In the evening we attended a play, also outdoors, and this time the governor did appear. Below the stage sat five musicians playing native instruments. The play consisted of sixteen acts, fortunately short, and in everyone's opinion was delightful. It was a story of two brothers, the personification of good and evil. The good boy begged his father to send him to the military school, while his brother lived a high life of crime, even shooting an official who took a long to die, uttering many admonitions to the young in the process. The good boy was in the twelfth and last grade when war came, so he and his comrades begged the head of the school to allow them to defend their country. They returned as heroes, grew rich and happy while the evil brother died in poverty. The end of the play showed the father dying, and telling his grandsons to unite and cooperate, using the age-old story of the arrows, easily broken when apart but strong when in a bundle.

The ruins of the ancient city of Balkh were about 14 miles away, but the next day I set off with my repaired bicycle on a road covered with at least eight inches of dust. Less than half way the front axle broke and I had to wheel the bike the rest of the trip. Upon reaching a caravanserai near the ruins, I drained many teapots, after which I walked around the ruins, talked to some peasants and then returned to Mazar in a *godi* with four others and the bike, pitying the poor horse all the way. It was the first day of the fasting month of Ramadan, but before the official announcement of its beginning could reach Mazar from Kabul, people already had eaten, and so were in a quandary how to atone for their mistake. Finally it was decided that they could take an extra day of fasting at the end of the month. People traveling were not bound by the rules of fasting, however.

Back in Mazar the chief of police came to the hotel to inform me I had to return to Kabul the next morning. The rest of the day was spent in the bazaar observing the matting procedure of felt carpets, the separation of cotton by a bow string which was continually twanged, and the making of camel hair ropes. It seemed we were back in the Middle Ages where everything was made by hand. Stuckert had finished his plans for the villa and was hoping to be able to return to Kabul, but the governor informed him that he would have to remain and design a cinema in Mazar. It would be the only other one in the country, which would resound to the prestige of the local governor. How he would obtain the films for his cinema was not explained. The trip to Kabul was long and arduous, but by now I had become used to the difficulties of travel in Afghanistan.

The war was moving to an eventual conclusion and several new teachers arrived from the USA, so Ingalls decided to leave, and he set out on the 16th of September 1943 overland for Herat, Tehran and Cairo. I resolved to follow him at the end of the school year in December, but there were still trips to be made, within Afghanistan, especially to Begram where the French had found many and varied objects, such as carved Indian ivories, Hellenistic glass, and objects from China, all testimony to the wealth of the site in the international trade of two thousand years ago.

Again I skirted the same barriers north of Kabul, but this time I spent the night with the family of a local policeman who knew nothing of restrictions on travel for foreigners. The following morning, cycling to Begram, the bicycle broke down near the archaeological site. On foot pulling a broken bike to the town of Charikar twelve miles distant was an ordeal, but just as I was about to collapse another policeman took me to his home, and after informing the women about the foreign guest so they could retreat to their quarters in the back, we repaired to the roof to eat and sleep. Mosquitoes made sleep difficult, and without netting a sheet was pulled over my head. The sheep and goats in the courtyard below woke us at four in the morning, and departure for Charikar, an hour away, gave hope of an early ride on a bus to Kabul. Four times we changed my bicycle from one lorry to another, since busses were not departing until late in the afternoon. Number four lorry finally left at eleven, but frequent stops in the middle of the road for no purpose which I could discern, made the trip last four hours instead of one.

Since the boys at Habibiya had no books, the first few days of school in the new session were spent in searching for used copies for various courses. Some of the students were really hostages from tribal chiefs who might prove troublesome for the government, and needless to say their desire to learn left much to be desired. They saw little use in learning English, but I tried to at least make the lessons enjoyable by translating them into Persian, although the head of the school disapproved.

Because it was impossible to conduct archaeological work during the war years, mainly because of the drying up of funds from Paris, on October 26, 1943 Ghirshman left for north Africa via Peshawar, saying that only archaeology was of interest for intellectual foreigners in Afghanistan, and if it were impossible to dig he would leave and join the forces of DeGaulle. His departure left a great gap in the life of those in Kabul who were interested in the past of the land. It was not covered by Pietro Quaroni the Italian ambassador, who had amassed a superb collection of gold coins during his long stay in the capital. His wife was Russian, related to the Romanoff family, and rather glamorous. The exit of Italy from the war increased the number of Allied foreigners in Kabul, and I frequently joined the Quaronis in searching for old buildings in the bazaar, for they were much interested in the architecture of the city. In the narrow streets, really lanes, the top story of houses extended over the ground rooms and the middle of the lane was the place of garbage. The smell from the lanes was overpowering, and to obtain photos we had to hug the walls of the mud houses and pick our way around refuse.

With the Nazis in retreat in Russia and in Italy there seemed no reason for me to remain in Kabul, so I decided to sell my belongings, including some furniture, and leave for Cairo at the end of the school year. Furthermore, the tall radio tower in the Italian embassy, which had served for communications between Berlin and Tokyo, was now no longer functioning, and I was hoping to see some action before the end of hostilities. In our isolation in Kabul little did we know that the war was far from over. The US consul Thayer was also leaving, transferred to London, and the Quaronis were hoping to return to Italy, so the foreign community was moving or hoping to leave. After many goodbyes, and advice from all not to return, I set out for Iran believing my Afghan stay was over.

CHAPTER 5

Kabul to Cairo

IT WAS November 1943, the beginning of the long vacation for schools in the country, which the government had frivolously called the Switzerland of Asia. Perhaps no one in the Afghan government had ever been to the clean, well-ordered European land, but many knew that it was mountainous like their own country. The mountains of one, however, were verdant and green, while in the other land they were barren and the color of sand. Yet many foreigners who lived in Afghanistan somehow had been charmed with the land and the common folk, even though hardships in living , restrictions on travel and a convoluted bureaucracy, did not make life easy. Others hated the land and people, and told stories about their foibles. The eastern and western neighbors of this mountain land, India and Iran, both seemed islands of comfort and plenty in comparison with the wildness and scarcity of everything in Afghanistan. "One should not think of the hardships, but revel in the adventure of living in such a wild and fascinating country," said Albert Engler, my former housemate. Or Chaudan, in a more dramatic way, declared that Afghanistan would either make or break one's spirit.

It was the beginning of December before all matters were settled, my books deposited in safe keeping with the newly arrived military attaché Major Fox for eventual shipping home, and a seat on a bus to Kandahar secured. The chassis and engine of each Afghan bus were imported and the body was made locally. If one found a bus with padded seats, it was a stroke of luck for most had only wooden benches and tin on both the floor and ceiling. Outside bright colors with pious slogans gave the bus a cheerful appearance, not to be confused with comfort in any way. The farewell trip was uneventful until the bus reached Karabagh, a village between Ghazni and Mukur, where several logs across the road stopped further progress. Soldiers appeared and declared the road unsafe because of bandits, and for three hours we waited for an order to the soldiers to accompany us.

After spending the night in Mukur, the poor road delayed entry into Kandahar until after midnight of the second day. The one hotel in town was deserted because of the holiday, Id-e Qurban, so instead I was invited to stay at the British (Indian) consulate until a ticket could be secured on a bus to Herat after a two day wait. Since the rains had washed away the bridges over both the Arghandab and Helmand Rivers the bus had to cross by ferry while all the passengers disembarked and crossed the rivers on small craft or on home made barges. The ferries were propelled by man power rather than any engine, and for both drivers and passengers time was immaterial.

After the Helmand region the landscape changed to desert, and at night the bus stopped at the village of Dilaram where there was a hotel for travellers. Each room only contained a *charpoy* with no mattress, but after a rough day's ride anything was welcome. There was nothing to eat, but I had several flat breads under my shirt which assuaged hunger. As we continued towards Farah finally palm trees appeared, which had I not seen since my arrival long ago in Karachi. Several times the passengers had to descend from the bus when it chugged up mountain passes for the motor was not up to the task. The next night was spent in Sabzawar (Shindand in Pushtu), the edge of the division between Pushtu and Persian speakers, and the dialect of the latter was more akin to that spoken in eastern Persia than to the Kabul dialect.

The Herat hotel was large and pleasant compared to those on the road, and I noticed an electric refrigerator in the hall, but there was no electricity in the city. "We are waiting for electricity which was promised before the war," explained the head of the hotel. This reminded me of a story told by Stuckert. It seems that some years ago the Afghan government decided they needed a boat on the Amu Darya, since they heard that even Switzerland had a small navy in the Mediterranean. A German company agreed to transport a small ship in parts across Turkey and Iran to Herat, and then north to the river. By the time the trucks reached Herat broken axles and many repairs had delayed and discouraged the Germans. The Afghans told them to assemble the boat in a tributary of the river near Akcha to the northeast of Herat and float it down to the river. "But the tributary is dry," came the puzzled question. "When the rainy season comes it will be a torrent and there will be no problem," was the Afghan reply. So the boat was assembled in the dry bed, but when the rains came the stream changed its course and the boat was left high and dry, a memento of misplaced expectations.

Fikri Seljuki was the person to see about the antiquities of Herat, and he had much of interest to say. Some time previously, peasants who had been digging an underground irrigation canal in the vicinity of Fushanj, a town to the west of Herat, had unearthed a small Buddha figure of stone.

At that time it was thought that no Buddhism had existed to the west of a line extending from Balkh in the north through Bamiyan to Kandahar, a line proposed by the French archaeologist Alfred Foucher. I explained to the surprised Seljuki that this discovery was sensational since it refuted a well established theory. On a later expedition into Afghanistan from Tehran we were to find caves beyond Obeh east of Herat, which suggested an ancient occupation by Buddhist monks. Some day after the war I determined to return to the Herat area.

To travel on to Iran it was necessary to change money, but how to do this since there was no bank in Herat to make an exchange for Persian money. "Go to the bazaar and ask for Hajji Muhammad Omar. Everyone knows him and he can help you," said the head of the hotel. Hajji was a title given to those who had made the pilgrimage to Mecca. Omar was an imposing white bearded figure sitting on the floor of his small shop. After tea and much questioning, he asked how he could be of service and I explained my dilemma. "No problem," he declared, "give me the Afghan money." I waited for the Persian *toumans* but he did not offer them. Instead he said, "When you arrive in Meshhed, ask for my friend Hajji Husain 'Ali in the bazaar next to the shrine. Everyone knows him and he will give you the equivalent in Persian money." I was perplexed and asked if he would put it in writing. "If you insist, but it is not necessary," he replied, tearing a piece of dirty paper and writing on it. I wondered if I would ever see the Persian money, but there was no recourse, because at that time, Afghanis were not accepted in Iran, and furthermore it was forbidden to bring local money across the frontier.

Fortunately a Turkish doctor was leaving for Meshhed in a car with an extra seat and agreed to take me with him. It was usual practice to travel with two cars in case of trouble with one of them, so another auto from the Turkish legation in Kabul accompanied the doctor. The trip over dirt roads took two days and we stayed at Turbat-e Shaikh Jam for the night, since one Russian and two Persian control points had slowed progress. At that time there was an American mission hospital in Meshhed, with a medical Dr. Hoffman in charge, as well as a missionary section headed by a Mr. Irwin who invited me to stay with him. He had made some converts, and that evening in his house a gathering of Christians and Bahais discussed the merits of their respective faiths, a discussion which was so different from any such conversation by Afghans in Afghanistan.

The next day was spent in the bazaar. I found Husain 'Ali sitting in a small shop near the shrine of Imam Reza just as described. An almost duplicate of the encounter in Herat took place, with tea (this time black rather than Afghan green tea), and questions about everything, including the health of his friend and my life story. When told about the Afghan money he calmly counted out the equivalent in Persian money without a glance at the paper I gave to him. At a remark that such a transaction would hardly happen in the West he replied, "We are the last to hold to old virtues such as trust; soon here too all will change." His words were prophetic.

It was necessary to obtain a permit from the Soviet military authorities to continue traveling to Tehran, and only the British consulate could write a proper letter to enable one to obtain a visa, as well as another note to get a seat on a truck going to the rail head at Shahrud. During the war transportation in the country was under control of the UKCC (United Kingdom Commercial Corporation) and busses had been sequestered by the military. In towns private cars were few, and the taxis were *droshkies*. These were four wheeled carriages, which the Brits called Victorias, each pulled by one horse.

The British consul, C. P. Skrine, was a Scot who had been posted in Kashgar before coming to Meshhed, where he had created a miniature golf course within the consulate compound. The governor of the province of Khurasan and Skrine were playing when I arrived and, enamored by the game, the governor declared that after the war he would make a real golf course in Meshhed. He was removed before the end of the war, however, and his plan did not come to fruition. At that time it was possible to photograph the shrine at Meshhed, provided a copy of each photo was given to the custodians. Also every male who entered the shrine was required to cover his head, not at all observed at present.

The train to Tehran began in the east at the railhead of Shahrud. A Persian *touman* was six to the dollar at that time, and the trip from Meshhed to Shahrud was fixed at 20 *toumans,* a considerable sum for the time. The truck was due to leave at nine in the morning with three passengers, but finally it set off at noon. At night we slept in a dirty tea house in a village called Mehr, which made the Afghan counterparts seem clean by comparison. Here tea was served in small glasses holding much less than the bowls used in Afghanistan, but sugar was available as it was rare in the latter land. Near Shahrud the truck came to a halt and the engine steamed, indicating it was overheated. When the driver opened the hood the engine broke into two pieces and the front part fell forward. This was the end of the line, for surely nothing could be done, but the driver took wire and re-attached the front part of the engine to the rest. In disbelief at the ingenuity of the driver, we moved slowly forward at ten miles an hour reaching Shahrud in the afternoon. Such was the creative ability of drivers in those days.

After questioning what I was doing there without father and mother, the Russian commandant told me to stay with the 'Englishman' until the train arrived from Tehran after three days, so I set off to find Jones, the representative of the UKCC in Shahrud, and the only Westerner in town. He was surprised at the visit but hospitable, together with his Azeri translator Dad 'Ali, whom he called Dudley. All of our meals were 'chips and beans,' until on the last day I asked Jones about always eating the same food. Jones told the following story; "I was an inspector on the London bus system when a call came for volunteers to go overseas. I volunteered and was sent here after a short time in Tehran to get my bearings. After eating *pilau* , meal after meal, I sent Dudley to Tehran to fetch some real grub. So don't complain about the food." Dudley had a voracious appetite and after bringing butter from Tehran, he consumed half a pound in one luncheon. There was no meat to be had during the war.

Beggars were plentiful on the streets, again in contrast to Afghanistan which, although primitive and with a poor population, yet had a certain attraction because of the dignity and simple virtues of its people. Most of the Soviet soldiers in Shahrud were Uzbeks, although the officers were Russians, and there was plenty of vodka available. The place was a rest area for Red Army soldiers on leave from the front, but they were not eager to talk with a foreigner.

The long train ride from Shahrud to Tehran was memorable for the cold and darkness, no heating or lights, and several instances of window breaking by drunken passengers which let in even colder air. In my compartment were several Russian soldiers, three Armenians and a Persian lady. Arriving at Tehran at midnight I was apprehensive about finding a place to sleep, but one of the Armenians was a missionary and invited me to sleep on the couch of his crowded home. It was a relief to arrive in Tehran where I looked forward to seeing friends.

Edward 'Tiger' Kennedy was the small, almost petit assistant US military attaché who had been a mathematics teacher at Alborz College, the American secondary school in Tehran, before the war, and he knew Persian and the country well. He received his nick-name from an overweight wrestler called 'Tiger' Kennedy, who had come to Tehran for a match. He had just returned from a long trip through the central deserts of Iran with the following story. It seems the Nazis had flown several planes from the north Caucasus to the deserts, and had parachuted down some spies. Kennedy was part of an expedition sent to find them, but they failed. When they arrived at the oasis of Khur they were told "The Almani (Germans) were here but they went east." At the next oasis, Pusht-e Badam, where in April 1980 Americans were to land, seeking to rescue the hostages in the US embassy in Tehran, they were told the same story, so the group continued east to the large oasis of Tabbas. Here they thought they found valuable evidence of the German spies, for they were told that they had stayed for a month with a leading citizen of the town. Kennedy became suspicious when told that they had been here for a month, so he questioned the host, an old man. He knew the *kharijis* (foreigners) well, even their names, one Hentig and another Niedermayer. Kennedy knew his Persian history and realized that everyone had been speaking about World War I. Needless to say, the concept of time in isolated villages of Iran is different from that in the West. Shortly afterwards the Germans who really had landed on the salt desert surrendered, unable to survive in that desolate area

In Tehran I met Gunnar Jarring, whom by correspondence I knew as a Turkologist. He was tending to German interests in Iran and living in their embassy. He said he had been a starving student in Istanbul when approached by the Swedish government to accept the job of caretaker in Tehran, and this launched him on his diplomatic career. At a Christmas party thrown by the Swedes in the German Embassy I found that their dialect was much more melodious and refined than the speech I had heard in Chicago and Detroit when I was growing up.

Rain for several days in Tehran prevented planes from flying, but finally a two engine eight passenger plane took off from Amirabad airport, and after two and a half hours we landed at Abadan, the oil refinery town, for lunch. The landscape on the flight, especially the steep drop from the plateau to the lowlands of Khuzistan, was impressive in its sudden change from the stark, barren snow covered mountains of the Zagros to cultivated lowlands with palm trees. The passengers changed to a larger cargo plane bound for Lydda in Palestine via Baghdad and the oil pipeline. Together with a sailor bound for New York, we sought a hotel in Tel Aviv. Unable to get into a cinema the sailor and I went to a night club, and thought we were no longer in the Near East.

The last leg of our flight was to Cairo, but the plane instead landed on a small military air field on the Suez canal. Here I was back where I had started a year and a half ago. Changes had occurred; now there were more Yanks than Brits, and the COI was now called the OSS (Office of Strategic Services), while the Cairo office was JICAME (Joint Intelligence Command American Army in the Middle East). All hotels were jammed full and I was lucky to obtain quarters with Edwin Wright, a former missionary in Iran but now with the OSS. Ghirshman was also in Cairo and surprised to see me, but he left shortly for Algiers. I hoped to return to the USA, get my officer's commission and hopefully go the Pacific, but fate decreed otherwise.

In spite of my protests that there was nothing to do in Afghanistan JICAME officials ordered me back to Kabul, since others who had been observing the scene had all left, and the OSS wanted someone to be in the country. Wright was driving by car to Tehran on my birthday, January tenth, and I agreed to go with him. On the last day of 1943, however, chills shook my body, with the result that I was sent to the 38th General Military Hospital in the desert to the east of Cairo. The diagnosis was amoebic dysentery and a spinal injection kept me horizontal, drinking only liquids for a week. Injections with dirty needles, however, caused jaundice, so the dysentery regime was halted The nurses joked that the deep yellow color was becoming, but the loss of 20 pounds in a week was dangerous. Slowly recovery came and one day Dr. Stone, the attending physician, asked if I could speak Arabic, and on my reply "somewhat," I was moved from ward 28 to 30 where Ja'far at-Tayyar, chief of the Camel Corps of Saudi Arabia, had been brought in from Jiddah. I tried to communicate in Persian, then in halting Arabic and finally in Turkish, which made his eyes light up. He spoke much about his life, born sixty years ago.

Ja'far was a Cherkess (Circassian) officer, who had fought in the first World War against the Russians in Anatolia, and then against Allenby in Palestine. He hated the Russians, who had killed some members of his family when they were living in the Caucasus. Since he was a follower of the Sultan, when Atatürk took power he left Istanbul and went to Saudi Arabia. His repeated wish was to see the islands of Marmara again, since he was tired of sand and the desert. But he had cancer of the colon, complicated with jaundice and knew he was dying.

Ward 30 was occupied by civilians, especially a number of American women such as WAACS, and the nurses. After Afghanistan even to be able to talk to females was heavenly. Upon leaving the hospital on March 4th, several days of recuperation were necessary, and there was time to visit several scholars in Cairo such as the Arabist from Oxford H.A.R. Gibb, Thomas Whittemore a Byzantinist connected to Harvard, and particularly very British Captain Wesley Archibald Creswell.

Capt. Creswell had been an officer in Allenby's army and had remained in Egypt after WW I, becoming an authority on Islamic architecture. His spotless and well-ordered apartment was located in a narrow lane next to the palace of King Farouq, his patron. The books in his excellent library were all bound in leather, and everything was in military order. He was a small, thin bachelor, a model of cleanliness to the point of obsession. He was known as an eccentric by the local population, who viewed him with amusement when he walked on the street with a large fly whisk, swinging it from side to side, and occasionlly beating locals who did not move out of his way quick enough.

"Where did you come from," he asked. "From Iran," was the reply. "Where is that?" he shot back. I was surprised and did not know whether he was joking or not. "Tehran is the capital, sir" came to my lips as though I were addressing a superior officer. "Young man, do we say in the English language that I am going to Deutschland for the summer? The name of that country in English is Persia, and please use the correct name." I had no reply.

A Swiss ice cream parlor in Cairo was a great favorite of all the soldiers who used to sing, "I'm a Middle East commando, I'm a Groppi grenadier", to the puzzlement of new arrivals. Groppi's chocolates were almost up to Swiss quality, and before departure I sent five boxes to my favorite nurses in the hospital. There was no time to say good-bye, for a BOAC (British Overseas Airline Company) was flying to Tehran on March 13, and it was possible to get a seat on one of the first civilian flights in this region. Over two months in the hospital left me with a resolve to keep away from one if possible in future illness.

The flight to Habbaniya airport, outside of Baghdad was uneventful, but when the plane climbed over the mountains to Tehran several passengers, including myself, lost consciousness and had to be administered oxygen. At that time the planes were not pressurized and the cabin was quite cold. New people had arrived in Tehran, including friends from America-Cyrus Gordon a specialist in Semitic languages, Joe Upton who had been an archaeologist from the Metropolitan Museum, and others. With snow blocking the roads south of Kabul it was necessary to return via Zahedan and India. There was no transport available to reach Zahedan by way of Yazd and Kerman so it was back to Meshhed. This time, after the Tehran conference, the Russian officers in the train were friendly and talkative, persuaded by gifts of American cigarettes. We were all convinced that after the defeat of the Nazis a new and friendly world would emerge, an indication of the optimism of the war years. When I showed them a copy of Time magazine with a picture of Marshal Tukachevsky on the cover, however, they only asked "why?"

In Meshhed, miniature golf in the British Consulate with Skrine was a relaxing pastime after the travels. A truck leaving for Zahedan only had room in the back which was satisfactory since it was possible to sleep in spite of the cold. Several times we met Russian soldiers on the road bringing horses from Sistan, and at Zahedan the Royal Indian Engineers provided food and shelter, which was especially welcome since bacillary dysentery laid me low for several days in a tent hospital operated by the Indian Army medical service.

The train from Zahedan to Quetta, built during the first world war, was tedious, since rain had made the tracks slippery, so difficult in climbing slopes. On one occasion we could not make it, so an extra engine had to be called from Zahedan, and we went on with one ahead and one behind. Twice the tracks were covered with water in floods, the first time stopping the train from 11 AM to 5 PM. From Quetta to the main line on the Indus was without incident, but rain caused delays on all trains which were also very crowded, both to Lahore and on to Peshawar. In Peshawar at Dean's Hotel Major Enders was preparing to leave for the States since he had been replaced by the dour, erstwhile geologist, Major Fox. Enders' malaria had returned and he had lost his verve and swagger. It was sad to see the change, and I was never to see him again.

CHAPTER 6

Last Days in Kabul

IT WAS a shock to many friends, as to myself, to return to Kabul, where I already had burned my bridges, and everything had to be started anew including lodgings. Two Czech engineers invited me to share their large house, but I had to go out to the bazaar to furnish them: a charpoy, table, chairs and several rugs. As I had arrived late in the academic year, new classes had to be arranged for me at Habibiya. But the two bouts with dysentery had weakened me and Dr. McGregor at the British Embassy gave welcome advice to take it easy.

In April-May of 1944 unprecedented rain and cold nights left pools of water and mud in all streets and yards, just when many foreigners were in the process of leaving. An American lady married to an Afghan, however, could not obtain an exit visa, to leave with or without her husband, and the American Legation could not, or would not, do anything in this matter. We, non-official Americans, helped to smuggle the two of them out of the country. We drove them to the frontier north of the Khyber Pass, circumventing the normal border crossing. The Italian ambassador Quaroni had been appointed ambassador to Moscow and was preparing for departure, but he still bought many ancient coins in the bazaar, elevating the prices for all antiquities. At a diplomatic dinner his very attractive Russian wife wore a splendid necklace of rare gold coins, and it was difficult to refrain from examining them closely.

Continued pains in my stomach were tentatively diagnosed as a duodenal ulcer. So, as an employee of the Afghan government, an examination by fluoroscope in the government hospital was in order. After eating over a liter of yoghurt (*mast* in Persian) the technician, who was examining me, claimed he saw the ulcers and recommended a trip to Delhi to a hospital with better equipment. Permissions had to be secured which now took more than a fortnight.

The same social whirl of bridge, parties with dancing, and picnics continued, as news of Axis defeats in Russia and the Pacific raised the spirits of the reduced foreign community. There was little for me to report to Cairo since communications between the enemy had ceased with the adhesion of Italy to the Allied cause. The tall antenna in the embassy could no longer be used by the Japanese or Germans, and Afghanistan soon came to be a forgotten backwater of the war. Finally on May 29, this seemed a good time to look after the ulcer, and so I left for Delhi and treatment.

Anyone who has been in India before the monsoons knows what an ordeal it was to travel on crowded trains without air conditioning. The 10th US Army station hospital of Delhi was not up to the comforts of the 38th in Cairo, and we were crowded with five in a room under mosquito netting, and hot and sticky. No ulcers were found, but weakened stomach muscles had caused a fall of some internal organs. Nonetheless paperwork for my release from the hospital took time, and it was only on June 21st in the midst of a strong rain, that I got on the usual crowded train back to Peshawar. It was a relief to leave the steaming plains of India for the highlands, even on an uncomfortable Afghan lorry with a hot tin lined floor. For some reason this time the Indian border officials at Jamrud Fort in the Khyber Pass carefully searched all baggage, sealed my camera, and sent back to Peshawar the uncensored books of an elderly hydraulic engineer bound for Kabul with me. It seems that some tribesmen had been aroused by a group of 'red shirts', a political organization in the Northwest province led by Abdul Ghaffar Khan agitating for independence from British rule, but not advocating partition of India. Even though the lorry left Peshawar at nine in the morning, because of extensive controls on both sides of the frontier we only arrived in Jalalabad at ten at night. Continuing to Nimla, at midnight we slept for four hours and then continued, stopping every five or six miles to let the motor cool and add

Last Days in Kabul 59

water to the radiator. Finally after three flat tires on the rocky road the lorry reached Kabul at four the next afternoon.

It became clear that absences had turned the Afghan officials in the Ministry of Education against me; they refused to pay me among other things. Furthermore Major Fox was unhelpful. So, despite the orders from Cairo, I resigned from the school and prepared to leave. But because the resignation had to be accepted in order to obtain an exit visa, I continued teaching. Nonetheless, with limited time much of it was spent with friends, especially with the Poles because of my passion for Yadya who continually rebuffed me. Here I was twenty-four and still a virgin, and only work and the constant social whirl kept me subdued.

To get an exit visa was an ordeal, for the first task was obtaining a letter from the head of the school. He asked me, "In the contract which you signed was a clause to the effect that you would obey all the laws of Afghanistan." After my agreement he continued, "and in the West it is said that ignorance of the law is no excuse," again my assent, "there is an Afghan law which states that if any employee of the Afghan government is absent from his work without excuse for one day he shall be fined three days salary. You returned from Cairo one month late, which means three months will be deducted, unless you obtain a medical certificate, signed by the Afghan minister to Egypt to the effect that you were sick there, which is another Afghan law." I sent a telegram to Cairo on July first but an answer did not come until August 5th, stating that a certificate had been sent. After much palaver, and obtaining written permission from the Ministry of Education, this did not satisfy the Ministry of Foreign Affairs, so finally Mathews the new American consul agreed to act as my power of attorney and handle the case if there were any problems or payments to be made. Much later I learned that the minister in Cairo had forgotten to sign the certificate. The salary had to be waived, and much heated discussion was necessary to get the visa.

I had already visited all of the archaeological sites in the vicinity of Kabul, and many times the museum had been visited, and the Afghan authorities were not about to let me go elsewhere in the country. Conversations with Ahmed Ali Kohzad, head of archaeology, with Pazhwak of the Pushtu Academy, and others soon exhausted scholarly topics of historical interest, so I turned to almost every foreigner in Kabul to find kindred souls to discuss the future, and the destiny of mankind.

Stories about the Afghans were numerous in the foreign community and Herr Plaut had a large repertoire. He told about the rise to prominence of Abdul Mejid Zabuli, founder of the National Bank of Afghanistan. It was claimed that he was a money changer in Herat at the time of the Russian Revolution, and he took advantage of the flight of many Central Asian notables to buy rare objects and then sell them to Indian princes at high prices. With two associates he founded the first bank, and also a company to import rubber boots and shoes, and export dried fruit, all monopolies at this time. He married a Russian woman, and in 1933 was in Germany where he reportedly admired Hitler. He spent the war years in Switzerland and Afghans said he was uncertain about returning to his homeland, where he might be either honored or executed. He ended his days at almost a hundred years of age in Nahant, Massachusetts in a beautiful house overlooking the ocean.

Since salaries were so low here, all servants had to find other ways to survive, an activity foreigners termed stealing. The native philosophy was that one should receive his due for services, obviously more valuable than the meager wages from an employer, Afghan or foreigner. The latter thought they were singled out for theft, but it was the accepted way of life for all underlings in private or government employ. The *bakhsheesh* which exists to this day is expected from all those in a higher position or with some wealth. As long as it does not get out of hand and become excessive, the removal of a small portion of money, groceries, or whatever, by a cook or servant is tolerated. Those on top follow the same practice but on a larger scale, as in the West.

In the summer heat two mountain areas to the north of Kabul were favorite retreats, one Istalif, which was noted for its pottery and the other Paghman, where the Afghan aristocracy and foreigners had summer homes or gardens. Trips to one or the other provided relief from the heat and chores of the capital. Afghanistan was a pleasant land at that time in spite of the lack of modern facilities. In Kabul it was hot under the summer sun, and every morning the boys of Habibiya had to perform calisthenics from 7:30 to 8 AM after which they went into classes with steaming bodies, the odor of which was overpowering, especially when mixed with the dust everywhere in the air.

By this time the American Legation had assumed a presence equal to the British and Russian establishments, which was apparent on the fourth of July. The American colony was recruited to prepare a lawn party for top Afghan officials, the diplomats in Kabul plus a few other foreigners. All of us put up flags, chairs and tables and prepared for an enjoyable afternoon to rival other national holidays. Somehow the spirit of fun was lacking at the official party, so the unofficial Americans looked forward to a better party. Several new American teachers had arrived, and we decided to hold a super party for them which would outshine even the Legation's efforts. We planned to invite over a hundred guests as a house warming party for MacWhitney, one of the new teachers. Everyone had been saving various spirits- beer, whiskey, rum, vodka and Cyprus wine in preparation for the party, which was held on July 16, 1944. A Czech called Feit, a former pugilist, prepared his own brew of cherry spirits which was a hit. Glasses, plates and silverware, as well as chairs and tables, had to be rented from the Kabul hotel. Many people helped us in the largest party given by private means in Kabul. It lasted from 7 PM to 2 AM and featured dancing, bridge, poker and much consumption of alcohol. Optimistic views of the postwar world neglected the baleful influence of Stalin, but at least conversation was interesting. It was a party to remember.

Our party influenced the Polish colony to organize several skits for the benefit of the Polish Red Cross, in which others were invited to participate. My role was as assistant to Engert, who played a stage director, and then in another role with a duel over Yadya, whom I shot after being rebuffed. My real infatuation with her was parodied, since most foreigners in Kabul knew about it. Money was raised and everyone had a good time, but it was in no way the equal of the American party.

I spent my last few days in Kabul buying books and lapis lazuli in the bazaar, where a camel knocked me down, to the amusement of the Afghans, and finishing teaching ancient history to Sheila Van Engert, the daughter of the American Minister. The last was important since I had no income for teaching at Habibiya.

The Indian transit visa and the Afghan exit visa finally in hand, I attended the *jashn* (celebration for Afghan independence), and a farewell party given by my Slavic friends, who insisted on it even though there was little time. At the *jashn* the new Russian diplomatic uniforms were dazzling, with much gold braid and gold daggers at their side, most un-socialist in the view of some. The Afghan bands played both native and Western music, but the main event was wrestling, a national sport. Two wrestlers clad only in knickers, red or blue, would perform several rituals before beginning the contest, first taking a handful of dirt and throwing it in several directions, and on their heads with various stylized gestures. They moved about the circle, slapping their thighs and uttering cries before grappling. The wrestling, just as the sword play, seemed more a kind of dance than combat. Tribesmen performed the *atan* or national dance of the Pushtuns, a circle dance done by men exclusively who would throw their heads from one side to the other while moving in step to the beat of drums and flutes.

The party given by my Slavic friends was interrupted by rain, unheard of in July, and it was moved inside, where though wet, the good time continued. They all signed a card in Russian saying "remember the devotion of your Slavic friends in Kabul," something I would remember the rest of my life.

I was ready to leave, but transportation to Peshawar was denied by Major Fox, until by intervention of Van Engert, the American minister, the major allowed me to ride in the embassy mail station wagon to India.

This trip was one to remember, for the storm had not only washed out bridges but flash floods inundated the road in dozens of places. Twice the engine failed because of high water, and twice we had to be pulled out by trucks whose carriage was much higher than the station wagon. A third attempt to ford a stream almost ended in disaster. The engine stopped in the middle of the stream, and because of the sandy soil the right rear wheel started to sink. In a flash the water was over seats and windows. The Legation courier and two other passengers and myself, in over our waists in water, had to unload the car and throw the boxes and luggage on to high ground. Again we were saved by a truck which pulled out the car, and we spent the next half hour in scraping mud from the inside. It was astonishing that the car actually started after being dried. We, however, were not dry and the heat and wet made steam rise from our clothes.

At the Afghan frontier stood a line of travelers waiting to have their passports stamped. Two Indians ahead of us did not understand the custom of placing a ten Afghani note under the passport when handed to the official. He put their passports aside and waved them away, so I explained to the Indians that they would have to get in line again and ask for their passports so they could follow the proper procedure. "Think of it as a tax, not as a bribe," I explained. They were indignant but followed my advice. Afghanistan was left behind.

Before leaving Peshawar, signatures by the passengers were necessary on a letter absolving our driver of responsibility for the difficulties of the trip, a requirement of Fox. Back in Delhi much time was spent in arranging for the shipment of books, rugs and other items back home. Censorship was still severe and written permissions from several bureaus were necessary to ship effects. After making these arrangements I headed to Agra to see the fort and the Taj Mahal. It seems that Shah Jahan intended to build a duplicate mausoleum for himself in black marble opposite the white one for his favorite wife, nicknamed Nur Mahal, but his son usurped the throne. The black structure was not built and Shah Jahan was simply buried beside his favorite.

One had to be ready to be called to the airport at a moment's notice for flight in a military craft, and luggage weight was restricted to a minimum. The first leg of my trip to Cairo was the flight to Karachi where passengers were billeted in a camp near the airport and put on wait until their names appeared on the alert list. Speaking with Indian customs officials revealed the universal dislike of British rule, but also cynicism about future prospects for freedom. With time to visit the city, Karachi seemed a small sleepy town in comparison with Lahore and Delhi. At that time, before the influx of Muslims after Pakistan, the population was predominantly swarthy Sindhis and Baluchis, The four-rubber wheeled carts pulled by camels were a distinctive feature of this town.

The next plane was a C-54 transport with two large airplane engines in it, being returned to the USA for repair, and room for only 12 passengers on benches on both sides. It was a relief for all of us to land at Cairo, after a stop in Abadan, because the large engines held by ropes swayed dangerously from side to side as we descended. In Cairo more changes had occurred since my last visit in February. Many friends had left for the campaign in Italy or for home. Perhaps now I would follow them. But it was not to be.

Several days of check-up in the 38th hospital gave me time to write doggerel verse, for the only time in my life. Unfortunately I lost the verses later and could not remember them. Other than sightseeing in Egypt, acquaintance with the Coptic community through George Rentz, a friend from Princeton seminar days, who had married a local girl, led to staying with their extended family, eating *fool* (horse beans) and honey for breakfast. It was necessary to wait for instructions from Washington. They soon came; go to Istanbul and interview several Tatars who had been taxi drivers on the island of Kyushu, the southern island of Japan. The Tatars recently had been repatriated to Turkey over the Trans-Sib railroad. Japan was now the new focus of attention, and my knowledge of Chinese, Turkish and a little Japanese was ideal for the assignment. Finally I hoped to be doing something significant for the war effort.

Since 1942 passport control, censorship and difficulties of travel for anyone in civilian clothes had greatly increased. To take my camera across the frontiers from Egypt to Turkey required turning it over to officers, usually British, to avoid trouble. The Free French, with their usual priority for cultural affairs, had assigned Daniel Schlumberger in the French Archaeological Institute of Beirut to be their representative in Afghanistan, so he was especially glad to talk about affairs there. After a side trip to Damascus a number of acquaintances advised me to visit the ruins of Baalbek in the Baqaa valley between Beirut and Damascus. But there was no transport to Baalbek, so I decided to get off the Beirut bound bus and walk to the site from the main road, not counting on the heat and the distance.

Sitting on a rock beside the road to rest, a British MP jeep picked me up and took me to their nearest headquarters where an interrogation proceeded, since I had left my passport and papers in Beirut. Suspicion had been because some German prisoners had escaped from their war camp in Palestine and were said to be heading for Turkey. Fortunately the American military attaché was in his office in Beirut and vouched for me by phone. My slightly Swedish accent had aroused suspicion, as it had previously on a train in India. I was admonished for walking alone in Lebanon.

Continuing from Beirut by train to Turkey, the Turkish border officials probably had been informed that I was going to teach at Robert College on the Bosphorus. Consequently there was no searching of my baggage, as with other passengers. Perhaps the Turks had been alerted by the Cairo office and had agreed to a long stay in their country, which at that time was unusual. At Ankara the conductor on the train collected 8 liras from each passenger as a tip, which annoyed several of them, but which seemed to me quite normal. At night the city was blacked out and there were only purple lights, a precaution in effect from the beginning of the war. In Turkey new experiences were in store.

CHAPTER 7

Spying in Istanbul

IN KARPICH'S notable Ankara restaurant two tables away, the German ambassador Von Papen and his aides were dining. This was the time when the notorious Cicero spy affair involving the butler of the British ambassador was underway, but that evening everything seemed benign in the still warm October evening. Ankara was a new town with much glass and cement in the modern buildings. Atatürk had made it the capital, but many bureaucrats preferred the bustling old center of Istanbul, even commuting to Ankara. On the pleasant train trip to Istanbul I joined President Black of Robert College, who had formerly presided over an American college in Sofia, closed by the war. He was told that I would join the faculty as a teacher, which would satisfy the officials there as well as the Turks. On seeing Istanbul across the water, I appreciated the remarks of Ja'far at-Tayyar, the dead Circassian general in Cairo. It was easy to understand his longing for the Ottoman capital after the deserts of Arabia.

The city in those days was a beehive of rumor and intrigue, for Axis and Allied sympathizers almost rubbed shoulders. But it also was an enjoyable place to sit in conversation at coffee houses, undisturbed by automobile traffic and air pollution. If you asked for tea, the waiter would stare at you with disbelief, for in those days only coffee was available in Istanbul. In many ways similar to Venice, the best way to travel was by boat, and a trip by *vapur* from one side of the Bosphorus to the other was a pleasure, for speed here too was unimportant. New friends were made and, and while some Westerners considered the city as an exotic but backward Oriental place, by comparison I felt myself almost back in Europe.

In Bebek, where Robert College sat on the hill overlooking the Bosphorus, I found living quarters quarters designated for teachers. In the village lived Helmut Ritter, a distinguished gay German Arabist, teaching at Istanbul University, who knew intimately the manuscript collections of Istanbul. He proved a helpful guide to the collections. Another Arabist in the city was Osman Rescher, a German convert to Islam, who turned out to be a hermit and sat every day in the Topkapï Saray library, speaking to no one. Another distinguished Orientalist philosopher in the French consulate compound was Henry Corbin, a Vichy appointee, and his lovely wife Stella. In spite of his deafness and almost unintelligible French, we formed a close friendship which lasted through his years as head of the French institute of Iranian Studies in Tehran, and his retirement in Paris. Frequently Stella Corbin had to interpose into the conversation with "*il a dit.*"Among the younger scholars, with whom I visited the many sights of Istanbul, was a German, Robert Anhegger and his Polish wife, and Austrian Andreas Tietze, both students of Ottoman history and literature. Adnan Erzi Bey, a young Islamics student and I walked from library to library, and through the manuscript collections, which at that time had not yet been united into the Sülemaniye library complex.

In the mid 20th century, one of the joys of Istanbul was the great number of specialty food establishments, like the highest acclaimed *börekci* (maker of cheese *baklava*) at the Pera side of the Galata bridge, the *bozajï* (maker of fermented drink made from barley, like a thick egg-nog), near the Sülemaniye mosque, praised by Atatürk, and many others. After Kabul, Istanbul was a culinary delight (see note at end of chapter). But I was here for work, and it was a strange situation, for I was forbidden to associate with Americans, other than an archaeologist called MacDonald, but whose cover name in Turkey was John Hoag, who served as my contact with Cairo. My name in Istanbul, for Hoag and Cairo, was Stephen, just Stephen, no family name. The procedure was to phone Hoag from a public telephone in a coffee shop, which sometimes took half an hour's wait in line. On the phone we would arrange a meeting at 2 PM Friday at an apartment in Beyoghlu, the new part of the city, but we really meant at 3 PM on Thursday in an apartment in Moda, a section beyond the former. What was the purpose of the meeting? It was to convey information about Kyushu, the southern island of Japan, which I obtained from the Tatar taxi drivers.

In the office of Rahmeti Arat, himself a Tatar Turkologist in the Türkiyat Enstitüsü in Beyazit near the university, I met Ibrahim Menger Bey, a leader of the Tatar community in Istanbul. Through him I contacted the Tatars I needed and interviewed them. In Cairo I had memorized the map of Kyushu and knew it better than any part of the USA. The detailed information about beaches and roads on the southern island of Japan far exceeded my expectations, but there was something else. Some demanded compensation for information, and one of the Tatars had started a small shoe repair shop, and wanted some equipment from the USA in return for information. Hoag promised to expedite a machine, and those arrangements were left in his hands. Menger Bey was himself a source of other information, which was duly passed to Cairo. For example, according to him Turkish officers had served with the Germans in the Ukraine, and now with the retreat of the latter from Soviet territory, they turned over their spy network to the Turks who wanted to sell it to the Americans. It was unclear who those Turks were, for the government kept a silence about such matters. The Americans, however, dropped this offer after the conference at Yalta when Stalin requested Roosevelt to remove all agents from Turkey. I hoped that the more experienced British were able to rescue this network.

My involvement with the Tatars opened vistas into pan-Turanian activities, which were being held in check by the Turkish government. They even had arrested some of the leaders including Zeki Velidi Togan. How Menger Bey escaped is unknown, but many sympathized with the ideas of those who advocated a union of all Turkic speaking peoples, culturally if not politically.

Later several visits to a distinguished scholar, Fuad Köprülü in his old but luxurious house in front of the mosque of Sultan Selim opened contacts with leading Turkish writers and scholars, such as Adnan Adivar and his wife Halide Edip. An old Ottoman charm still existed in the foyers of some of these intellectuals, who were a vanishing breed.

The first week in November I moved from Bebek. Robert College had no teaching position for me, and so I took the cover of being a student and moved to a room in the new part of Istanbul, Yüksel Apartment 48, Kumrulu Sokak, Cihangir Avenue. In the apartment of six rooms were another tenant Vehdat, a Cypriot Turk educated in England, and Mme. Tanet our landlady with Liane, an attractive daughter of 22 years. Mme. Tanet was from a French family which had lived in Istanbul for generations and one daughter had recently married an American soldier, so I was the target intended for Liane. The first two weeks in the new lodgings were spent in bed with a fever much of the time, while a Turkish doctor prescribed a liquid diet, as well as medicines. After recovery I had trouble with the police for not registering a change of residence within 48 hours of a move. The police were nervous and suspicious of foreigners, and I was arrested several times, once even when trying to board a crowded tram in the old part of the city. It seemed that in such matters knowledge of Turkish helped less than an innocence and lack of understanding with the police.

At that time the exchange rate was 2.3 liras to the dollar; prices were relatively low and the bazaar was tempting, for many refugees had sold their heirlooms to pawn shops. Byzantine and Russian icons, and manuscripts could be found, but my lack of funds prevented the purchase of both manuscripts and works of art. Still it was interesting to see treasures in the bazaar.

In the middle of December the flies vanished and cold winds from the north even brought snow. On Christmas Wehman, the Swedish consul, invited his countrymen and myself to a feast with aquavit and many sorts of fish in a smörgasbord. They asked me to explain my name. So I told them that my father, Nels Freij was born in a suburb of Malmö on 16 December 1886. His mother, to whom he was very attached, died when he was fourteen and his father re-married. Nels did not get along with his step-mother so his father sent him to America. At Ellis island he was told that a name like Freij was impossible in America so he changed to Frye, and because of resentment towards his father he never spoke Swedish again. This explained my deficiency in

Swedish, for we never spoke it at home, and only in visits to grand Aunt Josie and Uncle Oscar in Chicago was the language barely kept alive.

One day I wished to see the rest of the Top Kapï Saray, for only the library was open during the war, but it was *yasak* 'forbidden', according to the soldier guarding the gate. "But others have been allowed to see the treasures." I protested. His answer was, "Well, a little forbidden."

Fortunately my time in Afghanistan had prepared me for such a response, and after payment of a tax, I was admitted. I was not disappointed in the fascinating surroundings, which delight all who visit Istanbul. How could one live in Istanbul and not visit all of the splendid Byzantine and Turkish remains?

Mme. Tanet was determined to marry off her daughter and spoke to me about it, but I remained non-commital, even after Liane came into bed one night and pushed my head down between her legs to give us both orgasms. Afterwards we went many times to cabarets, danced and enjoyed each other's company. I studied Arabic paleography to keep up appearances as a student for the benefit of the Turkish authorities, but one day a policeman came to our door and said Cemal Bey wanted to see me in his office in Bab al-'Ali, a principal street in old Istanbul. He was quite surprised at my question, "Who is Cemal Bey?" "Everyone knows he is the chief of the secret police," was the response.

The large room was empty, save for a long bench and a painting covering the wall, showing Attila on horseback stamping on Europe. After a twenty minute wait Cemal Bey, a short but not stout man with an air of authority, entered and asked in Turkish whether I knew who the figure on the wall was. "The great Turkish conqueror Attila," was my reply which at once pleased him. He offered me a Turkish cigarette, while a servant brought in Turkish coffee. The interview lasted a half an hour, and Cemal Bay apparently was mostly interested in other Americans in Istanbul. Again and again I truthfully replied that I knew none of the names he mentioned, and in the end he was satisfied and bid me farewell. He certainly was aware of my reason for being in Istanbul, but nothing was said about that.

The advice, or more like an order, from the SI people in Virginia, had remained with me. Never give any information about your mission; never trust anyone, and only acquire as much information you need to accomplish your mission. If one heard of something, which might aid the enemy if it reached the ears of an enemy agent or spy, then dismiss it from your memory so it would not leak out. I was not to seek any Americans in Istanbul, but, of course, at the same time I could not avoid them if encountered. Nonetheless, I could hardly be counted a member of the American community, especially after moving from Bebek to Cihangir Street. This aided my practice of foreign languages, and persuaded me that knowledge of the local language was the first step in visiting any country. Even in speaking English with a foreigner, to this day almost involuntarily I copy his accent.

It was pleasant to ride the tram in the old city, usually not jammed full, so unlike Cairo. A good deal of time was spent with a Persian, Ismail Kouchan, who was dubbing American films into Persian in Istanbul. At that time in Iran there were no machines or studios for changing English sound track to Persian. His Mitra Film Co. was the first attempt to do this, the forerunner of a later distinguished film industry in Iran.

If Kabul and Tehran had many foreign communities, they were nothing compared to Istanbul. Passports too were manifold. I met a White Russian girl with an American passport who could not speak English, and a Hungarian with a Spanish passport who could not speak Spanish. As Adnan Erzi Bey said, "Everyone is spying on his neighbor for various reasons."

Since young Turks could not read Arabic letters, in which the manuscripts were written, most of the librarians in the mosque libraries in town were aged Muslim foreigners. For example, the librarian of Aya Sofya was from Badakhshan, Afghanistan, while in the Köprülü library I found an Uzbek from Bukhara. The many libraries of the city contained the largest collection of Arabic, Persian and Turkish manuscripts in the world, and most of the librarians jealously guarded their treasures. It took many visits and cups of coffee to win their confidence in order to view a manuscript.

Ali Enver, son of Enver Pasha of World War I fame, was a frequent visitor to Liane Tanet, and I wished that he might marry

Liane, but after the war she did marry a Swiss merchant. Social life, lunches and dinners were mixed with classes with Ritter at the university, and countless trips to all the mosques and churches in the city, and on the islands of Marmara. So the days passed, every morning being awakened by the Muslim call to prayer in Turkish -*Tangri uludir* 'God is great,' usually followed by a man in the street pushing a cart and calling *eski elbise* 'old clothes,' or another with a donkey carrying double baskets which held cabbages as large as basketballs. A newsboy would call *Ulus besh kurush yalniz*, 'five *kurush* only', a cheap price for the newspaper Ulus. When I tried to mail a Persian book home at the post office it was rejected because written in Arabic characters. After heated discussion, and emphasis that the book was published by the Turkish Historical Society in Ankara in that same year, 1944, the postal authorities relented. Afterwards I sent a number of older books by mail, having made friends with the postal people.

According to a local proverb, the Turk is by nature born good with infinite capacity for becoming evil, while an Arab or Persian is born with a mean streak, with the possibility of improvement. At the same time that I was enjoying their company, a number of foreigners, German and other refugees, feared they might be interred in camps, since Turkey entered the war on the side of the Allies on Friday, March 24, 1945. Wolfram Eberhard, the Sinologist at Ankara University begged me to recommend him for a position in the USA, which I did, and he later came to the University of California at Berkeley.

Allied prisoners, who had been released from their camps in Poland by the Russian advance, came through Istanbul on their way home, and they were full of stories. Not only about their prison experiences but also they told many jokes about themselves and their homelands. An especially garrulous Englishman showed a tattoo on his arm, and for benefit of Americans he supplied this anecdote. "An American black soldier was serving as a chauffeur to an English officer in England during the war. The colonel liked him so much he asked if he would like a job in England after the war. The soldier turned his head in surprise and said, 'Does you all mean that people live here when there ain't no war going on?'"

Fortunately many of the Ottoman sultans were cultured and even poets or scholars, so the treasures they gathered from conquests in Iran, Egypt, and elsewhere, were brought to Istanbul and preserved in mosques, museums and schools all built of stone and almost immune to fires. Also few were fervent, fundamentalist Muslims who showed fanaticism. The Turks, however, did plaster or paint over Christian symbols in churches turned into mosques, but Roman and Byzantine remains were not systematically destroyed. Consequently Istanbul (Turkish contraction of Constantinople) is still a treasure house of the past, worthy of many days of exploration. The destructive rage of the Taliban in Afghanistan later was nowhere manifest in the Islamic world at that time.

In a long conversation with Köprülü, we concluded that the USA would have to shoulder the burden of Oriental Studies until Europe recovered, and the establishment of an American Institute of Archaeology and Oriental Studies in Turkey was necessary. This later came to pass with the creation of the American Institute of Turkish Studies, in which I played a part.

All the information garnered from the Tatars having been sent to Cairo, there was little left for me to do. It was time to leave, but many formalities had to be passed before I could get an exit visa. In Istanbul it was declared that only Ankara could issue the visa, so back to Ankara I went. In Ankara, on visiting the US Embassy, there was a small uproar over the refusal of the local Istanbul Turkish police to issue an exit visa. The Foreign Office only handled diplomatic passports, while the municipalities issued visas for ordinary foreigners. A clearance from the Istanbul police had not been secured, but in the embassy a letter was written with the forged signature of Dick Gnade, the consul and a friend of mine, who was absent from Ankara at that time. The letter stated that the consul had my power of attorney if I needed to pay any taxes or fines. The assistant mayor of Ankara said it was against regulations to give a visa to one who lived in Istanbul without authorization from authorities in Istanbul, but because of Turkish-American friendship he would make an exception and issue the exit visa. Needless to say knowledge of Turkish was a great boon in dealing with intelligent authorities, who always were pleased when a foreigner spoke their language.

The next day on the plane to Cairo was an Egyptian Princess Iffet, whom I had met at Köprülü's house, and since she did not know English I served as her interpreter. After stopping in Beirut to refuel we flew to Lydda for lunch, after which the plane continued to Cairo flying low since it was not pressurized.

In the present days of high altitude flying in pressurized planes, we miss the pleasure of flying low where ancient walls, aqueducts and houses can be seen clearly. It was worth the discomfort of cold, and sometimes shortness of breath. The steep drop from the mountains of Syria to the plains of Palestine reminded me of the flight from Tehran to Abadan. The thick walls of Acre were especially impressive, a tribute to builders who saw the strategic value of a city built on a promontory jutting into the blue Mediterranean.

From Payne field to Cairo was a long stretch, and the princess was met by a group of notables, who whisked her away with every one of the vehicles at the airport. After searching for transport with an RAF officer, we finally found a car and chauffeur for hire to take us to the city. The city had changed, for most of the troops had left, but quarters were still difficult to find. It was the first of April 1945 and no orders had been received for me, to return home or back to Turkey. I found a bed in Ed Wright's apartment and had time to think of scholarly matters. After meeting Gaston Wiet, head of the Arab Museum, he made it possible for me to photograph some manuscripts there. I also contacted many local scholars, and at the Fuad al-Awwal University I helped Muhammad Amin, a distinguished Egyptian philosopher, translate a lecture from French into English which he was to give at the Cairo Orientalist Society. In general I tried to make myself useful. The most impressive scholar in town was the French Orientalist Louis Massignon, a religious mystic in his own right, but a devout Roman Catholic, who prostrated himself before the altar on entering a church.

Still no word from Washington, so after spending a pleasant day with George Rentz and Sophie, his Copt wife, I embarked on a trip to Luxor by train or Wagon-Lits. The train was slow and the dust was so bad it was difficult to sleep and even breathe in the train compartment. I remembered the dusty trips in Afghanistan. The temple of Karnak was most impressive in size, but in my opinion it lacked the grace and charm of Persian counterparts at Persepolis and Pasargadae. Here, just as in Persia, foreigners had carved their names in the ancient stone, especially up high, a large 'year eight of the French republic,' a memento of Napoleon's expedition.

The following day a boat trip on the Nile ended with a visit to the tombs of the pharaohs. Just as in the pyramids, false chambers had been dug to mislead thieves, but all in vain for the thieves dug everywhere and chipped the stone until they heard an echo which led to the real passage leading to the tomb. Only King Tut's tomb had defied detection and its contents were in the Cairo museum. The colors on the walls of the tombs were amazingly well preserved, and later in the prehistoric caves of Lascaux, France it seemed that such preservation was a common feature of underground chambers, but subsequent crowds of tourists led authorities to limit access to them.

The train trip back to Cairo was unpleasant, since no beds were available in the sleepers and the seats were not as comfortable as those on Indian trains. Many friends from Kabul had arrived in Cairo, Engler, the van Engert family, and officers from the Italian and Turkish legations. After several days of reunions and dinners, finally orders arrived to return home, but transportation was delayed for a week. This was enough time to send books to Turkey to Adnan Erzi and Ritter, and to prepare packages of my own books to be sent to the USA, which proved to be an ordeal.

A list of all books purchased had to be secured from just one bookseller, Bouquiniste Orientale, even though purchased elsewhere. They then had to be taken to the censor, who demanded to see every book. After all were passed, he said an export license had to be obtained from the Ministry of Finance on the far side of the city. There an official declared he needed three copies of the list of books, certified by the bookseller that all were printed in Egypt. In addition a special form, which was a request for export of the books, had to be purchased and completed, after which a special stamp had to be purchased in another ministry, to be placed on the form and returned to the Ministry of Finance. The books had been left with the censor who had them wrapped in six ten kilo packages and sealed and stamped. Then to the post office where the head in charge declared that packages of ten kilos or more had to pass through customs. Three new forms had to be filled out at the customs and more stamps had to be purchased at the railroad station, and then a special form X-2 for the Finance Ministry, had to be purchased from the National Bank. This was too much and had taken the entire morning from nine to one PM, and the customs officials were said to be rapacious and difficult to pass. The censor advised me to repack the books in two kilo packages, which then would not have to pass customs. After lunch, instead of a siesta I repacked the books into 25 bundles and with the aid of two boys carried them to the main post office which opened at 4:30. The packages had to be registered, and six of them were a little over two kilos. They had to be repacked and finally by seven-thirty all was done, and I was too tired even to curse the Egyptian bureaucracy. Anyhow, Turkish is the best language for curses in the Near East.

While visiting the Tulunid mosques with Engler, he told me that in his five years in Afghanistan he had only completed three architectural projects, a tennis court in the Indian Club, a private house of general Daud Khan and a fireplace in the home of the American consul. The old Islamic architecture of Cairo in stone was distinctive and pleasant, lacking the more somber massiveness of the great mosques of Istanbul. My Arabic improved but still left much to be desired.

The Arabic language mostly has tri-consonantal roots, and according to Egyptian wags, each root has five meanings-a direct sense, the opposite meaning, a mystical meaning, something about a camel, and something obscene. Egyptians seemed to resemble the Persians in many respects, their humor, their hospitality, and the ability of both to pull out the rug from under one without anyone noticing.

Finally at the very end of April I turned over my diary and other papers to the OSS officials to send home, and all baggage was carefully checked before boarding a C47 at 1:30 in the morning. We stopped for breakfast in Tripoli and then on to Casablanca, a French town unlike Cairo or other Near Eastern cities, where we spent the night. A larger plane, a C-54, took us over the Atlantic, first to the Azores, a six and half hour flight, where lunch was found. Then the longest stretch of ten hours brought the plane to Bermuda at midnight for refueling, and the last leg was again over six hours to New York. Rain almost prevented a landing at LaGuardia field, but finally the plane made a rough landing and I was back on home soil. My passport, phonograph records and films were taken, later to be returned in Washington, and I found an expensive hotel, the Governor Clinton, which charged an outrageous four dollars a night for a room. The Orient had changed my sense of prices and values at home.

A Few Turkish Culinary Delights (some inherited from Byzantium)
(spellings from ear rather than written)
Airan-yoghurt strained through a bag and cooled with ice.
Börek-like baklava made with cheese.
Boza- drink made from fermented barley, like a thick egg-nogg.
Cacïk- cucumbers and garlic added to airan.
Dondurma-ice cream in Turkish style.
Döner kebab-leg of lamb on a spit with slices.
Ekmek kadiev- dessert of dark brown bread-cake with syrup.
Hunkar sevendi-mashed egg-plant with butter and meat in the center,
Imam bayïldï-eggplant preparation.
Mahallebi-dessert pudding with powdered sugar on top.
Shire-drink similar to grape juice.
Sumada-juice of almonds and sugar served cold.
Solep-milk thickened with powder from an orchid type plant, served warm.
Tavuk göksu-a custard with chopped chicken in it.
Tell kadiev-dessert-shredded wheat or noodles with syrup.
Telatur-a sauce with eggplant, made of bread crumbs, olive oil and chopped walnuts.
Yoghurt shish kebab-kebabs with yoghurt and bread.

CHAPTER 8

1945 in Washington

BY THE END of May all eyes in the OSS had turned to the Pacific war theater and the Near East was very much relegated to the background. I had not received any orders and was at a loss what to do, for the Near East section had no openings. I was hoping to retrieve my second lieutenant's commission in the Signal Corps when I was transferred inside Research and Analysis. My assignment now was to the East European section of R and A, with the task of gathering information about the relations of the USSR with the Near East. First, however, a trip home was necessary to see parents after almost three years of separation. In the USA, unlike overseas in Europe, civilian airplanes were flying, but frequent stops were the rule. Also the airplanes were stripped down for the military with few comforts. This flight went from Washington to Cincinnati, then to Indianapolis and finally to Chicago, four hours flying time. Before taking the train to Danville a visit to the Oriental Institute of the University of Chicago revealed that many faculty members had remained there throughout the war. The director of the Institute, John Wilson, an Egyptologist, was an exception, since we had been roommates in Washington in 1941, but he had returned early to his academic post. Nonetheless, at many universities some who had left academia would never return, for the taste of action, or influence in government, made the ivory tower seem tame and uninteresting. This was also true of scholars in the ancient field, which at that time comprised the great majority of those in Near Eastern fields.

In Danville after three years absence both parents now had grey hair and father was unwell, a presage of his death in three years from leukemia. The town had stood still, for building materials were difficult to find and workers were in the forces, or in war factories. Only a few days vacation were possible and then I returned back to Chicago, with a long and very rough flight to Boston which caused several timid passengers to leave the plane at Hartford. Weather influenced passengers much more then than now.

At Harvard advice came from several friends to leave the OSS (dubbed Old Stuffed Shirts) and return to finish the dissertation, which I had carried with me everywhere, and which had caused problems with censors. But war with Japan continued, and only at its end could one in all conscience return to a normal life. I had only taken leave and was duty bound to return.

The draft board in Danville was supposed to have been notified of my status in the OSS, but Cairo forgot to inform them, so a draft notice was received in Washington after returning. Some in the office gave advice not to contest the call but to accept it, since benefits for veterans were discussed in Congress, especially for education. Even though I hoped to return to the university at the end of the war I was not happy with my record during the war, and resigned myself to further service as an enlisted man in spite of the old ROTC training. In any case, as it turned out a health exam revealed traces of amoebic dysentery, so the medical military officials joked that the government did not want to take care of someone who had health problems, and rejection was in order. I was free to leave the OSS, but resolved to wait until the end of the Pacific war.

The Washington I had left in 1942 had been one of parties, dances and concerts, although somewhat reduced after Pearl Harbor. It had seemed as though people wanted to enjoy life before a possible deluge. For then the future was uncertain, and anticipation of change had been evident on everyone's face. By the middle of 1942, however, the capital had become a vast bedlam, with people coming and leaving for overseas. Before leaving, I had an unfruitful 'puppy love' affair with Florence Day, ten years older, a specialist in Islamic art, who was a fellow at Dumbarton Oaks in Georgetown. This was a lovely estate of

Robert Bliss in Georgetown, which had been given to Harvard as a center of Byzantine Studies. The teas of Mrs. Bliss were famous and they continued until her death after the war. By 1945 the atmosphere had changed, for three years of war had left their mark. People were serious with little time for fun and frolics, and even Dumbarton Oaks was in use by the military. All old friends were gone, save those in the Research and Analysis branch of the OSS, no longer in the Library of Congress Annex. Even though the war in Europe was over, no one knew how long the war with Japan would last, and it was essential not to relax efforts to bring it to a successful conclusion.

Since in 1942 I had helped the East European section to compile a survey of the cities of Central Asia, it was easy to resume connections with the people there, such as Wayne Vucinich, specialist on Yugoslavia and later professor at Stanford. There always was an air of urgency about the preparation of reports which kept us busy, sometimes night and day. Also, because of my interest in Central Asia, as well as a fading knowledge of Chinese, the East Asian specialists borrowed me to work on a report on transportation in eastern Turkestan (Xinjiang), so many new contacts were made. Concentration on Central Asia had opened doors eastward to China, north to Russia, and to the Near East, and this expanded interest in Eurasia remained the rest of my life.

Brother Bill had been working in the Naval Research Laboratories in Washington since December 1941. He had married the following year and now was expecting a baby, so the summer of 1945 brought me closer to him and his cheerful wife Betty. Our younger brother Kenneth had been drafted and soon would be sent to Panama. Unfortunately we had never been close, and in later years he much resented that his older brothers, one with a doctorate in Physics from the University of Chicago and the other in History from Harvard, had followed different paths than he. We had left home early leaving him with our parents, and mother held on to him as a substitute husband after the death of our father.

By the end of the summer, suspicion of the motives of the Soviet Union in Europe had begun to appear in government circles in Washington, and the East European section of the OSS began to split into those who were friendly to the Russians and the anti-Communists. It seemed that one would have to choose sides, and with my love of Russian literature and culture, and with several Soviet friends in Kabul, perhaps it would be advisable to leave government service as soon as possible. It became unpleasant to act as a middleman between two camps. For, although I liked Russian people, the acts of Stalin had made me most critical of their government. I resolved to leave as soon as possible. The end of the war in the Pacific brought an opportunity to do so.

On the evening of VJ day in Washington crowds milled about in front of the White House, stripes were torn from the jackets of non-com officers, and girls indiscriminately kissed anyone in uniform. The small Iranian embassy, a shadow of the later ornate structure, was closed, while a visit to the Soviet Embassy only produced a laconic response that information about the end of the war had not yet been received from Moscow. Street cars were jammed with people hanging on outside, like shades of Cairo, so walking back to our quarters beyond the Library of Congress took many hours through dense crowds. It was time to wrap up work and return to the university. Government employment lured large numbers of academics to remain in Washington after the war, including many in the OSS, but I left Washington at the beginning of September 1945, happy to resume life in Cambridge. There changes wrought by the war years were apparent, not so much in the physical plant but more in the attitudes of both faculty and students.

As the only large country untouched by war, America's new role in the world was becoming clear and Washington already was beginning to have the aspect of an imperial capital. This change surely would have an influence on the ivory-towered universities, still mired in a Medieval approach to learning by methods mostly based on memory. But I was a product of that era and I wondered if I could adapt to the new world which lay ahead.

CHAPTER 9

Pre-War Harvard

> There were people in our time, not like the present breed.
> They were heroes, not you.
> —Lermentov, *Borodino*

THE WAR, which had just started in Europe, was far away, and most people were more concerned about the aftermath of the devastating hurricane which had caused so much material damage the year before in New England. Since scholarships were few and small, most graduate students had to scramble to find jobs. I was lucky to find work as a waiter in a small restaurant run by an elderly lady and her middle aged daughter. Every morning I would come early to serve breakfast to customers, usually graduate students. One student, Herbert Bloch, a refugee from Germany, appeared thin and hungry, so I gave him seven prunes, which brought a reprimand from Grace the proprietor's daughter. "Five prunes for five cents, no more," she scolded. "We will go out of business if you give more than the fixed amounts." Bloch later became a distinguished professor of Latin at Harvard.

"Did you know that undergraduates here live in suites, and in the dining halls they have table-cloths and are served their meals?" my classmate in Chinese said. "They are a privileged lot, not like us poor graduate students," he continued. I thought of my tiny room on the third floor of an old rooming house, and how when I rented it for an expensive sixty dollars a month, I asked how it was heated. "You must have matches to light the small gas heater," was the aged landlady's reply. She had never been west of Worcester, and thought that anyone coming from Illinois must be living in the wild west among Indians. At least it is a place to sleep, I thought; my studying will be in the Law School library, not too far away, and open every night until ten.

A Divinity School student, Larry Cox, was in the Chinese class, and I asked if he intended to become a missionary. "No I am in the Div School only because the tuition is much less. Many of us are really in other fields," was his retort. Such was the state of the Divinity school at that time.

The History Department, to which I belonged, had no money to aid students, so I was told to speak to Serge Elisséeff, a Japanese specialist and the director of the Harvard-Yenching Institute, which had an endowment from the Aluminum Corporation of America. "Yes, I will give you the $400 for the year's tuition, but you must study Chinese and Chinese History," was his genial reply.

Since I wanted to do this anyway, it was no hardship to agree. In those days Chinese was taught as a dead language, and the instructor, James Ware, even suggested that Latin or Greek should be a prerequisite for the study of Chinese. He was enough of an eccentric to drive students from his class, and finally he became a recluse who could not be fired since he had tenure. Memorization of Chinese characters took most of my study time to the detriment of other courses.

Harvard had a galaxy of talented professors, some of whom can only be described as unusual characters. My advisor in the History Department was Professor Robert Blake, a huge man who had a vivacious Cossack wife Nadia. He was a prodigious drinker, which he had amplified by his study years in St. Petersburg and teaching in Tiflis. He nurtured his students in guidance, and in studies of Byzantine history, but he was enamored of bibliography. Once in class he wrote on the blackboard the author and title of a book in Italian and advised his students to read it. One raised his hand and said "Sir, I do not know Italian." Blake merely turned and said, "Well learn it". It was at his house that I was able to meet savants such as Cardinal Tisserant from Rome, expert on Oriental churches. At the meeting many of the local

Catholic hierarchy were present, and they were shocked when Robert Casey, an Episcopal cleric and professor at Brown University arrived and shook hands with his friend the cardinal, instead of bending and kissing his ring. Professor Michael Rostovtzeff, a distinguished ancient historian, at that time at Yale was also a visitor, but he soon lost his mind and died. The many Europeans on the Harvard faculty made it a cosmopolitan center, so unlike the isolationist mid-West, where, as mentioned, it was more than frowned upon if one spoke a foreign language in public. For me it was a new world, intellectually exciting and overwhelming, especially because of the many books in the famous Widener library.

Arthur Darby Nock was a most learned professor of Comparative Religion from Cambridge, England, whose bawdy limericks amused or disgusted others. One such was the following: "the wife of the chronic crusader reproduced every bastard who laid her, till the amorous itch of that populous bitch so dismayed her crusader, he spayed her." He was full of limericks, but he swallowed his words so much, together with a heavy Oxbridge accent, that it was difficult for students to understand him, and his fastidiousness was ever apparent. He would cover a doorknob with his handkerchief to open it, and he always carried an umbrella, rain or shine.

George Sarton from Belgium, founder of the discipline of the History of Science, would descend the steps of Widener at night and greet students and colleagues with a cheerful 'good morning.' His daughter May was a prominent poet, and served as his hostess when people were invited for tea to their house just off Brattle Street. Otherwise she always retreated into her own quarters when students or colleagues of her father appeared. His first doctoral candidate was a Turkish student Aydin Sayïlï, who later became my roommate, and at any slight tremor of the earth would rush onto the street, a habit brought from his homeland.

Harvard was not only a home of *prima donnas* among the faculty, but of fascinating 'characters,' who lived in Cambridge. One of these was Alois R. Nykl, a specialist on Mozarabic, the mixed dialect of Christians living under Arab rule, as well as Arabic inscriptions from Portugal and Spain. He had come to the USA in 1893 as a boy wonder who could speak many languages, and was exhibited in the Bohemian village of Chicago's world fair. Later he had earned a doctorate in Romance languages from the University of Chicago, but had not taken an academic job. Instead he edited a Japanese newspaper in that country. He also translated the Quran into Czech, but he had an abrasive and arrogant personality. He would delight in showing language professors that he knew more than they. For example, once on the steps of Widener library, to Jerry Ford a prominent professor of Romance languages, he pushed a Catalan newspaper under his nose and asked if he could translate it. Ford was taken aback, and before he could answer Nykl took the paper away muttering that such professors were ignorant. He criticized native Russians for making supposed grammatical errors in their own language, and in general was a nuisance. Unable to hold any academic position, he was kept busy and alive editing the Arabian Nights for our Arabic professor William Thomson, a genial Scot from Glasgow, whose gutturals were ideal for speaking Arabic, even though it, similar to Chinese, was taught like Greek or Latin.

Every summer Sinologists would come to the Harvard-Yenching Institute to work on the Chinese language dictionary in Boylston Hall, an enormous project with thousands of cards. Prof. Duyvendak from Leiden looked and acted like an aged mandarin, while Peter Boodberg from Berkeley was an inspiration to many of us for his studies of Inner Asian nomads. Elisséeff, was a special treat with his ability to dance in Japanese fashion with fans, and his extra-curricular classes in calligraphy. His family had lost their department stores in Russia, but still in Moscow the old store was called by his name by local folk.

At dinners minute scholarly topics were often discussed. For example, one evening William Hung, a specialist in Chinese literature, proposed that the sound, and associations with the sound of a Chinese character, had more effect in poetry than the image of the character. This position was attacked by Duyvendak and a young student of Chinese Literature, Hightower. Hung was not to be fazed, and added an interesting suggestion that art was an artist trying to present his unconscious thoughts and craft to the unconscious appreciation of others, in which more might be obtained from the artistic creation than was originally conceived. Science, on the other hand, was an attempt to present the conscious, so that another person would see and understand, as nearly as possible, what the scientist sought. Such was the distinction of Harvard, fully the equal of Oxcam's high tables.

In the spring of 1941 I became more involved in Far Eastern studies since I moved into a Chinese students' house on Francis Avenue and Kirkland St., where a Chinese couple provided Chinese cooking, and I learned how to eat with chopsticks. My roommates were Chou-I liang, later to become head of Beijing University and Cheng-Te-kun, prominent archaeologist of ancient China. My move from the Near to the Far East pointed towards a career in which Central Asia would be approached from the Chinese side. For a time my model was William McGovern, a flamboyant professor of Political Science at Northwestern University, who wrote a history of ancient Inner Asia, and with whom I had many interesting discussions when he came as a visiting professor to Harvard.

The Peabody Museum and department of Anthropology was home to several retired businessmen who drew no salary, but whose devotion to teaching and research exceeded even regular faculty. A former businessman Lauriston Ward, was a first rate teacher of the archaeology of Asia, and inspired his students as only a passionate amateur could do. Another such private scholar was Eric Schroeder, a delightful Englishman who was a specialist in Persian Islamic paintings. Even though he did not teach, his home was always open to young and old interested in the Orient. In the Anthropology Department Carleton Coon, a physical anthropologist and former newspaper reporter, was rough and bearlike in manner, who also inspired devotion from his students. He wanted to measure Nock's large cranium, but was not allowed to do so. After the war Louis Dupree, later a specialist on Afghanistan, became his and my student.

Before the war Russian was taught in the Germanic languages department by Samuel Cross, who had served in the American Embassy in Moscow. He too was competent, and a good drill master, but not so much academically inclined. The department of Semitic Languages held only three professors, Harry Wolfson for Hebrew, who was a specialist on philosophy from Aristotle to Maimonides, Thomson for Arabic and Robert Pfeiffer for Akkadian and Syriac, also director of the Semitic Museum. Pfeiffer after only one stein of beer would become overly jovial, to the distaste of some of the opposite sex. His spouse was a charming Italian lady who was able to calm stormy sessions between guests at their house when disagreements arose. Once when W. F. Albright from Johns Hopkins University declared that his excavations in Palestine took precedence over students and family, a sharp retort from Nadia Blake was expertly controlled by Mrs. Pfeiffer.

In the Art department was Langdon Warner, who was interested in the art of Chinese Turkestan, and his assistant Ben Rowland, an Indian art specialist. They too provided a friendly and relaxed atmosphere for students. A contrast to the hustle and bustle of later times, Harvard was a genteel and fascinating place before the war with devoted teachers of broad interests. Later as specialization became dominant the professors appeared not as interesting as previously, even though they might be characterized as more serious, and more specialized, than their more urbane predecessors.

Inasmuch as there was no department of Near Eastern Studies at the university, and such languages as Turkish and Persian were not regularly taught here or at any university in the country, anyone interested in the lands between China and the Mediterranean, had to study on his own. Harvard College, however, seemed to be a glorified 'finishing school' for students destined for Wall Street or Washington, while the graduate school seemed to be only a place for future academics. In one French class a student asked why nothing was done to assist him to learn to speak French, instead of only reading literature. The astonished professor replied, "one doesn't come to a university to learn to speak a language, for that you should go to a Berlitz school of practical languages." The universities at that time were much closer to their Medieval ancestors than to the new institutions of higher learning in the post-war world. Today young college students find it difficult to picture the university world of the thirties, for computers and canned lectures, with fixed curricula dominate the landscape.

My second year Chinese class was fascinating for we began to read difficult classical texts, which required intense concentration on various meanings of characters. Our teacher was Edwin Reischauer, a specialist of Japanese, who many times had to bring to the class specialists on ancient philosophical texts for aid. In the class were students who were more advanced in Chinese than those who had only studied one year of the language. One was Ed Schafer, who later became professor of Chinese in Berkeley, and like me was interested in Inner Asia. Similarly, however, he never learned to speak Chinese well.

By the summer of 1941 my earlier loneliness had changed to a whirl of social teas and dinners with various professors and friends. The post-war specialization, and emphasis on practicality and future jobs, was a different world from the genteel Harvard of the past. To succeed, however, I realized that I would have to study harder than classmates from more prosperous and fortunate backgrounds.

CHAPTER 10

Post-war Harvard

AFTER the war great changes came to the university, even in sports. Before the war I had continued fencing at Harvard in matches using the three pronged, sharp attachment at the point of the épée blade. My right arm had a number of scars from previous contests, but now new electric plungers were attached to the end of the blade, and one had to wear wires inside his jacket attached to a cord on a pulley. It seemed to me cumbersome, and it changed the style of fencing, reducing speed. I reluctantly adapted to the new conditions. The French coach had retired and a new Yugoslav coach was in his place.

On returning to Harvard from Washington in the fall of 1946 I found that there were many girls in classes and only a few boys, the latter usually decried by the girls as having escaped the draft and thus unworthy of attention. All attempts to describe my experiences during the war to the fair sex at dances received only glances of disbelief, so any talk of adventures overseas was dropped. The first year was spent in Perkins Hall, an old graduate dormitory with a roommate who had somehow eluded war service, but at least I did not have to work in a restaurant or study Chinese language, art, and history, since now I had money from war work to pay for tuition and living expenses. It became clear to me that continuing in Chinese was a life's work, demanding more effort than I had to offer, and It was necessary to concentrate on my real interest in Central Asia and Iran. The war had returned me to the Near East, but I did not abandon interest in the Far East. In the spring of 1946 nomination to the prestigious Society of Fellows provided impetus to finish my thesis on Narshakhi's Persian History of Bukhara, and to receive the PhD diploma in June of the same year. Finally launched on an academic career, my time and energy were now devoted to scholarly matters.

Having finished all classes before the war, Blake put me to work on classical Armenian, and together we published a translation of an Armenian text on the history of the Mongols. We also made a translation of a Medieval Arabic text of the travels of Ibn Fadlan to the Volga. This provided material for a novel by Michael Crichton called *Eaters of the Dead*, and a film *The Thirteenth Warrior,* both significantly far from the text.

Blake was my mentor, and even more frequent invitations came to drink and dine with him at his home just off Brattle Street where many old professors lived, now inhabited by bankers and lawyers. Since Blake's wife was Russian, Professor Karpovich in the History Department, Elisséeff, and many other Russians, came to Blake's dinners. When our father died of leukemia on his 62nd birthday and Blake soon afterwards, it was a double blow which required time for me to recover. Soon followed the death of George Sarton; his daughter May sent me a poem, with an invitation to come to their home to take some mementoes by which to remember her father. One by one my teachers died, until only Harry Wolfson and William Thomson remained, but even they were marginalized in the new post-war world. This meant that their influence was gone, and they retreated to their studies and their own research. It seemed as though they could not adjust to the new students who had returned from the war who sought practical goals. All this time Iran and Central Asia eluded me at Harvard. Then I heard about Henning a German scholar who had fled his homeland and ended in the University of London.

I had read some of the articles of Walter B. Henning with admiration, and hoped to study with him, when the news came that he had been invited to Columbia University. An internationally recognized authority in the field of Middle Iranian Studies, Henning had been sent to a detention camp in England during the early part of the war, and in early 1946 crossed the Atlantic to continue his career in New York. I decided to arrange to take classes in Middle Persian and Sogdian with him, either by commuting or, if necessary, moving to New York for classes.

On entering his study room at Morningside Heights, I was startled to find almost a dwarf with a hunched back. He moved his somewhat enlarged head slowly and deliberately, but his dark eyes were penetrating with an air of complete control of any situation. If you asked him a question, he would deliberate and slowly respond with a minimum of well chosen words. He almost cast a spell over his listener, and it was clear he would not abide fools. At a request to study under him, he replied he would not stay at Columbia, but return to London were he was a lecturer, a junior position at the School of Oriental and African Studies of the University of London. "They offered me an associate professorship here," he said with a note of contempt, "and I asked associate to whom?" Possibly the American system had not been explained to him, for such a tenure post was given to younger scholars, rather than a full professorship, usually reserved for older academics in the Humanities or Social Sciences. But his dignity had been offended by Colonial types, and he would return to Europe where scholars were respected. Then he introduced me to one of his good students at Columbia, Donald Keene, with whom, as he advised, one should converse. Keene did not continue in Iranian Studies, and later was to become professor of Japanese literature at Columbia.

In September of the same year, as a new Junior Fellow at the Society of Fellows of Harvard University, I went to London to study ancient Iranian languages, and I came to know Hennning better. The senior fellows in the Society reluctantly agreed to allow me to go for my first year, saying it was most irregular, and only because of the disruption, which had been caused by the war, would they allow this exception to their rules. It was not easy to find a boat going to England for travel conditions had not returned to normal over the ocean, but eventually after much searching one was found.

On 30 August 1946 aboard a decrepit 'Liberty' ship called the Ferdinando Gorges, we sailed from Brooklyn for Southampton, with seven other passengers in four aft cabins which the gun crew had used during the war. This was the only means of transport to Europe in those days. The quarters were filthy, and the garbage and debris on our aft deck turned one's stomach, and not until we were well clear of the harbor could they be pushed overboard and the decks hosed. The voyage of fourteen days and thirteen nights was memorable only for poor food and uninspiring company. Just before leaving, a letter from Karl Menges, a friend and colleague, and a Turkologist in Columbia University, arrived asking help to rescue a prominent Soviet Mongolist living in hiding in the British Zone of Germany. Allied authorities had his name on a list of wanted refugees from the USSR. Many former Soviet citizens had joined the Germans during the war, and now Stalin wanted them back.

Since I had served in the Research and Analysis section of the East European branch of the OSS in Washington from June until September 1945, Menges thought I might be able to pull a few strings to go and find Nikolai Poppe. First, however, a stay in London to find a place to live was in order.

London in 1946 was recovering from the war, with ration coupons, a lack of quarters and also of heat in rooms. Since classes would not begin until October, and I could not at that time find living quarters in London, it seemed better to fly to Paris and then to Zürich where Engler and I would discuss editing a book about Afghanistan, and hopefully a trip to Germany might be arranged. Air service had revived after the war, but only for a few flights inside western Europe.

Paris had little of the austerity of London, and it was a pleasure to visit Henry Corbin and other friends, to go to the opera and museums, and to enjoy good food in restaurants. Zürich was even more flourishing than Paris, and a short stay in an old 17th century house in Wädenswil on the lake was pure delight. Meeting Rudi Stuckert, and talking of our time in Kabul, brought to mind the saying of the Persian poet Rudaki that there is no greater joy in life than seeing the faces of friends. My only disappointment was going to see a play by Gerhard Hauptmann, *Das Biberpelz*, but on entering found that the dialogue was in Schweizer Deutsch, although outside every notice of the play was written in Hoch Deutsch.

Back to Paris at the headquarters of the OSS, a trip to Germany for civilians was declared impossible at that time, even when I explained the urgency of such a trip. Hoping for a change of regulations in a short time, I returned to London to find a place to live and organize my year of study, which was realized. After a week, however, the possibility of a trip into Germany improved according to a friend in the Paris headquarters, and a return there was planned. A former OSS person in the US embassy helped in obtaining a pass, but a photo and badge were necessary which would take time. Relying on similar experiences in the Orient, with determination both were secured and, against expectations, even a berth on the night train to Frankfurt. From the train, as we passed through towns, the destruction on all sides was enormous, and in Frankfurt many streets were impassable because of the debris. Hardly an unscathed building could be observed, and I opined that Germany would never be rebuilt as it had been. Only near the railroad station, target of many bomber raids, a few apartment buildings seemed intact, and in one of them on Gutleut Strasse I found Heinrich Menges, father of Karl, who briefed me about Poppe and where he was living.

It was necessary to go to Heidelberg, US army headquarters in Germany, to obtain permission to travel in the country. Fortunately there was a sympathetic OSS civilian employee called Henry (last names were unmentioned), who agreed to go north with me to find our refugee. Leaving for Thuringia, we drove through Giessen and Marburg to a mountain resort, where we had lunch with Henry's British counterpart, for the British had to be informed of our intentions. Both the American and British secret services opposed the repatriation of Soviet citizens from Germany, and any moves against this policy had to be hidden from all of the armies of occupation. It was embarrassing for me to see the British chauffeur eat at a separate table from the rest of us, and later the bitterness between classes in England came out, when in private he decried the officers' snootiness, and speaking a different 'language' from the common folk. But with a Labor government coming to power it was a harbinger of changes to come in British society.

After a pleasant night at Bielefeld, in a hotel which had been requisitioned by the British army, in the rain we proceeded to Rittergut (estate of) Böckel where the elderly Gräfin (countess) served tea brought by an even more aged servant. During the tea she closely questioned us, to determine who we were. After half an hour she was satisfied and sent the servant to bring Poppe from a hut in the rear of the estate. He was very nervous until we were able to persuade him of our identity, and desire to bring him out of Germany. He was full of information about other Soviet citizens in Germany, which Henry was pleased to hear. Poppe selected the name Pushkin as the pseudonym under which he could be contacted. I agreed to be the middleman between him and American authorities. It was late at night and raining when we returned to Heidelberg. The Germans, with whom I spoke were either sullen or stiff, but at least willing to talk with a foreigner who appreciated their literature and culture. Fortunately not only was my German in good shape, but I had memorized many poems. The recitation of poems was a good entry into conversation with foreigners everywhere.

I missed my flight to Paris because of staying too long at the Oriental Institute of Heidelberg University. Planes were much slower at that time and, of course, low flying and not pressurized. More planes were now flying and the next day another one left Frankfurt for Orly where I remained over night, and flew the next morning to London, arriving late to the first class in Middle Persian.

Henning's Middle and Old Persian classes with classmate Mary Boyce were difficult, but even more was Sogdian with a classmate Dr. Godakumbura from the University of Ceylon, who was only interested in Buddhist texts, which to me were boring in their repetitions. As if this were not enough, Arthur Arberry, head of the Near Eastern Department, assigned me to a class in Arabic, since, he averred, everyone in his department should study Arabic no matter if they were interested in other languages or had studied the language previously. Our teacher was an Iraqi journalist Khulusi who claimed to have initiated the designation 'Arab Gulf' for the usual Persian Gulf, a designation which was to cause trouble in the future. A close friend was Bernard Lewis and his Danish wife, with whom many pleasant hours were spent. It was customary to give one's food coupons to a dinner host rather than bringing flowers or liquor, which in any case were not easily found.

Trips to Cambridge to meet a retired pro-Soviet Orientalist, Vladimir Minorsky, Sir Harold Bailey and Ilya Gershevitch, former prize student of Henning, were happy interludes from classes in London. Staying with Gershevitch, every night we had to put the bed sheets on a stove to see the steam rise, otherwise sleeping on them would have been damp and cold. One had to be careful not to burn the sheets, which required practice. These contacts in many respects were more important than the hours spent in libraries and museums.

Gershevitch, living in Cambridge was waiting for an academic position, and I was surprised to find him such a devoted emulator of his master, even to mannerisms. Henning's second student, Mary Boyce, was the same age as I, and in the same classes, yet she too was under the spell of the remarkable teacher, but I was not long enough in London to completely fall under his influence, since it was necessary to return to Harvard in 1947 to continue studies on my own. Nonetheless, the time spent in London provided good training for future teaching tasks.

In Oxford Gibb and Paul Kahle, a refugee Arabist from Bonn, were especially friendly. Staying in the Old Parsonage was a memorable experience, for the ancient stone structure was very cold without heat, and the boiled eggs for breakfast seemed made of rubber. Food in England in the post war period was neither plentiful nor tasty, and furthermore it was rationed, requiring coupons.

For Christmas vacation I resolved to visit relatives in Lidköping, Sweden, but the trip was more arduous than planned. The plane to Copenhagen was cancelled because of snow, so I hurried to catch a train to Harwich but missed it. A Dane, who also had missed the train, suggested we take a taxi, but the roads were icy and we arrived at the dock just as the boat for Copenhagen was leaving. Instead we boarded the night boat to the Hoek van Holland. Without a Dutch visa the authorities were perplexed and suspicious, but allowed me to go to Amsterdam to catch a plane to Copenhagen. Tickets could not be purchased with British pounds, and the banks were closed on Sunday. An American hotel in town changed my money into Dutch guilders, but on returning to the KLM office they insisted that, as a foreigner, I had to change money at an authorized bank. " But they are closed," I protested. Finally we compromised and I paid for the ticket half with guilders and half with travellers checks, an unusual event in post war Europe I was told.

It was a Swedish Airlines airplane to Copenhagen, and the pretty stewardess persuaded me to remain on the almost empty plane to Malmö, but it filled with Swedes returning from the famous Tivoli gardens, and it was impossible to talk with the stewardess. I took a train to Lund and visited Stig Wikander a professor of comparative philology and religion. When told that I had just arrived from Amsterdam he began speaking French until I remarked that I was from Harvard and an American, after which we shifted to English. It was Christmas eve, so an introduction to *glögg,* Swedish tea with raisins and alcohol, was proposed. He put me on a train bound for Stockholm, but the next thing I remembered was a group of naval officers standing over me, demanding what I was doing at a naval base on the Baltic. I had fallen asleep in the wagon which was detached from the train and sent to the base.

The officers put me on another train and I descended at Linköping at eight at night, taking a taxi to 12 Rudenskjöldsgatan. In surprise, the driver told me such a street did not exist there until I showed him a letter from my cousins. "Oh that is Lidköping not Linköping, and it is on the other side of Sweden," was his uncomforting reply. It was very cold so I sat in the cathedral church until the midnight train to Göteborg. In the church Bishop Tor Andrae gave a rousing sermon, punctuated by several vehement declarations of *Jag tror på Gott* (I believe in God), which awakened those of us sleeping in the back of the church.

The all night train ride to Göteborg was comfortable, compared to trains in Iran, but it was crowded. At the small town of Skjövde a transfer to what may be termed a Toonerville trolley finally brought me to Lidköping, and for the first time to uncle Eric and his wife Susanne, with two daughters Ingrid and Britta my age.

An old-fashioned Swedish Christmas is something to be remembered. One first noticed the blue flag with yellow cross everywhere, outside and in smaller versions on the Christmas tree. A rice pudding for breakfast had a ring in one serving and whoever found it was considered lucky. Also a pot of pork fat with bread in it, the name of which sounded like *doppy gritan*, was supposed to represent the food for the poor on Christmas day, but since now the Swedish welfare state took care of everyone, it became only a symbol for each family on Christmas day. The small red wooden horses, Dalarna *hester*, the significance of which no one knew, were supposedly brought to the homeland by Swedes from Minnesota, but this seemed to me unlikely. Everyone wrote a short poem attached to every gift to another. For example, Ingrid wrote for me "You my dear Dick are a funny fellow (rimes with Dick). You wanted to go to Lidköping but only came to Linköping." It sounds nice in Swedish, hardly in English.

On Saturday farmers came into the town square in wagons pulled by horses, and they sold their produce, meats, cheeses and liqueurs to the townsfolk. Swedes were considered liberal and uninhibited, especially in regard to sex, but the citizens of this small town were conservative and overly religious. Uncle Eric, a retired engineer, not only attended the Lutheran state church but a missionary church as well. What was one to do in a small Swedish town in 1946? There was only one foreigner in town - myself, wearing a long Afghan overcoat and a karakul cap, an object of interest on the part of the local population. Ingrid had the after effects of polio, and had to be carried most of the time, although she could manage with a set of canes. She had lost any ambition, but wrote poetry, and her mind was active. Britta was a nurse in Stockholm and was home only for the holiday. I returned with her to the capital and we attended an opera Turandot, but inasmuch as we were cousins, according to her we could not make love to each other.

I made a quick flight to Frankfurt, and by train to Heidelberg and back to Frankfurt, then by plane to Zürich and finally back to London. The entire vacation seemed to have been spent in traveling, and at that time planes were rarely full, and seats were easily obtainable at short notice. London was even colder than before Christmas, and at the British Museum readers had to wear gloves in holding books, while periodically one went to the washroom to wash hands in hot water. At least in Britain the water was hot. At a rag debate on 'Resolved that chewing gum is the cement of American civilization,' which Mary and I attended, anti-American feeling clearly was high, especially by young Brits criticizing local women who married or went with better paid American soldiers. My attempt to retort with the remark, "women of Britain are you going to take this lying down or standing up", was not recognized by the chair.

There was too much studying to worry about such matters, and every evening after the close of the SOAS (School of Oriental and African Studies) library I boarded an underground train for North Finchley, went into a pub for a glass of cyder and then home to a rented room in a house called Oakdene in North Finchely with a Jewish family. Fortunately the house where I was staying had central heating, even though I could see my breath in the still cold room. At least it was better than houses in Oxford and Cambridge, which were heated with coal stoves. Food rationing also was stringent in its restrictions. My stay in London, however, was cut short at the request of senior fellows of the Society, and it was back to Harvard at the end of April 1947. But wanderlust was not quenched and plans were made to go to Iran the following summer.

By this time most of the faculty had returned from Washington or from the army, and most students were veterans, serious about their future plans and with little frivolity, as existed before the war. Austerity was also a legacy of the military which had occupied Harvard during the war. Gone were table cloths and servants. Everyone now ate from plastic trays in cafeteria style, and in the dormitories and houses each was expected to take care of his own linen. But it was not so much the physical changes as the different atmosphere which had entered the ivory towers of the Ivy league colleges. Latin soon dropped from diplomas and other documents, and clearly moves in the direction of practical studies were in the making. Requirements were changed, for one no longer studied to become well-rounded or cultivated in the Classics, but rather for the real world of jobs. One might regret the passing of the genteel outlook, but change was inevitable.

In 1948 I served as secretary to a committee on Near Eastern Studies of the American Council of Learned Societies, composed of old professors who wanted no changes in their time honored methods. For example, Arabic was taught by all of them from an

English translation of a nineteenth century German grammar of Albert Socin, following a Latin model. Warning the members of the committee that it would be abolished if some action to adapt to the times were not taken, I for one could observe the coming changes in academia and realized that adaption was in order. John Marshal of the Rockefeller Foundation spelled out what changes the foundation would support. If departments maintained a focus only on the past, then new centers of area studies concerned with the present world would be created outside of the department. There were few specialists on the contemporary Near East at that time anywhere in faculties of universities.

One more year remained in the Junior fellowship, and already other universities were expanding their teaching curricula, and looking for young teachers. The future seemed bright for recent graduates in most universities, and the first university to accept the grant of the Rockefeller Foundation to create a Middle East Center, mostly devoted to contemporary affairs, was the University of Michigan which hired George Cameron, an Elamite specialist from Chicago, to be the new director. He had seen the writing on the wall, and led the way. Harvard, tardy as usual, waited until 1950 to begin discussions about the future. The ivory tower universities were changing, with support going to centers and programs outside of the academic structures or traditional departments.

Finally at Harvard an umbrella organization was formed with Professor William Langer as its head. This gravely voiced prolific writer of factual histories, had been the head of the Research and Analysis section of the Coordinator of Information in 1941, changed to the OSS then to CIA, and was a seasoned administrator. Under him were John Fairbank, head of the East Asian Center, Klyde Kluckhohn, an anthropologist, head of the East European Center, and myself as the work horse of the Middle East Center. Since I did not have tenure, Langer officially was head of the Middle East Center, but daily operations fell to me. In a dispute in the CIA in Washington, between Ted Lockhart a Harvard anthropologist and Kermit Roosevelt, the latter won and Lockhart became our executive secretary. All the centers were located in a building formerly a dormitory on Dunster St., now the large Holyoke center for administration of the university.

The first fellow in our center was Firuz Kazemzadeh, whom I, when a third year Junior Fellow in 1949, had examined on Persian history. He had received his doctorate in Russian history and returned to Tehran, expecting a post in the university, but was denied an appointment because of being a Bahai. He needed a position in this country, so the fellowship was welcomed. Later he became professor of Russian history at Yale and secretary of the Bahai organization of North America.

The Department of Semitic Languages would have nothing to do with the new center, so the teaching of modern languages was relegated to Comparative Philology. As mentioned, in the past all languages were taught as Latin and Greek, with the order to read and memorize. If one wanted to speak a language, he should go to a school of practical languages. Such teaching was not the business of universities, but now universities were being asked to revise their methods. Charles Ferguson, a linguist who had set up a school of spoken Arabic in Lebanon, was persuaded to come to Harvard and oversee the teaching of Arabic, Turkish and Persian, with native informants. The language departments, however, were on the whole uncooperative, and they controlled academic appointments, so much diplomatic activity was necessary.

Since there was no department of Slavic languages, a new one was created with people able to use modern methods of teaching languages. The department of Semitic Languages continued as previously, although the new state of Israel, and students from the Near East, put pressure on the three professors to admit the teaching of modern Hebrew and Arabic. They refused however and turned the task over to the committee on Comparative Philology. Although not a member of the Semitic department, I was asked to teach beginning Hebrew one semester when Robert Pfeiffer went on leave. This was especially difficult since the only Hebrew I had studied was before the war at the Hillel House in Illinois in 1939. Our teacher was Abraham Sachar, future first president of Brandeis University; only he did not teach, but had a rabbi from Cincinnati instruct the few students in the difficult book of Jeremiah. Also teaching classical Arabic was assigned to me for several years, for Thomson was ready to retire.

The East Asian duo, Edwin Reischauer and John Fairbank, were now in charge of the Harvard-Yenching Institute and the department of East Asian Languages. They were somewhat ruthless in clearing out the old order, for the Chinese dictionary project was terminated and countless cards were thrown away until they were rescued by Francis Cleaves, professor of Mongolian and Chinese, who brought them to his farm house in New Hampshire. It was sad to see the enormous amount of time and effort which had gone into the project go down the drain, and hostility between the old guard and the reformers was unconcealed. Since I was sympathetic to both sides, a role as middleman and conciliator was a proper course to follow, but it led nowhere since mutual feelings were too bitter.

One assignment, as a third year Junior Fellow, was to lecture on the eastern part of the Islamic world in a course on anthropology, organized by Carleton Coon. Subsequently a reward came in the form of office space in the Peabody Museum. As my three year fellowship was coming to an end several offers of employment arrived. One was to head the Near Eastern section of the Library of Congress, another was from Norman Brown at the University of Pennsylvania for a new assistant professorship in Iranian Studies, and another from Michigan from George Cameron. These offers enabled me to secure a joint appointment at Harvard as assistant professor in the History Department and in the Committee on Comparative Philology. The latter was presided over by a marionette of a professor of Classics, Joshua Whatmough, who proved to be a difficult taskmaster.

Many junior appointments to the faculty in those days were made by the provost Paul H. Buck, with scant regard for the wishes of a department, which in any case was happy to receive extra posts as gifts from the administration, but tenure appointments remained in their hands.

The year 1950 proved especially full, for my doctoral thesis on Narshakhi's *History of Bukhara* had to be prepared for publication by the Mediaeval Academy of America, the office of which was over the cinema at Harvard Square. In return, Charles Miller, head of that office, persuaded me to accept the job of book review editor for the journal *Speculum.* Following the common path of trying to make oneself indispensable, in order to secure promotion, too many tasks were accepted. Another was as assistant secretary of the newly founded American Research Center in Egypt. But I realized it was vital to turn attention to the contemporary scene if support for promotion was to be secured. Also, even though I had lived in Afghanistan and Turkey, I concluded that Iran was a key to understanding the past of the whole area, much as the Roman Empire served as a background for Europe. Luckily my old Turkish teacher, Walter Wright, again came to my rescue in 1948 by asking me to collaborate with him on a book called *The United States, Turkey and Iran*. At that time the two countries were not deemed important enough to devote a separate volume to each in a series The American Foreign Policy Library. The book was published by Harvard University Press in 1951 after the death of Wright. A year earlier a summer school program of teaching on the contemporary Near East was organized and directed by me. Charles Issawi came to teach economics, Majid Khadduri government and politics of the area, H.A.R. Gibb from Oxford on cultural and social problems, while Moshe Pearlmann taught modern Arabic. A conference on the Great Powers and the Near East was held in August, which resulted in a book by the same name. Issawi in his autobiography mentioned that his probably was the first course on the economics of the Middle East anywhere. As if all these projects were insufficient, an old friend from the New York University Institute of Fine Arts, Alfred Salmony, persuaded me to be book review editor for his journal *Artibus Asiae*. Since I was actively engaged at that time in collecting books, I accepted and wrote many reviews of books which came to these journals.

One day a telephone call came from someone called Henry Kissinger, who had returned to Harvard, with a grant from the new Ford Foundation to bring young people from various countries, who held promise to develop into leaders in their lands, for a summer at the university. It was a parallel to the State Department's program to invite prominent politicians or officials from various countries to conferences in Washington, followed by VIP treatment if they wished to tour the USA. Since there was no one else at Harvard to advise him on the applications from Near Easterners, this lot fell to me. I recommended well-known poets and literary figures, as candidates for the positions from

Iran, but after two summers Kissinger became annoyed and complained that future government officials and ambassadors were not being considered. An explanation that most public leaders in Iran were in fact poets, and nowhere else in the world was poetry so highly valued as in Iran, did not convince him. Prominent Iranian literary figures, such as Sadeq Chubak and Jalal Al-Ahmad enjoyed a summer at Harvard, and the former was especially entranced by the squirrels in the yard of the university since such animals were not found in Iran. Later, when from all over the world foreign representatives came to Washington in various capacities, or simply on visits, when asked if they previously had been to the USA, the answer was "Yes, Henry Kissinger invited me to Harvard." In this way the name of Kissinger became well known to government officials in Washington. It may be hard to believe, but Kissinger was much more 'Germanic' then than later, both in speech and demeanor.

In the summer of 1948 a trip to Iran was arranged with a Guggenheim grant to go to a Middle Persian inscription at a remote site in the south called Sar Meshhed, which had been discovered by Ernst Herzfeld, but the inscription had remained undeciphered. Iran at that time had recovered from the Soviet occupation of the north and the British in the south, and foreigners were welcomed, but the monopoly of the Anglo-Iranian oil company annoyed many Iranians, and it was soon to become a source of conflict.

CHAPTER 11

With the Aid of the Qashghais

THE TEHRAN airport was now the old Allied military one at Amirabad, since the small, old airport in the eastern part of the city, Dushan Tepe, was no longer used for commercial flights. Not much had changed since the war years, but innovation was in the air, for young intellectuals wanted to shake off the restraints which had been imposed on the country during the Allied occupation. Since the Arabian American Oil Co. (ARAMCO) had made a deal with the Saudis in which their company remained a Saudi institution, Iranians looked to the Anglo-Iranian Oil Company to move in the same direction. The Brits, however, had no intention of turning over ownership and direction of their company to the Iranians. Many newspapers and journals, including those of the Communist (Tudeh=people's) party, flourished in Tehran, and many groups were forming behind prominent citizens, indicating a prelude to political parties, but in the end without success, for personalities rather than platforms dominated politics.

From Majcen's pension just south of Takht-e Jamshid, the main street in the north of the city, before mounting to the summer residences in Shemiran, every morning one could see the snow covered peak of Mt. Demavend in the east. The air was so clear that one could not imagine the pollution of a half a century later. The Yugoslav owner of the pension asked me to interpret for several Japanese businessmen who had come to buy the famous *dumb-e siyah* 'black tailed' long grain rice, the best in the world, according to the Japanese. When asked how they liked

Iran the response was unexpected, "Goddamn Orientals." I was taken aback and asked what was wrong. "We have been here only two weeks, and both of our watches and cameras have been stolen," was the reply. There was nothing more to be said on that subject. It was the early summer of 1948 and the effects of the war still lingered among the people, especially the lack of imports in the bazaar. On one occasion, however, walking with a bag of oranges, a beggar approached and asked for something to eat. I offered him two oranges which he threw to the ground, saying he wanted bread not fruit.

Since my intention was to go to Sar Meshhed, far in the south, to copy the Middle Persian inscription there, and only one small plane a day, always booked long in advance, flew to Shiraz, it was necessary to go by bus. Much better than Afghan counterparts, because of competition between several companies, the bus took only one day to Isfahan, over a dusty dirt road with frequent stops at tea houses. Invariably at the rear of each teashop was an opium den, where at times poor people gathered and ate *shire,* the dregs of opium. Isfahan has been described by others often, but the contrast with Shiraz was striking. The former was a bustling city with artisans and craftsmen, all eager to sell their wares, while Shiraz was a sleepy town in the south, where a merchant hardly cared whether a customer bought something from him or not. Travel on the dusty roads in summer was no enticement for tourists, and breakdowns were frequent.

In Shiraz Rev. Norman Sharp had constructed an Anglican church, across from a synagogue on a lane behind a cinema on the main street, and near a Zoroastrian fire temple. The main street was named after Karim Khan Zand, the much beloved ruler of Iran in the middle of the eighteenth century, who had made Shiraz his capital. Sharp was much interested in the antiquuities and ancient inscriptions of Fars province, and had incorporated copies of some in his church built in a Persian style. He agreed to help me on my investigations and on trips. First, the Aramaic inscription beside the tomb of Darius at Naqsh-e Rustam had to be copied, and, with the help of 'Ali Murad, a worker at Persepolis, we were able to climb to the burial chamber, carved from the rock cliff, and make a squeeze of the inscription. In those days a squeeze was made by placing large white sheets of blotting paper over the inscription, and then hammering the wet surface with a stiff brush so the paper would form the letters. This was different from the Chinese method of copying, or rather rubbing, the surface with black ink or graphite and then making an impression of the inscription. The paper squeezes needed buckets of water to dampen the paper thoroughly, and to haul them up to the tomb chamber was no easy task. Fortunately there was an iron ladder leaning against the cliff and it was possible to reach the tomb, now off limits to tourists. With 'Ali's help, however, the job was accomplished, and a number of other inscriptions were copied.

The trip to Sar Meshhed, however, presented difficulties, since the government had no jurisdiction over the area at that time. Rather it was the summer quarters of the Turkish speaking Qashghai tribe, and the chiefs had to agree to permit travel, as well as provide an escort for protection against bandits. The head of the Qashghais lived in the palace and garden called Bagh-e Aram in Shiraz, and through the good offices of Sharp and others he agreed to help on the trip. We left by truck before dawn.

The road from Shiraz down to the Persian Gulf had been carved out of the mountains by the Indian Army in World War I, and it had deteriorated since, for it was not used by the Allies in the second war effort of sending supplies to the Soviets. I was told that the Indian Army had built the road and then put up an inscription reading "India took the trouble; Iran took the profit." When Reza Shah saw it he ordered the inscription blasted from the cliff on which it had been carved. My escort was able to reach the town of Farrashband by truck descending two long passes, one called 'the daughter' and the other the 'old woman.' Why they had such names I never learned, but they should have been called something relating to the devil or hell, for they surpassed all roads I had traversed in Afghanistan in fright and difficulty. Several times a wheel went over the edge, and if the passengers had been in the truck instead of only the driver, it would have plunged hundreds of feet below. Furthermore it was the beginning of August, and once off the plateau the heat was intense. Potable water always was a problem, and it was advisable always to drink tea, which had to have boiling water.

At Farrashband we left the truck and obtained horses, for there was no road beyond. Fortunately my old ROTC training proved useful for the trip of five hours. Nevertheless, for me it had been a long time since riding, and the saddles were not up to the much maligned US army saddles in comfort. On arriving at the spring of water by the bas-relief and inscription, completely dehydrated, I fell on my stomach and drank while the tribesmen looked on. "Why don't you drink," I asked, for they had taken their dirty leather bags containing water to quench their thirst. "There are little worms in the water which can cause problems in your stomach," was their unwelcome reply. Unfortunately the inscription was high on the rock, and without a ladder it was impossible to copy the top, so only the bottom was copied by squeezes, as well as by photos. Ever since Afghanistan I had jokingly remarked that a *jinn* always sat on my shoulder ruining my photos, for invariably trouble occurred with cameras, and here was no exception. After taking six photos the camera jammed, possibly because of dust and sand. Because the Qashghais wanted to return to Shiraz I was unable to copy much of the inscription by hand but it was late and we had to leave. I felt glad to return to Shiraz alive, for the trip had fully taxed all resources, and fortunately the spring water had no ill effects. Shortly after the trip a gun battle between the tribesmen and gendarmes had occurred near Farrashband, and it was fortunate that I had made my trip earlier.

On the main street of Shiraz were many *sherbet-khanes*, like tea houses, but serving all kinds of fruit juices, and it was a pleasure in the hot evening to sit in them and discuss many subjects with the local citizens. Invariably poetry was recited and composed, while the *kalyan* or water pipe provided a relaxing time. Women, who were with husbands or family members, would also engage in conversation. The belief among foreigners that Iranian women were shy and oppressed in my opinion was a myth. Not that conservative people did not exist, as everywhere in the world, but not many then in Shiraz. In the city one could find all kinds of citrus fruits, from a sweet lemon to a large *bi-htabi,* a cross between a grapefruit and lemon, but only good for preserves. There were few autos on the streets and not many victorias, which served as taxis in the provincial towns. Tehran already had automobiles and taxis, which comforts were slow in reaching the provinces. Because of the poets and scholars, as well as the many gardens in town and surroundings, Shiraz was an appealing place and I resolved to return for a longer stay.

In the morning several passengers went to the small airport, to the west of the town center, to board a plane for Tehran. It arrived from Isfahan and the pilot appeared at the door to say that the plane was not going to the capital but to Abadan. It was scheduled to fly to Tehran and tickets had been sold, but the pilot was adamant and the ground authorities could not change his mind. Planes at that time were usually crowded with passengers sitting on the floor, sometimes even with sheep or chickens, but this plane appeared almost empty. Perhaps some VIP had pre-empted the plane. So our tickets were refunded and three of us sought to hire a car to drive to Tehran. After much negotiation a chauffeur was found who agreed to take us to Tehran, but the fare for each was more than for the the plane. No other possibility presented itself, for plane schedules were unreliable, and no one could guarantee a seat on a later flight. Two companions had to arrive the next day and the driver swore he could accomplish such a feat. It was an all night twelve hour trip, a real *tour de force*, and we arrived in Tehran covered with dust and exhausted. No flat tires or breakdown made the trip memorable for the speed over dirt roads.

In the capital a number of associations or clubs of poets and writers were producing journals and newspapers. In one of the meetings on the street called lower Lalezar a group of writers had assembled to publish a new literary journal called *Sukhan* 'word' or 'speech'. It is impossible to remember all of the literary lights gathered to encourage the editor, Parviz Khanlari, with his new magazine, but one quiet figure in the corner, who did not speak, was Sadeq Hedayat, a prominent novelist, who was to leave for Paris where he would commit suicide. Sadeq Chubak, on the other hand, was ebullient, while Sa'id Nafisi was full of anecdotes. This was the beginning of friendship with many writers, which was to be sustained over the years. Others, such as the solemn Hasan Taqizadeh, an eminent political and scholarly figure, with his German wife, to me seemed overly *garb-zadeh* 'West inspired'. I preferred to speak with Iranians who had not been educated abroad, for they better preserved old traditions and were more interesting.

At that time there were several theaters on lower Lalezar, where both historical and political plays were produced, the latter usually with much satire. One historical play especially remains in memory, a play about Atabeg, a nineteenth century prime minister, who was imprisoned and then murdered in prison. When the dying man wrote a testament with his own blood on the wall of the prison, lights came on behind red paper on the wall as he traced his message, and the long applause of the audience indicated the moving effect on them of the little technological display.

Airplanes were improving in performance continually, so the return trip to Boston via Frankfurt, with a side trip to Heidelberg, had only two stops, in Iceland and at Gander in Newfoundland. Back at Harvard new tasks awaited. By autumn our father Nels was sinking from a severe case of leukemia, and before I could reach home to see him he died on his birthday, December 16 at the age of sixty-two. This was a trauma for me since I had been away from home so long and had missed his counsel and conversations. My younger brother and mother tried to keep the cinemas going, but debts and other problems soon brought an end to life in Danville. Television had also contributed to a decline in cinema attendance. They moved to Wayne, Michigan, while Bill remained in Los Angeles, now working on NASA's Apollo Mission for Rand Corporation. I had become engaged to the editorial secretary of the Harvard Journal of Asiatic Studies, Barbara York, daughter of Colonel Robert York of the Corps of Engineers, living in Cambridge. It seemed that life had entered a new phase, with roots now sunk in the east and no reason to return to the Mid-West. My efforts were concentrated on work at Harvard with little time for anything else.

As the only one at the university concerned with the Middle East , the task of presiding over Arab-Israeli debates devolved on me, a task which brought little comfort. On one occasion, trying to calm the passions of both sides, I said, "as an historian I suggest that one should look at the past and seek to put the dispute in a long term context. Perhaps, from the Arab point of view, the state of Israel represents the last attempt of European powers to impose a colonial entity on the third world, much like the Crusades." An Arab lady in the audience objected strenuously, saying, "What you said is insulting; have you been to Beirut? It is just as European as Western cities." An attempt to explain fell on deaf ears, but then a Jewish woman, shaking her umbrella at me, complained that I had allowed an Arab speaker to exceed his time by two minutes. After two years of trying to mediate between the two sides, the only course was to refuse to be a middleman in such acrimony. Unfortunately the situation in Israel since has deteriorated almost beyond hope.

Afterwards, in the Middle East Center all refrained from discussion of the Arab-Israeli conflict, concentrating instead on questions of education, commerce and cultural matters in the entire area. We felt that politicians could handle contemporary problems, while our task was to present a long-term vision. This was before the explosion in concern with contemporary political and economic affairs, which brought much money into institutes and centers, such as the Kennedy Center for Public Affairs. At that time, however, we could not ignore events in the region, but always emphasis was on long term vistas, as free from bias and incivility as possible.

Everywhere the term 'Middle East', derived from British nomenclature during the war, was replacing the long-established 'Near East.' Finally the former term came to be used for the recent past or contemporary scene, while the latter was reserved for classical studies of the same area. So 1948 had been a turning point in my life, leaving the Middle West behind and looking east across the oceans to Iran and other lands of the region. It was not too long before I could concentrate on Iran and Central Asia, leaving the Arab world and Turkey to others.

CHAPTER 12

Through the Deserts of Iran

THIS YEAR was the first opportunity to spend a long period in Iran and to get to know the people well. It was necessary to buy a special car in order to travel over the dirt roads and deserts, and the land rover seemed ideal. With GB plates and an international driving license, Barbara and I were ready to leave London and cross the Channel by ferry in the middle of July 1951. After driving through Holland, Germany and Italy we arrived at the border of Yugoslavia at Rieka, formerly called Fiume. We entered a Communist country and it seemed the beginning of the Orient.

Our visas to Yugoslavia had entry dates of several days previously, but I changed the dates, and the border guards did not notice the difference. The road along the Dalmatian coast was only dirt, dusty and full of holes, but the people though poor and dirty, were very friendly. Fortunately German or Italian was widely understood, but because of Tito's break with Stalin, Russian was not to be spoken. Several times we picked up people on the road seeking a ride, but we had so many punctures and blowouts on the road that the tires several times had to be vulcanized, while gasoline was sold from large drums by the kilogram. Again we had hitch-hikers from Knin to Split (formerly Spoleto) and from Split to Dubrovnik (formerly Ragusa), Near the latter the exhaust pipe, where it was attached to the engine, broke, but fortunately a welder was found who proceeded to weld the pipe back in place. Since there were several cans of extra gasoline attached to the land rover, as well as a full tank, I protested that the welder should be careful not to cause a big explosion and fire. Several Croats assured me it was no problem, since the welder was a Muslim who did not care if he blew himself up. Nonetheless we moved some distance away from the vehicle.

From Cetinje we climbed to Titograd (present Podgoritsa), like a rough frontier town, where we spent the night in a new but almost barren hotel, and then down to Pec and Djakovic where we passed the next night. In the latter there was only one inn in town, and in the bar on the first floor an air of hostility greeted us when we entered. After no response to my question if anyone spoke Italian, German or Russian, when there only remained Turkish, the atmosphere at once changed as if by magic. They were Albanian Muslims, and sullen in the presence of Serbian policemen, but when they heard Turkish and that we were en route to Istanbul, we became honored guests. It was a great surprise to find people who spoke Turkish, making me feel at home. The Serb policemen, on the other hand, were annoyed and questioned me about conversations with the Albanians. Even then the tenseness in relations between the two peoples in Kosovo presaged later unhappy events. Yugoslavia clearly was not a happy place, although Tito kept the passions of all under control.

Salonika seemed part of Europe after an uneventful trip through Pristina and Skoplje, but we had to reach Istanbul by early September to attend an international congress of Orientalists, which was directed by a friend, Zeki Velidi Togan. At the congress 'Abbas Iqbal, at that time Iranian cultural attaché in Rome, showed us several pages of a remarkable Persian manuscript, the *Andarz Nameh,* generally known as the *Qabus Nameh,* with the oldest Persian miniatures known. The paper, script, and everything seemed truly ancient, so I resolved to find the rest of the manuscript in Tehran. At this congress I proposed the establishment of a *Corpus Inscriptionum Iranicarum,* which was accepted, and later taken over by Henning. A former student, Greg Sarmanian, joined us in Istanbul to drive to Tehran, and inasmuch as Barbara was unwell with her pregnancy, he provided support on the way.

Traveling by car in 1951 through Turkey and northwest Iran to Tehran was not easy, for engine trouble, flat tires and dust on the unpaved roads made such a trip quite an adventure. So it was with great relief that we were able to settle down in an apartment in Tehran. The country had suffered losses in agriculture during the wartime Allied occupation, and poverty was endemic. This was impressed on us by many beggars on the streets, which was an unpleasant feature of Tehran, but it was a relief to find old friends, both foreign and local.

Late one afternoon I drove the land rover to the house of Kennedy, who had married and returned to Iran after his stint as assistant military attaché. We only stopped for a short time to pick up a book, but when I came out and turned on the lights of the car there was no response. On examination the two headlights had been torn from their sockets in the space of ten minutes. Reporting to the police, they advised me to wait until morning, and then buy back the very same headlamps from a nearby junkyard, which proved to be the case.

Barbara was uneasy, needing more attention in her pregnancy, and it was decided that she should return to her parents in Fort Peck, Montana, where her father, Col. York of the Corps of Engineers, was stationed, and I would remain in Iran until the summer. Our relations had not been happy, but now that a child was coming, separation was not contemplated, even though I felt like an S.O.B., in what seemed to be abandoning her. In any case, she left and I moved into the *bashgah* 'foreigner's club' at the University of Tehran. Here I first met the indefatigable Iraj Afshar, who remained a close friend. There were a number of students from various countries, as well as several older scholars, including Vladimir Ivanov, a specialist on the Ismailis, and Milocz Borecky a Czech Iranist. Also there was a Swiss linguist, Georges Redard from Neuchatel, who wanted to visit the oases of the central deserts to collect material on dialects, and I agreed to go with him using our land rover. Thus preparations began for an extensive expedition into little visited parts of the country.

Another American student at the university, red haired Murray Barr, had served in the Navy during the war, and was on good terms with the American naval attaché in Tehran, from whom he obtained loan of an old jeep and supplies. We had to buy six jerry cans for gasoline, which was unobtainable in many of the places we would visit. Finally, it was necessary to obtain letters of introduction to people who could help us on the way.

Especially important was a letter from Habib Yaghmai, editor of the journal *Yaghma*, to his uncle Honar, an important personage in the oasis of Khur. We hired Rahim, a Baluch as driver for the jeep, while I would manage the land rover. Barr could drive but not Redard, who had injured his leg in a skiing accident and limped. On Monday 17 December 1951 we left the university at seven in the morning bound for Qum, where we had our first flat tire, and encountered the first long caravan of camels. We decided to spend the night in a deserted caravanserai near Kashan, but Rahim protested that it would be dangerous, so we proceeded to the city, and, producing a letter from General Garzan, head of the gendarmerie in Tehran, were permitted to set up our cots and sleep in the local police station. The night was cold, but when the sun came out the change to a warm day was most welcome.

The road to Natanz deteriorated and even with four wheel drive the way was difficult. At Natanz we again produced our gendarme letter, but were referred to Perivahsh, the head of the local electric power plant, and a Zoroastrian convert to Bahaism. The power plant consisted of a 40 kw motor operated on diesel oil, but his house was warm and he was unusually hospitable. Outside it was freezing at night, so a warm shower in an underground bathroom was a much appreciated treat.

Natanz was the center of a fertile plain with many villages, which we were able to see from the minaret of the old mosque in town. After a pleasant lunch we continued on a washboard road to Ardistan. Just before that town we encountered four long strips of concrete in the desert, each about 400 feet long and about 25 wide. With our war memories still fresh, both Barr and I speculated that we might have found a secret air strip, but it was soon dispelled when the people of Ardistan laughingly told us they were the bases for a railroad station and engine yard, started by Reza Shah in 1940 but abandoned with the war. In every place where gasoline was available, our spare tanks were filled, and Nain was the last stop before going into the Biyabanak, the oases in the Kavir desert, where fuel would be difficult, if not impossible, to find.

Nain, though the administrative center for the entire desert area, with brackish water from an underground cistern *(hauz)*, had no electricity. The commander of the police was an opium addict who could not help us with quarters for the night. The head of the education department, however, spoke some English and obligingly allowed us to use the administrative office of the main school as our bedroom. He gave us information about the desert, and asked us to bring letters to his representatives in the various oases on our way. Food supplies were scarce, for Nain only grew barley, and the bazaar was poor, except for several additional fuel cans we purchased for our journey. A strong wind was blowing when we left, and Redard and I donned face masks against the dust and sand. The trail descended from Nain to the barren mining town of Anarak, where a surprise met us, a dispensary (*darmangah*) presided over by an Austrian doctor Karl Bartelmuhs. He told us about the area in which there were several mines of copper, lead, manganese and antimony, all worked in a primitive manner. Germans had built his dispensary and several buildings here before the war. All food had to be brought from Isfahan, and the thousand or so inhabitants were all undernourished. Bartelmuhs had cleaned the local spring, so potable, but salty, water was available. It was the nineteenth of December and Redard and I made notes of the local dialect, while Barr photographed and talked to Bartelmuhs about his war experiences on the eastern front. I should mention that the only common language between Redard, Barr and myself was German, for Georges did not speak English. The doctor was delighted that a Swiss and two Americans had to speak to each other in German.

Opium smoking was widespread among those who worked in the mines. The poor, who could not afford opium, ate the dregs, and life expectancy among them was the early thirties. The miners, over half the population of Anarak, lived much of the time in caves hollowed from the ground near their mines, and their food was brought by truck from Anarak. The mines had existed here since antiquity, since a Pahlavi inscription, probably from the sixth or seventh century, had been found on a stone in one of the mines. At a spring some 12 miles from Anarak, we found ten miners who operated a small smelting establishment for the various minerals. Needless to say, opium appeared to be a release from their miserable existence.

Several times snow appeared, with constant blowing of wind and sand, and a number of times we lost the trail, but continued to descend. It was a great relief to come over a hill and see the oasis of Chupanan with palm trees and green fields. The notables of the oasis related the history of the Biyabanak at supper. Chupanan had been only a caravanserai with a well until World War I when a *qanat* (underground canal) was built, bringing abundant water, such that barley, dates, wheat, grapes and some citrus fruit were grown. In1917 a war lord Naib Hosein Kashi from Kashan had terrorized the oases, killing and stealing until he was defeated, captured and executed in Tehran. But the real fear of the inhabitants were the raids of the Baluch, the last of which had been only twenty years ago. In order to warn the people of the oases of an approaching Baluch raiding party, towers were built each with a supply of dry wood, and if Baluch were sighted at daytime smoke signals were sent, at night fires. The raids were only in winter, but they occurred every year in the past. Trachoma was widespread among the inhabitants of the oases, but for most it was not considered bad enough to go to the dispensary in Anarak.

Our goal was Jandaq, the most remote of the oases, 41 miles to the north of Chupanan over a trail through the sand. We hoped to find a dialect even more unusual than those of Nain, Anarak and Khur, but another surprise greeted us; everyone spoke good Isfahani Persian. The local inhabitants explained that their oasis had been a place of banishment for notables from Isfahan in olden times. From Jandaq a camel postal service existed across the salt desert to Damghan, a six day trip. Jandaq was a center for making camel's hair cloth, and little else could be found there. How people survived was a mystery to all of us. The date palms appeared to be the main source of livelihood here, as in other oases.

Since there were no ancient remains in this oasis of 2,000 people, or dialect work, we continued south on a camel trail across the sands, several times being stuck, and only able to extricate one jeep through towing by the other. At last we had to unload both cars to move, and tired we decided to pitch our tent and spend the night in the desert. With us was a guide from Jandak, Hajji Mahmud, who was loathe to eat with us until Rahim convinced him we had no pork in our food supplies, which was true.

In the morning frost was on the tent, but at least the sand was much firmer at that time of the day. It was about seventy miles to Khur, our next destination, and the camel trail at times vanished. The sand frightened us, since we had to reach stony ground before sand lost its morning solidity. Fortunately we left the sand after two hours, or about ten miles driving, and reached a plateau where tamarisk was growing. It was with a great sigh of relief at noon that we saw the green oasis of Farrukhi in the distance.

In our standard procedure, while Barr took photos and Redard handled a 16mm motion picture camera, I engaged the local people in conversation. The women and girls wore a distinctive headdress, similar to that of the Arab bedouin, called *chepiye* in the local dialect. After lunch we continued to Khur over a salt plain with ruts in it for a trail, which made driving difficult. Khur was reached in the late afternoon. Outside of the oasis we asked for the home of Mr. Yaghmai, but the surprised reply was, "we are all Yaghmai here." So we had to specify Honar, and since the narrow lanes in the oasis forbade driving, we left the cars in the desert on the edge of the oasis and by foot entered a land of palms.

We had a letter for Honar Yaghmai, the patriarch from his nephew Habib in Tehran, but already he had been informed of our trip, and welcomed us in his house, which was to be our home for a week. On Christmas day Redard and I recorded the local dialect while Barr took photos. During questioning of two informants, they played a trick, claiming that the local word for 'no' was *yok*, which Georges duly recorded. I said to them, "wait a minute, where did you hear that word, from an Azeri gendarme?" They laughed and admitted as much, and we had to explain that we wanted the local dialect, not Persian or anything else from another language strange to them. We were told that everyone in this isolated oasis, before our coming, believed that foreigners were Turks, either Azeris or Turkmen, sent by Tehran as gendarmes or officials.

Khur was a relatively new oasis, and the principal sources of livelihood were products of the *mog* (date palm). Even clothes were made from the 'hair' of the palm, usually made into rope.

The water came from three *qanats* but was salty and strictly rationed. It was here that Rahim, our driver, refused to do any work, such as washing dishes. He said he wanted to return to Tehran, and demanded his salary for the entire trip. What was worse he began to spread rumours about us. People now seemed hostile and refused to have their pictures taken, even for money. Muhammad Amini, servant of Honar, acted as a middleman, and took us to the police station, where Rahim had made friends with several Baluch men who had come there. The police chief was an opium addict and only listened to the complaints of both sides, with no advice on what to do. We retired to a rooftop to drink bitter green tea. Amini suggested a compromise; we would pay Rahim four toumans extra for his food if he did not eat with us, and provide him with bus fare to Tehran from the first town with such service, if we could not settle problems. It was put in writing and signed by all. Rahim agreed to continue on our final day in Khur, so Amini had saved the situation.

On the last day of the year we set off from Khur, accompanied by Amini and a gendarme going to the oasis of Beyaze. The land seemed more propitious for life, since a number of oases were near one another. The first was a small one called Nishapur, then Garme, after 25 miles from Khur, and in the distance Mihragan, which we did not visit. Amini left a package with the opium smoking largest landowner at Garme, and we continued to Beyaze, an oasis of some eight hundred inhabitants.

Here we learned of the existence in each oasis of a book about a treaty with the Arabs, when they brought Islam to the region. The *Ahd Nameh* of Beyaze was a recent copy of a much older text, we were told, but still it was interesting in some details. According to it the Arabs came to the Biyabanak in the year 1030 AC and won a battle at Garme, when all the chiefs of the oases accepted Islam and gave 1/3 of their lands to the Arabs. The late date of the conversion is implied by other sources, but the book we saw could not be checked for authenticity of details, and I was able only to copy part of it by hand. Amini and the gendarme left us at Beyaze and we continued to the caravanserai of Pusht-e Badam on a miserable trail, but with a veritable symphony of colors in the *kavir* to the east. In the gendarmerie post, where we spent the night, the brazier of coals, consuming oxygen, gave us all headaches, and we were glad to leave. This was the site where American soldiers were to have trouble when they came to rescue hostages in the embassy in Tehran.

We were on the 'pilgrim road' across the desert to Meshhed, but one could only pity the pilgrims trying to navigate the salt plain and huge sand piles on the road to Tabbas. The 130 mile trip took twelve hours, but half way to the oasis of Tabbas the trail led over stony ground and we were able to make up lost time. We passed several abandoned caravanserais, but one Ribat-e Malik was a post of gendarmes, who were very surprised to see us, for the season of pilgrimage was in the spring, and now few travelers passed this way. This forlorn place brought to mind a story about Reza Shah, who inspected a similar post and asked how many men were there. The answer, from the sergeant, quaking in his boots, was "about six, your majesty." His majesty roared, "what do you mean about?" "Well sir, we were ten, but two ran away and three took sick leave, and we don't know who may return." One can only imagine the response of the shah.

Tabbas still had impressive walls and a large citadel, albeit in decay, and a public garden, called Gulshan, with running water, was our place of residence. Electricity had come to town only nine months previously, we were told, and since it was obtained from a diesel generator the supply was uncertain. The local dialect was Khurasani Persian, in many respects similar to Afghan Persian, so we made no recordings. Likewise there were no antiquities, but of interest were several deep underground ice houses where winter ice was stored packed in straw, to be used in the summer. In Tabbas a mullah, follower of Ayatallah Kashani of Tehran, spent several hours trying to convert us, and he told us there was no difference between Shi'ites and Sunnis, and that Islam was rapidly gaining ground in the West, which we did not dispute. There were date palms in town but also apples and oranges in the bazaar. We were told Tabbas was fortunate in having hills nearby where fruit of the temperate zone was raised, while in the town itself oranges and dates could be found.

The next leg of the trip was through Firdaus (formerly Tun) and to Gunabad, the longest day of 204 miles, over what might be called a passable dirt road. The Gunabad region had the deepest qanats, and the best opium in Iran, a dubious distinction. It was snowing heavily when we visited the shrine of the Sufi Salih 'Ali Shah in nearby Bedukht, a beautiful monument being restored by craftsmen from Shiraz. Eighty miles south of Gunabad we found an Austrian doctor in a dispensary in Qain. He had been with the Afrika Korps, and averred that improvisation on the battlefield well prepared him for service in isolated places in Iran. Austrian doctors, but not German, had been allowed to come to Iran after the war. After visiting a prehistoric cave near the road at Khunik, which Carl Coon of Harvard had excavated, we reached Birjand 141 miles from Gunabad, again in a snow storm.

Outside of town we were directed to a large hospital compound where another Austrian, Dr. Otto Jakober, with a Christmas tree and eggnog liquor, greeted us. Both he and his wife were doctors, with a five year old boy, and they were exceedingly cordial. Almost all of his patients were opium addicts, even the wealthy who were bored with life in Birjand. We learned that a Parthian rock relief and inscription had been found near Khosf to the west of Birjand and decided to go there the following day.

At Khosf we found a guide and retraced our steps to the mountain opposite two villages of Tagab and Mahsimabad. After six miles and two hours of driving over rocks and river beds still dry, we found a village with two houses and a donkey, which we hired and loaded with cameras and supplies. Finally the donkey could go no higher, so we climbed on for an hour and a half to reach the relief and inscription. A Parthian prince was depicted seizing a lion with his hands, and the inscription gave his name and title, 'Gari-Ardashir, Nohodar (governor) and Satrap.' On return the man with the donkey and his father fell on their knees and kissed our hands after we gave them ten *toumans*, which embarrassed all of us.

The road to Zahedan was better than any that we had seen since Nain, and we drove the 300 miles in one day in a blinding snowstorm. Geography books declared that no snow ever fell in Sistan or Zahedan, but we could revise that information, for it came in buckets such that the windshield wiper ceased to function and fell off. We had to tie it with rope and pull it back and forth, through open windows on both sides, a cold ordeal.

We stayed with Mr. Lal, the Indian consul in Zahedan, formerly called Duzdab 'thieves' water, most appropriate for this desolate frontier post, where smugglers from the east passed into Iran.

From Zahedan we then retraced our steps to the turn-off, to the low-lying province of Sistan. At the site of Malik Siyah Koh, where Afghanistan, Pakistan and Iran came together was a shrine with stones piled high, and many pieces of cloth fluttering from poles stuck in the heap of stones. Travelers, or pregnant women seeking a boy baby, would place a cloth on a pole and say a prayer for a safe trip. The Sufi attendant claimed that 'Ali, the son-in law of Muhammad, had stopped to rest here on his voyage to the east. We did not contradict him but continued on our journey. We descended through red cliffs and to the village of Hurmuk where the inhabitants spoke Brahui, related to the Dravidian tongues of south India. Other such villages were in the vicinity, and the origin of the Brahuis in Baluchistan has remained a mystery, whether they were ancient remnants of Dravidians who once lived here, or more recent immigrants from the Deccan. I believed the former, but research is needed on their dialects.

Arriving at green fields with winter wheat, we came to a customs barrier, and had to convince the officials that we were not bringing merchandise to sell in Zabul. The next stop was at the ferry on the Helmand (Hirmand in local parlance) River. Our cars presented no problem, but large trucks had to unload and pass their goods on the ferry to the other side where other trucks carried them four miles to Zabul. At the river we were greeted by Khazima 'Alam, the lord of Sistan, who spoke English but appeared to be an effeminate Tehrani. Zabul was a town of about 15,000, with electricity and wide streets, paved with crushed white stone. Our residence was at the dispensary, formerly the British consulate, where a Persian doctor, and head of the education department, assisted us. The town itself was uninteresting, so we decided to use it as a base for short trips in the vicinity. The first excursion from Zabul was to two dams on the river, some 17 miles from the city. Every year a dirt and log dam had been constructed, and every year it had been washed away. So now they were trying to build two cement dams to control the flood waters. An Italian engineer in charge of construction said that the flow of water rose from 43 cubic meters per second to

1400 at flood time, which was a problem. The second dam on the Afghan frontier was being constructed by Iranians with Afghan approval, but was smaller than the other.

At a banquet given by 'Alam it seemed as though I were back in Afghanistan, with bright red and yellow stuffed chairs facing each other in two rows and the chief presiding. The most interesting person at the dinner was Nasr Khan Irani, chief of the Nahrui tribe of Baluch, who had been converted to Christianity by Presbyterian missionaries. He told us about the ancient sites in the province, including Shahr-e Sukhte, where Italian archaeologists were to excavate later. "There is a legend", he said, "that under the waters of the Hamun was a ruined city called Savorshah, which is why the northern part of the lake was called Savori." Several months after returning to Tehran we heard that Nasr Khan had been killed in an riot, probably because of his conversion which he did not conceal from anyone.

Our host said his family had come from Birjand, and he had built many structures there and in Zabul. The dinner was a caricature of a feudal lord's festive board. Local officials fawned on him, and the head of agriculture acted as court jester, with stories about ducks which were numerous in the province. One such story was the following: a bald man painted his head to look like a stone, and he went under water, breathing through a reed. A duck would come to sit on his head and he could catch it with his hand, and in this way he made a living.

For a trip to the village of Adimi on the lake we had to bring two timbers to use as a bridge over brooks, and six times we had to drive over deep streams, using the timber as a bridge. In one case we had to dam the water of a stream with branches and earth so the car could pass through the reduced flow of water. At the village, cotton cloth was woven, but most of the inhabitants also made reed mats and rope. A cavalry captain accompanied us, and he became upset at our photography, until we assured him we had written permission from Tehran. The cattle were all humped water buffalo wading in the water marsh lands. Since the locals spoke Baluchi, dialect notes were made and two Baluch were promised money if they came to Zabul to be further interviewed. The car became stuck in the mud on our return trip, but local people pulled us out, while a fender was smashed by running into a mud wall.

In Zabul we registered the local Baluchi dialect with the Baluch from Adimi, and also recorded Sistani Persian. On my birthday, the tenth of January, I decided to go to the Parthian-Sasanian remains on Kuh-e Khwaja 'mountain of the lord', with our captain of cavalry. Redard stayed at home while Barr visited some ruins called old Zahedan near Zabul. One had to go by horses to the lake, but the captain thought horseback would be too difficult for an effete foreigner who only knew about automobiles. My ROTC stint in the horse-drawn field artillery, however, again stood me in good stead, except every time one sat up straight in the saddle the horse would break into a gallop. After a three hour trip we reached the lake, and had to sit in small reed boats, called *tuten*, to reach Kuh-e Khwaja, a plateau in the middle of the lake. The water was shallow, and a boatman stood in the rear of the boat with a pole to push us through reeds six feet high. Every now and then light blue colored birds would dart from the rushes to fly ahead of the boat. Our boatman caught a baby duck with his hands as we pushed through the reeds, and said he would bring it home to his children. At last we reached the plateau and started to climb. Only traces of colored wall paintings remained in the ruins of the ancient buildings, and excavations would be necessary to recover a plan of the ancient town. On top of the plateau was a cemetery and shrine to which pilgrimages were made at New Year, on the 21st of March. This strange plateau, rising out of the lake, was said to have been an important site in the early history of Zoroastrianism, and with the ancient ruins it might well have been.

The boatmen had brought old matchlocks with them, into which they put lead balls, rags and powder. Their attempts to shoot ducks, however, were failures, even though hundreds of ducks could be seen, but it was turning late so we started back. The trip back to Zabul was about 48 miles, and one of our horses fell off the ferry going over the river. Since the horses were hot after the long trip and the water was cold, the captain was afraid this one might become sick and he would be blamed, so the horse had to be thoroughly dried and massaged. We finally arrived at Zabul late at night completely exhausted.

Parviz, son of Nasr Khan agreed to accompany us on our trip to Baluchistan, and we returned to Zahedan in a dust storm. One restaurant existed in the town operated by a Greek called Kalfides, who claimed he had escaped from Turkish military service over forty years ago and had found his way here. Also we met an American sergeant called Kolman who was on his way to Baluchistan a day before we would leave. On the 12th of January we left Zahedan in rain which was foolish, for one should never drive in Iran after a rain storm. Crossing one flood after another on the road, finally the land rover stopped in the middle of a stream and Georges and I had to unload everything in water up to our waists. The jeep pulled us out, but mud was everywhere and we were soaked and cold. It was necessary to wait two hours for the water to subside, drinking vodka to keep warm. It was dark when only five miles from Khwash the land rover again went into deep water, and again we had to unload it and pull it out with the winch on the jeep. This time it failed to start and was towed by the jeep, which itself got stuck in mud at ten at night. So we sent Rahim to Khwash for help from Kolman who had arrived earlier, and the three of us fell asleep in our bedding rolls. At almost two AM Rahim returned with the sergeant and two soldiers in Kolman's jeep, but after trying to tow the land rover his jeep too became stuck in the mud. Several Baluch from a nearby village started to fill in the muddy road with stones, but it was slow work and not until five were we able to get the jeep out. Rahim repaired Kolman's jeep, and both of them with Barr were driven into Khwash while Georges and I remained with the land rover. We made a brush fire and watched dawn come over Mt. Taftan, the only active volcano in Iran. It was a beautiful sight with smoke coming out of the snow covered top, and we enjoyed the spectacle in spite of our miserable condition. Late in the morning Rahim returned, and this time Kolman's jeep was able to pull the land rover out of the mud and into Khwash. The sergeant worked on our engine and was able to start it, even though the starter was shot, and the car could only move after pushing or rolling down an incline. Rahim wanted to visit his home in Dizak in Sarawan district, so we rewarded him for his efforts with the cars, and told him to meet us in Zahedan in three days.

The principal tribe in Khwash was called Rigi, and Parviz stayed with the chief of this friendly tribe, while we were with Godarzi, the head of education in the town. The thatched roofs of houses of the Baluch were different from other village houses in Iran, and the people were quite dark but with thin, handsome features. We decided to continue, and the trip to Iranshahr was without difficulty, except the land rover could only be stopped on a hill. Parviz' uncle, Sardar 'Isa Khan Mubaraki, was governor of the province, so we were royally treated, with chairs, a table and beds, although the food was plain and monotonous, consisting of rice and a plain sauce on top. This was to be the end point of our trip because the tires on our jeeps were worn almost to the rim with countless punctures, and the starter on the land rover was not functioning. The loss of a telephoto lens in the wild journey to Khwash also dampened our spirits. Plans to reach the coast at Chahbahar were abandoned, so we recorded dialect and music at Iranshahr and prepared to leave.

The entire region of Iranian Baluchistan was patrolled by a camel corps, and we questioned several officers about ruins of a Greek theater near Chahbahar, reported by a KLM pilot who had crash landed near Tiz, a fishing village. He had spent his time searching for antiquities in the vicinity while waiting for a relief plane from Tehran. The likelihood of the fleet of Alexander the Great building anything on this wild coast was minimal, and I suggested that the pilot had only seen strange natural rock formations. No one had heard of such a structure. In any case, we could not continue and had to return to Zahedan.

Road gangs were working on the areas which had been flooded, filling the gulleys with dirt, so the trip back was relatively easy and uneventful. Lal was again most hospitable, especially since Pakistan was causing trouble for the transit of Indian goods which Iran needed, and he wanted to show his neutrality by solidarity with Europeans. There had been political demonstrations, but now Zahedan was relatively quiet. Rahim did not appear after three days, so we decided to continue without him. A gendarme, who wanted a ride to Bam, accompanied Barr in the jeep while Georges and I sat in the land rover. Then the accident happened, with a blowout of a tire on the jeep, which caused it to turn over several times. Barr was in shock but his passenger seemed unharmed. We returned to Zahedan with the gendarme at the wheel of the land rover and I with the jeep, which had a flat tire in sight of the town and had to be left with Redard. Barr was treated by a Sikh doctor and put to bed at a surprised Lal's house, while Sgt. Kolman, who had returned to Zahedan, and I returned to tow Redard and the jeep back to town.

A day was spent in searching for tires and repairing the cars, while Barr remained in bed. No bones were broken, but he had two cracked ribs which were not discovered until we reached Isfahan. By this time both the jeep and land rover had large dents, and in the West would have been abandoned. Barr could not drive, so we engaged a gendarme to serve as a driver of the jeep, when suddenly Rahim appeared and we were ready to go again.

The road to Bam passed through many colored mountain gorges until we descended to the desert of Lut, and here we encountered the notorious *reg*-e *ravan* 'moving sand,' which one would not believe until seeing it with one's own eyes. A small mountain of sand moved across the road and we waited ten minutes until it passed, moved by the wind. Farther on the road the land rover did get stuck in the sand but a nearby road gang obligingly extricated it. Without such help by Iranians our trip would have been impossible.

Near the village of Fahraj we passed the extensive ruins of a Medieval city called Narmasir, which we photographed, and thought it would be a good site to excavate. It was a surprise to find an asphalt street in the town of Bam, the first since Kashan, and we felt we were back in civilization. Election day was approaching, far from the minds of the people we had visited, but here the Tudeh party and others were active, and tension was in the air. We had returned to 'real' Iran.

The trip continued to the lovely shrine of Nimatullah in Mahan, and to Kerman where we found an American rug dealer George Bitar, who managed a rug weaving factory. In dark, damp rooms girls and women worked on horizontal looms. Wool was washed and dyed in nearby streams by men, whose arms were colored by the dyes. We were told that Kerman had about 5,000 weavers and they exported twice that number of rugs every year, many made to specifications by American and European dealers. In most other cities weaving frames are vertical, and other differences distinguish the rugs of Kerman from those of Yazd, Nain and elsewhere. At the end of January, we were told, the Zoroastrians of Kerman and Yazd build fires outside of town indicating the end of winter, although it seemed to us that winter was far from ending at the end of the month.

After another miserable road to Yazd, which so shook the land rover that it lost the bottom radiator plug, and we had to improvise with gum to stop water from leaking. In Yazd we stayed in the Godarzi hospital, built by rich Parsis of Bombay, where two gendarmes had been wounded in pre-election rioting, while others had been killed. The unique tourist sight in Yazd were the towers of silence, where the Zoroastrians exposed their dead. There were three towers, two still in use. We were able to crawl into the unused tower, for the small iron door five feet off the ground had no padlock. Inside, the stone paved ground sloped at a steep angle and at the bottom were many skulls and bones, but all picked clean by vultures or the elements. It was a wonder that any Zoroastrians were left in the country after centuries of persecution and massacres.

Back at the hospital we saw a wolf which had been captured and was being trained by an Englishman, with what success was most uncertain. Time was passing, so on we went to Isfahan. Barr complained of pain in his chest, so at the British hospital in Isfahan his chest was taped and he was advised to rest and not accompany Redard and me to Shiraz. The US consulate and information library in Isfahan were open, but soon to be closed by the government, so a number foreigners were still in town. The US consul J. Hall Paxton, with whom we stayed, had been consul in Urumqi, China at the time of the Communist victory, and had been forced to go on foot over Tibet into India, a difficult but interesting journey.

Redard wanted to see Persepolis, so an excursion to the south was necessary, even though the land rover was in poor shape. At that time in Abadeh delicate wooden spoons were made, to sell in the antique shops of Isfahan and Tehran, and we acquired several. At Persepolis we found Zakatali who was making a plaster model of the site, as well as 'Ali Murad my helper from 1948, and 'Ali Samii, director of Persepolis. While Georges photographed Persepolis I went with my helper to copy several small Middle Persian inscriptions south of the site. It was unusual to see many storks with nests in high places in villages all the way to Shiraz. There people gathered menacingly about the car, thinking we were British, but the police assured them we were not the enemy who was stealing oil from the country. The British consulate had been closed, and even Anglican Rev. Sharp was afraid an attack on his church might happen any day, for here also were demonstrations before elections.

The ride back to Isfahan was easy compared to roads in the east, and in spite of snow we arrived back in Tehran at night on the third of February, for Redard was prepared to return to Switzerland in a few days.

After returning from the long trip I had lunch with a friend in Shemiran. One of the guests had a daughter of twelve, who when told of the long strings on camels in the deserts, was amazed, for she had never seen a camel and did not know they existed in Iran! The difference between the southern part of Tehran and the lovely gardens of Shemiran was as night and day, and even then the great division between classes was apparent.

Together with Seyyed Hosein Nasr, who had been a student at Harvard, we paid court to Ayatallah Borujerdi, the *'uzma,* or head of the Shi'ite religious establishment in Qum. He presided over a religious government within a state, with representatives in London, Paris and Washington, and while sitting on the floor drinking tea envoys would report to him. On the way back we stopped at the home of the Imam Jum'ah, or leader of the local clerics and of Friday prayers in Tehran. Many religious leaders had gathered there to discuss matters of interest. One of the divines in anger said that everyone living north of the street called Takht-e Jamshid, in the northern part of the city, should have their throats slit. No one objected, including one at the session who, we were told, was called Khomeini. A few months later Borujerdi was dead and no one replaced him. Premonitions of the future were already here.

Later in 1952 a taxi ran into the rear of the land rover but caused more damage to the taxi, and this time the police took notice. The taxi driver and I were to appear in court within ten days to settle any damages. That was an interesting experience, for we had to wait until several cases were to be decided by a judge. He invited me to sit beside him while he judged three cases, including a domestic dispute between an Armenian man and wife. It was Easter time and the judge admonished the man, quoting passages from Persian poetry, and in the end he said it was sad to see such a dispute at the time of the most important Christian holiday. All the time he made sideway glances at me to exhibit his knowledge of poetry, as well as his qualities as a judge. After his eloquent speech, however, the woman said, "Your honor he doesn't understand Persian." The judge was deflated, and the case was dismissed, but at least the foreigner had been impressed by the judge's humanity.

When my case came before the judge, the two taxi drivers pleaded that they had no insurance, and were too poor to pay for the relatively slight damage to my car. The judge replied, "I am sure the esteemed foreigner understands, and will dismiss any charges against you, won't you?" What could one say?

On leaving Tehran I asked Kuhi Kermani, a popular story teller on the radio, for his address, so I could write to him about a student who was interested in Persian folklore. He replied, "Kuhi Kermani, Tehran." " But Tehran is a large city and a letter might get lost," I protested. "All right, then write Kuhi Kermani, Tehran, *Majles*," was the rejoinder. "But you are not a delegate to the *Majles*, how can that address reach you?" I remonstrated. "I walk in the garden of the *Majles* every morning and everyone knows this," came the response. Eternal Iran!

CHAPTER 13

Back to Afghanistan

IN TEHRAN most of my time was spent with various Persian literary people. Saʻid Nafisi was especially loquacious, and his stories always were amusing; he also allowed me to look at manuscripts in his large library. Sadeq Chubak, Parviz Khanlari and Mohammad Moʻin were also interesting writers with whom much time was spent. The last was engaged in two projects, an edition of the classic Persian dictionary *Burhan-e Qati ʻ*, and, with an older poet and author Dehkhuda, a large dictionary project in thirty or more volumes. I purchased journals and books for the Harvard library and for myself, and all booksellers in town knew the young foreigner well. I enjoyed going from one bookstore to another, talking to the proprietor of Danesh or another store. The bookstores were not concentrated as happened later near the university, but were to be found in various places of the city.

The capital in 1952 was a fascinating place, with election fever everywhere, and various groups were making propaganda for their candidates to the *Majles*. One, the Tudeh party was especially active, as we had observed in places as far away as Zabul and Bam. New plays on stages in lower Lalezar Street were also now frequently political, and usually leftist in nature. Anti-British sentiment was strong, and the nationalization of the Anglo-Iranian Oil Company was pushed by Dr. Mossadegh in the parliament. Passions were high, and I had to assure people that, although my land rover had GB plates on it, the driver was an American. At that time Americans were not linked to the British and had a high standing among most Persians. Stories about the British were widely circulated, and one by Mahmud-e Mahmud was typical of the prevalent tales.

I asked him why he had such a name, and he straightened himself and replied that his family name had been Pahlavi, but he had to relinquish it by order of Reza Shah. He had written seven volumes on relations between Iran and Britain, and when I marveled at the number of pages, he averred that he could have written twice that number, but dared not include much information. For example he said," Do you know that Iraqi oil which is refined in Kirkuk is really Iranian oil, which the British have siphoned in secret pipes from Iranian oil fields? And every fall when peasants in Khuzestan go to the fields to gather their harvests, British send agents to their empty houses to poke holes in the roofs, such that when the rains come in winter the roofs will not only leak but collapse." In response I suggested, "Do you know Mahmud-e Mahmud, that when Reza Shah cancelled the oil agreement with the British to secure new terms, actually he was doing this as a British agent?" He looked at me in disbelief and said, "You are the first foreigner who has realized that!" One knew then that Hajji Baba was not dead.

Food at the university was not especially tasty, so the foreign students there frequently ate in restaurants, where we soon discovered the best *chelau kebabs* in town. There were many taxicabs with cheap fares taking several passengers, like the *dolmush* of Istanbul, so it was not difficult to get around town. My routine of visits and study was broken by a request by Roman Ghirshman, now director of French excavations at Susa, to make a trip to Afghanistan. He had heard of the discovery of both a well preserved minaret at a site called Jam, and Parthian inscriptions on a rock at a narrow valley, called Tang-e Azao 'difficult gorge', on the way. Since he had several weeks free time before returning to Paris, he enlisted my help with the land rover, which had now recovered from the ordeal of the trip through the deserts. It was to be a difficult trip, but the car had been made proper by much work, so we decided to go.

We resolved to find both sites, and his capable chauffeur, Georges Sarkisian, an Armenian from Lebanon, would do most of the driving. Georges had married an Iranian Armenian, and had lived in Tehran for several years, where he had inherited the Persian dislike and fear of the wild Afghans, and consequently did not want to go, especially when I told him that at the frontier the Afghan officials would ask him to declare his religion. We calmed him, however, and on May 2 set off with two new extra tires and a new spring for the car in case of emergency.

Since we were going into the mountains we had to take warm clothes, as well as those suitable for the month of May. Rains had not helped the condition of roads, but we thought that they could not be as dangerous as in Baluchistan. Nonetheless, the road to Meshhed was covered with water in several places, but second gear in four wheel drive enabled us to pass streams where even busses were halted. In Shahrud I looked for the former Soviet army hospital and the UKCC office where I had stayed, but could not find them since many changes had occurred since the war. Now Iranian officials checked our passports instead of the Soviets, but we had no trouble in passing.

Beyond Shahrud, at the village of 'Abbasabad, we found a colony of Georgians who had been settled there by Shah 'Abbas. They were craftsmen who carved the green stone from nearby mountains, making ornaments for tourists. At Sabzevar, where we spent the night on the floor in a room over a garage, I found that in the local dialect the word for nose is not the usual *bini*, but almost *nos*. Could all of the local population have learned that from the British, or was it a relic from ancient times? Everywhere opium poppies had been planted, by permission of the government we were told.

As a child I remember going to carnivals where a popular ride was called 'the Rocky Road to Dublin,' in which children sat in a small model of a car which went over large bumps, enough to make one's teeth rattle. This was supposed to be a treat, and on the road to Meshhed this memory returned, except here many streams had washed away the road, causing delays, but washboard surfaces, caused by heavy trucks, gave us a heavy shaking.

The British consulate in Meshhed had been closed, and instead an American one had been opened in a house belonging to a wealthy merchant from Central Asia. In it the Russian influence was evident, with huge stoves built inside the walls, but the furniture was French Louis XIV style, which surprised

Ghirshman. The consul explained that the US had to spend excess francs from loans to France after the war, so furniture was bought in France even for a distant consulate in Meshhed. The consulate was to be closed in the following year, when Iranians learned of US support of the British in their oil policy.

Here, from the head of the shrine, we heard a story about the origin of a *ziyaretgah* 'place of pilgrimage,' where usually a saint is buried. "A *mullah* presided over such a place, and many students came to him because of his fame as a teacher. To his best student, who had learned all his knowledge, he gave a donkey as a present and told him to go out into the world and establish his own school. The student mounted his ass and set off across the desert. He lost his way, however, and despairing for his life, tied himself on the donkey but fell asleep. The donkey found his way to a water hole in a small oasis, took one gulp of water and fell over dead. The student had been saved and considered it a miracle. So he buried the jackass and made a shrine of stones over the grave. When a caravan passed he showed them the grave and said it was the grave of the saintly *ushakli baba* 'father jackass,' who had performed a miracle. The caravan men believed him and spread the word about the newly discovered *ziyaretgah* in the desert. In short, the student, now a full-fledged *mullah,* attracted students who came to him instead of to his old teacher. The latter was curious and decided to visit the new site, and there found his former student, who in great embarrassment told him the whole story. Hanging his head, he asked forgiveness from his former teacher. Instead of a reprimand, however, his teacher said, *al-hamdu lillah* 'God be praised,' know my son that the jackass buried in your *ziyaretgah* is the son of the jackass buried in my *ziyaretgah.*"

On the way to the frontier we passed a model town of Fariman, built by Reza Shah with European style buildings in it, but it was now abandoned, with only a few inhabitants. On questioning they said that no one had liked forced settlement in the town, and at the death of the shah most had left. Georges became worried at the prospective questioning by Afghan officials at the frontier, and sure enough they asked his religion. "*W'allah* 'by God' I am a Mussulman Catholic," he declared. When questioned further he explained that it was one sect of many in Lebanon. When they heard that he was from Lebanon and spoke Arabic, he was treated with great respect. I told Georges always to speak a little Arabic when talking to locals, for it would fascinate everyone. Because of this, his impression of the people changed for the better after the trip. Speaking Arabic to Persians, however, would not produce a similar feeling.

While drinking tea in the customs house a hail storm began, and ice drops as large as eggs broke every window and completely destroyed the flower garden by the house. At first we thought it was gunfire and dropped to the floor, but because of the damage everywhere our car was not inspected by the preoccupied officials, and we were allowed to proceed to Herat on a new dirt road, much improved over the path I had followed during the war. The hotel had acquired a small power generator, for lamps as well as several small electrical appliances. Unfortunately, it was not functioning, so the old kerosene lamps were in order. The only foreigner permanently living in the town was the Iranian consul who was quite happy to see us, and at once invited us to dine with him while we were in town. This was the second day, while the governor of the province tried to contact Kabul for instructions to allow us to proceed into the mountains. Rains had disrupted all telephone connections with the capital, but assuring him that he would not be responsible for any accident which might happen, not only was permission given but Fikri Seljuki, whom I had known previously, was asked to accompany us to Obeh, where he would inform the chief official to aid us in our continuing trip. We left the following day.

After about twenty miles traveling on the rough roads, the radiator twice had to be filled with water, otherwise our trip to the hotel at the hot springs of Obeh, six miles in the mountains north of the town, was uneventful. Georges, Fikri and I had hot baths, but Ghirshman warned us that people with skin diseases bathed here, and because of infections thought we had made a mistake, but no one suffered as a consequence. The next day back at Obeh the *hakim* 'governor' advised us to go by horse since the road was pronounced impassable for a car. Ghirshman, however, said he had to return to Paris by a certain date, and we should try to push ahead with the land rover. The *hakim* thought it foolhardy, but sent a soldier with us as guide and helper, plus extra shovels and picks which were necessary, since the road had been washed away in eleven places. We rebuilt the road with the help of local people, commandeered by the soldier, and arrived in Chisht, a distance of forty miles in nine and a half hours. Several horsemen from Obeh had beaten us to Chisht, and advised us to turn back because, they said, the road to Tang-e Azao no longer existed. Ghirshman, however, was determined to continue and the *alaqadar* 'mayor' of Chisht was persuaded to go with us, against his better judgment.

Muhammad Zaman Khan was thirty-eight years old, originally from Kabul, and had not seen his family for three years, serving in remote areas. In Chisht he felt himself in exile, a miniature Siberia. He was indispensable for our trip, since an official was needed in order to secure assistance from villagers and nomads to construct a road.

At Chisht was the shrine of Maudud Chishti, the spiritual teacher of Mu'in Chishti, founder of an order of Sufis or dervishes with followers mainly in India. The relatively recent shrine stood beside the ruins of a mosque and school built in the eleventh century. A group of nomads of the Chahar Aimak tribe, who had stopped for a day at the shrine, spoke Mongolian as I learned, and consequently recorded some words. This appeared to me surprising, but was not unknown to scholars of the language. Equally unexpected were the rice paddies which supplied much of the rice needs of the country. We had not expected to find rice growing in the temperate climate of the Herat region. After Chisht every horse we passed was frightened and reared up almost unseating its rider, and we also met villagers who had never even seen a car for no Afghan officials had ventured into the mountains.

We continued from Chisht following the Herat River until we turned into a small dry stream bed. Stones in the stream bed we followed made driving most difficult, for many had to be removed by shovel and pick. Twice telegraph poles had to be taken down to provide a bridge covered with brush and sticks over gullies, but the poles were then replaced. This could not have been done without the orders of our host. About thirty miles beyond Chisht we reached the end of the line according to local people, and retreated to a nearby mountain nomad encampment, where a *chappar* 'hut of reeds covered by felt' was prepared for us to spend the night. We hoped to find horses in the morning, but none were available, so we decided to cut a road from the side of a mountain and continue by car. The difficulties encountered were beyond belief, but always workers were secured, or rather commandeered, to help in our tasks. As usual time and distance had little meaning for the local people, except for the five times of daily prayer. I was ready to turn back but Ghirshman insisted on continuing. The unit of distance in this region was the *ribat* or *sarai,* in the past those structures built to house caravans but no longer in existence. The distance between them varied according to the terrain, longer on a plain and shorter in mountains. If the traveler looked tired he would be told a smaller distance to his goal to hearten him on his trip.

Finally fifty-three miles from Chisht we arrived at our destination Tang-e Azao, at 2500 meters high according to our altimeter, but a swiftly flowing river separated us from the inscriptions on the rock. A camel was secured from a camp of nomads, and Ghirshman and I faced each other on its back to cross the river. The inscriptions seemed to be Parthian, but they turned out to be much younger, Judeo-Persian in an Aramaic script, and merely mementoes of Jewish merchants who had passed this way. Since it was late afternoon we could not work or photograph, so we recrossed the river and spent the night in a black tent of the nomads. It rained at night and water came through the tent so we were completely wet by morning. Soon the sun dried us, however, and we returned to the inscriptions to photograph and copy them with latex, which took most of the day. It was impossible, however, to continue to the minaret of Jam without horses, and camels would take too long, so disheartened we set out on a return trip to Herat.

The return trip, however, was a nightmare, for the rain had washed away our road, and especially a bridge we had constructed over a gorge. To reconstruct it would require many hours, and it was almost dark, so we spent the night in the open, and the following morning began the reconstructing of the bridge, which was finally accomplished after six hours work. Yet that was far from the end of our problems, for other sections of the road had been washed away, but we finally reached Chisht utterly exhausted. It appeared to us like a return to civilization, such was our relief at reaching a familiar place. The ordeal was not over, however, for the road to Obeh was also gone and all springs of the car were broken, including the extra one we had brought with us. It is difficult to remember the number of times that the car became stuck in mud or water, but always various gangs of Afghans pulled us out. Even though we paid them, such assistance was more than one would receive elsewhere. Without their help we would not have made it back to Herat. Since we had to follow a different path along the river on the return to Obeh, a series of caves were visible on the bank of the Herat river. They reminded me of Bamiyan, and later of Dunhuang, Bezekilik and Qyzyl in Xinjiang, possibly evidence of the presence of Buddhist monks who built such caves, facing south and above a river in all cases. I resolved to return later to investigate them, for now it was impossible to descend to the raging river from the cliff above.

The trials and tribulations of the return voyage to Tehran need not detain us, for they were minor repetitions of the flat tires, floods on the road, and repairs which we had experienced in Afghanistan. When we finally returned to the capital I resolved never to make such a trip again, and only to hire horses where there were no roads. The land rover had made a remarkable *tour de force*, but a new complete overhaul was needed. Ghirshman left for Paris and I returned to the university. The two trips in this year of 1951-2 were more than enough for me, and I was happy to initiate preparations to fly home. More airplanes were coming to Tehran and the planes were much faster than those just after the war, and several airline companies had jet planes.

The trip to Afghanistan had brought back memories, but more it revealed the great differences between the two lands. Iran was far ahead of its neighbor in all respects, sophistication, material progress, and more. Yet for different reasons both appealed to me, the Iranians because of their culture and the Afghans for their simplicity and traditional way of life with few outside influences. As enemies, however, Iranians would use a stiletto while the Afghans would prefer an axe.

CHAPTER 14

Dr. Mossadegh and Irandoost

A PHONE call from the Metropolitan Museum in New York brought a request to catalogue the Persian manuscripts of Hagop Kevorkian, an antiques dealer, who had sent his collection to the museum, presumably eventually to donate it to them. He had established a foundation and was using it to evade taxes as a collector of manuscripts and antiquities. In any case, I spent much time in New York and became friendly with Kevorkian, so much that he asked me to go to the Near East in the summer on a mission to seek antiquities and manuscripts. Although I had not intended to return to the area at that time, his mission was intriguing and I agreed to go as a representative of the foundation.

This trip was an opportunity to see friends and give lectures, the first of which was at the London School of Oriental Studies, then at Frankfurt University and finally in Rome at the Institute for the Middle and Far East. In Cairo it was a shock to find old haunts, such as Sheapherd's hotel, Groppi's ice cream parlor and other buildings gone, destroyed by riots in 1952 which had also toppled King Farouq. At first, book dealers whom I knew were contacted, to find out about manuscripts, but only quantities of Coptic papyri and a few Greek leaves of Gnostic texts were found. Inasmuch as Kevorkian was not interested in such items, and furthermore I was unable to judge their value, attention was turned to Arabic manuscripts and miniatures, but these were few and of little value. At least I made notes of all written materials, if Kevorkian should be interested in them. Many old acquaintances, such as Creswell, had left and archaeologists were gone, awaiting favorable policies of the new government to return. The king's collection of antiquities was being auctioned later in the summer, but it was not possible to wait for this event. Instead I inspected two small warehouses in the *suqs* where Kevorkian had stored objects he had purchased before the war, and made a list of the antiquities. Most were pottery and statues from Pharaonic times, but none really of top museum quality.

A flight by Misr Air to Damascus brought me to more pleasant encounters with dealers. On the 'street called straight' was a veritable palace of the Dahdah brothers, who provided a headquarters for persons bringing antiquities or manuscripts to sell. The severe Shishakly government had frightened collectors and dealers, so they had to be very careful in meeting foreign buyers. Much inflated prices for inferior goods after hours of drinking coffee, and exchanging pleasantries, led to nothing, until a distinguished looking sheikh appeared with a list of old and important Arabic manuscripts. Fortunately Nikita Elisséeff, then at the French Institute, explained that the sheikh recently had been released from prison for stealing manuscripts from mosque libraries, and the list he had was of items now in various libraries. I decided illegal transactions were out of bounds, and, furthermore, my instructions were only to report not purchase anything. I decided to go by taxi to Beirut, and at the frontier the guards could not understand how a foreigner could come to Damascus without first passing through Beirut. After lengthy discussion it was possible to purchase a visa and proceed to Beirut.

Asfar and Sarkis in their store for antiquities almost beat me, when told that I represented Kevorkian, but they calmed down and explained why they were upset. In the 1930s they owned an antiquities shop in Damascus, where Kevorkian bought from them a room with furnishings, reputedly from Mameluke times (15th century), for Doris Duke Cromwell and her house in New Jersey. When it was unpacked it was declared by experts to date from the late 19th century, and Kevorkian sued the dealers. The French protectorate government sequestered all of their assets, and in effect drove them out of business, such that they moved to Beirut and engaged in other affairs. After the war, the independent Syrian government was in no hurry to settle the lawsuit and it languished to the present. Such was their story.

A rich collector of Beirut, Firaoun, had created a museum in his home, and his prize was a parchment with Kufic lettering, a letter of the prophet Muhammad to Chosroes, ruler of Sasanid Iran, calling on him to convert to Islam. A local scholar had written an article in the newspapers authenticating the letter, but I said nothing to disturb the owner, who probably had paid much for this forgery. It seemed that the only result of my trip would be the contacts established with collectors and dealers, and only a long stay would bring forth hidden objects. The next stop was Baghdad which proved even more barren than Egypt or Syria. Manuscripts with miniatures, items especially prized by Kevorkian, were not to be found.

Because of disturbed conditions in Iran in the summer of 1953 it was impossible to fly to Tehran, and busses were full because of the pilgrimage season for Shi'ites to go to the shrine in Meshhed. Finally a converted hearse was found, going to Tehran, and a seat was secured in it, with two other passengers, Armenians returning home after years abroad. Coming into Iran at this time was different from the past, for the people were no longer friendly to Americans, evidenced by signs and grafitti, saying 'Americans go home', lit. 'get lost'. We passed from the realm of coffee to that of tea drinking, while mountains and deserts replaced the flat fields of Iraq. We spent a chilly night in a tea house at the base of the famous inscription of Darius at Bisitun, where the proprietor explained that after the departure of the British the Americans were now the target of a Communist campaign of xenophobia. Good news was that the melon crisis of 1951 was now over. In that year too many cucumbers had been planted, or had grown, in the melon patches with disastrous consequences to the flavor of the melons.

The hearse ran out of fuel near Qazvin, so it was late at night when we arrived in Tehran, as usual covered with dust. Many Americans had left the country, and those who remained were fearful of their lives. In Isfahan windshields of their cars had been shattered by stones, and in Shiraz Point Four employees had to take refuge with the police. In Tehran the American ambassador forbade the ostentatious gatherings of large automobiles at the frequent parties of Americans. The inability of Iranians to sell their oil after nationalization, as a result of the British boycott, brought an inflation of four hundred percent in less than a year. Many merchants were ruined and unemployment was at an all-time high, with resulting unrest and a feeling of desperation among all levels of society. Most taxi drivers were Armenians and Azerbaijanis, many of whom had come from the Soviet Union, and they were not hesitant to predict the coming revolution.

As a representative of Kevorkian, I made the acquaintance of many dealers and forgers in Tehran. For example, in a house in southern Tehran, managed by a Zoroastrian, a small 'factory' existed which made pre-Islamic pottery in one room, and lovely Islamic pottery in another. Genuine potsherds would be collected and reassembled in expert fashion. "We are no different from museums," I was told, "They also reconstruct pottery, but with white paste showing the reconstructed parts. We go one better by filling in the new, white areas, restoring them and making the pots more presentable." He also said they made Etruscan pots for Italian dealers, which were then smuggled into Italy and buried near Citta Vecchia and later excavated. It was cheaper to make such articles in Iran, and smuggling them into Italy presented no problem. This seemed unlikely to me, but in this business anything was possible.

One of the great copiers of manuscripts in Iran was the father of one Fakhr al-Din Naseri, and his son was a shrewd operator and dealer. He had some genuine manuscripts in his library, but he would place an 'eleventh century' forgery among them and then invite a scholar, such as Mojtaba Minovi, to lunch and show him his newest acquisition. If Minovi told him he had been fooled, and the manuscript was a forgery because it had lined borders, which did not exist in early manuscripts, Naseri would express feigned dismay. After the savant left he would resolve to correct the forgery or omit the lines in a future work. Miniaturists would copy illustrations for some of his manuscript forgeries, and they were very competent in their knowledge as well as craftsmanship. For fear of possible attacks, either physically or legally, for several years I refrained from writing about forgeries I had seen.

Ancient silver plates, bowls or jugs were also beautifully forged by several workshops. In Isfahan it was claimed the forgers melted Sasanian coins and used the old silver in their superb craftsmanship. In the Karaj workshop genuine excavated plain objects would have designs or even inscriptions engraved on their rims or interiors. A smaller factory of such forgery existed in Shiraz, but when the master craftsman of silver objects died, his art went with him. A talented miniaturist in Isfahan called Behzad, signed his productions in the same fashion as his famous namesake of Timurid time, so Iran was a center of remarkable forgeries as China had been. Perhaps today in China such crafts have been revived.

The National Assembly had balked at some of Mossadegh's plans, so he resolved to appeal to the people by a referendum to dissolve the parliament, leaving his hands free. By so doing, however, he would be subject to removal only by order of the Shah. Every day street demonstrations revealed the organizing abilities of the Communists, and all Americans were advised to take refuge in the new embassy compound. Instead I visited 'Ali Akbar Dehkhuda a friend and distinguished scholar, who had bestowed upon me the sobriquet *Irandoost* 'friend of Iran'. He urged me to talk to Mossadegh about American-Iranian relations, and the prime minister agreed to see me on August 9, the day before the referendum. I decided to present him with a small book I had written called *Iran,* and in the dedication I called him the savior of his people, which proved annoying to both Iranian and American officials after the fall of Mossadegh.

Austerity was the key word in his house, but his bedroom was air-conditioned. He was in bed in pajamas when I entered. Taking my oustretched hand in both of his, he motioned me to a comfortable chair beside his bed. After an exchange of compliments I presented him with my volume which he pressed to his heart, lips and forehead. He was grieved at a recent pronouncement of Secretary of State Dulles that Mossadegh had a deliberate policy of giving the Communists free rein. He showed me a letter he had written in reply, protesting that Persians will never submit to uniformity and discipline which throttles their individualism, and there was no danger from Communism in Iran. Also he disclosed a letter from President Eisenhower which refused any monetary aid to the country because Mossadegh was supporting Communists. "How could a scion of the Qajar royal house support Communists," he declared. After an hour I left feeling I had spoken with a well-meaning man, sincere in his beliefs, even though he may have been naive in his estimate of Communist strength, or in the bogy of the British. He feared the Right more than the Left, and in light of subsequent events this was understandable. He was an ailing man, and probably out of touch with the realities of both internal and foreign affairs. Business was left in the hands of his lieutenants, some of whom were not known as scrupulous men.

The referendum was a farce, for those who wanted to vote for the government went to one square, while opposition votes were cast at another square, next to the parliament. This procedure reminded one of the introduction of a 'secret ballot' in the time of Reza Shah, when voters were handed ballots, which could not be opened since they were secret, and were ordered to put them in a polling box. The National Assembly was dissolved and Ayatallah Kashani, who had been its head, sharply criticized the prime minister. Sides were being drawn and the future was unclear.

Since I had received an offer of assistance from Mossadegh, I requested a letter to a bus company to permit me to go to the Caspian Sea, one part of the country I had not visited. Foreigners were forbidden to leave the capital, but the letter enabled me to buy a bus ticket, to the surprise of the bus driver. At midnight on Saturday August 15 tanks rumbled into Tehran, and in the morning it was rumored that the Shah had dismissed Mossadegh, but the latter refused to accept this order, and officers sent to arrest him in turn had been seized. Then the Shah left the country for Baghdad and Rome, and crowds in the streets carried signs in English and Persian 'death to the Anglo-American imperialists.' A driver asked me to get on the floor of his taxi in order to avoid an attack by angry demonstrators in the streets. Foolishly I decided to leave Tehran for the Caspian the next morning.

At the first large town in Gilan I thought we had arrived at Bandar Pahlavi (Enzeli), but at the hotel they told me it was Resht, and one should not go to Bandar Pahlavi where six people had been killed the preceding night, and Communists were in control of the town. Advice was given to stay in Resht for the night, and go east to Ramsar on the morrow, but the hotel keeper told me not to leave the hotel, or even show my face at a window, while he telephoned the chief of police. When the latter came, he explained that the entire province was under martial law, and the Communists would welcome the presence of an American to start a riot. He declared he could not be responsible for the protection of a foreigner's life. So with three gendarmes we drove to a teahouse to the east of town. A truck, which was driving east, was stopped by the chief, and he ordered one of the nine Persians in the double cabin to give me his place, surrounded by others so as not to be observed.

In two small towns we passed crowds carrying signs reading 'death to the Shah,' and 'the people are victorious; we want a republic.' At Ramsar, after spending the night in a small hotel, in the morning I was advised to return to Tehran on the next bus. In the bus were young Communists on their way to the capital, and I became a Swede rather than American, for there was a Persian on the bus who had been in Stockholm and we exchanged memories, quieting the young hot-heads who sang Communist songs all the way to Tehran. There statues of Reza Shah, as well as of his son, had been demolished. At the bus garage in Tehran, before boarding a taxi I could not resist a parting shot at the Communists, saying to the other passengers, "Do you know what these sons of burnt fathers say? there is no God but Lenin and Stalin is his prophet, may God curse them."

In the center of town, in front of the Firdosi hotel, where I was staying, police were using tear gas against crowds in the streets, and the situation seemed chaotic. About nine at night, however, several cars passed with occupants shouting "long live the Shah," and soon a crowd from the bazaars, led by a famous wrestler called Bimugh 'brainless', had overwhelmed the Communist led groups. Ayatallah Kashani and the bazaar had triumphed over liberals and leftists. The rest is history.

To end the saga, the day after the fall of Mossadegh, I flew to Zahedan, and by Himalayan airlines to Kandahar and Kabul, by car to Peshawar, by air to Karachi and back to Beirut and Istanbul, ending in Paris, then finally to New York by 10 September. In each stop several days were spent contacting booksellers and dealers. It was soon apparent that the antique business was almost Mafia-like, and it behooved one to keep a distance from the intrigues and abundant forgeries, but not until a break with Kevorkian occurred, did involvement in what promised sometimes to be unsavory matters come to an end. That rupture happened sooner than predicted.

CHAPTER 15

Iranian Studies in the USA

HAGOP Kevorkian was an Armenian from Kayseri like Gulbenkian, and over years he had graduated from a rug to an antiques dealer, and finally a collector, with his foundation created to build the collection. He was a shrewd dealer and lived with an adopted 'daughter' in a building which housed his antiquities on 67th St. near Fifth Avenue. Short of stature, he at times appeared pompous, and categorically refused to give any contribution to any Armenian organization, and, in short, was rather self-centered. In Tehran I had introduced his nephew, Vahram Kevorkian, to Fakhr al-Din Naseri the owner of the infamous *Andarz Nameh,* pages of which we had seen in Istanbul in 1951 in the hands of 'Abbas Iqbal, a writer and editor of Persian texts. After returning from a summer in Iran I learned that Vahram had purchased about half of the manuscript, while Arthur Upham Pope, an American specialist on Persian art, bought the other half for the museum of Cincinnati. This manuscript was to cause a breaking of ties with Kevorkian.

The Harvard rare book Houghton Library, at my recommendation, had purchased a Persian manuscript with miniatures, the *Divan* of Amir Mu'ezzi, dated a few years after his death in 1148. The rare miniatures in the book were consistent with the date, according to several art historians. It was later proved to be a forgery because of the lines enclosing the text, a phenomenon which had escaped my attention. It was, however, a masterpiece of forgery, but no match for the *Andarz Nameh* or *Qabus Nameh* of Kay Ka'us grandson of Qabus ibn Vushumgir 'quail-catcher', a ruler of the Caspian coast, with over a hundred miniatures, and reputedly older than the preceding book by almost a century. I was anxious to work on the *Andarz Nameh* and, after receiving photographs of the text, started to read it in class. It soon became apparent, however, that there were anomalies in the text. I had lectured on the manuscript at the Cincinnati museum, where a special room had been devoted to their half of the manuscript, and also in New York on Kevorkian's part of the book. Art historians were ecstatic about the miniatures, even declaring that the presence of Egyptian blue color, which had gone out of use for almost two centuries, insured the authenticity of the ms. Nonetheless, reading of the text in class suggested otherwise.

At that time Kevorkian was trying to entice me to come to New York to work at his foundation, but only a professorship at Columbia would be a successful lure. As a result of tortuous negotiations, in which I was both middle man and object, a professorship was established at the university. As the first incumbent of the chair, I delivered a series of lectures and taught two courses at Columbia. Schuyler Wallace, head of International Studies at Columbia tried to secure my assent to come to New York, and many luncheons and conferences with him almost persuaded me. In the end, however, a decision to remain at Harvard was tied to uncertain relations with Kevorkian, as well as to the manuscript. But Columbia, with many friends, always remained as a second home for me.

As mentioned, on reading the manuscript in class a number of word forms appeared inconsistent with the date of the manuscript. At the same time, Henning also discovered that the Pahlavi forms of some words in the text, apparently had been copied from a textbook on the history of the Persian language by Malek al-Shu'ara Bahar, poet laureate of the country. The book in my opinion was a masterpiece of forgery, although others, especially art historians such as Ernst Kühnel in Berlin, for a long time remained unconvinced. Richard Ettinghausen, my teacher of Islamic art at the Princeton summer school of 1941, however, maintained a noncommittal attitude.

Minovi wrote a pamphlet entitled *Kapusnameh-e Frye*, in which he berated me for having purchased *Andarz- Nameh* and spirited it out of Iran, but at the same time declaring it to be a forgery. Later he repeated the pamphlet in the journal *Yaghma* with corrections which I sent him about my role in the matter. I had sent photos of the manuscript to my teacher Henning and he had informed Minovi that the manuscript was fake, whereupon Minovi decided to publish this information. Neither he nor Henning wanted to mention the forger Naseri for fear of legal problems, so Minovi decided to use my name instead of Naseri for the title of his writing. The authorities at the National Library in Tehran probably had known that the *Divan* of Amir Mu'ezzi was a forgery what they stamped it with the seal of permission to export the book, but the *Andarz Nameh*, before it was known to be a forgery, even caused Taqizadeh to write to the Prime Minister requesting that microfilms of the manuscript should be acquired by Iran.

At a symposium devoted to the manuscript in New York in April 1955 there was no other course for me except to declare that it was a forgery, to the intense anger of Kevorkian. He was also furious that I had persuaded him to create a professorial chair at Columbia, and then had not accepted the invitation, which instead went to Ehsan Yarshater, who had no relations with Kevorkian. The whole episode of the manuscript left a bad taste and convinced me to leave the arena of manuscripts and antiquities, and instead to concentrate on the early history of Iran and Central Asia. In the future classes would be devoted to these subjects, plus Iranian ancient languages.

Support of Mossadegh had antagonized both the Iranian government and the US State department, and I was advised to keep away from the country for the next few years. Instead attention was turned to Central Asia, inasmuch as a return to Iran appeared inadvisable. In 1954 promotion to associate professor assured tenure at Harvard, which provided confidence to concentrate on my specialities. Nonetheless, as I frequently told my students, in a variation on a well-known theme, "to understand the past one should also observe the present." Consequently trips to the field were part of the learning process and should not be neglected. In the area of study of Central Asia and Iran not just book learning, but first hand acquaintance with land and people was necessary.

Personal affairs unfortunately were not encouraging, especially after Barbara's father retired and moved to Winchester,

Mass. This proximity to her parents gave her support which she refused from me, although it must be said that my preoccupation with work was not conducive for reconciliation. I always thought that the little things in life were more destructive than major crises, which frequently united people. Instead we went our own ways.

An interesting group of foreign students at Harvard was to have an effect on university matters. Karim Aga Khan and his brother Amin were here, as well as Sadruddin, his uncle, who was in one of my classes. On questioning whether his father would be interested in establishing a professorship in Iranian Studies at Harvard, he suggested writing a letter in this regard, which he would take to his home on the Riviera in the summer vacation. On July 5 a reply came from the aged Aga Khan saying, "where should I send the money." The administration of the university was both surprised and quite pleased, but recommended that the chair be broad to include oil economics, or at least modern Persian government and society. I convinced the old Aga Khan that it should not even be Persian literature, but restricted to old Iranian languages, history, and religions, rather than anything to do with politics or business. The administration was unhappy with this interference but nevertheless accepted the gift.

The grandfather of Karim died shortly after establishing the chair, and his father 'Ali was passed over in succession, but he was killed in an automobile accident, thus averting a split in the Ismaili community regarding succession. When Karim was installed as leader of his community in Karachi I was present and tried to be helpful in suggesting procedures. For example, Karim was uncertain whether to kiss the Quran when presented to him in the ceremony, or simply touch it to his forehead. Uncertain of Ismaili traditions, my advice was to bring it to his forehead since Sunnis would probably kiss it, and Ismailis probably should be different. Whether this was correct or not I never discovered.

Another student was 'Pinky' Bhutto, a lovely, vivacious coed who then had no plans to become the political leader of Pakistan in later times. An attempt to build a mosque in Cambridge almost succeeded, and it would have been an architectural attraction, built in a tiled Persian style, designed by Eric Schroeder, our gentleman scholar of Islamic art. The plans were ready, and money was put down for a site on the corner of Concord and Garden Streets, while finances were assured by support from the Aga Khanids and John Goelet, a wealthy student from New York. Then the Egyptian president of the Islamic Students Association, Muhammad 'Abd al-Hayy Sha'aban, put a monkey wrench in plans, when he declared that a clubhouse with a bar in the basement was better than a mosque, and the project was dropped. It was a great disappointment to all concerned.

It was a pleasure to see some of the older students, who had been in my classes, attain distinguished professorships in various universities. Oleg Grabar in Islamic art was at Michigan, but soon to be called to Harvard after Karim Aga Khan established a program and professorships in Islamic architecture. In some of the large classes on the Near East were students who later made a name for themselves elsewhere, such as Michael Crichton in Hollywood, and Frank Huddle and John Limbert in the State Department, both of whom became ambassadors to countries of the area. There was always a conflict between scholarly work with official duties and family affairs. The struggle to obtain tenure bred a kind of workaholic frenzy, which continued even after tenure was achieved. Perhaps it was the setting of a pattern which became hard to change, or maybe it was in the genes, an inheritance from my father. Whatever, I probably secretly reveled in it and did not attempt to change. An autobiography or memoirs, however, cannot simply relate adventures, but should at least mention personal concerns and events.

Our first son Jeffrey Lawrence was born on May 6, 1952 in Fort Peck, Montana, where Col. Robert York had been assigned. I remained in Iran until the middle of June, and then flew to Austin, Texas where the Colonel had been transferred. Back in Cambridge we settled down in a University house now replaced by a dormitory on DeWolfe St. A routine soon developed.

Work was long and varied, for an assistant professor had to show cooperation and flexibility, as well as achievements, in order to obtain tenure. Since I had been appointed to the History Department and Committee on Comparative Philology I had to teach in both disciplines. Lecturing in Comparative Religions on Islam and Zoroastrianism for Arthur Darby Nock was easier.

Nock was the prime mover in an old university religion club, where faculty members interested in the field of religion held dinners at their homes, and where a paper was read by the host. Some of the dinners were sumptuous, such as those hosted by Fred (Fritz) Robinson a Celtic specialist and by Giorgio LaPiana, a former priest, specializing in the history of the Catholic church. Renowned they were not, but interesting characters they were. Stories from the personal experiences of each were fascinating in the eyes of a young academician.

LaPiana told us how, after being ordained, he had been sent to a small fishing village in Sicily, his homeland, where he had to give sermons to rough fishermen in their small clubhouse, since they were too poor to have a church. At Easter time, in order to keep their attention, he had to be dramatic, and in the story of the prelude to the crucifixion, with talk and gestures, he related how Judas gave his master a kiss of betrayal the night before the event. He raised his voice to a high pitch in describing the scene and waited for a reaction from the fisherman. After a few seconds of silence their leader slammed his fist on the table and cried 'son of a bitch'. LaPiana then knew he had overcome their doubts about him, and he could work with the reticent fishermen.

Everything seemed to settle down to a life of teaching and research, with a belief that extensive travel in Iran and Afghanistan was over except for a conference or two. A change in direction, however, came in the summer of 1955 when out of the blue a letter arrived from the Soviet Embassy in Washington on the fifth of July with visa forms, saying that a visa was available if I wished to go to the USSR. My spoken Russian had grown rusty since Kabul, and several weeks were spent reviewing and preparing for the trip. At that time Intourist, the state agency which later arranged trips for foreigners, had not become organized, so I did not know what to expect, either in regard to necessary funds for a month stay, or what destinations were allowed. At all costs it was necessary to visit Bukhara, which had been the subject of my thesis and a published book. Nevertheless, it was with considerable trepidation that a trip into unknown areas was planned.

CHAPTER 16

Breaking Soviet Ice

BUKHARA is far from Moscow, and to get there in the past was not an easy task. One could never predict the eccentricities of the Soviet bureaucracy, and twice I experienced them in the summer of 1955, after the death of Stalin with the relaxed period of Khrushchev, first in the USA and then in Moscow. Lightheartedly, I had applied for a visa in Kabul, Afghanistan before leaving that land in August 1944. The eastern front had receded from the Caucasus and the Nazi armies were in retreat, which might have made Central Asia a possible place to visit, especially since the Soviet ambassador was friendly, and correspondence with Bernshtam, an archaeologist in Frunze had raised hopes of a trip. Almazov, a cultural attaché spoke on behalf of the ambassador, explaining that this hardly was the time to travel anywhere in the USSR, where shortages of food and lodging were everywhere. Perhaps later, he consoled me. Again in the summer of 1954, after the death of Stalin and the time of Krushchev, another request for a visa, in reference to the first one, was made, but there was little hope of receiving an answer. So it was a great surprise to receive a letter the fifth of July from the Soviet Embassy in Washington, saying that if I wished to visit the Soviet Union my passport, with necessary enclosed forms and photos, should be mailed to Washington.

The Russian Research Center of Harvard University was even more amazed than I, since their members had not been successful in obtaining visas. They were willing and did pay for my air fare to Helsinki on a four engine propeller plane, for in those days jet engines were still rare. Airports, like airplanes, then were small and near cities, and the flight from Bromma airport in Stockholm to Helsinki lasted almost two hours. Another two hours in the waiting room for the Leningrad plane were spent in looking over the twenty-five passengers who appeared to be waiting for the same flight. Already here the ubiquitous reserve and suspicion prevalent in the USSR seemed to have penetrated, for no one spoke in the room. The twin engine Aeroflot plane, I was told, only had places for 21 passengers, and I wondered how all would be seated. But on boarding there were only five passengers, an American man called Bradshaw from the US Embassy in Moscow, a girl from the Canadian Embassy, two Norwegian girls and myself. When I spoke to Bradshaw and told him I was an American, disbelief was registered on his face, especially when the co-pilot came back to smoke, and we conversed in Russian. The girls too were what can best be described as 'up tight', and unwilling to talk to a stranger. Joking with the co-pilot, I explained that I was a 'real Russian', a Varangian or Swede, whose ancestors had conquered Russia and even given the land its name. I explained that the Finns called the Swedes Ruotsi, and the area formerly about Stockholm was Roslaget, while the Finns called Russians Venäjän after Vendi, the name of a Slavic tribe, all of which he did not believe.

After a flight of an hour and a half we saw the large expanse of Leningrad with the Neva River cutting through it. From the airplane, walking up the broad walk to the airport building in the distance, with white pillars in front, we all followed an English speaking guide. The rooms of the spacious room were large with high ceilings, but one could not determine whether the structure had been built last year or forty years ago. The rooms, with their worn dark red carpets and stuffed sofas, reminded me of Afghan embassies in various capitals of the Near East. In the largest room a uniformed official sat by a table to which our young guide led us. After filling out currency declarations and other forms we went to baggage control, but the inspector did not open any luggage, only questions about the contents. The only item which aroused a passing interest were the five copies of my translation of the Persian history of Bukhara by Narshakhi, which I was carrying as gifts in a canvas shopping bag. The other passengers reboarded the plane for Moscow leaving me alone and somewhat apprehensive of the future. Fortunately an official brought my much needed raincoat, which had been forgotten on the plane.

A sturdy looking Volga car finally came from the city, and the guide and I departed for the Astoria Hotel, probably the leading hotel of the 19th century. This was a city of the tsars, with its broad streets and sprawling, yellow colored buildings with huge gutters and down spouts. People were already filling the streets after work, while the number of cars on the streets was a surprise, since everyone outside supposed that automobiles were relatively scarce in the USSR.

The hotel room reminded me of Parisian counterparts, worn and Victorian with a shared bathroom, but on the whole respectable. At the restaurant below, my perilous monetary plight became apparent when a few sausages, brown bread and tea came to an expensive six rubles, over a dollar and a half at the official rate of exchange. At that time both a dollar and a ruble were valuable, and there was no black market in currencies.

Wearing a bow tie, and obviously Western clothes, caused some patrons to glance at the foreigner for a second, but always they lowered their eyes, and never spoke, since the memory of the Stalin era had not receded. At night streets were well lighted, and some stores, especially bakeries and food stores, as well as beauty parlors, were open until ten. Women swept the sidewalks and streets, as girls in pairs wandered by holding hands. One sensed the effects of the war in the smaller number of men on the streets. Female pulchritude, in spite of the beauty parlors, however, was conspicuous by its absence.

At breakfast on the 27th of August two Americans, John Curtis, who taught Russian at Duke University, and a certain Mr. Browder appeared, which reassured me that other tourists were in the Soviet Union. They had been here for two weeks and were leaving that afternoon for Finland. They too expressed surprise at finding another American in the restaurant of the hotel. It is difficult to remember the feeling of suspicion and uneasiness which permeated every contact made with any Russian, or even foreigner in the country, at that time. The hotel could not change foreign currency, so I had to borrow five rubles from the desk to pay a taxi to go the Bank of the Soviet Union on Fontanka St., where fortunately there was no customary long line waiting in the exchange section. At the Public Library I found my way to the manuscripts section, but an enormous, sullen woman said one would have to obtain permission from the director in another office around the block to see the mss. There a fierce, mustached man in uniform said no one could have a *propusk* 'permission' unless he were properly introduced as a scholar by someone in authority, and who that might be, was never explained. The most commonly heard words in the Soviet Union, for either citizen or foreigner, were *ne propuskaet* 'it is not allowed'. After a walk on the crowded streets I resolved again to tackle the library, but this time directly to the section of Oriental books, and success was at hand. The director had lived in Iran ten years before the war and spoke Persian, which finally opened a door. "It is a pity that the university is not open and the faculty are all still on vacation in their *dachas* 'summer cabins'," he said. But the Oriental Institute of the Academy of Sciences on the bank of the Neva River surely had some people with whom one could speak.

Nina Pigulevskaya's eyes almost popped out when she saw me at the institute, for we had met in Cambridge, England the previous autumn, when a delegation of Soviet scholars had attended an international congress of Orientalists for the first time since the war. She was a specialist on Syriac literature, and after introducing me to a comrade we spoke of colleagues and the need to exchange information, as well as visits. Here too most people were away, many on archaeological expeditions in Central Asia or Siberia. Emboldened by contact with Pigulevskaya, I decided to try the Hermitage Museum, but it was clear that no one would speak to a foreigner without another person present in the room. At the Hermitage only an Islamic numismatist, Bykov, and his assistant, were available and his memories of other Russians who, after the revolution, had left St. Petersburg, as he inadvertently called Leningrad, were countered with stories of such colleagues now abroad. It was late so it was necessary to return the following day, when Bykov, and an Islamic art specialist Guzeliyan, would show me the various parts of the splendid museum.

At the time it was not apparent to me that Intourist would be quite unhelpful; the guide had left on arriving at the hotel, and I had to change money and buy food in shops or on the streets by myself. To give an idea of prices, the hotel room was 30 rubles a night, 40 rubles for a taxi to the train station and 179 rubles for a ticket on the night train to Moscow. Today these sums might seem piddling, but then they appeared very expensive because of the rate of exchange. I resolved to buy a ticket for the train to Moscow, and this time I was assisted by the hotel people, since they told me if I went to the station myself it would be difficult if not impossible to arrange travel. The train wagon had a compartment with a samovar for tea, but otherwise it was similar to trains in western Europe. In the train, before dusk the two engineers in our compartment pointed out fields where once forests had stood, the headquarters of German General Mannheim in a village near the city, and several still destroyed bridges, as well as trenches and shell holes. Again and again the effects of the terrible war were emphasized. Every compartment had a small radio, the volume of which could be controlled but not turned off. It ceased at 11:00 P.M. to begin again at 7:30 A.M. and on reaching Moscow the loud strains of a popular tune, 'My Moscow,' filled the train. The bunks on which we slept were comfortable, in part because of the wide gauge of the tracks. For all of the passengers hot glasses of tea from a large samovar were provided by a large woman attendant.

The National Hotel in Moscow was a center for reporters and diplomats, but I was more interested in meeting colleagues and scholars, so much time was spent in walking from one institute to another, or travelling by bus to more distant buildings. At the Institute of History of the Academy of Sciences an American lady, called Emily Kazakevitch, appeared, and we had interesting discussions about the USSR. She had received a doctorate in Classics at Yale and had been married to a Russian from Columbia University, who had been attacked for his leftist views such that both had taken refuge in Moscow. "Is life better for intellectuals in the USA now that Senator McCarthy had been defanged?" she asked. At my assurance that the McCarthy era was definitely over, she continued, "Americans do not understand much about life in the Soviet Union, where the group spirit of scholars, for example, is wonderful. When the husband of an Armenian girl in the institute died last week, the entire institute arranged the funeral and took care of everything as a group." No doubt the old Soviet spirit of group cooperation was praiseworthy, especially when compared to the present situation in Russia. Life certainly was not bad for academics in the Soviet Union, since they were well regarded, especially if they just did their own research and refrained from politics.

At a table in the restaurant in the hotel that evening I sat with a young Ukrainian who had come to Moscow for the first time to see the sights, and the loud toasts we shared amused several Chinese in uniforms sitting next to us. Later Adamov, an Armenian from New York, who had returned to the USSR after the war, came to my room and asked if I would give my impressions of the country on Radio Moscow, whether I had troubles, or was frightened, and such questions, for which I would be paid. Since my funds were being used more rapidly than anticipated it was not difficult to agree. First, we drove to the university on a hill, with a ski jump on front, where the lights of the city below were beautiful to behold, then on to Gorky Street and the radio station. The interview was short and without political overtones, and mostly positive since frankly I was enjoying myself. In spite of some bureaucratic barriers to meet people or see manuscripts, as well as the miserable service in restaurants, people were pleasant and friendly to an American.

Perhaps it was an impish impulse, but to pass as a Soviet citizen, perhaps from Estonia, provided several interesting incidents. One was trying to enter the US Embassy when the guard outside told me to get lost. He was surprised when an American passport was produced, but still suspicious that a Soviet citizen was trying to fool him. There were many Soviet citizens who spoke Russian poorly or with an accent. By this time my clothes had become somewhat bedraggled and ties no longer were worn. Another time a German businessman at the dinner table thought I was a local inhabitant, and probably spoke in a different fashion than if I had admitted to being an American. He grumbled about high prices for little value, of traffic which disregarded the rights of pedestrians and other complaints. Adamov returned and gave me a most welcome 394 rubles, (minus 6 for taxes) as payment for the interview. I felt positively rich.

Chip Bohlen, the American ambassador, had been to Central Asia, and since my card had been left at the embassy, he wanted to talk about that region, so he sent to the hotel an invitation for dinner. His brother-in-law, Charlie Thayer, had been the first American consul in Kabul, which provided an entry for conversation. Bohlen believed that the days of one dictator were over, and henceforth the Soviet Union would be governed by the Politbureau, not one of whom would become another Stalin. He mentioned how the Chechens had been invited to a great victory celebration, at the end of the war, and then surrounded by MVD troops who shipped them ên masse to Kazakhstan. No wonder the Chechens, after returning to their homeland, were anxious someday to fight for their independence! Irving R. Levine of NBC at that time was in Moscow, and as an interpreter, on Sunday I was to accompany him to a monastery at Zagorsk near Moscow. Unfortunately, because of his orders to cover another story that trip did not materialize.

All attempts to secure permission to go to Central Asia having failed, at last at the suggestion of the lady in the tourist bureau of the hotel, I wrote to the president of Intourist explaining the need to visit Bukhara since I had written about its history. In all visits to institutes and conversations I had not been upbraided because of American politics vis-a vis the USSR, nor had any personal attacks surfaced, until meeting a Buryat Mongol, Sanzheev, in the Oriental Institute on Armenian Lane. He asked how Americans could honor an irresponsible, stateless person like Nikolai Poppe who had joined the Germans during the war, and now was a professor of Mongolian in the University of Washington. I was not about to tell him that I had helped spirit him out of Germany to the USA several years after the war. "Why is the USA building bases all around the USSR, and why did Americans write about the starving Mongols?" he exclaimed. It was unclear whether his outburst was for the benefit of his companion Komissarov, or whether he believed all that he said.

One cannot simply walk into the institutes or libraries, but always a gamut of several individuals, a guard, a secretary, or director, needs to pass on the suitability of a meeting. Since it was difficult to telephone for an appointment, much going and coming was necessary. The Museum of Anthropology with its famous curator, Gerasimov, was a most interesting experience, for he was able to reconstruct facial features from skulls. He had reconstructed the heads of Timur, his son Shah Rukh and grandson Ulug Beg, with the first a Mongol type, while Shah Rukh, the son of a Tajik woman, had Europoid features. The third was a mixture of the two, with the Mongol type predominant. Gerasimov explained, "It was nothing new, only a continuation of old principles, the study of both halves of the face, careful measurement of all of the cranium features, and finally extensive use of x-rays on living specimens, then projected back on the old skulls." Then he continued, "look at the Cro-Magnon and Neanderthal features which I have reconstructed, the former more like homo-sapiens than Western reconstructions. What I need are negroid skulls, which we don't have in the USSR." I assured him of my interest but inability to help.

Vasilii Abaev, an Ossete in the Institute of Linguistics, was more friendly than any other scholar, for he invited me to his apartment and gave me an apple and breaking it, offered half of it with the remark, "In Ossetia breaking an apple with anyone is a sign of great friendship." Then he handed me a Caucasian drinking horn, saying," You must empty the horn, filled with vodka, with one draught, because it will spill if it is set down." I could not comply or compete with Ossetian prowess, so he excused me. An American company was coming to Moscow to play Porgy and Bess, which he would not miss for the world. The other Iranian linguists at the institute, a majority of them women, were also pleasant and visits were most enjoyable.

In the evening a car came from the embassy for dinner with Justice William O. Douglas, his young, blonde southern wife, and Robert Kennedy. Bohlen sparkled, but Douglas was glum, as he explained, "In Alma Ata (today Almaty) I wanted to drive to the Chinese frontier, but they told me that the paved road only went a hundred kilometers from town, and then one would have to take a mule for ten days to reach the frontier. But I saw a map which showed the road paved all the way, and I mentioned this to the mayor and police chief of Alma Ata. Without blinking an eye, they then told me that avalanches had blocked the road and no one could get through them." Again in Petropavlovsk he had wanted to fly to Karaganda but was told there was no air service.

At the airport, however, planes were arriving and departing for that place. Justice Douglas was most unhappy that he had not been allowed to go where he wished, and the rest of the evening he kept silent. If he had had an experience living in the Orient he might have better understood the Russians. Robert Kennedy was intent on listening to the ambassador and said little, while my place also was to keep quiet for Bohlen was a compulsive speaker.

The following day, Friday 2nd September, a Russian who spoke Persian came from the radio station and asked me to record an interview for the Persian service, with similar questions as in the Russian interview, plus greetings to friends in Iran. Again the hope of earning some rubles, combined with a wish to speak Persian caused no hesitation. The hotel was now full of visitors, the sister and wife of Kennedy who had come from Helsinki, several new correspondents, senator Kefauver from Tennessee, Sparkman of Alabama, a senator from Nevada and several congressmen. To calm some of their complaints of poor service directed at foreigners, I told them of my attempt to be served at the restaurant in the Kurskii railroad station for lunch. At noon there were four of us at the table, including an artillery officer who had to catch a train at 2:00 P.M. A few minutes before that hour he only had the first course of his lunch, which he bolted, and smashing his fist on the table which almost overturned, he swore at the waitresses before running to catch the train. The other two at the table upbraided the waitress, making such an uproar that I finally left at 2:30, only having received *kasha* and bread. "So you see," I remarked," nothing is directed against foreigners; the local people have to suffer much more."

Because of my lack of complaints and bothering her, now even the lady in the service bureau of the hotel became friendly, and after the senators and others had gone to the Bolshoi theater, we had a long conversation, in which she affirmed that Theodore Dreiser was the greatest contemporary American writer because he had understood so well the society in which he lived. Afterwards she lent me a Latin letter typewriter so I could type some letters to send to the Boston Globe, and for my diary.

At the Tretyakov gallery paintings by Russian artists were exhibited, but sometimes the explanations of guides, leading groups past the large frames, left something to be desired. The artistic qualities of the painter usually were ignored, while any social consciousness was praised, which was not difficult since there were many paintings showing the poor lot of serfs under the tsars. For example, in front of one huge tableau was depicted the boyarin Morozova being led to her execution through the snow covered streets of Moscow on a sleigh, with chains on her hands, one lifted in the sign of the cross of the Old Believers. The guide explained this gesture as a sign of protest of the Russian people against feudal tyranny, while the work of Vereshchagin on the horrors of war, especially a pyramid of skulls, was ideal for social exposition. All paintings were from the pre-Soviet period and modern art was exhibited at another museum.

At that time foreigners were impressed with the tight controls and the power of the Soviet Union. A Swiss businessman at the hotel averred that the eastern European countries would never break away from the embrace of the bear, and that this bloc would only grow stronger. Bohlen also had some fears for the future. "Think", he said "what would happen if there were a Chinggis Khan with a telephone." Today we would say computer.

The Pakistan embassy gave an address for the only functioning mosque in Moscow, and a long trip by bus revealed a ramshackle, low roofed building, in a courtyard filled with trash, and locked all the time except Fridays at one P.M. The streets were unpaved and the log cabins around it were hovels, a part of Moscow not seen by tourists. Later in the treasure rooms of the Kremlin the reputed helmet of Tsar Alexander Nevsky, made by an old Russian master, had an Arabic inscription around the base. Such sights revealed the strong influences of the Islamic world on medieval Russia. But Central Asia, that part of the USSR which was Islamic, eluded me. I declared I would return home before the expiration of my visa if it were impossible to go to Bukhara.

Every day I had asked about permission to fly to Tashkent and always the same answer, but wonder of wonders, came an unexpected surprise when coming down in the morning to the service desk and asking the same question, there came a different answer. "You can go whenever you want, but you will be entirely on your own," said the lady. "I have always been on my own here," said I, giving her 1397 rubles for the round trip air ticket. I prepared for the trip, but my money was almost exhausted. I phoned Adamov and said I needed money for my trip which required another interview, which, duly performed, netted another 394 rubles. For the Persian language radio interview a further 591 rubles came, which made the trip to Central Asia possible.

Even though it was only the beginning of September, on the bus to the airport at 1:00 in the morning I shivered in the cold wearing a sweater, and regretting my coat left with a suitcase in the embassy. After a long wait we finally took off at 3:40 A.M., and there were only fourteen passengers on the small propeller plane. We flew low and sleep took over until we landed at Uralsk, where breakfast was only a bottle of synthetic apple juice. After an hour we continued to Aktiubinsk, which was reached at eleven in the morning with a small lunch at the airport. In both places the runways were only packed dirt, and one wondered how they would look in the event of rain.

After an hour we continued to Dzhusaly, a port on the north bank of the Syr Darya, not far from the Aral Sea, which at that time was still a large sea. Several passengers claimed that this was one of the richest agricultural areas in the USSR, where rice and cotton were grown. From the tall smokestacks the town appeared to be also an industrial center, but today it has suffered the fate of many towns around the once expansive Aral Sea. Although on the map Tashkent did not seem far away, the last leg of the flight took almost three hours over a sandy, lifeless desert. The largest city in Central Asia was reached at four Moscow time or seven in the evening, Tashkent time. All flights in the Soviet Union flew on Moscow time rather than local time.

Before the earthquake which happened the following year, Tashkent looked like Kabul or Meshhed, with rows of one story, shack-like buildings, and a similar bazaar. The morning of next day, the ninth of September, was spent in arranging train travel to Samarkand, and for the return, a seat on the plane to Moscow on the 18th. In the afternoon a four hour visit to Mikhail Masson, dean of archaeologists in Central Asia, and professor at the university, proved most informative. He was an effusive, bald headed man, about 65 years, wearing a skull cap and large glasses, all of which reminded me of Vladimir Minorsky, an Orientalist friend in Cambridge, England. Both were large in frame and not shy to tell of their achievements. Masson had begun his first excavation in 1913 at the site of Afrasiab, old Samarkand, and since that time had participated in fifty-five expeditions, all in Central Asia. He told that in tsarist times archaeologists had little support, but under Soviet rule money was available, and many specialists had been trained. There were a few problems, however, he admitted. The archaeologists worked on a five year plan, and were fairly free to choose sites to excavate. If, however, the Uzbek republic was to celebrate, for example, the millennium of the Samanid dynasty, then they might request the archaeologists to concentrate on Bukhara, even though they were engaged elsewhere. Another problem was wooing workers from local state farms to dig on the sites, and always the teams were small. Masson was now engaged on a long term plan to excavate a site called Nisa, a Parthian city in southern Turkmenistan. Ten years earlier his wife had died and he married a prize student assistant, Galina Pugachenkova, a stunning beauty, who spoke French. Vadim, his son by his first wife, was studying archaeology in Leningrad, and in later years I was to have much to do with him, as he followed in his father's footsteps.

Masson was very open, and with pride showed his laboratory, where many students were reconstructing objects found in various excavations. "My students must study soils and geology," he declared, "and then they have to learn to eat dirt on the desert sites of Central Asia." He disagreed with the reconstruction of Kushan history by Roman Ghirshman, and rightly declared that the excavations in Central Asia were changing all old views of the past of the region. All the information he gave was revealing, but clearly of little interest to my readers.

Azimjanova, the directress of the Oriental Institute of the Uzbek Academy of Sciences, was even more surprised to see me than Pigulevskaya in Leningrad, and the atmosphere here was more tense than at the university, with people greatly restrained in their speech. Afterwards I took a trolley bus to the old city, much of which was levelled later by the earthquake. Turkish was somewhat understandable to educated Uzbeks, and its use aroused great interest in crowds around a mosque. On a question whether children learned anything about the Islamic religion, the universal answer was no. In the old city, with open stalls similar to those in Kabul, and elsewhere in the Near East, a first beggar in the USSR was encountered, but later in Samarkand and Bukhara many appeared, surprisingly most of them Russians.

My costume of a woolen Afghan cap and sweater did not set me apart from Russians who lived in Central Asia, only they did not deign to learn the local languages. A night at the opera in Tashkent was the occasion for some worry that perhaps I was tempting the future of travel to Bukhara.

The Alishir Navoi opera and ballet theater in Tashkent was an interesting mixture of old Islamic architectural motifs and new techniques in plaster work. Each room was in a different style, corresponding to the various provinces of the Uzbek SSR. The opera was a local one, Majnun and Leila, but it was far from the brilliant performances of the Bolshoi. In the vestibule an elderly Russian was noisy, and obviously drunk, so the blue uniformed police quietly ushered him outside. In Russia the police wore white tunics in the summer but not in Central Asia.

An Indian delegation of textile workers was also in the outer halls of the theater at the intermission (they looked like managers rather than workers), and they wanted autographs on their programs from the Uzbek leading lady. I acted as interpreter for them, but a request for the same autograph only brought the response, "Go away; this is not for you, but only for foreign guests." This response actually pleased me to be regarded as a local. After the performance a midnight snack was arranged for the delegation and I joined them. Three Russian interpreters, one a woman, took a dim view of my intrusion, and they were even more uneasy when I told them I was an American, but the fruit on the tables was fresh and inviting, unlike the miserable specimens in the bazaar, and I was hungry. One of the Russian interpreters vanished, and when I came out of the theater he accosted me with great agitation. "How is my pronunciation of final -n in English," he requested. Had he been to my hotel room across the street, or what was involved? I was uneasy and hoped that nothing would come of this incident, which might hinder my trip to Bukhara.

The next morning at the railroad station a large crowd was waiting to enter the RR yard, which gates opened at eight, with a stampede towards the train. A guard approached and asked for my papers, since I had been photographing the train. With my passport in hand he walked towards the station, but his superior told him to forget it and return the passport. The seats on the train were wood and not very comfortable, and the train got off to a very slow start but went at a snail's pace. Three Russian beggars came through the train, one of whom was a girl in her 20s with a missing right hand. In the adjacent compartment were two girls, one a Ukrainian, who had just received their diplomas from a technical school in Moscow, and were on their way to a hydro-electric project at Kuy-e Mazar, near Bukhara. This was the first time they had been to Central Asia and were fearful of the future. One said she did not like the Uzbeks, and when we stopped at every station she would ask whether Russians lived there. Truth to say when the Uzbeks in the next compartment removed their boots the odor from their unwashed feet was overpowering. I consoled the girls by describing conditions in Afghanistan, asserting that living conditions here were much better, and that the Uzbeks really were friendly and hospitable. But it did not seem to make much of an impression.

Traveling by train was a great opportunity for talking, and an elderly Russian RR engineer was full of stories, some far-fetched, such as the one about a scientific expedition to the Caucasus. It seems its purpose was to study longevity there, and they found an old man who claimed to be 92 years old. By questioning him about past events in his memory they established that he was in fact much older, about 110. He begged the members of the expedition not to tell anyone in the village because he was hoping to marry, and no woman would have him if they found out he was 110 and not 92.

At the station in Samarkand, which we reached in the evening, as I waited for a tram, a young man accosted me while his companion picked up my suitcase and started off with it. It was either too heavy with books in it, or he realized it belonged to a foreigner, hence a possible problem for him. In any case, he put it down and both of them vanished in the crowd.

Suddenly the lights went off in the city, including the tram, so I walked to the darkened hotel, and was shown to a room by a Russian concierge holding a kerosene lamp. Although the room only had a bed and a chair in it, everything was clean, unusual for Central Asia.

In all stations along our route here and there Russians could be seen, as well as, of course, in the cities. Many Uzbeks preferred to speak Russian instead of their own language or even Tajiki, and it seemed clear that Russification was proceeding apace. How wrong one could be, for the changes of the nineties were many years ahead! Incidentally the same radio program was heard all over the USSR, every day beginning at eight in the morning from Radio Moscow. Radio speakers were not only in hotel rooms but in public squares and on railroad platforms.

When my film became stuck in the camera a Bukharan Jew in a local photography shop fixed it. After some conversation he spoke about the status of Jews in Central Asia. There was one mosque, one synagogue, and one church in operation in the city. All other houses of worship had been turned into offices or warehouses, and young people knew nothing, and were taught nothing, about religion. What happened in secret, in this regard, was not revealed until the 1990s, which was a surprise to outsiders, as well as to Russians themselves.

At that time Samarkand was a dusty Oriental city with camels on the streets, and old men with turbans riding on donkeys, similar to Afghanistan. Side by side with taxis and trams were droshkies, carriages pulled by horses, acting as taxis, and many carts drawn by donkeys. Green tea in small bowls in tea houses also brought back nostalgic memories of Afghanistan, but the Russian overlay here revealed some contrasts, especially in the old and new parts of the cities, except in Bukhara which did not have a new, or Russian, section.

At the hotel, radios blared throughout the night, and in the room above an Uzbek made much noise and finally vomited out the window onto the porch of my room; it was an unpleasant night. The monuments of the city, of course, were spectacular, but only the tomb of Timur had a complete, restored dome; all others were in various states of decay, unlike later years when tourism promoted a wave of restorations, most of which were decried as shabby by local master craftsmen and builders.

At the local university I again heard that Dreiser was the top American author whom they read, and my protests that I had not even read his books left the Uzbeks somewhat crestfallen. "What a pity that you cannot read Russian authors, while we are free to read all of your publications," commiserated the dean of the history section. With almost 13,000 students, the university in Samarkand had many departments with a wide range of courses, including the universally required study of Marxism-Leninism. Nonetheless it was apparent that the least restrictions, and the best brains, were to be found in non-political subjects such as linguistics and archaeology.

Walking back from the observatory of Ulug Beg, a few kilometers from town a funeral procession came down the street led by a mullah. They went to the extensive cemetery where I was resting, and all listened to the recitation of Quranic verses. The mullah, with irony and some contempt in his voice asked, "I suppose you find this interesting." I replied in Tajiki that I was not a Russian, but happy to see Muslim practices in Central Asia. The group warmed up considerably, but remained suspicious until we parted with many exclamations of peace and "God protect you."

The last leg to the goal of the trip was by night train to Kagan, the station of Bukhara, a six hour trip, with arrival at three in the morning. A wait until late morning was necessary for the antiquated train from Kagan to Bukhara some fifteen kilometers distant. It took an hour for the trip, and passengers still had to walk some distance from the Bukhara station to the city. A 'so-called' hotel, but in reality a large tea house was to be my home in Bukhara for several days. The rooms were primitive with only four beds (really *charpoy*, as in Afghanistan), but they were clean. The museum of the citadel (*arg*) of Bukhara, like that of Samarkand was disappointing, for moth eaten specimens of stuffed animals and modern Soviet art, mostly propagandistic, were the mainstays of both. Again at present how different the onslaught of tourists with money has made on new museums in Central Asia! No paved roads, but only dust, thistles, and darting lizards on trails led to the famous mausoleum of the Samanids, at that time in a field on the outskirts of town, but now in a well-kept park. Everywhere questions about antiquities brought no responses, only that young people were not at all interested in such matters.

At a tea house, where I shared canned hamburger and cigarettes with Uzbeks and several Russians, conditions in Afghanistan and Iran came up for discussion. When I mentioned that every tea house in Iran had an opium den in the rear, but that the worst was *shire*, the dregs of smoked opium which poor people ate, they laughed and replied that *shirak,* as they called it, was also found in Bukhara. At my astonishment that such conditions should exist in the Soviet Union where it was against the law, they laughed again, and a Russian remarked *Moskva daleko* 'Moscow is far away'. There were few Russians in the city, and most people spoke Tajiki rather than the Uzbek language. It was interesting that no one wanted to hear about the United States, only about their neighbors to the south. The stay in Bukhara was the high point of my trip to the USSR and I felt more at home here than in Moscow.

When I asked for the hotel bill, a woman told me it was an outrageous 30 rubles a night. At my strong protest she explained that each bed was seven and a half rubles a night, and there were four beds in the room. "But I only slept in one bed, " I protested. "Ah, but you kept others from sleeping in the other beds," was the rejoinder. "Nonsense," I replied," I did not prevent others from sleeping there; you did." Not convinced she exclaimed, "but you are a foreigner and had to sleep alone." Since we were getting nowhere I asked to see the director and explained that if I returned to Moscow and said that I had paid thirty rubles a night for a bed in Bukhara, everyone would think that I had stayed in a palace instead of this miserable hovel. In the end the price was only seven and a half a night (really a *sutki* or 24 hours, or any part thereof.) In Moscow at the National Hotel the price was only 12 rubles, which fact I impressed on the director. Maybe he had a monopoly as the only place to be called a hotel in town.

At Kagan, a few hours before the train for Samarkand was due, an attempt to put my suitcase in a left luggage room failed because my passport had been left in a strong box in the 'hotel' in Bukhara. All attempts to telephone the hotel having failed (and one pays for a telephone call if there is an answer or not), I took a taxi to the hotel in Bukhara and retrieved the document. Then back to Kagan where a delayed train provided much time to inspect the town. Beggars were plentiful in Kagan, which was a rather dilapidated railroad town with nothing to recommend it.

The return train did not stop in Samarkand but went directly to Tashkent, and there I made broadcasts for Radio Tashkent in Persian and English, with the usual questions, how I liked Central Asia and what did I see. But we worked hard on preparing a polished text, since they were more concerned about content here than in Moscow. A visit to the Oriental Faculty of the university revealed a class in the history of Iran taught by a Russian, G. Bondarevsky. He gave a lecture on the rise of the Safavid state in 16th century Iran, and at one place remarked, "As great Stalin said, tribal confederations can never make states." Perhaps the death of Stalin had not quite sunk into the psyches of some people in Central Asia. After class he explained many things about education in the USSR, but few students were interested in the past. A conflict exists among students of Islam, he explained; one camp proposes that Muhammad rose in a slave society, while the other asserts that it was a following feudal society.

A visit to the chief *imam,* or leader of Muslims in all of Central Asia produced some interesting items. He had a book of Arabic lessons, printed in Kazan in 1913. Much later I was to see the same book with Dungans, Muslim Chinese, in Gansu province. He claimed that 18 small mosques were active in Tashkent, and confirmed that only one existed in Samarkand. When I switched from a mixture of Russian and Arabic to Persian, he became agitated and warned me not to speak in that language, looking outside of his door and windows to see if anyone were listening. Already the enmity between Uzbeks and Tajiks of post Soviet time was apparent.

That night I stayed too long at the opera where Tchaikovsky's Mazeppa was on the stage, and when I returned to the hotel everyone was upset, saying a taxi had been waiting more than an hour to go to the airport. Actually the plane was delayed, and we left after one in the morning, flying the same route with the same stops as on the trip to Tashkent. Two generals were passengers on the plane, and in Moscow we shared a limousine to the hotel, which was a relief since airports were far from the city.

That evening the Moscow Art Theater's production of Gorky's 'The Lower Depths,' was a masterpiece, and confirmed that the Russians were masters of stage and theater. Back in the hotel Adamov phoned and asked for an interview on my trip to Central Asia. He was particularly anxious to have my views about relations between Uzbeks and Russians, and he wanted to dispel the notion that Central Asia was a Russian colony. I answered his questions as best I could, with the belief that the Uzbeks now could handle their own affairs, which was hardly the case in the past. Subsequent events, however, have shown the truth of this remark. This interview, however, was to have repercussions in the future.

Several articles which I had written for the Russian language journals *The Messenger of Ancient History*, and *The Nations of Asia and Africa*, had been translated into Russian by an interpreter in the US embassy for 50 rubles an article. Writing about my trip was my chief task in the hotel after return from Central Asia. In conversations at the hotel Cliff Daniels of the New York Times, Levine and others, agreed that Americans were fooling themselves if they thought there was even a remote chance of rolling back the 'Iron Curtain.' It took a long time, but how wrong we were!

The train trip to Leningrad was uneventful, and there many scholars had returned from their vacations, so it was a real privilege to be invited for lunch by Mme. Kratchkovskaya to her *dacha* north of the city, where a neighbor, Josef Orbeli, director of the Hermitage, proved to be a fascinating person, and we quite enjoyed the chance to talk about matters of common interest. Returning to the Astoria hotel my luggage had been placed in a taxi, and everyone was upset that I had returned so late. At the Leningrad airport I was the only passenger from town who boarded the Moscow-Helsinki plane, which was full of diplomats, especially Swedes returning from Moscow to Stockholm. In that city at lunch my old friend, Gunnar Jarring remarked that there were sixty-seven Soviet tourists in Sweden, whom the Russians had wanted to come as a group under one passport, but the Swedes had declined, so a week later they all appeared with individual passports. This shows that the Soviets could change and adapt themselves to new conditions.

CHAPTER 17

A Year in Germany

THE YEAR 1956 brought changes to my academic position. Thomson had retired as Professor of Arabic, and I was the most informed member of the committee to search for a successor. A friend from Princeton reported that Hamilton A.R. Gibb was leaving Oxford for Princeton, which information was reported to the committee, with the recommendation that Harvard invite him, and let him choose. That evening Thomson telephoned to Fritz Jewett of Weyerhauser Lumber Co., whose father not only had established the chair, but had occupied it for many years. Thomson, in his Glasgow accent: "They've invited Gibb but he w'ont come. " Jewett: "Why not?" Thomson: "He is Laudian Professor of Arabic at Oxford and only a University Professorship would tempt him to come to Harvard."

Jewett: "I hear that is a prestigious appointment with a high salary; well I will put up the money for such a post just to bring Gibb."

A short time later President Nathan Pusey called me and asked who Gibb was, saying that "University Professors are distinguished scholars who are Nobel prize holders, or those who for their accomplishments are interviewed in journals such as *Time* and *Life*". My experiences in the Middle East were useful in the arts of persuasion, which had to be utilized with the president of Harvard. It took convincing, but Gibb was appointed and came, at which I resigned from the Middle East Center to give him a free hand, and I turned to research on Iranian subjects, as well as constructing a department of Near Eastern Languages and Civilizations as well as a Center for the Study of World Religions. It was also a good time to apply for a sabbatical year.

Rebecca or Becky was born on March 9 of this year, after an unusual one night stand with Barbara. With two children, and tenure at the university, we had to leave a rented university house on DeWolfe Street, long since removed for a dormitory, and purchase a house in Winchester not far from her parents. Commuting to the university by car was a new experience, but which at least caused a better organization of time. Repairs on the house, including the roof, and fencing épée with students at the university, kept me in fair physical shape, but early rising and late returning home left little time for the children. My bedroom was on the third floor of the large old frame house at ten Fells Road, while Barbara and the children were on the second floor, a strange situation as the children later remarked. But such were our relations, not conducive to reconciliation.

Much was happening at Harvard, with Dean Douglas Horton of the Divinity School seeking to establish a Center for World Religions, against the wishes of his faculty. The story, which was current, had Spalding of tennis products fame unhappy about the appointment of Robin Zaehner as Spalding Professor of World Religions at Oxford, after Radhakrishnan, the first incumbent had returned to India as vice-president of the new country. Zaehner, a convert to Catholicism, had given an inaugural lecture called 'Foolishness to the Greeks,' in which he openly derided the idea that all religions were the same, or at least that all should cooperate in working for such a goal, which idea his predecessor had embraced. It was said that Spalding sued Oxford for appointing Zaehner, against the terms of the professorship, but he lost and turned to American friends to persuade Harvard to accept funds from American friends to create a center for world religions, with the express purpose of having practitioners of various religions living and studying together. In order to override the votes of the old Divinity faculty, opposed to the center, Horton appointed several professors of the Faculty of Arts and Sciences, friendly to his plans, as voting members of the Divinity Faculty. We carried the day and Horton got his center. It then was proposed that the Chinese Jehol temple, which had been erected at the World's Fair of Chicago in 1933-4, and which after the Communist control of China remained in box cars in this country at Oberlin, Ohio, could be secured as a building for the new center, especially since the temple was free for the asking. The only difficulty was how, and who, could reconstruct the many miniature parts of the temple, a daunting prospect. This plan, however, finally was vetoed and a more practical structure was proposed. Until the building was constructed, however, the center would rent a large private house.

Another problem was the recommendation from the donors that a retired English missionary to Burma, Robert Slater, should be appointed the first director. The faculty balked at being told whom to appoint, but since he would only serve for five or six years, his appointment was pushed through the faculty, over objections. I strongly defended this decision.

One of the first group of fellows to the center was an ayatallah from Iran, who insisted on wearing his turban and robes, even when walking at Harvard Square. He returned and complained that people stared at him, at which I suggested that he change his costume. He refused, saying it was imperative that he always wear his robes, so finally he resigned and returned to Iran. Later another more liberal religious leader came, Haeri-Yazdi, who was even more learned than his predecessor. He wore ordinary clothes, and when told of the action of the first ayatallah, Haeri-Yazdi's retort was simple, "He was a jackass."

The Center for World Religions was designed by a distinguished architect Jose Sert, and all religions were accommodated in the building with various symbols, and even a special place for ablutions. As advisor on both Zoroastrian and Islamic practices, I had to research many facets of the religions in order to secure approval from various leaders who were invited as fellows. Peshotan Anklesaria was the first Zoroastrian priest to come from Bombay, and through him I later was introduced to many of the Parsi community in that city.

A Fulbright grant, plus an invitation to teach at Frankfurt University, was finally arranged for the academic year 1958-59, and the family flew to Paris just before Bastille day. A Volkswagen minibus was purchased, even though we were warned that the motor, made for a beetle, might not readily push the minibus up hills. We had been invited by Mary, Barbara's sister and her army husband Lt. Dick Gorder stationed in Madrid, to spend a week at a house they had rented in Bourgette near Pamplona. Jeff enjoyed the bull run in the latter town, and later especially a bull fight in Madrid, but the rest of us had a sympathy for the bulls. Inability to speak Spanish hindered our stay, although using Italian sometimes provoked understanding in listeners.

Arriving in Frankfurt, we found quarters difficult to rent but finally secured an apartment but only beginning late in September. Since we would have to find a hotel for several weeks, and classes would not begin until October, we decided to drive to Moscow and return through Sweden to introduce the children to relatives in Lidköping. After lengthy negotiations visas were secured, and on the 24th of August we entered Czechoslovakia, duly observing the barbed wire and guard houses on the frontier with western Germany. The beautiful city had not been harmed by the war, and colleagues such as Jiri Becka, Jan Marek and others were delighted to talk to a rare American visitor and were helpful in making more contacts. Austrian friends had told me that they spoke German but acted like Slavs, while the Czechs spoke a Slavic tongue but acted like Germans. Orderliness was apparent, and Charles University professors, although formal, were both friendly and helpful. Both here and in Poland many people preferred to speak German or French rather than Russian.

At the Polish frontier we were surprised to find the same barbed wire and guardposts as on the frontier with Germany, but none on the Polish side. On questioning, the Polish border officials remarked that if they let their neighbors handle frontier defenses Poland did not need any. "We like the French and try to copy them," was a remark made by a Pole who dared to speak to an American visitor. Ravages of war were apparent in Poland, and the Stalin style buildings in rebuilt Warsaw contrasted with medieval Prague. Polish colleagues were more open than the Czechs, and did not conceal their dislike of the Russians. Just before reaching the Soviet frontier at Brest, Jeff accidentally dropped the large key to open the rear of the car, where the motor was, down the space between the dashboard and windshield in front. The Poles asked me to open the rear, and I explained what had happened, whereupon they said to forget it, and instead give them cigarettes, which I did, and they waved me through. On the Soviet side, however, they had to break the lock for inspection, and an Intourist guide sent to escort us to Moscow angrily said we should have arrived yesterday, for he was about to return to the capital. I apologized for being late and we set off as fast as the car could travel for Smolensk where we were to spend the night. He was necessary to guide us on the dark road without any lighting, for several times I had to slam the brakes to avoid falling into large ditches across the road. Finally we arrived in Smolensk at two in the morning exhausted. We had to travel fast to make up for the lost day, the first of September, according to our guide.

In the morning I told the children we would eat tasty *blinchiki*, or Russian pancakes for breakfast, but when they appeared on our plates even a knife would not cut them, for they seemed to be made of hard rubber. I had forgotten that food in restaurants outside of the large cities usually was awful. Although the car had no problems on the flat land, several times on the trip it had to be repaired, and payment to mechanics had to be negotiated with an Oriental bazaar method. In Moscow we were turned over to a girl from Intourist whom Becky called Catherine lady. She stayed with us until the Finnish frontier and became much attached to Becky. If Czechoslovakia and Poland had made a bad impression on Barbara, because of the unhappy and depressed look on peoples' faces, she was almost terrified in the Soviet Union, always fearing that we might be arrested and held for no cause. We were only nine days in the USSR, and with Intourist control, I was unable to meet colleagues to show her a kinder face of Russia.

At least we had a tourist view of the land, and Novgorod especially revealed a view of old Russia different from the Stalin style buildings elsewhere. The children were unconcerned, however, and did not share the extreme relief that Barbara felt on crossing the frontier into friendly and clean Finland. Speaking the language gave me a different view of the Russian people and I felt much like the children. The boat trip to Stockholm was exciting for them, and the trip to Lidköping pleasant without car trouble. The lack of castles, similar to those in Germany, however was disappointing for Jeff who was in a 'castle stage' at that time. My mother's brother, Eric Hagman, who had built his own house, was an engineer now retired. His eldest daughter Ingrid, now more crippled by polio was soon to die, while the youngest Britta, was hoping to be married, and finish her course in Stockholm to become a registered nurse. Lidköping had little changed since 1946, for farmers still brought their large carts to town on market days; great changes were to come in the eighties. After two days we continued to Frankfurt and settled in our new home for the next nine months. The apartment was not far from the university, and one could easily walk to classes, while the Volkswagen could be repaired by experts.

At every class hour only two or three students appeared, and not the same ones every time. At the end of the term, however, over thirty students appeared and asked me to sign their books, indicating they had attended the course. I was perplexed and went to the new head of our Oriental seminar, Rudolf Sellheim, who had replaced Helmut Ritter, to ask what one should do. "Sign all of the books, for which you will receive eight marks for each student." Against my better judgment, all the books were signed. In the floor above the Oriental Seminar was the Indoeuropean Linguistics Seminar, and in the libraries of both there were many duplicates, especially of journals. I spoke to Prof. Bernfried Schlerath, head of that seminar, as well as to Sellheim about the duplication, but both replied that they had separate book budgets and bought whatever they needed, with no need for consultation, even though the money was limited for both. There were other surprises in the university, such as the exalted station of a head of a seminar, but most of my time was devoted to the children, which I hoped would make up for neglect back home. Jeff began an American school in Frankfurt, while Barbara became engaged in Episcopal church matters.

Many times we visited the botanical *(Palmengarten)* and the zoological gardens, and strolling around the city revealed how wrong I had been on my first trip to Frankfurt, when I said that the city was so ruined it never could be rebuilt. Buildings and monuments in the old city were restored, but American style skyscrapers also were being built in a kind of parallel to the Stalin style structures in East Germany, referred to as the 'Zone' in the west. People were hard working and helpful, and many friends were made. With the Volkswagen, trips to castles, and to the restored Roman fort on the Limes in the Taunus mountains, were the fare for almost every week-end. It always was a disappointment later to realize that young children remember virtually nothing of such trips, unless reminded by their parents, and even then it is not a real memory.

Some refugees from Hitler's Germany had returned from Britain or the USA to occupy posts in universities, and in Frankfurt the Institute of Sociology, financed by American foundations and headed by Professors Horkheimer and Adorno, was especially active, and with stimulating public lectures. The intellectual milieu, however, was nothing like Paris, where I had interesting conversations with Georges Dumézil regarding Indoeuropean religion and folklore, or with René Grousset on Oriental history, or my special friends Henry Corbin on Sufism and philosophy, and with the Dominican Jean Pierre DeMenasce on ancient Iranian matters. These were always memorable occassions. Grousset was charming and, like Louis Massignon the specialist on Islam, a fervent and devout Catholic. Protestant Corbin, who would never ride on the underground Metro, was even more hard of hearing, and his lovely wife Stella had to repeat most of his sentences. His passion about philosophy, however, was impressive, similar to Harry Wolfson a teacher and colleague at Harvard.

Scholars are divided between those who specialize in one discipline and are not concerned with other matters, and those who aspire to the status of a 'Renaissance person,' interested in many fields while concentrating on one. To the former belonged such Iranist savants in Cambridge as Harold Bailey and Vladimir Minorsky, whom his Russian colleagues dubbed Majorsky because of his conceit, and in London my mentor Henning. To the latter category one could assign H.H. Schaeder in Göttingen and many French scholars.

A Kurdish scholar in Paris, Bedr Khan, taught that language, and once when I visited him Mohammed Mokri, who had left Tehran after the fall of Mossadegh, also appeared at the apartment. He had received his Ph.D. degree from Tehran University on Kurdish dialects. When he mentioned this to Bedr Khan, the latter glared at him and said there were no dialects in Kurdish.

How he explained the differences between Kurmanji and Sorani, mutually unintelligible, was never revealed.

In the spring of 1957, while in Frankfurt, an invitation came from ARAMCO, the American oil company in Saudi Arabia to deliver several lectures in Dhahran and Riyadh. On arrival in Riyadh the debris on the desert of plastic bottles, tinfoil, paper and cans was shocking, especially since the trash would not disintegrate and be absorbed into the ground in such a dry climate. In the American ghetto of Dhahran, chemists competed with each other in the production of various spirits, and they were most competent in everything save scotch, which failure they wrongly attributed to inability to secure the water of Scotland, which could not be duplicated here. This first trip to Saudi Arabia did not allow time to visit ancient sites or villages on the eastern sea coast, but it established connections for future trips. The money pouring into the country was visibly making great changes in the land, and luxury cars were replacing camels on the streets. An old friend and Princeton seminar classmate, George Rentz, had become a country specialist and interpreter for ARAMCO, which made the short stay both informative and pleasant. He was happy to explore the country, after having to spend much time on a dispute between Saudi Arabia and Abu Dhabi over the oasis of Buraimi.

Back in Frankfurt time passed quickly and the onerous task of packing boxes to send by sea from Bremen took longer than planned. Although it had been a strenuous year, everyone enjoyed their experiences, but strained marital relations soon returned to the pre-trip norm.

CHAPTER 18

An Armenian Guidepost

AS A POSTSCRIPT to the saga of Poppe and his escape from Germany, he finally was able to come to the USA where we had hoped to find him a position at Harvard. But Francis Cleaves was teaching Mongolian and not even Serge Elisséeff, director of the Harvard-Yenching Institute, could raise the funds to keep Poppe. Fortunately at that time Henry Jackson was building a Slavic and Oriental Center at the University of Washington and endeavored to offer Poppe a position. Later it proved difficult to raise funds to bring Omeljan Pritsak to Harvard. This is a story in itself, which can reveal how university appointments were made in the past.

The living room of Hans Heinrich Schaeder in Göttingen was a meeting place for many of his students; one was Omeljan Pritsak from Lvov, who had been the last student of a noted Ukrainian Orientalist Krimsky in Kiev, after the USSR annexed his part of Poland in 1939. At the outbreak of hostilities between the Nazis and Soviets he was drafted into the Red Army, but fell into captivity by the *Wehrmacht* in 1941. Shortly thereafter, relying on Krimsky's former contacts with German Orientalists, he engineered his own release from the German army prison and went to Berlin as a student of Richard Hartmann. At the advance of the Red Army in 1945 he left for Göttingen to study under Schaeder, where I met him.

Several years later while Pritsak was a lecturer at Hamburg University I succeeded in securing an invitation for him to teach Ukrainian as a visiting lecturer at Harvard. The real object was to show colleagues that he was the Turkologist we needed to complement our staff of Near Eastern language and area specialists. It was the fall semester when Nixon and Kennedy were running for president, and the dean of the college of Arts and Sciences was MacGeorge Bundy. After impressing colleagues whom Pritsak met, we were able to assemble a group of the faculty to go to Bundy with the hope that he would approve an appointment of Pritsak as Associate Professor of Turkic languages. Roman Jakobson of Linguistics, H.A.R. Gibb, Profs. Whatmough of Comparative Philology, Setchkarov of Slavic Languages, and Cleaves of Far Eastern Languages all supported the proposal and Bundy was sufficiently impressed to say he would approve. It was shortly before Christmas, and Pritsak was lecturing at Seattle when I phoned to announce the good tidings. But Bundy went to Washington after new year's day to serve on the team of the new president, and two months later the president of Harvard, Nathan Pusey, called me to his office to ask what had happened in regard to Pritsak. When I replied that Bundy had approved the proposal to appoint Pritsak, Pusey, with obvious annoyance, replied that Bundy was gone, and had acted without any authorization. Furthermore there were no funds for such a post.

To Pusey's credit, he spoke with Pritsak and explained the situation, saying that in two years Harvard would be able to move ahead with an appointment. Pritsak, however, had burned his bridges at Hamburg and it was imperative that he be found a place in the USA. Jakobson called his former student at the University of Washington and explained the situation, asking if something could be done for Pritsak. The reply was indicative of the time of the 'Cold War.' If Pritsak could make a proposal which had strategic implications, funds might be secured. Pritsak proposed to make a grammar and dictionary of the Yakut language.

An imposing brochure was prepared with an outline of the USSR on the cover, showing in red the borders of Yakutia, an impressively vast area. The main title of the proposal was 'Strategic Languages of the Soviet Union'. Jackson explained at that time only the Ford Foundation and the US government were in a position to fund such a project, and since they were in communication about such matters, a proposal to one would preclude a similar request to the other, so it had to be a one shot affair. But to which organization should one apply? In his wisdom he decided on the government, since the Ford Foundation might ask how many Yakuts there were in the USSR, while the government would hardly go beyond the title. Money was received at the University of Washington, and Pritsak spent two years there before accepting Pusey's invitation to return to Harvard.

It was a gift of the administration to the department of Near Eastern Languages and Civilizations, and accepted with gratitude. His efforts to build on Turkic Studies in the department, however, failed, and he soon devoted his energies at Harvard to establish the Ukrainian Institute, modelled on the similar Armenian effort to establish an academic presence in universities by funding chairs of Armenian Studies.

That effort began in 1950 in a class on the history of the Near East for the night extension school, when Manoog Young, a young Armenian in class, asked why the Armenian language was no longer taught in regular courses after the death of Robert Blake. I replied that an endowment was needed to secure the continued offering of courses on Armenian history, art and language. Blake and I just after the war had tried to interest the Armenian community in supporting such a program, but the politics of the nationalist Dashnaks, Ramgavars, and other quarreling groups, ended our efforts. Young was energetic, and succeeded in persuading some members of the community to help in creating an endowed chair of Armenian Studies at Harvard. Manoog and I together launched the program which not only created the chair, but led to the establishment of the National Association of Armenian Studies and Research, as well as endowed chairs in ten other universities and colleges in the USA. For example, Tufts University now has a chair of Armenian art and architecture and another in Armenian history. It took over fifty meetings and banquets all over the country to convince Armenians that they should get out of their ghetto and show their contributions in cultural matters to world civilization. Many times I was accused of trying to secure an endowed chair for myself, and statements to the contrary were greeted with skepticism. But we persisted.

An Armenian Guidepost

On November 7, 1999, at a banquet in Cambridge for the 45th anniversary of the founding of NAASR, a plaque was presented to me which read as follows: 'In grateful appreciation of a lifetime of dedication to the furtherance of Armenian Studies, and his active participation in NAASR as a Founding Member, Director, and Advisory Board Chairman, and for his continuous efforts to bring greater recognition and understanding of Armenian history, and the contributions of Armenians to world civilization.' Needless to say, this justified the hours spent in bringing the above goals to fruition.

Empire building always attracted some professors, but most of the time the university did not support such efforts. Nonetheless if a professor brought outside funds to the university for various programs, then the administration usually accepted the money with gratitude, although unrestricted money was even more welcomed. Endowments, or 'hard money', were always preferred over 'soft money', since the university consequently would not be obliged to support or rescue any program which faltered in its endowment. As a result the various centers and institutes, which after the war had become attached to universities, especially those which were private, were constantly searching for outside funds, or 'soft money', to continue their activities. The sources of money were usually made public, but sometimes a scandal might arise. For example, when the Center for Middle East Studies, later under the direction of Nadav Safran, received money from the CIA for a conference to which several participants from the area had been invited, a leak to the student newspaper caused a storm of protest, and a subsequent cancellation of the conference. Even the hallowed halls of academia were not spared from juicy revelations of misdeeds. The Middle Eastern field, of course, was especially prone to unusual scrutiny, and Harvard's center was no exception.

The success of the Armenian enterprise persuaded the Ukrainian community in Canada and the US to follow suit, and Pritsak became the leader in the effort which led to the creation of the academic Center of Ukrainian Studies at Harvard. Later the Assyrians were also to take heart from the two programs and embark on a similar, but more modest effort to secure community support for entry into the academic world. Ethnic Studies, as they frequently were called in academia, became established in university programs.

In passing it might be mentioned that the accomplishments of the Armenians induced the Turkish government to match their efforts by establishing chairs of Turkish Studies in a number of American universities. Unlike the others, there were few Turks in the USA, and they had no unity or organizations to promote such efforts. Although many objections were raised regarding outside influences on academic objectivity, in my opinion the fraternity of scholars would insure not only impartiality, even though personal prejudices might exist, but also would help to promote an atmosphere of understanding among various ethnic or national groups.The unification of Europe, beginning with introduction of the common coinage-the Euro, would go hand in hand with the cooperation of various academic programs relating to various countries, ethnic groups and religions. If universities would not lead the way, who would?

With the establishment of a large center for Jewish Studies, attached to the Department of Near Eastern Languages and Civilizations, it was feared by some that pro-Israel sentiments would dominate activities of the department, and a split would occur between the faculty. This did not happen because the solidarity of scholars in support of reason and fairness precluded any empathy for extremism or fanaticism in any form. Cooperation continued, as it had in the past, even after the retirement and deaths of old colleagues. If only others would follow the example of our department.

CHAPTER 19

Sturm und Drang

MANY students came to classes on Iranian religions and the history of Iran; fewer enrolled in Avestan and Old Persian, and usually only one or two elected Pahlavi (Middle Persian) or Sogdian. Avestan was the favorite of students in linguistics, and they were interested in questions of grammar and phonetics above all else. To match a song of the Iranists of Leningrad, which Livshits had given me, I composed a short song for Harvard as follows: "No Persian, Pahlavi or Pushtu for us, we want Avestan, we want Avestan. You don't have to understand it. No Sogdian, Saka, or Shugni for us, we want Avestan, we want Avestan. You take a locative, I make it vocative, I stem U stem our stem, and reduplicate, reduplicate." Once several students, who were not linguists, wanted to study Kurdish, so it was necessary to secure materials, recordings and books for this course. More time, however, was spent on joint courses in Ottoman history, with William Langer and Robert Wolff, as well as comparative religions with Nock. I spoke both on Islam as well as Zoroastrianism for the latter, and classes were large.

Bookbinding classes in the evening provided a diversion from teaching and reading, as well as being needed for my many paper bound books purchased abroad. I had to purchase equipment for this craft in London, since locally little was available. Hand sewing of books was tiresome, but instructive as it proved useful later for sewing of buttons and torn garments. For physical exercise, fencing with the épée kept me in trim, although young team members usually won bouts.

Foreign students and professors came in numbers to the Center for Middle Eastern Studies, which was able to handle them better than the department. Two Iraqis from Baghdad were especially noteworthy. One, a professor of Islamic history, was Salih al-'Ali, a Sunni, who had received his PhD in England, and was studying the early caliphate. At a luncheon, together with an Iraqi student, Taqi Dibbagh, Salih explained how he had found new sources, which revealed how the caliph 'Ali at the time of his death had accumulated enormous properties in the Hijaz. Taqi, who was a devout Shi'ite, said not a word, but walking on the way home, he turned and said,"You see what is wrong with our country. Even learned professors lie about their research." Taqi had been sent by the Antiquities Department, and he complained bitterly that there was no special program on the archaeology of the Near East, and that he would have to go to Arizona or New Mexico in the summer to participate in excavations. "If I return to Baghdad and say that I learned about Navahoes and Hopi Indians at Harvard, everyone will laugh at me." He had to be assured that he would learn the techniques of 'dirt archaeology' or excavations, and the basic principles were the same anywhere. Actually, after his field work he was mollified and even enjoyed it.

A Sunni student made the following remark after hearing the above. A Persian Shi'ite entered a mosque in Baghdad to pray, but glancing at the large plaques on the wall, he saw the names of the first four caliphs. Realizing that he was in the wrong mosque he cleared his throat to spit on the name of 'Umar, who had ordered the conquest of Persia. But his spit landed on the name 'Ali which shocked him. Regaining his composure, he waved his finger at the plaque, scolding, "It serves you right for being in the company of this scum." This, I observed, was an exaggerated remark about the enmity between followers of the two major branches of the Islamic religion, but close relations certainly did not flourish.

Two Iraqi girls, Pakiza Hilmi, daughter of a leading Kurdish intellectual, and Wasma Chorbaji were studying History and Fine Arts respectively, and Wasma remained in Cambridge, finally becoming a specialist in making fine ceramics, as well as studying Arabic inscriptions in China. They, and a girl of the prominent al-Turki family of Saudi Arabia, gave a feeling of vivacity to the Center. Iranian students, on the whole, were studying the sciences, but there were a few in Social Sciences such as Majid Tehranian, who was editor of an Iranian student newspaper for a time. He later became a distinguished head of a Japanese Institute for peace when he was a professor of political science at the university of Hawaii.

Wanderlust was by no means quenched, and in 1960 a large international congress of Orientalists in Moscow brought friends and new acquaintances together. Harold Lamb, author of popular books on Central Asia, attended, and was pleased to learn of the effect his writings had on me when a boy. The Soviets, like the Iranians, were lavish with arrangements for international meetings, and caviar with vodka were both abundant. This was the first meeting with Bobojan Gafurov, former secretary of the Communist party in Tajikistan, and now head of the Oriental section of the Soviet Academy of Sciences. We became friends, for I openly admired his building of the Oriental section, even though Russian colleagues criticized him for bringing many Central Asians and Caucasians into his institute.

The Leningrad section of the Oriental institute was filled with new young scholars of high capabilities. Older Alexander Markovitch Belenitsky, excavator of Panjikant in Tajikistan, with its remarkable wall paintings, was a joy as a conversationalist, because of his wide knowledge and command of Arabic and Persian. In the 1960s there existed an Orientalist counterpart of the famous band of musical composers in St. Petersburg of the late nineteenth century. Yurii Borshchevsky had learned colorful British soldier's English, as well as Persian, during his stay in Iran in World War II, and he was especially helpful to foreigners. Sergei Sokolov, teacher of Iranian languages in the university, was the son of a priest, but he was proficient as a *muezzin* in Arabic and a cantor in Hebrew, as well as having a beautiful singing voice for the Russian Orthodox service. His only problem was the Russian vice of drink, and in the absence of spirits he would drink hair tonic if it had sufficient alcohol. It proved his downfall and he died young. Such wastes of talent occurred frequently in the Soviet Union. Sergei believed religion required pomp, pageantry, incense and chanting, which made Protestantism unworthy of being called a religion in his eyes.

Josef Oranski and Volodya Livshits were other Iranists whom I knew and admired the most, but unfortunately the former also died relatively young. The members of the Orientalist section of the Hermitage museum were especially friendly and exciting. Volodya Lukonin was a close colleague in Iranian art and archaeology, and Boris Ilich Marshak, assistant of Belinitisky at Panjikant, remained a close friend after the deaths of his chief as well as Lukonin. Lunch in Lukonin's office was ever a pleasure, when all gathered to partake of food and fruitful conversations. Every foreigner who came to visit Lukonin was asked to bring a bottle of an unusual liqueur, and he was especially fond of calvados, which he had found in the writings of Hemingway. His long row of empty bottles stood on a shelf above bookcases and desks. Especially attractive was Ada Adamova, specialist on Persian miniatures, but she was not alone, for other young ladies made both the Hermitage and the Institute colorful.

Life was not easy in Leningrad, but there was a remarkable camaraderie among scholars, who had suffered not only during the war but afterwards. Many had been evacuated to Central Asia during the war where they worked and studied in the field. The city of Peter the Great had remained the center of classical and theoretical studies, while Moscow was more practical, and applied sciences flourished there. The 'Camelot' of Oriental Studies, which existed in Leningrad in post war days, followed the fortunes of the USSR in its decline at the end of the eighties. Nostalgia may color one's recollections, but I for one enjoyed my partnership with the scholars of Leningrad.

Back home I insisted on having a native assistant for teaching Persian, so a search for a teacher of the Persian language brought Heshmat Moayyad from Frankfurt, but after a year he was invited to Chicago. Amin Banani from Athens also lasted only a short time before leaving for UCLA. In 1962 I turned to Gafurov for help, but received no reply to my letter. Luckily Peter Avery from King's College of Cambridge U. had a sabbatical and came for a year. Just before Christmas, however, a telegram arrived from Moscow, saying that Rustam Aliev, from Baku, would arrive in a week to teach. Now we had two teachers of Persian and insufficient funds for both. Such an unusual event of a long stay in the USA by a Soviet scholar surprised the Russian specialists at Harvard, and they agreed to help pay part of the extra salary for such a visitor, but we had to find tasks for Rustam. He taught a course on Persian literature and prepared a catalogue of Persian manuscripts in the Houghton Library. He learned a bit of English while here, but his classes were held in Persian.

Rustam was lionized by the Russians in Cambridge, among them the linguist Roman Jakobson. One night after a typical Russian dinner at his house Rustam collapsed in a drunken stupor before I could bring him to his room in Kirkland House. Unable to carry him, he was deposited in my car, locked, but with an open window. On awakening he became frightened and thought the American equivalent of the KGB had found him, and only after many explanations was he calmed. Aliev was envied by the Russians in Leningrad, who considered his trip an affront to them by Gafurov, complaining that he favored Orientals, which of course he did.

The teaching of Persian presented problems because of the limited stays of native speakers, who were much in demand in the US at that time. Not that Persian speakers were rare, but those with experience, who could teach American students, were in short supply. So it was necessary again to turn abroad, and contacts with colleagues in Germany seemed appropriate. Finally Manuchihr Mohandessi from Hamburg was sent by Professor Lentz, and remained, even though he could not speak English. At first students had trouble understanding him since he only knew German and Persian, but emphasis on the spoken language gave Manuchihr an advantage in teaching. I initially took care of grammar and introduction to the language, but later the entire language teaching of Persian fell to the instructor. There were functions other than teaching and research, however, which occupied my time and energy.

As one of the board of scholars of the Byzantine Studies Center at Dumbarton Oaks in Washington DC, many happy occasions were spent in after dinner discussions with colleagues. Mrs. Bliss, whose husband had donated the estate to Harvard, entertained at tea every afternoon, when not only scholars but musicians and literary people, who happened to be in Washington on visits, would be present. Among the scholars a Czech priest, Father Dvornik, was one of those who could be called the 'life of the party', but there were many others. Once, when explaining the system of Middle Persian writing in Aramaic yet pronouncing a word in Persian, using the word *malik* 'king', as an example, a sound on the floor caused all to look in that direction. An art historian, Ernst Kantarowicz, exclaimed 'malik the mouse,' and for several years this sobriquet was my lot at Dumbarton Oaks. After the death of Mrs. Bliss social and musical activities declined, and in time the atmosphere became 'stuffy', as one fellow remarked.

All of these activities meant a neglect of family, and again it was a second most unexpected one night stand, which brought our youngest son Bobby into the world shortly before New Year's day in 1960. Writing, and probably teaching, consequently suffered reduced attention as a result, while more tasks, such as putting new shingles on the roof, entailed learning new skills. It became clear that owning a house was much more demanding than renting.

My office in the Semitic Museum on Divinity Avenue was a lonely place until the theologian Paul Tillich moved into the library on the first floor, but he only remained a year. Unfortunately our conversations were only about the museum and its problems rather than any theological discussions. The new center for international affairs, with Henry Kissinger, not only caused Tillich's departure but also mine, and the museum was completely changed. The books and manuscripts of the library were sent to other libraries, my office was changed into a ladies room and small kitchen, while the objects of the museum were put in the attic and basement, and a large plaster model of the temple at Jerusalem, and another of Baalbek, were given away. From an out-of-the-way building, little visited by any save Sunday school classes and the like, the museum now became a bustling center of would be politicians and diplomats. My desk and books were moved to the Divinity School, and then to a wooden structure built during the World War, cold in winter and hot in summer.

A spate of construction and remodeling at the university began, and the Middle East center was moved to a former hotel, the Ambassador, at 1737 Cambridge Street, where my office also finally landed. The frequent moving, however, was not conducive to research and writing, and again, because of new tasks, family relations suffered.

The cold war was in full swing in 1962, so my invitation to a Russian Orientalist, Lev Ivanovich Miroshnikov, to give a number of lectures on contemporary Iranian history, was viewed by some as inappropriate. Miroshnikov, however, was well received and we became friends, meeting him again in Paris and Moscow. Several friends cautioned that Washington was beginning to consider me a 'fellow-traveller.' Well they might have, for only two months after return from the first trip to the Soviet Union in 1955, a letter came from the State Department asking my comment on a recorded broadcast by Radio Moscow in Albanian. It went as follows " This past summer the Soviet government invited two distinguished Americans, Justice Douglas and Robert Kennedy, to travel in Central Asia and climb mountains. On return they wrote two scurrilous articles for the magazine *Look* in which they claimed that there was racial discrimination in Central Asia, where, for example, Uzbeks had to go to Uzbek schools while Russians attended much better Russian schools. Fortunately at the same time another American was in Central Asia, a professor from Harvard University, Richard Frye. In an interview on Radio Tashkent we asked him if he had observed racial discrimination in schools in Central Asia. He replied that he had visited Russian language schools in which Uzbeks who knew Russian were enrolled. In the Uzbek language schools, however, there were no Russians as far as he could see, since they did not know the language. Textbooks were much the same in both languages, in the Uzbek schools usually translated from Russian. Dear listener, whom do you believe?" At the bottom of the page, written in ink was the State Department query "Whom do you believe?" I did not answer that letter.

Sir Hamilton Gibb, director of the Middle East Center, had brought money to the university, but his choice of associates was not always fortunate. He fired the Arabic teacher Charles Ferguson, and instead George Makdisi from Michigan was brought to teach beginning Arabic in the old style of reading classical texts. Advice to Gibb that Makdisi, a fine scholar in the French tradition, would never teach beginning Arabic since it was beneath him, fell on deaf ears. Makdisi, however, did teach first year Arabic for one year and then refused to continue, instead offering seminars on texts he was editing. Bill Polk was recommended to Harvard by the Rockefeller Foundation and seemed to be groomed as Gibb's successor, until it was clear that the History Department would not offer him tenure, so he left for Chicago. The same was true for George Kirk, who went to the University of Massachusetts in Amherst.

Gibb had an unwarranted fear that his scholarship was not respected or valued, a kind of inferiority complex. It was said that he left Oxford because he was never accepted there, being a graduate of Edinburgh and not Oxford. Once after a meeting of the religion club at Harvard, in which he gave a critique of Montgomery Watt's two books on Muhammad, he defensively said to me, "I suppose you don't believe anything I have said." I assured him, on the contrary, that his arguments were compelling, but he did not appear convinced, however we remained friends.

Early in 1963 a letter arrived from Nathan Pusey, president of Harvard asking me to reply to an enclosed letter to him from a lawyer in New York called Mr. Cherry. The latter was brief, asking if Harvard were interested in a project to translate the poetry of Ghalib and Mir into English verse in the style of Fitzgerald's translation of the Rubaiyat of Omar Khayyam. This was the desire of his client, a Pathan called Ozai Durrani, who had invented minute rice while living in Colorado. Cherry had first called Columbia in New York, but the reply had been that Ghalib was a second rate poet, which ended that contact. I had heard of Ghalib, a poet in Persian, who lived in Delhi in the nineteenth century. Mir was an unknown poet to me, but research in the library revealed that Mir Taqi Mir was a master of Urdu poetry, who lived in Lahore in the eighteenth century. I composed a florid styled letter, in which I assured Mr. Cherry that Harvard naturally was delighted to undertake a program to translate the works of such eminent poets as Ghalib and Mir, but it would not be a short or easy task. A committee on Indo-Pakistani Studies would have to be formed, and a professorship of a specialist in Persian and Urdu poetry created. Translations from everywhere would be solicited, and the committee would pass on them, then edit chosen translations for publication.

Negotiations and luncheons lasted more than a year, but in the meantime Durrani had died, and Cherry finally at the end of 1964 agreed to give funds to establish a professorship as suggested. To conclude this story, at first Ralph Russell, an Urdu specialist at the University of London was proposed. When Cherry discovered that Russell was a member of the Communist party of Britain, he strenuously objected, so Russell's name was withdrawn. Next Alessandro Bausani of Rome was suggested, which again aroused Cherry's ire, "how is an Italian able to translate Oriental poetry into English?" he demanded. On being told that Bausani knew English well, but would only pass on translations of others, Cherry was somewhat mollified, but still suspicious of our motives. In any case Bausani declined the invitation. Cherry became more annoyed when Annemarie Schimmel, an old friend of mine, was the third proposal. "First an Italian and now a German, what are you doing?" was his angry response. He agreed, however, to talk to her in New York, and when they had luncheon my hopes were confirmed; she charmed him and was appointed professor at Harvard. Her account of how she came to Harvard in her autobiography, *Morgenland* und *Abendland*, is different and somewhat embellished, but after all she was a poet.

Annemarie was a remarkable scholar who lectured with her eyes closed, for her memory took the place of notes. At the same time she was quite feminine, although marriage was out of the question since she was wedded to her writing, together with the acquisition of honors and adulation from important persons. In the spirit of an European much like Ernst Herzfeld, she was not happy in Harvard and arranged that she would only teach one semester every year while the second would be spent in travel and writing. In that one semester, however, her classes on Sufism and poetry were attended by many students. Poetry was her passion and after she took my course in the Pushtu language, she composed poems in that language. To say that she was a workaholic would be an understatement, and her production of books was matched only by that of a former student Jacob Neusner in the field of Jewish Studies. Undoubtedly Annemarie was the jewel in the crown of Islamic Studies at the university, and she was much sought after by museums, other universities and Islamic centers, for her talks always roused interest in large audiences. Rumors that we might be married were unfounded, however, since she would never change the life she was leading.

In February 1964 I suggested to Mr. Battle, head of Cultural Affairs in the State Department, that an American Institute, similar to the British and French establishments, be established in Tehran. It could be called the 'Jordan House' after the late beloved former head of Alburz college. This proposal was politely greeted but not implemented, until later a number of American academicians created a private American Institute of Iranian Studies, which flourished until the revolution. Accommodations for visiting scholars and the library were prominent features of the Institute, but after closure in 1979 the library was taken to a religious library in Qum.

I had always considered the acme of objectionable bureaucracy to be that of Egypt, since the experience of trying to send books from the country during the war hardly could be matched elsewhere. India in 1964, with its mixture of Moghul, British and native bureaucratic complexity, however, proved a worthy competitor. In January an international congress of Orientalists was held in Delhi, and I resolved to spend the Christmas vacation and reading period afterwards to visit Beirut, Baghdad, Tehran, Kabul and India, including Parsi friends in Bombay.

The congress was not only tiring, but full of heated controversies, and when I brought an inebriated Indologist, Professor Paul Thieme, back late to his room at the Janpath hotel, his wife upbraided me for his condition. He replied to her, "don't blame him, I was chairman of the Vedic section this afternoon", and that explained everything.

On departing from Delhi by air, one had to pay an exit tax, but this required visiting several offices in the city, one for forms and another for payment. Then one had to change money, and explain expenses, purchases, all with receipts, at another office. The forms and stamps took all morning. Finally at the airport a lengthy passport control was followed by a similar ticket control at another site. Afterwards came a customs control, and at another counter a security check of all baggage. Seat assignments and another check of tickets brought this ordeal to an end, for it had lasted more than the customary two hours before departure. Was this the result of an Indian bureaucracy imposed on an older English one, which in turn had inherited a Moghul system? One could only hope that in time more efficiency would prevail.

In December 1964 an invitation to lecture at Chatanooga College gave a first opportunity to visit the South since birth. At the college the reception was cool for a Yankee, and only the following day at the talk did everything change, after I gave my CV to the chairman of the history department for introduction. With a booming voice he said, "he was boan in Birmingham, Alabama," and that made me one of them. This change in attitude was indicative of the tensions of the time.

Also at this time Barbara and I became even more estranged, for she began searching for different spiritual avenues, and joined a group called Mind Dynamics, a kind of elaborate yoga movement. Middle age ennui had set in for both of us and it boded ill for the future. It was with relief that a Fulbright grant arrived to go to the Soviet Union in the fall of 1967, but this time it had to be alone.

CHAPTER 20

A Cultural Stay in the USSR

THE REASON for a stay in Leningrad was simple; it was the world center of Iranian Studies, with more people engaged in those studies than in the rest of the world put together. For example, there were ten specialists on Kurdish alone in the Kurdish cabinet of the Institute of the Peoples of Asia and Africa of the Academy of Sciences, the new name of the Oriental Institute. Other specialists were in the Institute of Linguistics, not to mention many in Moscow, Erivan and elsewhere in the USSR. In the western world at that time Kurdish was taught only in Paris and London by part-time instructors. Furthermore, friends were in the city, close friends like nowhere else, for so strong was their desire to meet visiting foreign scholars in the old USSR.

On the twelfth of October 1965 I flew to Paris for several days and then to Copenhagen where a talk on 'Israel and Iran in Antiquity' was presented at the university, with only a few persons in the audience, but dinner with an old friend Jes Asmussen equalled Soviet banquets in spirits, but far superior in the food. At the airport twelve bottles of scotch and bourbon, and calvados for Lukonin, were purchased, as well as several cartons of cigarettes. Also several boxes of books had been mailed to Leningrad to distribute as gifts.

On the Aeroflot plane to Moscow, unlike previous flights, the plane was full of Russians, and Rustam Aliev was waiting at the airport late at night. No questions were asked by customs, who smiled at the number of bottles, but who spirited me through

A Cultural Stay in the USSR 197

passport formalities, quite a difference from my first visit. Then the airport had seemed far from town with large expanses of open fields, but now buildings had been erected filling the once empty spaces. Tall building cranes were everywhere building identical apartment blocks on the way from Sheremetyevo airport to the city.

After checking in at the Leningrad Hotel we went to Rustam's apartment where his wife, who was a Persian commentator on Radio Moscow, and his two boys were waiting with the usual vodka, cognac and food. The next day at the Academy of Sciences, Korneev, head of the foreign section, spoke about the bombing of north Vietnam, surprisingly not at all belligerent or hostile, but, as his assistant remarked, the situation in Viet Nam was like a classical Greek tragedy, and just as complicated. With that one could only agree.

On a brief stay in Paris a notice at the Sorbonne had informed readers that Vasilii Abaev, the distinguished Ossete linguist from Moscow was coming to Paris, but he was still in Moscow so I went to his new apartment of three rooms and kitchen, and had dinner with him. He had prepared the French texts of several lectures, but was bitter that he had not been allowed to go. On my question why, he said it was nothing political, but only the terrible bureaucracy in the Soviet Union, where a minor official had refused to take responsibility to allow him to leave. Many times complaints about the bureaucracy and corruption were forthcoming, and these above all else appeared to be the bane of all intellectuals. From the wall Abaev took down the drinking horn, which he said was reserved for me, and this time he filled it with cognac rather than vodka, the former having replaced the latter as the fashionable drink of the USSR.

At the house of Shikali, an Azerbaijani writer and friend of Rustam, a Jewish engineer assured us that secular Jews endured no discrimination in the USSR, but all religion was frowned upon by the authorities. Again and again, as previously, the great losses of the Soviet Union in the war were emphasized, and the Russians feared Viet Nam might lead to another world war. Once previously in Leningrad I suggested that the Russians should do more toward influencing the Chinese, but the reply was, "this is our greatest problem. We can't do anything about the Chinese." Chinese students, who had been studying in Leningrad in the past ten or fifteen years, had maintained an isolation from their Russian colleagues. When invited to parties they had not come, and they had never invited Russians to Chinese gatherings. In other words, the Chinese had treated the Russians much like the latter formerly had behaved with foreigners. After two days in Moscow I left by train for Leningrad.

It was touching to arrive at the railroad station in Leningrad at 7:30 AM to find a delegation of four friends waiting as a reception committee. We had breakfast, with cognac toasts, and then to a room in the October hotel opposite the station, which was to be home for several months.

It was a pleasure to go with a pass to the Hermitage museum, where a desk in the Oriental section *(Otdela Vostoka)* was assigned to me. Photos of coins, seals, inscriptions on silver objects, and manuscripts were obtained with friendly cooperation from all. Also in the Iranian section of the Institute of the Peoples of Asia and Africa, Petrossian, the director provided a desk where I could study and write. If someone in the USSR was working on a manuscript, or was interested in doing so, no microfilm would be given to a foreigner, but otherwise it would be allowed. This time it was a pleasure to work in Leningrad. Colleagues gave me manuscripts of articles to read and criticize, while no one hesitated to ask me to revise the English of articles or resumés. I gave two talks in the Hermitage, on 'Forgeries in Persian Art,' and 'Persepolis, national shrine of the Persians,' but my pronunciation of Russian brought a note from the distinguished cuneiform specialist, Igor Mikhailovitch Dyakonov, "Wer kann wissen wie die Enten pissen." Accent is very important in Russian and a misplaced accent can cause trouble as it did for me, in placing the wrong emphasis on the verb 'to write' is *pisat'*, where the accent is on the -a, whereas *pisat'* with accent on the -i- means 'to piss.'

On familiar terms Russians are addressed by their patronymic, as Boris Ilich for Marshak, but a nickname for close friends, such as Volodya for Vladimir Lukonin, was also proper. A talk in the Institute on the same subject as Copenhagen fortunately produced no bloopers, while another at the university was given in English, at the request of the professors. It was apparent that English would attract fewer students and the reason became clear, for the talk was on 'The Rise of New Persian Language and Literature,' and there were only a few Tajiks in the audience who understood English. In the Stalin era the Tajiks had claimed that Tajiki was a different language from Persian, and always had been the native language in their land. My thesis was that Tajiki was nothing but a dialect of Persian, which had been brought to Central Asia from Persia at the time of the Arab conquest. This provoked much discussion and controversy, which was always prevalent in talks in the Soviet Union.

Especially entertaining was the defense of his doctoral dissertation (called *kandidat*) by the numismatist Evgenii Zeimal. He had prepared a massive catalogue of Kushan coins in the Hermitage, with a thesis that the ruler Kanishka lived in the 3d or perhaps even 4th century, instead of the usually accepted second. The chairman of the examining committee was Prof. Artamanov, an archaeologist, specialist on south Russia. He held up the two fat volumes of Zeimal and said, "I know nothing about the Kushans, but this is an impressive work. Does anyone know anything about the Kushans? Fray, can you say something?" I replied that it was an enormous labor, and with a thesis which required much discussion, for which we had not enough time. Artamanov was satisfied, ended the examination, and afterwards we had a party, with the present of a book to Evgenii from the examiner, while I gave a much appreciated bottle of bourbon to the successful candidate.

"If you see anyone drunk with a bottle of vodka on the streets of Leningrad, it will be a Finn and not a Russian, for cognac is the Russian's favorite drink,"was a common remark. At the time of the celebration of the October Revolution some 5,000 Finns came to town and bought every bottle of any liquor in town, with a resulting lack of spirits for several weeks. Someone suggested that one reason the Russians did not absorb Finland after the war, as they did the Baltic states, was their admiration for the drinking prowess of the Finns. One story had two Finns sitting at a table drinking vodka for an hour without saying a word. Finally one lifted his glass to the other and said the Finnish equivalent to 'cheers'. The other glowered at him and replied, "I thought we came here to drink, not to talk." Such is the Russian opinion of Finns.

Jokes and stories were well received by my friends, such as the following. Two American businessmen had come to Moscow, and they were most fearful of spies and wire taps, so at dinner they agreed to search their hotel rooms before sleeping, to uncover any bugs or wires. One found two crossed wires in a hole in the middle of the floor, after he lifted the rug. With his penknife he cut the wires and went to sleep, satisfied that he had thwarted anyone listening to him. The next morning at breakfast he excitedly told his friend how he had found the wires to a listening device. His friend was even more upset and frightened, saying,"They tried to kill me last night. I was asleep in bed when the chandelier in the ceiling fell down and just missed me."

The month of November, they said, was the coldest November month on record, for the Neva River froze solidly even before Revolution holiday, and a policeman recommended to rub snow on one's nose to prevent frostbite. The hotel room was so cold that something had to provide heat, or water in the glasses on a table would freeze. The old lady in charge of the rooms (*dezhurnaya*) advised everyone to run the hot water in the bathtub all night long. One can imagine the waste and cost. Everyone slept with overcoats on them and several pairs of socks. Russians have been characterized by many as half or more Oriental. Scratch a Russian and underneath you find a Tatar, is an old saying. Tajiks add, "keep scratching and under all is an Iranian."

Russians are too happy-go-lucky, and anti-rules, to suit Westerners. For example, before leaving Leningrad I took some phonograph records and a fur hat to the post office to mail back to the USA. After filling out the customs forms, and placing everything in the wooden box provided for mail, the girl at the window declared it was impossible to send fur by mail because it was forbidden to export fur from the Soviet Union. On explaining that it was foolish to carry the fur hat to warm Central Asia and leaving the USSR via Kabul, she phoned the head of the foreign section of the post office and explained the problem. His reply was to scratch out the word 'fur' on the declaration, and send it.

I had brought a copy of Solzhenitsn's book on the Gulag in Russian, but was afraid to present it to anyone, so I simply left it on a window in the Hermitage. The next day I was told that the book was well-known by all through private printing (*samizdat*) in the USSR, and I should not have been so stealthy. Many foreigners, as well as Russians, had exaggerated fears of breaking a law and being arrested, but the Stalinist past was dying and every year saw relaxation in controls as well as the atmosphere of fear.

As a foreigner, it was possible to buy tickets to plays which were popular, and very difficult to attend for locals. There were several Intourist offices for foreigners in Leningrad, and, on behalf of friends, tickets for the same play were purchased on different evenings. The Intourist people became suspicious and annoyed, asking why I wanted so many tickets to the same play. My reply that I only wanted to practice Russian, brought the response, "Aha, we know; you are getting them for your friends," so afterwards it became more difficult to buy them. One of the popular artists was a man, like Jean-Louis Barrault in Paris, called Arkadi Raikin, whose satires on bureaucracy and life in the Soviet Union made him much sought after. Much of his quick repartee, however, was over my head, but my friends enjoyed him greatly.

On past visits I had never succeeded in inviting my friends to the hotel for dinner or visits, but there was no problem on this occasion, and they even came when I was not in the mood to see them. They were able to secure a room for me in the deluxe Intourist hotel Europa, for the October hotel was a local cold and run down unattractive place. Even in the Europa it was still so cold I decided to leave the city for warmer climes, and the last evening in Leningrad was the occasion of a feast held in my honor at the hotel by Petrossian. It began at six, but by ten we were under the influence, and while dancing with a friend from the Institute, Mme. Vorobeva-Desyatovskaya, another couple collided with us, such that a scuffle ensued. The police, or militia as they were called, came and, after scolding for hooliganism, escorted me to the railroad station where the train for Moscow left at midnight. Everyone seemed to consider the episode as normal and of no consequence. Indeed brawls were not unusual, but being charged with hooliganism, however, was bad for one's reputation.

In Moscow Bobojan Gafurov, the head of the Institute of the Peoples of Asia and Africa for the entire USSR, asked me to convey a message to the cultural officer of the Shah in Tehran, suggesting that an international congress of Iranists be convened, proposing Moscow as the site. After discussion, however, it was agreed that the first meeting should take place in Tehran. On another matter I told him of a problem; in the USA some people think I am a spy of the Soviet Union while in the USSR I am considered an American spy. He answered, "Fray, don't worry; we all know that if you are a spy you must be a spy of Iran, Afghanistan and Tajikistan." Fortunately he allowed me to publish lectures in his journal *Azii I Afriki*, and, over objections of many to publishing any book by a foreigner, he agreed with Nauka Press that the *Heritage of Persia* should be translated into Russian and printed. Oleg Konstantinovich (OK) Dreier, head of the publishing office, later refused to pay any royalties, saying I had no use for them, until friends intervened. With the meager funds received I had to open an account in rubles at the Post Office since they could not be converted into hard currency.

Abaev and his young wife kindly made recordings on tape in Ossetic for the use of students, and later in Dushanbe recordings of Tajiki were made.

An interview with the editorial staff of the journal *Literaturnaya Gazeta* was published in the December 23 issue of 1965, and time was spent also in correcting English language articles for various people in Moscow. The round of dinners and invitations in Moscow continued, with a relaxed atmosphere, so unlike previous times. Not only Orientalists, but people from various walks came to dinners. For example, one evening near the university, at the cooperative apartment which a Daghestani colleague, Nuri Osmanov, had purchased himself, his neighbor, the head coach of the Soviet Olympic team for acrobatics, brought dessert and described how the athletes trained intensively, even though they were not paid for their efforts.

One afternoon at lunch with Gunnar Jarring, the Swedish ambassador to the USSR, he told how the Soviet ambassador in Stockholm tried to telephone Michael Shokolov, author of *And*

Quiet Flows the Don, at his home in the Don region, to tell him he had received the Nobel prize for literature. For two days he was told he could not speak to Shokolov. Meanwhile reporters in the world were speculating about political implications of the prize, whether the Kremlin would allow him to accept the prize. On the evening of the third day the Soviet ambassador was able to speak to the writer and inform him of the prize. The reason he had not been able to speak to Shokolov for over two days was that the writer was dead drunk during the entire period.

It was clear that the main stumbling block with scholarly exchanges between the Academy of Sciences and American universities was money, and the little amount available was allocated to the Natural Sciences rather than to the Humanities or Social Sciences. When I told Korneev that I wanted to go to Baku, Tashkent, Samarkand and Dushanbe before leaving for Afghanistan, he was angry, "This was not in your original proposal. You only wanted to go to Leningrad." On my response that in Leningrad I heard about certain materials which were necessary to see elsewhere, he declared that Baku was difficult since a new university was being built, and colleagues would not be available to help. Then I mentioned that my airplane ticket, purchased in the USA, was from Moscow to Tashkent to Kabul. An internal ticket would not be required. At this news he smiled, "Oh, in that case there is no difficulty in changing your ticket to Baku, Tashkent and Dushanbe."

In Leningrad my close friend, Volodya Livshits was going to Samarkand, and asked if I could request Korneev if he could accompany me to Baku, which he had never visited, and then on to Tashkent. Korneev's reply was, "You speak Russian and don't need anyone to accompany you, and don't expect us to pay for Livshits' ticket. Let him buy his own ticket if he wants to go." This did not work, but fortunately Gafurov had both funds and authority to send Rustam along as a guide and companion, which meant a great deal to me in Baku.

The hospitality and friendliness of Leningrad and Moscow paled in comparison with that in Baku, in some degree because of speaking Turkish. On one occasion a conflict in invitations caused overindulgence at two dinners. On another day, scheduled to talk on television regarding Turkish Studies in the USA at 4 PM in Baku, found us at Sumgait, the oil town on the Caspian, an hour's drive from Baku at lunch with the mayor. Lunch did not mean a snack, but a banquet, beginning at noon, and by 3:30 Rustam and I had to break away and dash for the TV station an hour late, which did not seem to faze anyone. Apparently the many toasts of cognac loosened one's tongue, for Rustam assured me that the Baku talk was much better than the same one had been in Moscow, especially when I ended with *yashasin Azerbaijan* 'long live A.'

The final day in Baku deserves to be recorded. A plane was scheduled to leave for Dushanbe at 11:00 AM, and about ten friends came to the hotel, bringing a garland of flowers, expecting to continue to the airport. A call to the airport, however, revealed that the plane was delayed, so we had a banquet lunch which lasted until 6 PM. It seems no one knew where the plane was, and the airport said the pilot was not giving them any information. Finally the airport revealed that the pilot had neglected his schedule and flown to Mineralnaya Voda in the north Caucasus to pick up some VIP Azerbaijani officials. Memory of the old Shiraz airport returned. I checked in again at the hotel at 8 PM, assured by all I should go to sleep, having been told that Soviet planes do not fly late at night. At midnight Rustam woke me to say that he was sure the plane would arrive the following morning. At 2 AM Rustam returned saying, "hurry get dressed, the plane is here and will leave in half an hour." At the airport no one was found to take tickets or handle baggage. We saw the plane and went to it where the stewardess took the ticket and put the baggage on the plane. It was full, however, so someone had to be ejected since I had a reservation. Rustam remarked, "You see what a problem we have here, rugged individualism, and disregard of rules."

Dushanbe was like returning home, and everywhere people were surprised that a Russian could speak Tajiki. "No I am not a Russian," but then you must be a German. On being told American, several asked if Tajiki was widely spoken in the USA. At the Dushanbe hotel a suite of rooms was assigned, but shortly a knock on the door revealed an American correspondent and his wife with several guides. He had been assigned to Moscow, and was just making a trip to Central Asia. The hotel manager gave him the suite, and brought me to a small room, whereupon my Tajik guide protested. I soothed him, however, and told him, unlike the USSR, in America journalists were more important than professors, which surprised him.

Dushanbe then had a 'wild west' aspect, with many Russian engineers, miners and construction people, with little contact between them and the locals. A number of North Koreans had been settled in Tajikistan to aid with the rice culture, and I attended an elaborate Korean wedding of a Russian boy with a Korean girl. It was colorful, especially the girl's clothes, with a mixture of Russian and Korean customs. Invited to see a Tajik film on the life of the eleventh century poet Rudaki, at the cinema I found Sa'id Nafisi who was visiting from Tehran, and we had a joyful reunion. Rudaki was a blind poet, like Homer, and the story of his life was sad, such that both Nafisi and I were crying at the end of the film.

Invited to go to a kholkhoz (collective farm) and see the countryside, I declined, and instead worked on manuscripts and museum collections. Tajik writers were especially prominent in the society, especially Jalol Ikromi, a novelist who later was to visit Shiraz. Talking to many I felt I was back in Iran.

Samarkand was skipped, since there were many manuscripts in Tashkent collections which required attention. Tashkent had suffered an earthquake since 1955 and much planning and building was under way, but the city was still on the whole like ten years previously, but soon to change. In the same old hotel, across from the opera house, the old ladies of the hotel recognized me, but I had to share my room, first with a Russian professor of agriculture and then with an Uzbek engineer. Both in Dushanbe and Tashkent talks were given and friends visited, but fortunately with less of the many toasts and liquor of the Russian cities or Baku.

When leaving Tashkent no official asked about baggage, or taking rubles out of the country, only surprise at the *barbud*, a five string guitar-like instrument purchased in Dushanbe. There was no other passenger on the Ariana Afghan propeller plane from Tashkent to Kabul, and it seemed we almost scraped the Hindu Kush mountains before descending to Kabul. Fikri Seljuki from Herat was now in the capital, and building activity and cultural affairs were much more developed than during the war. After a few cold days in Kabul at the end of January, the trip to Tehran was set. But on the day we took off in a small plane, a snow cloud over Ghazni persuaded the pilot to return to Kabul, and again the plane flew uncomfortably close to the mountain walls in turning. It seemed more prudent to abandon the Afghan planes for a more modern airplane of Iran Air, but that too turned out to have difficulties.

Our first stop was to be at Zahedan, but a dust storm there obscured the field and the plane continued to Kerman. There was no radio response from the field and it was getting dark with low fuel in the tank, so we had to land at Kerman blind. On landing, however, the pilot saw several large holes on the runway and zoomed back into the air. A second try, avoiding the holes, succeeded. But something had to be done about the cold and fuel, which was not available at the airport. Finally three cars came from the city and the passengers, crew and the starter for the plane, were brought to a warm hotel in town. The pilot explained that the starter had to be kept warm or it would not function in the morning. Airplane fuel was secured from a depot in town, and we awaited the morning. The night was cold, but it was with an audible sigh of relief from all the passengers when the engines did start in the morning and we arrived in Tehran in the afternoon. This had been a trip to remember, but it was a pleasure to be back in Iran. Here too changes in the panorama of the city were found because of much building. I wondered how long the old customs would continue and old buildings last before the modern world took over.

CHAPTER 21

Prelude to Change

OLD STUDENTS finished their studies and left. Sha'aban eventually secured a post in England; the Iraqis left, and with the death of Professor Mark Dresden at Pennsylvania, his student Koji Kamioka came to Harvard for a few years. One day a young Iranian came to my office in the library and said he wanted to study Persian. It was our practice, initiated by Gibb, to require students to study Arabic before another language, so the question was put to him. "No I don't want to study Arabic, only Persian, and even though I speak Persian I cannot properly read or write it, since I was educated in Switzerland," was the reply. Using the argument of Arberry, years ago in London, I tried to persuade him that Arabic was necessary for anyone interested in the area. "I am going to be a diplomat, and it is unnecessary," came the retort. "But Iran has posts in many Arab countries, and it would be useful for you." "No", he exclaimed, "I am only going to be a diplomat in Paris, London or Washington," This was annoying, and I asked his name. "Shahram Pahlavi," he said. "That's the name of the Shah," I objected. "Yes, he is my uncle," which deflated me. He actually secured a private tutor and studied his native language on his own.

On another occasion another student, Sheikhalislami Isfahani, came and said he wished to obtain a doctorate, even though he already had one. "When did you get your doctorate and where?" was my question. "Recently at the University of Meshhed, but it is not called a doctorate in Persian, rather the degree of *mujtahid*." This seemed an affront to one's intelligence, so I replied,

"Even though it is well-known that the university offers no such degree, to assume the rank of *mujtahid* at your young age is an insult to venerable scholars holding the title of *mujtahid* in Iran." He left in a huff, and it was reported that later he had formed a 'world university' in Washington D.C. Although more at home in Iran than other countries, at every opportunity a trip to anywhere in the east was tempting. Activities with NAASR, even after the founding of the chair in Armenian Studies, persuaded me to go to Erivan in September 1966 to discuss the holding of an International Congress of Armenian Studies there in 1967 or 1968. Armenia was a new experience, for it revealed an ancient Christian Near Eastern society and culture which was not Islamic, but still existed in many forms, secular as well as religious. A visit to the Matenaderan, a treasure house of manuscripts, the museums, and especially talking to the Catholicos in Etchmiadzin, stimulated thoughts about the past of this area. The architecture was distinctive, mostly of stone with some brick, unlike the Islamic structures elsewhere in the east. On the other hand, Armenia was part of the Soviet Union, and frequently over the native features was the drab, uniform culture of socialism. In order to enable Armenian scholars to come to the West on visits, the Academy of Sciences was the only organ capable of responding, and reception there was encouraging.

Trips to monasteries on Lake Sevan, and archaeological sites such as Garni, reinforced the impression of Armenia's surprising survival in the Islamic ocean. One did not need to be lured for a return voyage to Armenia, and a desire to see neighboring Georgia was the result of this trip. A report was given to audiences of NAASR on return, which induced others to go to the land of their ancestors. Another surprise was a subsequent visit to Bombay.

A young Parsi, Peshotan Anklesaria, who had received his PhD from London, and then had been a visitor to the Center of World Religions, sent an invitation to come to India. A journey to Bombay to talk to the Parsi community also revealed a new non-Islamic world. He had become the head of the Athornan, or school for priests outside of Bombay, but was worried about the decline in number of students. Peshotan joked about his dark color, unlike most light-skinned Parsis, living proof that the Parsi community was not pure but mixed with native Indian stock. He said Parsis, because of their inbreeding, either produced geniuses or morons. Nonetheless, all were proud of their descent from Zoroastrians who had fled from Iran after the Arab conquest. Later, Zoroastrian connections were to become very important for me, for I participated in many meetings in the USA and in India. My advice to the minorities of Zoroastrians, Armenians, Assyrians, or even Persians in diaspora, was always the same. Have your sons marry girls of the same community while daughters can marry whomsoever they pleased. The reason was that boys usually were uninterested in preserving their heritage, while girls on the contrary preserved it while living abroad. In this respect if males were interested in a heritage they followed their wives.

In June 1965, with the help of my student, John Moyne, who had worked for IBM, a conference was arranged at the Villa Serbelloni on Lago di Como in Italy to discuss the use of computers for Iranian Studies. Two years before the conference an Episcopalian minister, John Ellison, had presented a concordance to the Greek New Testament as a dissertation for the PhD in religion. The committee, on which I was a member, was in a quandary, whether we should award him a degree for such an enormous task, for which he had used a new method of punch cards on something he called a computer. Finally it was decided that he should receive the degree for the new methodology rather than for the end result which was no thesis. The conference in Italy was of value to several people, including Ronald Emmerick of Cambridge University, who produced a concordance of Khotanese Saka texts later in Hamburg, and became an expert in the use of the computer. Most of the scholars attending, however, echoed the sentiments of Henning, who did not attend, since he considered computers useless. In his opinion scholars only needed more time, and release from tasks such as teaching, to do their work. At that time no one foresaw the new world which would emerge as a result of developing technology.

At home our eldest son Jeffrey was becoming interested in his father's field of study, so in the summer of his fourteenth birthday he went on an archaeological expedition to Baba Jan Tepe in Iran, run by an English lady, Clare Goff. It was difficult for him to endure the jibes of older Brits, but he wished to return to the area the following summer and continue his interest in that part of the world.

Because of a trip to Austin, Texas that I made to review the nascent Middle East program at the university, Robert Fernea, an anthropologist, and Paul English, a geographer, asked me to organize an expedition to Herat in the summer of 1967. I hoped to return on the path Ghirshman and I had followed, and this time, after the rainy season, to reach the minaret of Jam. To the crew was added an archaeologist, Robert M. Adams, head of the Oriental Institute of the University of Chicago and later of the Smithsonian. My plan was to buy a VW bus in Heidelberg, and Jeff and I would drive through Germany, Austria, Hungary, Yugoslavia and Turkey, to reach Herat by the 25th of June.

All went according to plan until we left Samsun on the Black Sea, where to the east, at the village of Terme, an old man walking at the side of the road unexpectedly stepped in front of the car and was hit. He was taken to a local hospital but after a short time died. A police investigation was undertaken, and we were remitted into the custody of the US Air Force radar base at Samsun. From June 17 to 23d we remained at the base, exploring the ancient remains on the site. Thousands of potsherds covered the area, and a Byzantine mosaic floor had been unearthed by peasants. It was the ancient town of Amisus, founded by Greeks from Miletus, but traces of an older city, destroyed by the Phrygians, could be seen underneath the top debris. Otherwise we had to wait for a court decision.

Finally the police court decreed that a payment of $950 should be made to the family of the dead man, after which we were allowed to proceed. It had been a harrowing experience, especially for Jeff, and the accident was reported in newspapers at home, after the US embassy in Ankara contacted Barbara. The rest of the trip was uneventful but slower than planned, because of the accident. On reaching Herat on July fifth, we found English happily studying the bazaar, while Fernea was at a nearby village. Adams had returned to Chicago in disgust at the lack of cooperation of Afghan authorities in allowing him to survey the Herat region for archaeological sites. Unfortunately, by being late I had not been present to act as intermediary with the Afghans. A Peace Corps volunteer, Blair Brainard, was in Herat and he wished to join our trip to find the minaret of Jam, using his land rover, since our minibus could not negotiate the mountains. Faiz al-Haqq Nawa, a local guide, agreed to accompany us and we gathered supplies and departed over the same route as previously.

The usual car problems, punctures, leaking radiator, etc., plagued us on the trip into the mountains. It was July and water was especially a problem. The local word for 'crazy' is *bi-ab* 'waterless,' an indication of the importance of water in this parched land. In the village of Zamanabad we again met speakers of Mongolian, and this time I was able to record more of their words, such as *morin* for horse. In Obeh we learned that many Kazakhs from the USSR had settled in the region, but there were Baluch and Pushtuns as well, proving Herat a fascinating field for anthropologists and linguists. About 38 km from Obeh we stopped at the caves noticed on the former trip, which were now accessible from the river below. A number of them had yellow plaster on the walls, indicating permanent residence rather than places of refuge for nomads. They were man made rather than natural, and some had a series of connecting rooms. The caves were high above the river, but traces of steps had been carved to access them, most steps having fallen into the river. A passing caravan leader informed us that a fine spring of water existed above the caves, an ideal condition for Buddhist monks to establish a settlement. The red earth reminded me of Bamiyan, and it seemed a good place for excavations.

The car developed symptoms of a breakdown at one *ribat,* or six km. from Chisht, and could haltingly only carry one person. Jeff, was elected to drive, while the rest of us walked in the blazing sun. At Chisht the carburetor was cleaned and repairs made, but the engine still made strange sounds. The former official was gone and now Chisht had a police chief; also a government rest house had been built, which was our home for several days. Chisht was a small oasis in a desert with many apple trees, mulberry bushes, grapes and walnuts, but especially apricots, here called *zardalu* but *mishmish* in Iran.

All attempts to hire horses failed, for the only nags available were lame or blind. Nonetheless, we started with the car up the river to the old bridge over the river, but beyond was a nightmare. The road was even worse than years ago, and there was no way to get across the wide and deep gullies, so we had to admit defeat and return to Chisht. It was a disappointing repeat experience, but at least the caves had proven interesting. On the other hand, there was much to see in the city of Herat to keep us occupied.

One Herati told us that the original Friday mosque had been built of wood by the Arabs on the site of a Buddhist monastery, but the present structure of stones and bricks was erected by Ghiyath al-Din Ghuri, a twelfth century ruler of the region. We were surprised to find most of the bazaar population of Herat were Shi'ites, although outside the Turkmen, Baluch, Pushtuns and Mughals, as the Mongolian speakers locally were called, were all Sunnis. At the shrine of Gazergah, near the city, were many old beautifully carved marble and alabaster tombstones, and on trees and bushes many pieces of cloth tied to trees by women to obtain children. The villages around Herat had high mud walls, designed for protection against marauders or animals. In Iran, for the most part, such old walls had been destroyed.

About 36 km. to the west of the city, on the river, was the village of Zindajan where several shrines existed. The tilework on the shrines, as well as extensive mounds covered with potsherds, testified that this village once had been a town of some importance. Local people said it was ancient Fushanj, which seemed to me correct, and moreover they spoke of several Buddha figurines which had been found in the area. Buddhism should have left some traces, so this was not a surprise, even though the common opinion at that time was that Buddhism had not penetrated so far west.

The continuing trip of Jeff and me to Kabul was uneventful except for an overnight stay at Lashgargah or ancient Bost on the Helmand River, where an American company was building a dam, and where a bout of bacillary dysentery hit me. In Kabul we were able to sell the minibus to an official in the American Embassy, but it had to be registered in Pakistan, so a trip to Peshawar was necessary. Jeff and I spent a week in Kabul arranging visas for the USSR and Iran, and we flew to Tashkent and then to Samarkand, and to the excavations at Panjikant. Belinitsky and Marshak greeted us warmly and Jeff was impressed by the excavations. Afterwards we flew from Tashkent to Baku, and by boat across the Caspian Sea to Bandar Pahlavi. We did not remain in the fascinating jungle of northern Iran but went by bus to Tehran. It had been an interesting summer experience for Jeff, and he had learned much, but we were tired and returned to the USA by air.

Jeff was moved by a desire to learn more about the Orient, especially India, which appeared to be more exotic to him than the Near East, but he had to finish his studies. Family affairs remained cool, for Barbara and I spoke less and less with each other, but it appeared that other couples found themselves in similar situations. Instead of going to a counsellor or psychologist, however, she turned to spiritual group organizations, while I buried myself in work. The children suffered as a result of their parents' inability to function as a team. I considered the possibility of leaving, going to Lidköping, Sweden, to be with my relatives there, or to Germany, where many friends would make such a move less strange than elsewhere. But how could one live without a job? The answer came in April 1968 when I was in Iran at a conference. It was an invitation to become the successor of Professor Wolfgang Lentz at Hamburg University who was retiring. At the same time it was rumored that Berthold Spuler, head of the Oriental Seminar was moving to Vienna, since retirement conditions for professors there were more favorable than in Hamburg. Ultra-conservative and dictatorial, Spuler was the bane of underlings, who could only rarely talk to him by brief appointments. Annemarie Schimmel, a close friend, now half every year at Harvard, cautioned about Spuler, whom she blamed for blocking her appointment to a professorship in Germany, which she was never able to obtain.

The news came that Spuler, on the way to Vienna, had learned that Austria had aligned its favorable conditions of retirement with those Germany, as a result of which he returned to Hamburg. Lentz, however, strongly urged me to accept, and I agreed to come for a year to see whether conditions would be favorable to remain. It would be a time of change, and uncertainties were numerous, but perhaps a move would resolve problems at home. The children now were old enough to fend for themselves, although Bobby was going to high school and might have to choose between mother and father. It was a move that might prove satisfactory for all concerned, since at home the situation was anything but happy.

CHAPTER 22

Hamburg Upheavals

IT WAS not only family problems which brought dissatisfaction, but also at Harvard contention developed. Gibb had left and the Middle East Center was successively directed by various faculty members, while the Department of Near Eastern Studies returned to its previous dominant interest in Semitic languages. As mentioned my closest colleague, Pritsak abandoned Turkology for creating a Center of Ukrainian Studies. The Committee on Inner Asian and Altaic Studies, which Pritsak, Cleaves and I had created, was being neglected by the administration, and in general a marginalization of Iranian Studies apparently was progressing. Students also were demonstrating against the war in Viet Nam, and the academic atmosphere in the USA became distasteful, so Germany beckoned. I never had an assistant at Harvard, but at Hamburg an assistant and secretarial help was promised. The exalted status of the Ordinarius in Germany also was a lure, even though it was soon to change. Coming to Hamburg in September 1968 it was fully my intention to remain there, but events and people decided otherwise.

Before departing riots broke out at Harvard Square, originally launched by students, who attacked the Semitic Museum where the International Affairs Program was located. They were protesting the Viet Nam war as well as the activities of all international organizations. Soon the students were joined, or apparently displaced, by rowdy elements from the town who threw stones, broke windows and looted shops at the square. A solid wall of police with shields pushed the rioters back and a semblance of order was restored. I was caught inside the Harvard Yard when all gates were chained so no one could enter. I had to climb the wall and in the process tore my trousers, so it was with a feeling of relief that I left for calm Europe, although that was to change.

The Pension on Johnsallee was not a prepossessing building, a row house with windows only in front and back. But at least it was built of stone rather than bricks and was warm in winter. Since an office was provided in the Orientalisches Seminar on Rothenbaumchaussee, just around the corner, a bedroom was sufficient for the winter semester, which lasted until March, as well as the summer semester from May to August.

According to German academic rules Meyer-Ingwersen, a gifted linguist who was the assistant of Lentz, could not remain, so a search was made for another assistant. Another linguist from Cologne, Georg Hincha presented himself, and was at once hired. Hincha was from the east, a Slavic Sorb or Wend by origin, but completely Germanized. As all good assistants should, he carried my briefcase and luggage to station or airport when the professor went on a trip, which was an embarrassment for me. Also a half-time secretary Frau Dannenberg, was assigned, both privileges rarely found with American or British professors. It was a heady experience, and an auspicious start to a career in a German university. But then the faculty meetings of the Philosophical Faculty began.

Faculty meetings were held in a room with a large table, such that the twenty or so professors of the Philosophische Fakultät could all sit around in intimate discussions. The Dekkan was elected, and much like the chairman of departments in the USA, this position was considered an unwelcome duty. At least here you could cast a vote for someone whom you disliked, while in the USA chairmen usually were appointed by the university administration. The latter in Hamburg, die *Behörde*, exercised the same functions of fiscal control as at Harvard, but added a few. Once I had enough of faculty meetings, held every other week, and skipped a session. The following day Frau Dannenberg received a call from the administration inquiring whether I was sick. Faculty meetings lasted from 4 PM sometimes to midnight, and professors were expected to bring their sandwiches with them, for no one was excused. My German greatly improved, but the discussions were interminably boring. An hour might be spent on parking privileges for certain classes of students, whether science faculty students should be towed from spaces allocated to the philosophical faculty. Other trivia made attendance at faculty meetings an ordeal. Furthermore, student unrest brought longer and more frequent meetings to deal with problems relating to students.

Several students in Islamic Studies were excellent, including Heinz Gaube, who later became professor in Tübingen, but for Iranian no one appeared, although old students remained. One hanger-on was Klaus Schippmann, who had a degree in law, but had become interested in the archaeology of Iran after a trip there. He could not study for a doctorate in Iranian Studies since he already had one, but would have to apply for an advanced degree, German *Habilitation*. Lentz had refused to accept him as an advanced student and I was unable to change that decision, so he was advised to apply to Walther Hinz, a born again Christian professor at Göttingen, where he was accepted. In the meantime, in Hamburg he was a jolly beer drinking character who introduced me to popular German music and words, of composers Georg Kreisler and Franz Josef Degenhardt, similar to that of Tom Lehrer in the USA, mostly on 33 rpm discs, but at times live in a theater. Later he became a professor in Göttingen, after a tour with the Asia Institute in Shiraz. The pleasant teacher for the Persian language was Gulshani from Gilan, who was finishing a thesis on Safavid history. He recorded Gilaki proverbs and grammatical notes for Hincha and me. Another student, Monike Dahnke, later became associated with the Pahlavi Library in Tehran under Shoja ed-Din Shafa, a minister of court.

At the local mosque the imam, Ayatallah Beheshti, later to be the brains behind the Islamic revolution in Iran, frequently met with students from eastern Germany, who gave Behishti ideas about party cells, which the Ayatallah later put into practice in Iran. The radical students, who opposed the Shah's regime, probably were not the largest component of the Iranian colony in Germany, but they certainly were the most vociferous. Other students were restless, and by the end of the year demonstrations began, and the student movement or uprising was under way.

Especially clamorous was a leftist student group, the SDS, which began to organize activities against the administration of the university and the professors.

Faculty meetings took place now every week, and debates about the students dominated every session, until the invasion occurred. In the middle of one such meeting the locked door was broken down, and a horde of wild eyed, disheveled and unkempt students not only disrupted the meeting but danced on the large table. The faculty fled in disorder. Then came the police with armor and clubs in a phalanx, marching down the street, while stone throwing students slowly retreated. Windows were broken and a police car overturned, but the riot did not end. In the occupied psychology seminar on the third floor of the Philosophical Tower, students had barricaded themselves behind barbed wire. On sympathetically talking to them, their grievances were aired, condemning the professors for being little dictators, who carried the dust of a thousand years in their robes, and did nothing to help long suffering students. I thought I had left demonstrations behind, but here they were again.

Other students, including ours in the Oriental Seminar, were passive, or even opposed to other students, but it all came to a climax when one opponent of the radical students was killed by being thrown out of the eighth floor of the tower. This tragedy brought an end to the riots, and the faculty and administration promised to change the system and condition of students, so the revolt subsided. It was not completely over, but an overhaul of the faculties and student affairs was put in motion. Since I had sympathized with students on many occasions, they urged me to remain in Hamburg. Several matters raised strong doubts, however, but the most important was dependence on Spuler. Not only students, but also colleagues, had to obtain an appointment, at his discretion, for even a short time to talk to him. On inquiring of the administration about a budget for Iranian Studies, I was told he would control the allocation of funds for the library and any travel, assigning what he thought sufficient for Iranian Studies. Another was a feeling that the privileged position of German professors was over, and the perks of a position at a university would be curtailed. Also as an employee of the state other duties might be required. For example, on several occasions I was called into court to testify about conditions in Iran, and one remains in my mind.

An Armenian doctor, who had practiced in Hamburg for a number of years without obtaining citizenship, was to be sent back to Iran. His lawyer had pleaded that as a minority he would be persecuted. In court under oath I had to tell the truth that he would not be persecuted, and probably would do well in practice, since many Muslim Iranians would trust an Armenian doctor more than one of their own. At other times translations from Persian into German were required by city authorities, which frequently were taxing. Nonetheless, with support from our students, a decision to stay was almost made, if another factor had not entered the scene.

A letter came from Arthur Upham Pope, who had moved to Shiraz and reestablished his Asia Institute in the newly organized Pahlavi University with aid from the University of Pennsylvania. Previously in 1952 I had declined an invitation to become chancellor of the Institute in New York, but the possibility of a connection with Shiraz was an attraction. Negotiations with the administration at Hamburg began, with a request that in the vacations I could go to Shiraz as director of the Institute there, claiming that such a connection would benefit students. This request was denied, so, returning home during the spring vacation, I spoke to Harvard officials to negotiate a similar deal. That administration was more receptive, and swung the balance in favor of the old school. Also I hoped that perhaps a better family situation could be reconstructed by moving the family to Iran.

Pope was a controversial figure, although even his critics acknowledged his great organizing ability and persuasiveness. The congress of Iranian art and archaeology, the *Survey of Persian Art*, and his creation of the Institute of Iranian Art and Archaeology, later renamed the Asia Institute, all testify to his capabilities. But his dealing with art objects and antiquities brought accusations of fraud or even theft. His answer was that the acquisition of art objects and antiques was legitimate since collectors, whether in Iran, such as Mohsen Foroughi, or foreigners, eventually would leave their collections to museums, and this would spread the fame of Iran's culture and handicrafts throughout the world. He claimed only to be a middle man in such transactions and, together with Foroughi and Ghirshman, rejected imputations that he sponsored illicit excavations of ancient sites. His love of Iran and its arts, he asserted, dominated his actions even though other may have disapproved.

It was with strong regret that I prepared to leave friends and happy memories of Hamburg, which had been rebuilt with good architectural taste after heavy destruction during the war. This old Hanseatic League city did not have the charm of more picturesque towns of the south, such as Munich. On the other hand, it had a reputation of cosmopolitanism and liberalism. Since the death of the Danish king in a brothel of Hamburg in the early twentieth century, a well-organized red light district had been organized by the town officials. The Reeperbahn on Heribert Strasse was unique in its handling of prostitution, for girls exhibited themselves in open booths to lure customers, and they were continually checked for any disease. It was and is one of the tourist sights of the city. The university towns of Heidelberg, Göttingen or Tübingen were more pleasant, but Hamburg, like Berlin, had more to offer in worldly attractions.

In December 1968 Bobojan Gafurov organized an international congress of Kushan Studies in Dushanbe, Tajikistan, and asked me to be head of a small American delegation. In those days every such meeting was composed of 'official' delegates from various countries. Although Gafurov had a Russian wife, he insisted that the head of the Soviet delegation should be a Tajik or Uzbek, an obvious play for local sympathies, if he should ever return to Tajikistan, where previously he had been chairman of the party for several years. It was decided that Kabul should be the center for an international organization of Kushan Studies, and the next conference would take place in Afghanistan. It did take place ten years later in different circumstances in that mountain kingdom.

Fate sometimes intervenes to influence one's life, and the call to Shiraz, out of the blue, was a major change. Germany and Sweden always remained as my secondary homelands, while Iran became even more the guiding light of activities. Travels in Iran and Afghanistan had made knowledge about those lands far greater than about the USA, which remained more an ivory tower retreat from activities in the east. On the other hand, just as

Russians retreated to their *dachas* in the summer, so did I go to Shiraz. After the summer semester came to an end in Hamburg I flew to Shiraz to discuss conditions of employment with the officials of the university, for the Asia Institute, although under the patronage of the Queen whose office provided funds, was administered by the university. Since Pope was in his dotage, his assistant Jay Gluck, a capable but abrasive person, was the one who would be the liaison between the university and Pope. It soon became apparent that his ideas of the future of the Institute and mine were different. He wanted to maintain complete independence from the university, relying on Pope's prestige to override any actions of the university, with which he did not agree. Understanding Iranians better than Gluck, I saw the future of the Asia Institute as cooperation with the university, rather than an adversarial model. Serving Iran should be the ultimate goal, not just Pope or even the Institute, was my opinion.

Pope died on September 3, 1969 and everything was put on hold until he was buried. An account of his death has appeared in the book *Surveyors of Persian Art,* with several inaccuracies by Gluck and his assistants Noel Siver and Charlie Penton. A new regime was in order, for a new chancellor Houchang Nahavandi had arrived at the university with an order to fire Jay Gluck, who was accused of illegally exporting antiquities from the country to sell in Japan. He had a house near Kobe which was full of Iranian antiques and art objects. Gluck took the news badly, and asked me to go to the royal court in Tehran to intercede for him to rescind the order. Only when it was revealed that the order had come from the court did he bitterly accept his fate.

Pope had been installed in a Qajar house, with a large garden, down the street from the famous garden, Bagh-e Aram, attended by a cook and loyal servant Rahim, aided by Namaki, a pleasant young lady, his assistant. My quarters were in a large room built on the flat roof, and meals were taken with Pope and his wife, Phyllis Ackerman, in the small dining room on the first floor. Gluck and Sumi, his Nissei wife, lived elsewhere but came daily to the Pope house, as did many notables in town. It was necessary to get bearings and learn ropes in a new job, but fighting the bureaucracy, even though distasteful, would be unavoidable. A number of Iranian women helped in the library, as well as at the

Pope house. Janet Bolandgiray, wife of a medical doctor, was a kind of secretary to Pope, and she became our new liaison with the university. One of the immediate tasks was to finish and furnish the Naranjestan, a nineteenth century Qajar palace, near the bazaar, home of the Asia Institute, and to build the library. Cataloging was done by the Dewey decimal system, but I proposed the Library of Congress model, since we could then buy cards already printed. At first opposed, finally the change was made and the library grew.

At the end of September I had to return to Harvard and come back to Shiraz in the Christmas vacation to begin a new career, which could be considered as a worth while extension of teaching at Harvard, giving field experience to book learning. We hoped also to bring students to Shiraz, and this did happen, although most came from institutions other than Harvard. Little, however, did I realize the pitfalls which awaited one in dealing with the Iranian bureaucracy.

CHAPTER 23

Shiraz Successes

ON RETURNING to Harvard a new group of students and visitors had appeared. Wojciech Skalmowski, who had studied in east Berlin and obtained a doctorate in Iranian languages, came as an exchange scholar. He stayed with us in our old house at 10 Fells Road in Winchester, MA, and was a great help both at home and in classes, especially when I went to Shiraz. This was not the case with Josef Adamik, a student from Slovakia, who became a thorn in everyone's flesh, with his complaints and constant demand to be appointed a full professor after receiving his degree. Badri Gharib, who had studied at Pennsylvania like Koji Kamioka, also had a year's fellowship at Harvard. Finally David Utz from the University of Missouri, was a beginning graduate student who proved to be a hard worker, learning readily, and finally producing a dissertation on one of the Buddhist Sogdian texts in Berlin. This was a welcome change from the past, and a good transition from Hamburg, confirming that it had been the right decision.

Still my heart was in Shiraz, with a resolve to build a center for archaeology and other fieldwork in the province of Fars. By concentrating on the province as the domain of the Institute, it might be possible to make Shiraz a rival to Tehran in activities and publication. This was bucking the tide of concentration and centralization of all decisions in the capital, but for a time it appeared to be successful. On the other hand time doubts loomed in the background, for one could not forget the lesson of the fate of lovely Persian gardens, so well expressed by Gertrude Bell in her book *Persian Pictures*, "the stream is turned off, the water ceases to flow into the tanks and to leap in the fountains, the trees die, the flowers wither, the walls crumble into unheeded decay, and in a few years the tiny paradise has been swept forgotten from the face of the earth, and the conquering desert spreads its dust and ashes once more over it all." This was the fate of many projects begun in Iran.

The new chancellor of the university, Houchang Nahavandi, more than anyone resembled Gorbachev in appearance, only more roly-poly and with evasive eyes. Jay Gluck had overseen the restoration of the Naranjestan, a nineteenth century Qajar palace near the bazaar of Shiraz, and now the finishing of work devolved on me.

"Agha," said the chief brick layer, "what bricks shall we buy to finish the work?" "What have we done in the past?" "Well, because of lack of funds we used local bricks, but they contain much salt and will not last as long as bricks from Isfahan. Those bricks are more expensive, but the best, and most expensive bricks are from more distant Nain." At that time transport was a great expense because of the poor condition of roads. Having experienced the poor road from Nain I decided "Buy Isfahan bricks and I will get extra money from Nahavandi," I rashly decided. On entering his office, however, he averted the subject by saying that the head of an institute in his university could not travel around town on a bicycle, rather I should buy a reputable car. Eventually money was provided for the bricks, but only after months of constantly reminding the chancellor, and proposing to enhance his reputation by organizing the first summer school in Shiraz, if not in the country. To secure his good will I suggested that such a school would only be taught in Persian, not English as in most of his university. Iranian scholars would teach instead of foreigners, and this gave him pleasure, although he considered it an impossible task. I told him it would take time, but was worth the effort. I explained that classes would be designed not only for students at the university, but also for employees of the Ministry of Culture and the Arts or other government employees. The classes could be held at the Naranjestan, where every course would be given in the Persian language. Nahavandi was dubious but finally agreed and I set to work.

Classes were given in Akkadian and Elamite cuneiform, the history of Islamic Fine Arts, archaeology and early history of Iran, and a survey of Middle Iranian languages. Majid Arfai, a graduate student of the Elamite specialist Hallock at the University of Chicago, was secured for the cuneiform, and Firuz Bagherzadeh from CNRS in Paris for Fine Arts. Shapur Shahbazi, who had finished his degree at the University of London, gave the early history, while I taught the ancient languages. All courses were held in Persian to the admiration of many who thought it could not be done, since only foreigners would be qualified to teach such classes, never given elsewhere in the country.

The summer school was a great success, so much so that Tehran took Bagherzadeh to head the antiquities section of the ministry of Culture and Art, while Shahbazi also went to a post in Tehran, and Arfai back to Chicago. In passing, I was quite exhausted in fighting to obtain adequate salaries for the teachers, and this time the bureaucracy beat me, for poor Arfai, in student status, frankly was robbed, while the others fared little better. I did gain experience with the administration of the university, which helped in the battles to obtain funds to print issues of our bulletin, each of which required a prolonged contest.

That project, which required much of my time and energy, was the publication of a *Bulletin of the Asia Institute* in English, the first issue of which was ready for printing in Tehran. It had been suggested that proper printing could be done only abroad, but at my insistence local printing was decided in spite of difficulties of printing English, but at the capital rather than Shiraz, which did not have proper facilities. I was determined to show Iranians that I for one was promoting Iran and its capabilities rather than assuming that printing had to be done abroad. Other plans for special monographs were discussed, and an exhilarating time in Iran was forseen. My goal was not to promote myself, or a reputation at Harvard, but to make of our institute in Shiraz a model which could be followed elsewhere in Iran. It was difficult to persuade the administration of the university, or most Iranians, that such was my object, but I remembered the Armenians in the USA and resolved to continue in spite of difficulties.

On the way back home, a stop over in Rome revealed a new distinction, become evident because of my position as director of the Asia Institute in Shiraz. The grand *capo* of Oriental Studies in Italy, Giuseppe Tucci, a Tibetologist, invited me to his home in the mountains to the southeast of Rome, where his house was a veritable museum. Not many foreigners were invited to his mountain home, so it was an honor. The powerful drink of *grappa*, made from his grape orchards, was a specialty of the region, which left one gasping for breath. It was said that he had changed sides during the war when Italy surrendered, and it became apparent that the American army would enter the eternal city. The *Bersaglieri* 'elite troops' had abandoned their headquarters in the plush villa Brancaccio, and Tucci met the American troops with the assertion that the *palazzo* was his institute for Oriental Studies, so the US army confirmed him in its possession. In any case, as a fellow institute director, my prestige rose in his mind and in the minds of many in Europe as well as in Iran. It was clear that administrators, more than scholars, were highly regarded everywhere.

The writing of articles and books was not neglected, even though more energy and time was now devoted to building the institute in Shiraz. An Austrian pathologist, Werner Dutz, who had lived many years in Shiraz, advised that Iranians never say no. When they say yes it means maybe, and when they say maybe it means no. Furthermore they were experts on pulling the rug from under you such that you do not notice its absence. He was a character, who would eat food which fell to the floor, saying that disease came from other people not a little dirt. With him I went on trips to archaeological sites in Fars and elsewhere in Iran. In spite of his cynicism, persistence and patience, I hoped, would bring results in spite of doubts of the foreign community.

A delightful writer, and teacher of English at the university, was Terry O'Donnell, who had lived many years in Shiraz. He wrote a short history of the Naranjestan for us, and it was a joy to hear his stories of life in the villages and among the tribes. The lure of Iran on some foreigners, present company not excepted, was always a surprise, but also a comfort. On the other hand, having lived in Afghanistan, Turkey and the Soviet Union,

England and Germany, the similarities among people, their common concerns and problems, joys and sorrows, impressed me more than differences. Such a view was much older than the economic 'globalization' of today, spreading superficial, outward conformity around the world. Differences among peoples and nations certainly exist, but basically how similar we all are. I felt at home everywhere I lived which unfortunately made me a poor recorder of particular characteristics of other people.

Most foreigners living in the country maintained an existence apart from the older and poorer parts of a city, except to venture into the bazaar for purchases, while villages were only to be passed on the way to other towns or tourist sights. Since the Institute was in the old part of town, with its narrow lanes and mud walls, surrounding gardens and houses, it was our fortune to meet and learn about the common folk. With little of the polish and sophistication of upper class Persians, the people of the bazaar, or villages, were almost a race apart, speaking rough dialects almost incomprehensible to the elites of Tehran, who lived in the rarefied atmosphere of Shemiran north of Tehran. The distinction between classes in Shiraz was not as pronounced as in the capital, but the gap between social classes was to widen everywhere in the country before the revolution.

In addition to the summer school, I launched the first yearly conference on archaeology, when in September foreigners and Iranians who had excavated or surveyed sites in Iran came to Shiraz to report their finds. Just as the summer school, the conference also was a great success, so much that after two years officials in Tehran took both projects from Shiraz and brought them to the capital. The summer school, however, could not be duplicated, so it remained a one time accomplishment. After so much effort in starting these projects it was somewhat bitter to lose them. I wanted to imitate the old inscription on the Shiraz-Kazerun road, *hind zahmetesh kasheed; Iran faidesh burd*, and resolved on my tombstone to have carved in Persian 'Frye took the trouble, another took the profit.'

Especially pleasant were the evenings spent at the tomb of the poet Sa'adi listening to Persian poetry and drinking wine, in the style of the *Rubaiyat* of Omar Khayyam. Bill Royce, head of the United States Information Office in Shiraz, was a boon companion, even to trying the smoking of opium, although it must be confessed that it only left a bad taste in my mouth rather than a pleasant dream. Visiting foreign scholars were introduced to the pleasant pastime of imbibing wine at the tomb, and on one occasion Professor Eiji Mano from Japan was properly initiated to our carousing by an overdose of Khollar wine, specialty of Shiraz. How many times the Persian expression *che 'ajib shabi* 'what a marvelous night,' rang out in the warm Shiraz nights!

A further project which took much exertion, was as the editor of volume four of the *Cambridge History of Iran,* and it did involve a number of trips to Cambridge, England on the way to or from Iran. High tables at King's College, or other colleges at the university, were still lavish banquets with much liquor and snuff, perhaps a reaction to the austerity of post-war years. This too was soon to change. Arberry, who had moved from London to Cambridge, and was a director of the history project, proved cantankerous and difficult, but others, including officials of the Press, and Hubert Darke, secretary of the project, on the contrary were both relaxed and most helpful. It was now a different world from the immediate post-war period.

My usual path to Tehran included a trip to Germany, Sweden, and Leningrad, such that the Soviet consulate in Tehran invariably granted a ten day transit visa with a minimum of delay. In the Hermitage museum Volodya Lukonin declared I was really on a *komandirovka* 'scholarly mission' from Leningrad, since the city was a regular stop, both coming and going.

In the summer I invited cousin Britta, and her striking blonde teenage daughter Susanne, to come to Shiraz, but the heat was too much for the Swedes, and they did not care for the sand and dust on roads as well as in houses. Those who know the ease of travel today find it difficult to envisage the problems of travel a generation or more ago. There were some advantages in the past, however, for a breakdown of a car on the road always elicited help from the next vehicle, a kind of code of the road. Also a Persian villager, like the Afghans, would welcome a foreigner into his home if he were stranded on the road. The American adage that time is money meant nothing to the villagers or *bazaaris*, but again the elites were Westernizing at a fast pace, leaving the common folk behind. Seeds of future trouble were growing in the land.

Americans already were beginning to inundate Iran, in both the military and businesses, eager to earn money in building the oil rich country. A resentment among the people about the influence of foreigners, especially Americans, was also increasing, and those of us who had known the hospitality and friendliness of Persians, and the life styles of the past, sympathized with many of these sentiments. In Shiraz, where many small sherbet parlors had provided places for rest and discussion among the people, they were now replaced by bars with vodka and other spirits. Rituals of traditional wine drinking were replaced by Russian style heavy drinking, simply to become inebriated. Vodka was becoming the national drink of Iran and drunkenness, hitherto rare, now became more common. Old genteel Iran was becoming a Westernized copy of some of the worst in that world. More was yet to come.

CHAPTER 24

Fading Hopes

ON DECEMBER 16,1970, on arrival in Tehran and a visit to Shoja ed-Din Shafa, influential Minister of Court, I was met with a request. "You are just in time," he said, "we need someone who speaks English and can aid our delegation going to an international congress for the Study of the Peoples of Africa and Asia, taking place in Canberra." There was no time to go to Shiraz since we were to leave the next day. Already under the weather from jet-lag, a trip to Australia did not hold any attractions, but the advisability to conciliate Shafa overruled any inclinations, and furthermore Australia was not far away, according to the map. I forgot that the world is just as round north-south as east-west, and the flight to Canberra via Bombay, Singapore, and Perth was anything but short and restful. A talk, which was intended for Shiraz, was changed somewhat for Canberra, and the conference was successful, but the double jet-lag left me in a state resembling a zombie, such that memories of Australia only include annoying flies, and of course the kangaroos.

Finally back in Shiraz work on the Bulletin, and plans for archaeological surveys of Fars were made. Klaus Schippmann, who was now in Göttingen, came as a fellow of our institute, while Pierre de Miroschedji in a kind of French 'Peace Corps,' instead of military service, also joined the group at the Institute to investigate Elamite remains in the province. All the activities required money, and the administration of the university was loathe to allocate any funds to the Institute, other than the salaries of local workers, or those with contracts, such as myself and Professor Khoobnazar the executive officer of the Institute.

It became clear that if any plans were to materialize, external funds would have to be secured, and this was no easy task. Several attempts to obtain support from Manucher Eqbal, powerful head of the oil company met with stern rebuffs, saying that all money would go to the university and Nahavandi would allocate those funds as he saw fit. Relations with the latter were cordial but hardly friendly, especially after his refusal to properly pay for the summer school, allocating low salaries which were insulting to the teachers who had been brought to Shiraz from abroad. Since he had declared that riding a bicycle was unbecoming the head of an institute, it was necessary to satisfy him in this regard. He rode in a Chrysler, so I resolved to trump him by buying a Mercedes-Benz in Hamburg and driving it to Shiraz .

Both the trip to Afghanistan and the archaeological dig had awakened the interest of Jeff in the Orient and he wanted to go to India. This gave an opportunity to propose that the entire family should come to Iran, and perhaps being in that country might save or rather resurrect our marriage. Everyone thought it a good idea, so we sold our house and prepared to leave. It was necessary to make prior arrangements, however, so the first task was to fly to Amsterdam to talk with Robert Vandenberg of the oil consortium to obtain funds for the Bulletin and archaeological surveys. He usually was in Tehran but returned to his home for the summer. Afterwards I went on to Hamburg where a 1960 Mercedes sedan 300 SE was purchased. The low price of $3000 should have warned me that something might be amiss, but the leather seats and fine running condition were reassuring.

The drive to Tehran presented no problems, and this time the roads were better and I was able to drive faster than on the previous trip, and there I met the rest of the family who had flown by air. We would drive to Shiraz in relative comfort, or such was our hope.

The road from Tehran to Qum was paved, so the car went at a fast pace until what appeared to be a white paper or box in the middle of the road. With a truck coming from the other direction it was not possible to swerve, so the low slung Benz hit the white washed rock underneath and ground to a stop. The transmission had been badly damaged and the car had to be towed to a Mercedes garage in south Tehran. On entering the compound the mechanics gathered and pointed at the car. "There's another one." My question as to the meaning of their remarks was answered by the head of the garage who pointed to a duplicate of our car at the far end of the field. "It belongs to the governor of Mazanderan and has been here for a year." "Why?" was a natural question, and the answer was unnerving. "Only a few of this model were made, and parts are impossible to find. We finally found the part which we needed in Canada, cannibalized from a wrecked specimen, and hopefully it will arrive soon so we can fix the governor's car. We will have search the world for your transmission." Actually it only took ten months to fix our car, so we all went to Shiraz by bus, an interesting experience for the family.

After a few weeks living in Pope's house, a delightful early nineteenth century two-story house, we were able to rent a house with a garden on Qasr al-Dasht, the road with many lovely gardens leading north from the city. The owner was Dr. Faroukh Sa'idi, an eminent surgeon who had studied at Harvard, who became a close friend and consultant on ancient Iranian matters. With such pleasant, though austere, living quarters life seemed to head for a pleasant time in Iran. Becky and Bob were enrolled in the local international elementary school, but Jeff had to go to Tehran where a similar high school existed, with room and board. Many foreigners lived in Shiraz at that time, some teaching in the university, which also had instructors and professors coming from the University of Pennsylvania every year. When the president of Penn came to Shiraz to receive an honorary degree, the faculty turned out in splendid gowns with gold tassels, more impressive than any similar academic gowns in Europe or America. As head of the institute it was incumbent on me to welcome foreign visitors, as well as prominent Iranians, and never before or since had I worn so much finery.

During vacation Jeff went to India with some Iranian friends, and at the site of Buddha's birth he listened to teachers and became interested in Buddhism. On the return trip, however, he landed in jail in Meshhed for possessing hashish, and a trip to the eastern city, with much pleading for his release, resulted in the payment of a fine and his return to school in Tehran. His trip to India also brought him into contact with yoga exercises, which were to influence his future life. Another incident happened at this time with a bizarre ending.

Why would anyone smuggle gold into the Soviet Union when that country owned the largest reserves in the world, and the mining of gold was well developed? I asked this question when my friends Rustam Aliev and Kamol ad-Din Aini, both Soviet citizens, got into real trouble at Moscow's international Sheremetyevo airport. Rustam, if we remember, was an Azeri from Baku and Kamol was a Tajik from Dushanbe, and both were respected academicians in their home republics, but both lived in Moscow, a privilege accorded to such people.

In the seventies Iran's money was a hard currency, which one could change into dollars at New York's Kennedy airport. Both Rustam and Kamol had received 'prizes' of cash from the Shah of Iran for translations of Persian classics into Russian, and on my advice wisely they had deposited their money in bank accounts in Tehran. Rustam had travelled widely, but his last trip to Tehran proved most unpropitious.

As an academician of the Azerbaijan Academy of Sciences on his trips he was entitled to special treatment by Soviet embassies. All international flights to Tehran arrived late at night, including those from Moscow. On this occasion the Aeroflot plane was due to arrive at 1:00 AM, but it had been delayed and did not arrive until 3:30. The chauffeur of the embassy car assigned to meet the plane, and bring Rustam to the embassy compound, was a Russian who became tired of waiting, especially for an Azeri who threw his weight around, as he had learned from previous trips. So he went home. When Rustam arrived no one was waiting for him and he had no hard currency to pay for a taxi. So he walked to the embassy, some 7 or 8 miles distant, at each step becoming more and more angry. Later in the morning he upbraided the ambassador for allowing such a breach of conduct on the part of his chauffeur. The Russian ambassador, however, was very annoyed and resolved to get even with the bumptious Azeri. Both Rustam and Kamol had come to Tehran for a conference, but Rustam's boss, Bobojan Gafurov, told him that in future he should restrict his international travel and stay at home on the job for the next few years.

I came to Tehran from Shiraz to meet Rustam and Kamol, to aid them as they had for me in the USSR. Rustam revealed that after this trip he had to stay at home in Moscow, and would not be able to travel abroad for some time. He wanted to close his bank account in Tehran, and buy gold to bring back to the Soviet Union, which was against the law. I suggested to Rustam that I could handle his bank account, if he so desired, and use it for books, or whatever he wanted, to bring when I came through Moscow, or to send by mail. He explained that any foreign hard currency imported into the USSR would have to be changed into rubles at a poor rate of exchange, which was why Soviet citizens who earned money abroad would convert it into gold rings, jewelry, or even teeth, which they could pass through customs. "Everyone was doing it," he said, for only the value of gold was trusted by Soviet citizens. He would do the same and rejected contrary advice. Kamol wanted to stay a few more days in Tehran, but he was influenced by Rustam's action to do the same. I concluded that they must know what they were doing, since it was the common practice of Soviet workers at the steel plant in Isfahan before they returned home.

The ambassador, however, had sent someone to follow Rustam, so when he went to one of the Armenian jewelers on Naderi Street, who made gold objects for Soviet citizens, the ambassador had his chance for revenge and reported Rustam's action to Moscow. I learned about the incident at Sheremetyevo airport from Oleg Akimushkin, a Russian friend who accompanied Rustam on the plane. It seems the customs officer asked Rustam if he had anything to declare, to which he replied in the negative. "Think again, comrade, are you absolutely sure you have nothing to declare," asked the officer again. Oleg added, "How long does one have to live in the USSR without knowing the jig was up." Rustam, however, took umbrage at this demand, shouted that he was an academician, and no one should doubt him or touch him. The customs officer was taken aback but called a colonel of the NKVD or MVD (later KGB) who searched Rustam, found the gold and arrested him. Two days later Kamol arrived at the airport and also was arrested.

"What happened afterwards?" was the question to Oleg. Wryly he replied, "You see what progress we have made in the Soviet Union. In Stalin's time they would have been sent to Siberia, and you would not have heard from them again. Rustam was demoted from the academy and sent to Baku, where he was made director of manuscripts in the library of the local branch of the academy, while Kamol was forbidden to reside in Moscow and had to return to Dushanbe, where he too received a prestigious job. " But the Soviets working in Iran, who heard of the incident, were furious with both of them, since for several months afterwards they did not dare to smuggle gold into their homeland, declaring they would hang the two of them if they caught them. Such is the story of Rustam and the smuggling of gold.

Volodya Lukonin also came to Tehran, where I entertained him in Leningrad fashion. He had upbraided me there, saying I behaved wildly as a hooligan in the USSR, which I would not do elsewhere, but I wanted to prove him wrong and did so in Tehran. Drunken singing and dancing was tolerated in the capital in those days, and Russians felt at home there. As mentioned, transit trips through the USSR caused no visa problems, but extending one's stay was another matter, as I learned on one such trip back to Tehran.

At the Academy's Oriental Institute in Leningrad Yuri Borshchevski's colorful English was a constant source of amusement for foreigners coming through Leningrad. Because of an insult to Gafurov, Yuri was never granted permission to travel abroad. On one occasion, happily imbibing cognac with him, the time for departure for the airport and a plane to Moscow arrived. Yuri said we need not hurry since he too was flying to Moscow, and we could go together on the same plane. He called a taxi, patiently explaining that his name was like *borshcht*, and we had a pleasant flight to Moscow, but our plane was delayed. At the Moscow airport the Aeroflot plane to Tehran was on the runway and it was impossible to board it. I proposed that I could wait for the next plane after two days, but officials refused to prolong my visa which expired on this day. Instead they put me on the next plane, which was flying to Bucharest, and I arrived at that city's airport with my ticket for Tehran and no Romanian visa.

Passengers from the USSR did not require visas, so there was no problem, and cigarettes were accepted as a fee for stamping my passport. After a night and day in the city in a private home assigned by the tourist bureau, a plane flew to Ankara and then to Tehran. The Romanians in character seemed well suited to use the name of Romans, unlike their Slavic neighbors, and the unhappiness with their leaders was openly expressed, much to my trepidation. "We are not like Russians, and foreigners should not forget this," was their assertion.

At the end of summer the ostentatious celebration of 2500 years of monarchy took place at Shiraz and Persepolis, and the Asia Institute was designated to organize a conference of scholars in Shiraz to accompany the pageantry and celebrations at Persepolis. The foreign tents which were erected at Persepolis, the food and water flown from France for the distinguished foreign visitors, such as Spiro Agnew, vice-president of the USA, and the colorful historical costumes of soldiers marching by the podium on which sat the Shah and his invitees, all are well known, for it was reported in the world press. Other than the conference, I was assigned to take care of Barbara Walters, a well-known reporter and television personality from New York. My main job, however, was to care for foreign scholars.

A crisis arose because of the Israeli scholars whom we had invited for the conference, and the inability to put them in the same assigned hotel as Arab visitors. After much persuasion, the faculty club of the university agreed to accept them, and in this regard the conference ended without incident. The great cost of the celebration was a source of criticism among many Iranians, even though they were proud of the attention of distinguished guests who came to the country. The tents remained at Persepolis and the site now became a much visited tourist attraction by foreigners but few Iranians.

Many sophisticated Tehran officials had been impressed with the success of the activities in Shiraz, and decided to open a yearly Festival of the Arts in the city. As director of the Asia Institute I was invited to serve on the board of the Festival, with such prominent people as Qotbi, the director of radio and television in Iran. At the first meeting of the committee in charge of the Festival, I offered the suggestion that we should invite musicians and dance groups from our neighbors, Pakistan, Tajikistan,

Armenia, Uzbekistan, etc. The other members of the committee maintained a stunned silence until the chairman condescendingly spoke, "Mr Frye, you don't understand; we are *avantguardists* not folklorists." Keeping my peace I listened to the debate, whether they should invite a notorious group of nude dancers from the left bank of Paris, or a hard rock lesbian group from Greenwich village. The next time I was dis-invited from the committee, but the Tehranis had either not understood the feelings of the people of Shiraz, or they did not care, and this was to backfire on the ultra-modernists.

The festival of arts continued every September in Shiraz, with ever more far out programs to tickle the fancies of the *avantguardists* of Tehran, and to the dismay of the Shirazis. Once a pick pocket lifted my wallet, but when I went to the chief of police whom I knew, he threw up his hands in helplessness, "thieves from Tehran have invaded Shiraz and we can do nothing." When Stockhausen, a 'modern' German composer was invited to the festival, and set up his loud speakers in the Saraye Mushir, a traditional tea house in the bazaar, with loud noises at midnight, a revolt of the local people almost occurred. Bare breasted girl dancers from Senegal were offensive enough, but sexual intercourse in a play in the bazaar caused an uproar and a temporary retreat by the organizers. They decided to also look for local talent, but it had to be unusual.

The next year they brought a group of exorcists from the island of Qeshm in the Persian Gulf, supposedly to appease local tastes, and all of them were dark, almost black, descended from African slaves. The ceremony of exorcism, to drive the evil spirits or winds, called *noban* and *zar*, from several who were possessed of them, brought expressions of disbelief from several sophisticated ladies of Shemiran who were present. "These people cannot be from Iran, where did they come from?" was the incredulous remark of one of them. The clerics of Shiraz were outraged at the invasion from Tehran, and soon the people were to follow their lead.

When I had to fly to Tehran, seeking funds for our Institute, or urging the printing press to hurry with the Bulletin, a taxi would take me to the British or American centers where rooms were available. A driver frequently would ask from where I had come. My usual reply "From Iran," always surprised the driver, with the response "Isn't Tehran in Iran?" "No," I would say, "Tehran is an international cesspool; it is not part of 'real' Iran."

Another time at the Tehran airport I spoke to an American sergeant who had missed his flight to Isfahan and was at a loss what to do, as he did not speak Persian. His ticket was corrected to a later flight, which gave an opportunity to find out his attitude towards Iran and its inhabitants. He had been in Isfahan for two years and was quite happy, since he received extra local pay for teaching the Iranian army about tanks, as well as receiving an extra bonus on his normal salary for serving overseas. And he lived free in a US compound outside of Isfahan, surrounded by barbed wire and guard posts. As for work, he had little, since the 'gooks' couldn't learn anything. With such attitudes one could understand slogans of some students such as 'Yankee go home', and the religious leaders were not slow to take the lead in fanning such sentiments. Some of the civilians working for American companies had come from Vietnam after the war ended, and needless to say their manners frequently did not endear them to the local population. One story had a pilot, who worked for Bell Helicopter Co., becoming angry at the Iranians, such that he left his helicopter on the road to Shiraz to spite the Isfahanis just before leaving the country. Not that some Shemiranis themselves were not guilty of disdain and scorn for their own common people. And often they spent more time in Europe than in their native country. It seemed one would have to go to eastern Iran and Baluchistan, or to Kurdistan or Luristan, to find traditional values of the people. The split between affluent and poor people had widened considerably and was ever growing.

In the autumn of 1971 it was necessary to return to Harvard, while the family remained in Shiraz. They had learned enough Persian to fend for themselves, and had made friends who would support them. Fortunately back home it was possible to rent a room at the university in Kirkland House, of which I was a faculty member. The separation from the family, however, did little to heal the divisions between mother and father, but even turned worse because of separation. They all loved Iran as did I, but it was not enough to heal the ever growing breach between the parents.

CHAPTER 25

Life Changes

SOMETIMES a period in one's life which is filled with upheaval remains unclear in details, and such in my case is the period from 1972 to 1974. Becky had been sent to a school in England since she could not get into Iranzamin school with Jeff in Tehran. She did not like the school and in the summer of 1972 came back to Shiraz vowing not to return to England. In July of 1972 the lease on Sa'idi's house in Shiraz ended, and it was difficult to leave the garden on Qasr al-Dasht street to return to the Pope house. There was not enough room there for everyone so Barbara, Becky and Bob decided to return to the USA, while I remained until the middle of September. The same routine of summers and Christmas vacations in Shiraz was beginning to have an adverse effect on my stamina, and on hopes for developing the Institute. The library was being built, but it took much time, and the concentration of teaching in the university left the Institute with no input from students. We maintained teaching in the Persian language, but students could not receive credit for classes of the Institute so the teaching was abandoned. Furthermore, there were no graduate students in Shiraz, and undergraduates had their programs filled with requirements. On one occasion, however, a course in Japanese was offered in the Asia Institute by Koji Kamioka, my student from Harvard, who had returned to Tokyo where he became head of a Near Eastern section of a center devoted to the Orient, not including Japan. This course was requested by some traders in the bazaar rather than university students, so the university was not interested in its continuation.

Nonetheless, we encouraged students to use our library, but the Naranjestan for the most part came to be a hostel, where foreigners who were doing research in Fars, would establish their headquarters while they worked in the field. It was frequently difficult to explain to the foreigners the problems of obtaining permission to work in the field, for example among the Qashghai tribe. "Put yourself in the place of an official who has to give you permission. He thinks to himself, why should I give this foreigner my approval. Suppose something happens to him, I will be blamed and may even lose my job. It is better not to take any risk." What to do? My answer was to assure the official that he would have no responsibility for you, and this should be put in writing, while a gift would not hurt, to expedite obtaining the permission. Above all be patient but persistent, and remember the saying here, "yes, yes, if God wills, by my eye, after tomorrow (I will do it)". It sounds better in Persian " *bale, bale, inshallah, cheshm, cheshm, pas farda.*"

Andrew Williamson, a young British specialist in pottery, was especially helpful in arranging our collection of potsherds. Later unfortunately he was killed by a land mine in Oman. Bill Sumner, who was excavating the site of Malyan Tepe, or ancient Anshan, always brought students with him from various colleges in the USA, some of whom used our facilities. To the Naranjestan came people from everywhere, but mostly from Germany, France, England or the USA. Professor Honda from Hokkaido University would come every summer to Iran with students, and occasionally would show up in Shiraz. Professor Onu, an anthropologist, came from Tokyo. The latter returned to Iran every few years, and he told us about his studies.

He was making a comparative study of three villages, an Assyrian village near Rezaiyeh (Urmiya), a Zoroastrian village near Yazd, and a Muslim village near Marv Dasht. At the last village the young people had left to seek work in Shiraz, and only women, children and old people remained. He told them that the Zoroastrian village was flourishing and clean, while the Assyrian village was not far behind, but the village in Fars was unkempt and neglected, and asked if they knew why. The answer surprised him. "Of course the Zoroastrian village is better than ours, for they are true Iranians, while we have been contaminated by the Arabs." Thus this attitude was not confined to the elites in Tehran but had penetrated to the villages.

At the same time in the towns and cities economic conditions were deteriorating, for the price of oil, which sustained the Iranian economy, was falling and unemployment was soaring. In Tehran discontent among the young was led by leftist students, and it was the most important concern of Savak, the Shah's secret police. But elsewhere the leaders of opposition were the religious hierarchy, ordinary mullahs, *ayatallahs,* and other religious people. Most people in Tehran did not know, or care, about affairs in the countryside, and for many of the upper class their hearts were in Paris or London rather than even in Tehran.

In the summer Jeff copied grafitti for David Stronach on his excavations in Pasargadae, and became interested in studying archaeology, but India also lured him. The car in Tehran was finally fixed and, after considerable negotiation on expense, driven to Shiraz. Nahavandi was satisfied to see me in a vehicle worthy of an institute director, and on the street in his car he beamed on seeing the Benz. As ill luck would have it, after I made a trip to Tehran seeking support for the Bulletin, Charlie Penton, who was still in Shiraz, borrowed and drove the car with a cadaver in it back to a village which he had adopted, and again the transmission was broken and had to be returned to Tehran, where it had to be sold to pay the expense of repairs. Penton shortly thereafter left and joined Gluck, but he was not replaced in the Institute.

On one occasion I made a trip alone to the British excavations at Siraf on the Persian Gulf, and was surprised to find that one village would have a Shi'ite mullah while the next would have a Sunni. Perhaps it was intercourse across the Persian Gulf which caused this mixture, unlike Shiraz, Isfahan and other cities and villages in the center of the country, where all were professed Shi'ites. In a hotel in Bushire a Japanese looking person was in the next room, and I suspected he was a representative of Sony or Honda, or another Japanese company, but he spoke excellent Persian and was a Berberi, called Hazara in Afghanistan, and was insulted that he was considered to be Japanese.

I was told that small colonies of Swahili speaking villagers existed on the coast, possibly having been brought from east Africa years ago. Southern Iran was a fascinating, but little known area, and much investigation would be needed before dialects and customs vanished in favor of the ubiquitous Tehrani dialect on radio and TV.

On returning to the USA in the autumn of 1972 I found the family in an apartment in Back Bay Boston, where there was no room for me. Luckily a one room apartment was found in Cambridge, but it was clear that Barbara wanted not a separation, which we always had, but divorce so she could pursue her own life, which more and more was turned to spiritual groups or cults.

Since I participated in the Thursday evening seances of the Khaksariyya order of dervishes at their center in the structure of Chihil-Tan 'forty persons' (martyrs?) in Shiraz, spiritual affairs were not scorned, but also far from dominant in my life. As a matter of fact, one day when back in the USA and driving on a highway, a voice seemed to come saying, "you think that 'Ali is just a man, a caliph, but he is more-the name is the foundation of the universe." On reporting this to Anwar, our *murshid* or leader of the order, he was not at all surprised, and, of course, very pleased. Shopkeepers, intellectuals, and laborers used to gather on Thursday evenings to sit in a darkened room, while the leader began to recite Persian poetry, frequently of Jalal al-Din Rumi. Soon everyone would be transported by the rhythm and words, and in unison raised their voices, calling 'Ali, 'Ali, until all reached a state similar to hashish, but not opium, which subdued people. The leader was careful to keep his followers from going over the edge, and when it seemed that a kind of frenzy would take over, he would stop and turn on the lights. Afterwards we would have dinner together at the shrine.

Once the overall head of the order in Tehran complained to our leader that he should not allow a non-Muslim into the seances, but his advice was ignored. My failing one time was not to properly read an Arabic text handed to me by our leader, which reduced my standing in his eyes. There were several other dervish orders in town, but I kept to our group.

Separation spurred me to more travel and participation in congresses, in Budapest and in Paris in 1973. Meanwhile both in Shiraz and at Harvard changes occurred. In Shiraz Shapur

Shahbazi returned to be head of Persepolis, and married Theresa, a blonde Canadian girl, who was an exchange student at the university. He, as well as Werner Dutz, were companions in interest for the antiquities of Iran, but Dutz was soon to leave. Other students came as college exchange groups, and one of my duties was to advise them.

One day a request came from Nahavandi to introduce a group of Tajik writers who were visiting the university. At that time the cold war was in full swing and relations between the USSR and Iran were strained, such that no one wished to introduce the writers to students and faculty. Since being acquainted with several of the Tajiks, especially Jalol Ikromi, head of the delegation, as well as general fear among the Iranians to be connected in any way with Soviet citizens because of Savak the secret police, Nahavandi persuaded me to be master of ceremonies. Ikromi gave a talk in the hall of the university, named after the late Pour Daoud, a distinguished scholar of Iranian languages, and afterwards asked if there were any questions. One faculty member raised his hand and timidly asked where Ikromi had learned Persian so well. His indignant reply that it was his native language, and also of the people of Tajikistan surprised the audience. Their knowledge of their neighbors was abysmal, for all eyes were directed to the West. It was necessary to explain that Tajiki was a dialect of Persian but, contrary to popular belief, Pushtu was a separate Iranian language.

One of my tasks was to teach about the areas of Central Asia and the Caucasus, where Iranian peoples had lived and remnants still existed. Later, when teaching in Dushanbe, Tajik students, on the whole, knew much about Russian history and literature, but little about the past of Afghanistan and Iran.

At Harvard new students brought up a new field of endeavor. Folklore flourished; Margaret Mills had returned from Herat with much material for her thesis, while Mahasti Ziai was concerned with Persian folklore, and helped to establishe a center of folklore in Tehran. An attempt to secure an endowment for a professorship in Iranian folklore, by Qotbi, head of television in Iran, was thwarted by the administration which tried to have him give money only for the teaching of Persian. This he would not do and the project collapsed. Also interest in religion blossomed and Laal Jamzadeh, a Persian Zoroastrian, enrolled to study this field. In general. Interest in Iran again flourished, and more work seemed an appropriate answer to domestic problems.

Returning late in 1974, the only college open for Jeff was the University of Massachusetts in Amherst, where the Harvard faculty had advised in the establishment of a small department of Near Eastern Studies. Another project which occupied the interest and time of Harvard professors was the establishment of a new university in the Caspian area called Reza Shah Kabir University. This necessitated additional trips to Iran, acting as a guide for the administrators from the USA. It was amusing to accompany newcomers into the bazaar in Isfahan, where the aggressive sales actions of the local folk, well-known for their abilities throughout Iran, intimidated the foreigners. One of the group found an English language book he had been seeking for years and began to bargain, as he had been advised to do. When it seemed that the seller would not come below a price equivalent to 120 dollars, the American said he would think about it over in the night, and maybe return in the morning. The Isfahani was up to that stratagem, and said tomorrow was a holiday of the birthday of Fatima and his shop would not be open. Not wishing to lose the book in spite of a price he hesitated to pay, the declaration persuaded him to give the asking price. The next morning as he came down the stairs of the hotel, he remarked that everything must be closed because of the holiday of the birth of Fatima. The desk clerk in surprise answered, "Who is Fatima? Today is no holiday." After the revolution everyone knew about Fatima, daughter of the prophet, and her birthday was a holiday.

The difference between the bazaar of Isfahan and Shiraz was striking, for the merchants of the latter were noted for their indifference and even laziness in contrast to the Isfahanis. Various cities in Iran had characteristic reputations, and the Reshtis from the Caspian coast were regarded as obtuse and the butt of jokes, somewhat like the reputation of radio Erivan in the Soviet Union. The Turks of Azerbaijan were regarded as dull, but they upheld their reputation as good soldiers in the army and gendarmerie. The spread of Turkic speakers at the expense of spoken Persian was especially noteworthy in villages to the west of Tehran. A similar phenomenon could be observed in Pakistan, in areas of overlapping languages, where Baluchi was spreading at the expense of Pushtu. The reason probably was the far simpler grammar and phonology of the former.

Every morning at the chapel of Harvard university a fifteen minute mini-service was held at which a professor would deliver a five minute sermon. Several times a semester I had tried to deliver words of inspiration and comfort to students and faculty who attended, but with life somewhat in limbo I decided to dispense with the pablum usually heard there. Instead I offered the following advice to students, "you study the sciences in order to learn how to control nature, and you study the social sciences and even the humanities in order to learn how to control people, why do you study religion, or come here? It is to learn how to die." That was the last time an invitation was given to speak in the chapel.

In the spring of 1974 the divorce became final and we went our separate ways. If an application to become professor at Göttingen had been successful, visions of a permanent move to Europe and marriage to a German girl friend, or even Britta in Sweden , who was divorced, might have been realized. Since that did not happen, and not happy living alone, instead search for a wife in America began. It did not last long, for engagement to an Assyrian young lady, born in Iran, who was working on her PhD in Uzbek-Tajik literature at Columbia was proposed in the fall of 1974. Very different from Barbara, Eden Naby was strong willed and practical, and incidentally not in favor of popular religious cults in America, since she was the daughter of a Presbyterian minister in Philadelphia. A new phase of life was to begin at the age of fifty-five.

CHAPTER 26

Japanese Idyll

AT THE instigation of Professor Minobu Honda an invitation came to spend a month in Japan, which was not only unexpected but most welcome at this time, for it gave me an opportunity to slow down and reflect about the future. January 1975 opened a new world, and I wanted to speculate about the shape of things to come.

On Christmas eve 1974, aboard an almost empty Japan Airlines jumbo jet, several cups of *sake* brought on sleep which ended by landing in Honolulu. Since the plane was only continuing on Christmas day, a hotel had to be found to spend the night. Every vacation or resort hotel was full to overflowing, so only a small but clean and well-ordered Japanese hotel on the mall in the center of town had a last room for a mere $7.00 a night, a surprisingly low price for Hawaii even then. Tokyo was to prove quite different.

Japan even more than Germany had a special fascination for me, since both countries had been studied during the late war, and the order and discipline, combined with a certain harshness in both of them, had held a special attraction. The seemingly great difference in temperament between the individualistic Chinese and the socially minded Japanese called for explanation, and now was a chance to investigate it.

The combination of East and West in Tokyo appeared unique, for other cities may have an old or Oriental part and a new Westernized area, but here they exist together and yet not homogenized. The first night was spent in a completely modern hotel room near the airport, but ever afterwards only in Japanese *ryokans* or inns. The room at Atami-so *ryokan* in downtown Tokyo revealed the delight of the Japanese in small touches, which raised the pedestrian to something beyond the ordinary. The small space of the room was divided by sliding opaque paper covered doors into three parts, a modern bathroom, a bedroom with no bed, but in a closet bed clothes and a futon for the floor, and the third part a living room with a low table, cushions and TV, plus a garden of small stones a meter square. The last changed the room into a residence, where one could rest and contemplate while drinking green tea. The Japanese penchant for tasteful arrangements seemed to be universal, for everywhere the same meticulous attention to detail, with meals, flowers, decorations, packaging or whatever. The Japanese businessman in London styled suits and briefcases would come home, remove his shoes and outer clothes, put on a kimono and sandals and perform an ancient tea ceremony.

Although on several occasions Japanese friends complained that they borrowed much but always Japanized what they adopted, it appeared otherwise to me on several occasions. An Italian restaurant in Tokyo, for example, could have been in Naples so authentic was it, but mostly frequented by Japanese rather than foreigners. The beer fed cattle produced the most tender beef I have ever eaten. In my opinion more than all others, the Japanese keep the two worlds, their own and the outside, quite apart, even though they exist side by side. On the other hand, there were signs that even this separation was breaking down, and I wondered how long the old and the new could be kept so well distinct, with the Japanese changing from one to the other so deftly. But there appeared a down side to the preservation of the past, which was making simply a repository out of popular old fashions and objects.

Already traditional arts and crafts were pricing themselves out of existence, for ordinary kimonos easily cost six or seven hundred dollars, and were almost museum pieces, to be used, if at all, only once or twice a year. Old palaces and temples too were presented as dead and lifeless, since they were empty of objects, which had been removed to museums. Mass produced objects and new gadgets filled the stores, and the disappearance of small shops and restaurants was happening at a fast pace. The many one room restaurants in Kyoto, with seating space for only half a dozen, were doomed to extinction. Did the young really appreciate what their ancestors had wrought, or were they so 'modern' that old traditions seemed out of place, to be endured but hardly honored?

Another face of Japan was revealed when Honda and I visited the Mikazuki collection of antiques from Iran, including forgeries, in a private gallery fully as pretentious as any in Paris or London. The collector, a cool, reserved and completely correct individual was feared by Honda for the influence and power he wielded behind the scenes. Such people brought us into war, claimed my friend, an admission out of character with the close-lipped Japanese. Iranians were different in their criticism of their own country, as expressed by one of their diplomats in Tokyo. In the Iranian bureaucracy one cannot be fired for doing nothing, but only for doing something, rocking the boat in which his indolent colleagues sit. In activist oriented Japan, on the contrary, incompetence is a cause for firing, which, however, rarely happens, but in attempting an innovation if one makes a mistake, his colleagues rally to protect him, as in a family. The innovator in Iran is a threat to the system and should be discouraged, for maintenance of the status quo is the aim of those in power. Young Iranians are bitterly aware of this and want to change, but the establishment knows that the way to handle innovators is to buy them, corrupt them and render them impotent. This is why many leaders in Iran, who were once members of the Tudeh party, later were co-opted and brought into the government. To our surprise such sentiments came from an Iranian in government service in Tokyo.

At Nagoya the massive castle belied the Japanese style of the diminutive, while the boat ride on Ise bay revealed beautiful vistas of traditional landscape scenes, as found in old Japanese scrolls. Without the help of Professor Eiji Mano, who had visited me in Shiraz, many fascinating sights, such as Mikimoto's island of cultured pearls, would have been missed. Kyoto, where Koji Kamioka joined Eiji Mano, was a treat, from the moss garden of Kokedera to the silver and gold of the Ryoanji temples, and the royal Katsura villa, each with large and small stones arranged to make a garden. Was the permanence and strength of stones the reason why the Japanese favored them in their gardens? Here simplicity was the key word to a very sophisticated culture, where a single scroll on a barren wall enormously enhanced the wall. Even in food the principle of simplicity, or one dish only after another is finished, was maintained, unlike the Chinese who heap various foods or sauces on their rice bowls, while the combination, sweet and sour pork together, would hardly conform to Japanese tastes. I hoped that such differences would be maintained against the leveling wave influences of globalization.

Japanese gardens were impressive, but the royal Shugaku-in, with three levels, like terraces, surpasssed all of the others. With a traditional bridge at the small lake on the top level, one had a splendid view of Kyoto. Incidentally, at that time, only foreign tourists were allowed inside the royal gardens, so my friends had to wait outside. The most impressive experience in Japan, however, was the annual tea ceremony of the Muro sect of Shinto in old Kyoto which lasted almost three hours. Koji and I took off our shoes and, without usual slippers, signed a book with brush and black ink, whereupon, after much bowing, sat on the floor of a small room for twenty minutes contemplating the calligraphy on the wall. In the next room, which we reached crawling on our knees, a pot, chop sticks and a few characters on the wall, written by a former emperor, were admired, not because of their beauty, but because of distinguished former users of the objects. Then we passed into another room to drink bitter green tea and eat small cakes, but this was not the real ceremony. We passed into another and larger room which was filled by women in their elegant kimonos and men in their Sunday best. We all sat or rather knelt with our knees extended and legs bent back under us in the old Persian manner.

The master of the sect entered with several young monks in kimonos, and knelt in front of the middle of one wall, in the floor of which room was a square hole with a pot of boiling water over the fire in it. He carefully washed a beautiful lacquered bowl with a gold interior, with flourishes three times, drying the bowl with a purple cloth, unfolded in a traditional way. With great ceremony he measured spoonfulls of green tea powder in a silver ladle into the lacquer bowl, adding water in a similar fashion. With a bamboo whisk brush he stirred the tea into a froth, and an assistant brought the bowl to the first person on his right, who turned it slowly three times while admiring it. After sipping the tea three times and wiping the rim with special small cloths, the bowl was passed to the next person who followed the same procedure.

Each bowl had tea for only six people and the master again prepared the brew, which tasted like thick green pea soup, after which cakes came to counter the bitterness of the tea, all with great ceremony and care. Finally a flat bowl of sake was passed with usual small cloths to clean the rim. The ceremony being at an end, the forty or so people went into another room to be served dried fish, cake and soup, all in the exquisite manner typical of Japanese food. It had been a memorable experience.

The last evening in Kyoto was notable for two events, first, meeting a real geisha, who was persuaded to give me the sheath of wheat from her hair, and then a talk with the son of distinguished history Professor Haneda. His only son had not finished college but had gone to Iran where, after five years he returned home with a pregnant Iranian wife. She was only nineteen, from Azerbaijan, and had not finished high school. After fourteen months in Japan she still could not communicate with his family, who were much distraught by the affair. At the request of the elder Haneda I talked to the girl, and my first advice was to begin to learn Japanese, or at least English, if the former proved too difficult. She objected, saying the newly born baby girl occupied all of her time. I suggested to Koji that he should appoint the boy his assistant in Tokyo, so he would be away from his family, which did happen. Since he spoke fluent Persian but had no academic training in the subject, I further recommended that the young man seek a scholarship in the USA or Europe, to at least raise his standing with his father. If he remained in Japan I feared the breach between the generations could not be mended.

Nara restored my faith in the practicing, as well as preservation, of old traditions in Japan. The deer park and museum were fascinating, as was the university and library of the Tenri sect, founded by a woman a century ago, similar to Mary Baker Eddy and Christian Science. The head monk of the Todaiji shrine, with the Daibutsuden, the largest known bronze statue of the sitting Buddha, Dr. Morimoto, the monk, was also lecturer in Arabic at Kyoto University. He had studied the language in Cairo, but was famous for his recitation of Buddhist sutras, which had been recorded commercially. In the Nara temples, Horyuji, Toshodaiji and Yakushiji, worshippers were active with candles and incense, giving the impression of a more religious populace than in Tokyo or even Kyoto.

Osaka, the Chicago of Japan, had the most impressive castle in the country, a much used locale for motion pictures of old Japan. A dinner with Jay Gluck, near Kobe, in his large house filled with antiquities, confirmed the suspicions of Nahavandi that Jay was a dealer. The puppet theater or *bunraku* of Osaka was justly famous for its performances, and has been described many times by travelers to Japan.

A boat trip on the Inland Sea to Beppu was memorable for the scenery depicted in old Japanese prints. In Fukuoka, or Hakata , as it was previously called, the *ryokan* was heated by an electric light bulb under the quilt covered table, just like the *sandali* in war time Kabul. From Kyushu University came Okazaki, an archaeologist who had visited Xinjiang and Iran, and at the present was excavating the fortifications built by the Japanese against the invasion of Kublai Khan's Mongol army. He assured me that it was a typhoon, rather than Japanese samurai, which had defeated the Mongols, contrary to some Japanese history textbooks, which also neglected to mention the dominant role of Koreans in the Mongol army.

The flight from almost tropical Kyushu to Sapporo in Hokkaido was like going from Rome to Stockholm in winter. Professor Honda was my host again, and he showed me his enormous collection of photographs of Ismaili castles in Iran, which he and his students had made on summer trips to Iran. At a natural question, he replied he had no idea what he would do with the huge collection. Everywhere the penchant of the Japanese for details was revealed, the trees rather than the forest. I have not read Ruth Benedict's book on Japan, *The Chrysanthemum and the Sword*, but the symbolism of the two would be a good characterization of Japanese society. On the other hand Japanese scholars of the Orient are curious about everything in the world, whereas their Chinese counterparts are mainly interested in China. The level of literacy and education is probably the highest in the world, yet they rightly regard China as the source of their culture and civilization. China is now beginning to match and perhaps soon surpass Japan in all fields of material development.

The continued use of Chinese hieroglyphs by the Japanese is probably similar to the arrogance of the scribes in the ancient Near East, who sought to keep the art of reading and writing within their own circles. Anyone who has spent hours and hours memorizing Chinese characters has a sense of accomplishment inaccessible to those unable or unwilling to devote much time and effort to such memorization.

What is presented here is absolutely not based on any study of Japan or long residence there, but rather always on strictly personal impressions, based on comparisons from a Near Eastern background. Some Americans in Japan were critical of my views with admiration of things Japanese, expressed in several articles, published locally. Nonetheless I am sure different people have different impressions and experiences, and all that can be done here is to report what I saw and how I felt.

After the endless toasts with the salutatory word *kampai,* and the spell of the Japanese land and people, Thailand seemed a modest contrast, although as everyone who has been there, it is a fascinating land. It was only a brief stop to meet Eden's brother, Dante and Aun, his Thai wife, with four year old daughter, Dang, who was completely shy or frightened of the strange western adult who had appeared. The Thais appeared to me very relaxed in comparison with Japanese.

The trip continued to Pakistan, where I gave lectures in Islamabad, Lahore and Karachi. Noteworthy was the separation of male and female students at the universities by a curtain between them. The speaker from the dais had to turn his head first to the left and then to the right, with the curtain before his face. In general everyone was interested in talks about Iran and Central Asia, but when I described the Arab conqueror of Sind, Muhammad ibn Qasim al-Thaqafi as a rough soldier concerned with booty rather than a saint, as the locals considered him, strong objections were heard.

An interesting discussion with a brilliant lawyer in Karachi, A.K. Brohi, revealed a split in allegiances between intellectuals and the common folk. Brohi saw Indians as close relatives, which they were in culture, while Afghans and Persians were strangers, with little in common with Pakistanis. The religious common folk, however, claimed Persians and Afghans as brothers, while Indians were idol-worshipping foreigners. The difference in attitude between the secular upper classes in the Islamic world and the religious masses is perhaps one of the most pressing problems in that part of the world for the future. On the other hand, among some of the secular and educated elites, the native inhabitants of ancient Pakistan, with sites such as Mohenjo-Daro and Harappa, were considered their ancestors, while the Aryan invaders they regarded as terrible destroyers of culture, which they probably were. The Arabs really fell into the latter category. How long such an attitude would last, however, especially among the younger people, is questionable.

With honoraria from the lectures it was necessary to open an account in a Habib Bank in Karachi before leaving the country, since money could not be taken from the country, so this left me with bank accounts in Moscow, Karachi and Tehran. The next leg of the itinerary was to Tehran where I felt back home, but was unable to remain for only a few days, and to learn that a Zoroastrian, Farhang Mehr, had become the head of Pahlavi University. I arranged with him to return in the following year to teach at the university, much to the astonishment of Mahyar Nawabi, the new head of the Asia Institute. It was customary that once a director left his post in Iran, either he is advanced or he leaves permanently. So my willingness to accept a minor post was viewed with considerable astonishment. My new book *The Golden Age of Persia* had not reached Iran, but it was to create strong opposition among many intellectuals in 1977 after I returned to Iran.

CHAPTER 27

Wives and Children

The female of the species is more deadly than the male.
—R. Kipling

LITTLE did I realize the difficulties which might arise between a new wife and children from a previous marriage, especially if they were of teen age. Being a middle man is always problematic, but the strain on a person who is called upon to choose one side and reject the other, bears witness to the unwillingness or inability of each to accept a shared role. Eden was the daughter of an Assyrian couple from Urmiya and her father was a retired Presbyterian minister. We were married by a Nestorian priest on April5, 1975 in Philadelphia. She was thirty-three and I fifty-five, and the difference of twenty-two years in age caused considerable hesitation, but in the end we decided to try living together.

After a short honeymoon, a longer one was planned for a trip to Shiraz for the summer. From the start a problem appeared in the inability of Barbara to take care of Bobby, who was fifteen years old. He was skipping school, and not responding to any requests or orders. After consultation with a psychiatrist we decided to take him to Shiraz, where the change might change his attitude, and he could enroll in the international school there. Eden went with him ahead of me, since several tasks needed to be done at Harvard university, while she, alone with him, hoped to convince him of the need to heed adults.

The novelty of a new country at first calmed Bob, especially as he took driving lessons in an old Toyota land cruiser, which I had bought from an American archaeologist, and in spite of many kilometers it did function. Once, on the way to school, Bob ran into a Mercedes, driven by a leading religious leader of the city, and both adults had to go to the police, while he continued to school. The chief of police was surprised to see two reputable persons, saying, "what can I do mediating between a professor and an *ayatallah*?" The latter had insurance coverage and declined to pursue the case, and we parted friends.

Relations between Eden and Bob worsened, so much that he had to be sent home in January 1976, while my commitments obliged me to remain.

Pressures to choose between my new wife and children made life almost unbearable, for not wishing to offend or hurt either party, I was appreciated by no one. Eden taught in the university both history and English, while I lectured at the Asia Institute, now removed from the Naranjestan. It had become the linguistics department of the university, and had eliminated its concern with art and archaeology. In addition I also accepted a position as adviser to Shafa's Pahlavi library in Tehran, where a former student from Hamburg, Monika Dahnke, was working.

With Farhang Mehr, the new chancellor of the university in Shiraz, came some insights into Zoroastrians in Iran. For example, at a dinner given in honor of a Parsi medical doctor from Bombay, a chic lady from Shemiran happened to sit next to him, and after a few pleasantries remarked, with a note of disdain or even disgust in her voice, "is it true that you people expose cadavers to be eaten by vultures?" The doctor turned to her and in a clipped English accent replied, "madam prefers worms?" The reason for her question was the banning of such practices in Iran by the Shah. It seems a French journalist had written about the Zoroastrian practice, and many sophisticated Iranians had persuaded the ruler to ban the exposure of bodies in the elevated, enclosed areas called *dakhma*s. The ban, however, made no sense, since the Zoroastrians in Iran had not been able to follow this procedure for several years. The truth was that vultures had vanished, or flown to the east, since their steady diet of dead horses, camels and other animals had suffered, because of the reduction in numbers of the beasts of burden in the desert. After all the birds could not eat cars and tractors. There were too few Zoroastrians as well. In India, especially in Bombay, *dakhmas* still were put into use, but even there both protests from neighbors and the decline in vultures caused problems.

My book, *The Golden Age of Persia: the Arabs in the East* stirred up much controversy in the press, and one paper declared that the author should be expelled from Iran and not allowed to return. How could a specialist on ancient history ignore the Achaemenids and Sasanians, or even fail to realize that the era of the Safavids in the sixteenth and seventeenth centuries was the golden age of Iran, while the invasion of Arabs was a dark period? It was in vain trying to defend the new thesis, by saying that, against a previous position, I was forced to admit that the remarkable flowering of culture and learning in the pre-Mongol period in Iran was indeed that period when Iran gave an international character to the developing Islamic civilization. It had begun as a society and culture bound to narrow Arab mores and outlooks, but Iranian and Central Asian scholars had expanded Islam onto the world stage as never before, and it became clothed in the mantle of a world religion and culture. Needless to say, the only people who were pleased with this position were the religious leaders and their followers, even though I had by no means sought to gain favor with them.

Feeling in the dog house, only the support of the bazaar and common folk of Shiraz raised spirits, for the course of events easily could have been forseen. Only the inhabitants of Shemiran, Americans, and other foreigners did not see the writing on the wall. The need to conciliate the population of Shiraz, tired of the excesses of the *avantguardists* in their festival of arts, finally came home to the organizers when they turned to local popular *Taziyeh* or 'passion plays,' in their repertoire. But it was too late; economic conditions had deteriorated, and several events brought people onto the streets. A cinema in Khuzistan had burned with the audience inside since the doors had been locked, and the secret police were blamed for this act, although there was no evidence for this. Suppression of demonstrations, which resulted in deaths, was followed by even larger gatherings after the usual forty days of mourning.

The events snowballed while Eden and I investigated Sasanian inscriptions and ruins in Fars province with an anthropologist Sikander Amanolahi, a Lur from Khorramabad and his wife Lilie. We came to know Fars better than our home town areas. Even as the storm was gathering, the time spent in Shiraz was fascinating and invigorating.

We decided to take a trip to the Caucasus and Central Asia early in June, since Eden's studies for the doctorate in Columbia University had been on Uzbek and Tajik writers of the early Soviet period. On the overnight boat from Bandar Pahlavi to Baku, the only other passengers were a group of Afghans, but all attempts to speak with them were met with stony silence. From Baku we flew to Ashkabad and then to Tashkent, on to Frunze (now Bishkek) and to Alma Ata. In the former we met an Armenian who helped us to see the sights, but the most interesting institute we visited was that of the Dungans, or Chinese Muslims, who edited a Chinese newspaper in Cyrillic script! This belied the Chinese assertion that Chinese characters could never be transformed into alphabetic script. The Chinese government was unhappy about such an institute, but could do nothing about refugee Muslims from their country. After the fall of the Soviet Union, however, they were able to twist the arms of the Kyrgyz rulers to clamp down on Dungan activities.

In Alma Ata we drank kumiss and saw the famous 'golden man,' an ancient prince of the Sakas or Scythians, whose tomb had been excavated in Issyk kurgan near the lake. The tall, elaborate headdress, and the gold accouterments on his clothes, had been well preserved, so that a good model of what the original had been was possible to reconstruct. Kazakh scholars seemed better acquainted with European scholarship than their Kyrgyz counterparts, but this may have been the result of greater resources in Kazakhstan as contrasted with Kyrgyzia. The farther we went from Iran the differences in culture, between those with a nomadic heritage and settled folk, became greater. Frunze, but especially Alma Ata, was in a different world than the Uzbeks and Tajiks, who owed so much to their Iranian backgrounds.

At the end of summer, on the way home, we again went the same way as before, to board the boat to Baku, and lo the same Afghans were there. This time in surprise they laughed and talked to us, believing we were in the same business of trading as they. And what were they bringing to Moscow? They had started from northern Afghanistan with karakul furs which they brought to Tehran to sell. Then they bought panty hose and luxuries for the Russian market, which they sold in Moscow, and bought industrial diamonds to bring to Germany. The next goal of the journey was Stuttgart where they sold the diamonds and bought Mercedes Benz cars, which they drove to Tehran and sold them there, because of the great demand in Iran for that make of car. After their long trip back to Afghanistan they obtained more karakul skins and set out on the same journey. In the morning at the customs in Baku it was clear that the Afghans had an arrangement with the Azeri officials to expedite their passage. They were only following an age old tradition in that part of the world, to trade where the highest rewards were to be found, even if it meant long distances and much trouble.

The next year we went back overland, through Erivan and Tiflis, this time staying with an Assyrian family in a village near the capital, for many Assyrians had migrated to Armenia before World War I, and during the late war as well. Eden became interested in Assyrian matters, and prepared several articles about her compatriots in the USSR. Tbilisi or Tiflis was a lovely city in a green flourishing countryside, and Georgian scholars, such as Konstantin Tsereteli, a Semitist and specialist in modern Assyrian, were especially cordial and happy to meet American colleagues. In the post office we noticed a large bust of Stalin, the only place in the USSR where his memory was revered. The wine, but especially champagne, was a surprise and unexpectedly good, and the food was also better than elsewhere in the Soviet Union.

In a fit of daring we bought bus tickets to go over the mountains to Orzhonikidze, soon to be re-named Vladikavkaz, for the officials in the Tiflis Intourist hotel would never approve. The Georgian military highway was spectacular in its twists and turns on a narrow road over the Caucasus. Near the top with small stones, letters had been formed in Russian, saying 'long live the great Stalin.' In north Ossetia the local people were surprised but pleased to see Americans, and we had two days of pleasant discussions and sightseeing until ordered back to Tiflis by the local police, at the request of their colleagues in the Georgian capital.

It took much calming, and disclaimers of any ulterior motives, before the Tiflis police were satisfied. My argument was the need to see the Iranian speakers of the Caucasus since, after all, I was an Iranist. The Georgian police were happy to see us leave. We flew to Moscow forgetting my passport in the Tiflis hotel, but the efficiency of the Soviets, when any official business with a foreigner was concerned, was remarkable, for the next day the passport arrived, shortly before leaving Moscow for home.

Later, after returning to Iran, a *noruz* (new year's day, 21 March) trip from Shiraz to Kabul was a memorable experience. The Toyota land cruiser, which Eden dubbed *bishe Satana* 'wiles of satan' in her language, reminded me of a ditty in Persian:
"in mashin-e Hajj Mohammed Khan, ne rol darad ne roghan, miravad fakat ba komak-e Ya 'Ali, 'This is the car of Hajji Moh. Khan which has neither steering wheel nor oil, and only runs with the aid of (a cry, help us) oh 'Ali!' It had an old Chevrolet carburetor, and odds and ends cannibalized from various sources, yet it actually ran. Since Eden had been in the Peace Corps in Afghanistan, she was looking forward to a return to her former haunts during spring vacation at the local university.

Becky had returned to Shiraz, and with her friend Prudence, at that time in Shiraz, wanted to go to Pakistan and possibly India, since Jeff had regaled them with stories of his experiences there and in Katmandu. So four of us crowded into the car and started east over a dusty and bumpy road. On a desolate spot beyond Neyriz we encountered a young American couple who
had been hitchhiking across Iran and were on their way to Bandar 'Abbas. They had been waiting since early morning for a ride but no car appeared and they were at the end of their rope. Somehow we loaded them on to the land cruiser, which now had six people plus luggage. It was getting dark so we stopped at a tea house to spend the night sleeping on the floor. The next day when we reached the road from Kerman to Bandar 'Abbas they left us with a hope to find a ride south. The next night we slept in a field to the east of Mahan and had to drink vodka and sleep almost on top of one another to keep warm. The next night was a

happy change in the lowlands of Baluchistan where we slept in a dry qanat. Early in the morning a caravan of camels passed and the leader called to us, "What are you doing there?" I simply answered "We are sleeping," which satisfied them that we were not bandits and continued on their way.

The road had not improved since 1952 but fortunately we had no problems with the car. The food we had brought with us was exhausted and there was no sign of habitation in this desolate southern end of the Dasht-e Lut. No moving sands were encountered, but the road became a trail and I wondered if Baluchistan would ever be integrated into the rest of Iran. Again I was proved wrong, for later modern technology and communication promoted the importance of this sparsely inhabited land as a transit route to the sea from Central Asia and Afghanistan.

Almost miraculously we reached Zahedan without mishap, where food and shelter was found, and the girls continued east by train, while Eden and I turned north.

The car now began to cause trouble, first with a hole in the radiator through which the water leaked. In desperation we used our drinking water, and then urine, alone in the empty desert. Fortunately, at wits end, the car brought us in spurts to a camp of Greek road builders who were able to fix the radiator. Then in forgetfulness of the dangers of the rainy season, streams over the road caused not only delays, but on two occasions a tractor had to pull us through the water. On this little traveled road, trucks and cars were in the same situation, so we felt a companionship with other drivers. As I was the sole driver, the trip was beginning to wear on my energy and nerves, especially since we encountered snow after reaching Turbat-e Haidari. Just like the old Land Rover in Baluchistan, this car also would only start if rolled down a hill, so at night we always had to park on an elevation. The car obviously needed much work, so after being towed the last few miles to Meshhed we had to leave it to be fixed, and go by bus to Herat, for we both were going to give talks in Kabul and had to reach there within three days.

In Herat, late at night we roused the head of a new government hotel; there was no heat in the hotel and snow was everywhere, and it was too cold to sleep without some warmth. On asking for some heat to be provided by a stove in a room, the answer was that by government order no heating was to be provided after *noruz*. As reason could not prevail, warmth trumped over any comfort in privacy, so we left the hotel and in town were permitted to spread our sacks on the floor of an already crowded area in a dirty tea house.

Shades of Tiflis, we forgot to ask for our passports from the tea house owner when leaving on a bus for Kabul, and the Afghans were not as efficient as the Soviets in recovering them. In Kandahar the bus stopped for the night in a miserable garage with bedbugs in the *charpoys,* but again our sacks saved us from their onslaughts. The stench in the place, however, kept us awake, and the bus departed early in the morning.

Kabul was a real haven after the miserable bus trip, and our short time there was one of reunion with friends, Louis and Nancy Dupree, Max and Deborah Klimburg, and others. Little did we know that the following year Daud Khan, who had overthrown his cousin Zahir Shah, would be killed in a Communist led *coup d'état.* After a breath taking experience on a small airplane, which had to return to Kabul on meeting a storm in the mountains, shades of a former trip, we finally were able to fly to Herat. Then we went by bus to Meshhed, where the car was sufficiently repaired to bring us to Tehran and Shiraz. After this trip it was clear we should take no more chances with the car on long distances, but keep to local driving. Political events, however, were to change much in our lives.

CHAPTER 28

Revolutions in Iran and Afghanistan

PERSONAL affairs were taking front stage just when momentous events were transforming Afghanistan and Iran. When changes in one's life demand attention, larger pictures recede into the background. To indicate that family matters were always in mind, a brief mention of them may not be amiss, before turning to the theater overseas where history was being made.

In 1977 Jeff, who had graduated from college and started graduate school at Harvard in archaeology, gave up his field work in Saudi Arabia to go to India where he became first a Buddhist and later back in the States an American Sikh practicing yoga. He took the name Satpurkha, with, as all American Sikhs, the surname Khalsa. Barbara became involved with the Sikhs too, and for a time brought Becky into the circle. Britta's daughter Susanne came to attend the University of Massachusetts with Becky, and Bob continued in high school in calmer conditions, living with his mother. I tried to maintain relations with everyone, which was a most difficult task. Shortly, however, international events occupied our attention.

In Afghanistan the Communist party, divided into two branches Khalq and Parcham, in a *coup d'ètat* seized power and killed the ruler President Daud, his family and close followers. Since at the Kushan Studies congress in Dushanbe, Kabul had been designated as the international center for such Studies, in order to obtain recognition in the scholarly world, the new government organized an international congress on the subject in

November 1978. As a sign of the importance of such a meeting, and in a desire to exalt notable past events in the history of the country, Nur Mohammed Taraqi, head of the Khalq, and president of the country, was active in speaking to the delegates, and from the Afghan point of view the congress was a success. At least it seemed to give cultural legitimacy to the new government. The Afghans began to write about their ancestors the Kushans who had established a brilliant empire in Afghanistan and northwest India two millennia previously.

The scholarly purpose of the congress was to affirm a pre-Islamic identity for all of the people of Afghanistan, comparable to the Cyrus celebration of 2500 years in Shiraz. The Afghans now had a symbol comparable to that of the Persians, and the government wanted to show foreigners the progress made in the country under the new regime. They arranged expeditions to the archaeological sites of Hadda and Begram, the former of which was later completely destroyed. At the resort area of Istalif, a demonstration of support for the regime by the local people was replete with red banners and shouts of praise for the new leader. A local parade was also organized. One was reminded of the parades on a much larger scale in Russia in celebration of the October Revolution. As in the Soviet Union, all foreigners had guides assigned to them, and we travelled as a group of VIPs with a motorcycle escort. Also, as in Russia, local people were very up tight in talking to foreigners. A night curfew existed, which made visits to friends in the capital difficult, and every Afghan appeared nervous and uncertain about his future.

Soviet style buildings were going up in neighborhoods of Kabul, called micro-rayons, after the practice of their northern neighbors. Uzbeks and Tajiks from the USSR had arrived in numbers to teach the Afghans how to turn their country into a Communist state. One Uzbek, Osman, whom I had met in Tashkent, now had an office in the Ministry of Education, and was busy directing a revision of textbooks in all languages of the country, including an attempt to write the hitherto only oral Nuristani tongue.

The high point of the congress was the arrival of Soviet archaeologist Viktor Sarinidi from his excavation of Tilla Tepe in the north of Afghanistan with a wealth of gold objects found in tombs. Later he published a book on the remarkable finds, *The Gold of Bactria*, which was translated into a number of languages. I joked with the Soviet visitors that they had a penchant for finding gold objects in excavations while other archaeologists did not have that gift. The attention of all at the congress had been diverted from political or propagandistic concerns to the remarkable discovery.

It seemed to most delegates that the minions of the Soviets were in firm control, and Afghanistan would fall behind the 'Iron Curtain,' if it were already not there. Central Asians, sent by Moscow to Afghanistan, were happy to leave their homeland, and considered their work in Afghanistan a distinct service to disadvantaged neighbors. On the other hand, reaction to the entry of such people from the north was received with mixed feelings by the Afghans. The two factions of the party, the more intellectual emphasis of Parcham, and more pragmatic of Khalq, already showed signs of disagreement in rule. Some Afghans had fled to Pakistan to organize opposition to the government and soon many more were to follow.

On a trip to Peshawar at this time I met four of the leaders of the parties forming the *mujahideen* to fight against the Khalq take over. The Tajik Rabbani, a teacher, was the most unassuming; Mojaddedi was a religious leader whose family had been from Central Asia; Gailani owned an automobile dealership and was secular minded even though of a religious background, while Gulbedin Hikmatyar was a silver-tongued orator, a rabble rouser, according to his enemies. These were the leaders of the four main groups of 'freedom fighters.' After talking to all of them, I thought Hikmatyar would be the most successful because of his dedication and persuasive qualities, but his emotional and fundamentalist views repelled many at that time. At first the outside world paid little attention to these 'politicians' in a refugee situation. There were others, but the four groups, as they should be designated rather than parties, were busy enlisting support among the Afghans, as well as Pathans in Pakistan in resistance to the new Communist government in Kabul. While this year had been momentous for Afghanistan, in its neighbor to the west calm had not prevailed.

Back in Iran unrest was spreading, and we were still involved with the university, but when Eden and I returned to Iran in the summer of 1978 it was apparent that rats were abandoning the sinking ship. Shafa had left for a summer vacation in his home on the Riviera, and the workers in the library were at a loss for want of directions. Pahlbod, brother-in-law of the Shah, and head of the Ministry of Arts and Culture, also was gone, reportedly having taken the budget of his ministry with him. In any case, government workers were not paid, and tension was apparent everywhere. Yet the general feeling was that the army and police would uphold the rule of the Shah. Many signs of 'Americans go home' appeared on walls, for the close relationship of the US government with the Shah had strengthened the old Iranian belief that foreigners were to blame for ills in their country. In Shiraz we felt no animosity, since Persian friends had heard me more than once criticize American behavior in the country, but we were unsure of reception in other places. There were demonstrations everywhere and the populace obviously was aroused. We left in September with foreboding about the future.

After the congress in Afghanistan I returned to Iran in December 1978. Chaos was rampant and it was clear that Khomeini would soon return to the country, while the Shah had lost the confidence of much of the military. The events of the revolution are well documented, and there is no need to repeat them here. I realized that my services were over and it was time to leave, but the only airplanes flying into Tehran in January 1979 were those of the Soviet Aeroflot. Bus and trains were non-functioning, and schedules were non-existent, so a trip to Moscow was the only quick way out of the country. It was not so quick, however, and took some time to obtain a seat on a plane. In Moscow everyone was interested in events in Iran, and the information any one could impart. At dinner one evening in the hotel restaurant the only available chair was at a table with three Russian engineers. After all had become somewhat inebriated, I could not resist a light remark. "It is a pity you will never become communists." In disbelief they retorted, "so you are a provocateur." My reply was, "No, no, didn't Marx say everyone should give according to his ability and take according to his needs, and that the state would wither away? That cannot happen on earth but only in heaven with angels, not among humans." They laughed and agreed, but I continued, "there is another way one could approach communism, but you still won't make it, nor will Americans, Chinese, or others. Only the Japanese, and far behind them the Germans, can do this- with strict discipline." We parted friends.

It was with sadness that return to Iran was now out of the question, but events in Afghanistan now occupied our interests. Taraqi had been murdered by his second in command, Hafizallah Amin, and some Parcham leaders had taken refuge in the USSR. The Russians, seeing their control in the country in danger, because of Amin's flirtation with the West, invaded the country and killed Amin, his family and associates.

Dan Rather of CBS came to Harvard to interview me about Iran, but at the suggestion that he should go to Afghanistan an adventurous cord was struck. He agreed to go, even though his boss forbade the 'million dollar man' from entering the country. Assurances from me that *mujahideen* would guide them, clinched the deal. Eden and I left for Peshawar with a film crew and Rather in December 1979.

My height of 6'3", blue eyes and fair skin, did not make a passable Afghan, so it was decided that Eden would act as interpreter for the group, and they would go in disguises to the outskirts of Jalalabad with several guides. My job was to remain behind and lure the Pakistani official, assigned to us, away from the group, so they could slip across the frontier. The first attempt failed, but on a Sunday we drove to a field beside the Kabul River to have a picnic. While food was being prepared by an Afghan servant brought from Peshawar, I asked the Pakistani officer to take me to Charsada, an archaeological site a few miles to the east. He was loathe to do so, but at my plea that I had come to Pakistan to see such sites, he agreed and we left with our car. Several *mujahideen* had been waiting for this time and appeared with a truck, on which the group mounted and changed into Afghan clothes. The servant was bribed to keep quiet and they left for the border, explaining they would return in a week the same way. When we returned from Charsada the Pakistani official realized what had happened, but, after complaining that this act reflected upon him and his job, we ate at the picnic site and returned to Peshawar. I had to explain what happened and exonerate the official who had accompanied us, but since everyone was sympathetic to the Afghans this lawless event was forgiven.

After a week passed, during which time contacts were made with various Afghans, and attendance at a rousing speech by Hikmatyar in the Friday mosque of Peshawar, worry about the fate of Eden and her companions grew. On the tenth day they straggled into Dean's Hotel and recounted their adventures, which have been related in short in Rather's book, *The Camera Never Blinks Twice*.

At the end of January 1980, after Rather and his crew had departed, Eden and I decided to return via Tehran, and fortunately the Iranian consul in Peshawar at that time was an acquaintance, so visas were easily obtained. Tehran was still in turmoil, for university students had seized the US embassy in November of the previous year. It was unclear what was to happen, since the new president, Bani-Sadr, was busy following the movements and activities of the Shah in the US, and Khomeini had not pronounced any decisions about the hostages. People we met on the streets were convinced that it would soon be over, since we had been allowed into the country, a sign of coming change. How wrong we all were!

In front of the university, and extending for blocks, were stalls with publications, leaflets, books, and tape cassettes, proclaiming messages from communism through socialism to fundamentalist Islam. Newspapers and booklets in Arabic, Kurdish, Armenian, Azeri Turkish, and even Baluchi, as well as European languages, were for sale, and the enthusiasm of young people was exhilarating. On the other hand, many friends had left the country, while others were fearful of the future. When we rode on an English double-decker bus past the US embassy students with rifles could be seen on the walls; we decided not to stop.

Since at that time we were engaged with the Afghan crisis, attempts to photograph anti-Soviet posters in the central post office brought a speedy arrest. After discussions the police were persuaded that we only wanted to show the solidarity of the people of Iran with the Afghan *mujahideen*, but a tense hour passed before we were permitted to leave with the film. Already signs on walls reading 'death to the great satan' were seen. Joking about this to older folk brought forth customary smiles, but younger people were serious and belligerent. Yet they did not threaten us, since they assumed we were in the country with the approval of authorities. Some air flights had resumed to Tehran, and we were able to leave on an Iran Air plane several weeks before the ill-fated American rescue mission in the desert, near the tea house of Pusht-e Badam, which we had visited in 1952. On leaving the question rose, when would we come back?

We returned home to find a number of organizations being organized to promote the freedom of Afghanistan from the Soviet embrace. In the Boston area our organization was called the 'Free Afghanistan Alliance'. Both Eden and I were busy with lectures, making posters, bumper stickers, badges, and supporting relief organizations who were helping the refugees pouring into Pakistan. This activity was to last until the Soviets withdrew.

In Iran the revolution followed the same path as the French and Russian revolutions, overthrow of the rulers, civil war, time of terror and finally success of the revolution. In Iran, however, there was a difference in that the time of terror was really a conflict not of individuals but of two groups- the religious leaders and the liberals, or even communist-socialists, mainly students. Just as Naopleon and Stalin issued from their revolutions, so Khomeini became the Iranian counterpart, and just as time brought the European cases back to normalcy, so eventually much the same happened in Iran. Yet our hearts went out to the poor people of Afghanistan and Iran.

CHAPTER 29

Free Afghanistan and Beyond

SOON occupation with foreign affairs reversed the former personal attention to historical or linguistic details of study. It is interesting how concentration on one problem or situation can dispel other concerns, possibly as a kind of defence mechanism. Personal affairs can take a back seat to world or national upheavals, and with two of them in our lands of special interest, one was able to turn to them and relegate private matters to the realm of inattention.

Common interest in the Soviet-Afghan war, for such it now was, kept Eden and me united in a common cause, free Afghanistan. Conferences in Stockholm, Paris and Washington kept the plight of the Afghans in our thoughts and actions. At a conference in Washington on Central Asia I shocked many by a suggestion that if I were Andropov, the Soviet premier, I would unite the Tajiks and Uzbeks with their brethren to the north and leave the Pushtuns to Pakistan. In spite of support for a free Afghanistan I thought the country would not return to the old domination by Pushtuns and it would be better to divide the country. At the same time I wrote a long article on Baluch intellectuals, and presented it at a State Department meeting in Washington, where much attention was devoted to Afghanistan and surrounding areas.

Unable to go to Iran, or Iraq because of the miserable government there, I turned my attention to other parts of the Middle East, where in June 1980 a conference on early Islam took place in Jerusalem. At that time enmity between the Arabs and Jews had not developed into the implacable hatred of later times. Arab scholars participated in discussions of common interest, but such cooperation had been true in the past, before the age of fanaticism forbade any cooperation.

In Iran Ayatallah Montazeri had been selected as successor to Khomeini when the latter should die, and many stories of his dullness circulated, such as the following. The statue of the poet Firdosi, in the square with his name, had been changed from a sitting to a standing figure. Several policemen who passed by one evening thought they heard a voice from the statue saying, "bring me a horse to ride." In fear they went to tell Montazeri, who accompanied them back to the statue. A voice was heard,"I said bring me a horse, not a jackass." Another tale was his attendance at the university, where Montazeri heard that various faculty members had MS, PhD, or other titles, at which he replied, " well my son has a BMW." The ability of the Persians to joke, even in grim circumstances, was not forgotten. Later Montazeri was deposed, when he expressed disapproval of excesses of the regime, and in his place a conservative cleric Khamenei took his place.

In 1980 retirement at the age of 66 was obligatory, but shortly afterward the age was moved to 70, which provided more time to plan for the legacy to leave to my successor. A conference in Damascus in April 1981, with outdoor lunches beside a stream, brought back memories of picnics in Iran and Afghanistan. Unfortunately lack of practice in Arabic proved embarrassing in trying to speak with locals.

The birth of Nels on May 9, 1981 also brought a new vista into home matters, for it was necessary to move out of the Boston area and search for a house somewhere between the University of Massachusetts, where Eden at that time was teaching, and the University of Connecticut, which was showing an interest in establishing a Near Eastern program. Many days of searching yielded no results, for Eden was determined to have considerable land with a house, unlike crowded city houses with small yards. Finally we bought a wooded area of fifteen acres in Leverett, Mass., and hired an architect to build an underground house. Although seemingly competent, the young man had succumbed to the culture of the time and fell under the influence of drugs.

Unable to complete his task, in discouragement we purchased a decrepit 1700s Colonial house, with later additions, in Brimfield, with an aged barn and thirty acres, mainly woodland. Local people averred that city folk could not survive such rural conditions, especially as the house required extensive renovations. For three years, however, we kept this place as a week-end and summer house, while living in an apartment in the city until Nels became more self sufficient. Moving to Brimfield meant a completely new way of life, with much carpentry and garden work. Commuting to Cambridge and staying over night there became the new pattern.

Meanwhile in Iran the course of revolution reached the time of a terror in full swing, with leftist students battling the Islamic forces who were in control. Arrests and executions of the former increased daily throughout 1980, while the war ground on in Afghanistan. In September of the same year Iraq launched its attack on Iran, hoping to gain territory in the south in the face of the demoralization of the Iranian army. Saddam Husain further hoped that Arabs living in Khuzestan would join their compatriots across the border, which they did not. For eight years the bloody struggle continued, with enormous loss of life on the Iranian side. Only the threat of chemical and other weapons from Saddam forced Khomeini to swallow a bitter pill and sue for peace. American support for the Iraqi leader played a role in his decision, according to several Iranian friends.

In December 1985, when Nels was four years old, both Eden and I, as lecturers, went on a long trip by ship, sponsored by the Harvard and Yale alumni associations. We flew to Cairo and then by bus to Suez where we boarded a Greek ship, the Illyria, with stops in Sana, Yemen, Mogadishu, Somalia, Mombasa, Kenya, with an excursion to an animal preserve, near the Serengeti forest, where Nels saw his first lions, elephants and hippos in the wild. Although most elderly people on the tour were tolerant of a four year old boy, some were annoyed, because he did cry at times and needed attention, especially when we talked. Unfortunately our lectures on Islam did not fit well into the itinerary of the ship, and we were new to most of the lands visited. After Somalia, we left Islamic realms and sailed to places where we could not contribute a knowledge of local customs.

Nels became strongly attached to certain objects for long periods, or he pursued some goal relentlessly. For some time he had worn a round yellow plastic strainer with the handle broken off, in place of a hat, even when he went to sleep. On this occasion, in January 1986 in the Seychelles, after being intrigued by the giant tortoises, he walked on the beach and picked up shells. He became so absorbed that he did not notice when the strainer fell off his head. When as a group we boarded a bus to go to the center of the island to observe rare flora, he remembered his hat and began to cry. It was a crisis and I elected to stay behind to search for the strainer. What would we do if it could not be found? Another strainer would not do, for this one had some mysterious hold on him. After retracing the places he had walked it finally appeared amidst some sea weed, and when I rejoined the group back at the ship, the expression on Nels' face was enough reward, even though I missed the exotic flowers, bushes and trees of the island paradise.

The Maldive Islands were almost as intriguing as the Seychelles, mainly because of the beaches which extended far into the Indian Ocean, but which must have posed problems for the inhabitants of the low land, subject to flooding during storms. At Colombo, Sri Lanka, Eden had to return home, as she was teaching in Amherst, and I was alone with Nels. At Kandy he refused to go into the temple which housed the tooth of the Buddha, but instead outside was greatly frightened by a cobra drawn up from a basket by an old man playing a pipe. From that time he has had a fear of snakes, and then for long could not be comforted. At Aceh in Sumatra, we returned to an Islamic land, and again I was able to contribute something to discussions. It then was not the rebellious province of later times, but underneath one could sense tensions with the government in Jakarta. The boat tour ended at Singapore, and we took plane to Hongkong, Honolulu and back home, ending a strenuous trip.

At home such activities as investigating Near Eastern Studies at various universities, Arizona, Penn and UCLA, and writing reports, kept me in touch with colleagues, while conferences proliferated. Jamsheed Choksy, a Parsi from Sri Lanka obtained his doctorate and became a Junior Fellow, writing extensively about Zoroastrians. Also at Harvard it was the high point of Inner Asian Studies, with growing interest in that part of the world. One brilliant student, Jan Nattier, organized with me a joint seminar on Buddhism in Central Asia, in which she did most of the work. Faculty colleagues such as Maas Nagatomi, professor of Buddhism and Francis Cleaves, our Mongolist participated in the seminar. It was a fitting end to a teaching career and I felt I had accomplished something which younger people could continue.

Francis was a bachelor, who can only be described as strange, for he had purchased an old, run down house near Acton, New Hampshire to raise domestic animals there simply for the joy of being with them. A neighbor had given him land, such that he had acquired a thousand acres of mountain and woodland, over which the animals roamed. He had two dozen horses, and almost as many cows, six dogs who lived with him in the house, and several goats and sheep. He didn't milk the cows, which brought on him the ire of local authorities, who once arrested him for cruelty to animals, in spite of his plea that in nature calves took care of the milk. He did not sell his animals, but when the herd increased he gave horses or cows as gifts to neighbors. He always said that Mongols would do the same in their homeland.

His large Chinese and Mongolian library, which he kept in his house, was well protected with fine bindings on most of the books. In addition he had collected sixteenth and seventeenth century Greek and Latin texts, for he had studied the Classics in Dartmouth college and was an avid bibliophile. All attempts to bequeath the land and library to colleges or universities failed, for they wanted to sell them, rather than to preserve them on his land as a summer retreat, which is what he wanted. He was at a loss what to do with his possessions.

We used to camp on his grounds and talk to him, especially in my case, about Mongol history and inscriptions, his specialty. He was a world authority on Mongolian, but he mostly had taught Chinese before retirement. The house was primitive with no running water or indoor toilet, yet he had lovely glass covered wooden bookcases made for his books. In short he lived as a hermit, with assistance from local boys and neighbors. He finally gave his library to the priest of a local church, who agreed to keep his books in glass covered bookcases, while his land and house went to the young man who helped him in his last years. Cleaves was an old-fashioned scholar, who could not be reconciled with the changes happening in Harvard, or indeed in the world around him. Even an electric typewriter was too much for him. I wondered how many other scholars were similar, and felt myself to be a kind of bridge between the old and the new, sympathetic to old traditions, but conscious of the need to make peace with the new world of technological change and speed.

Meanwhile at home, and in Europe, meetings and conferences about the Afghan situation continued. Soviet friends, who had berated us for the Viet Nam debacle, now felt themselves in the same position. The senselessness of both conflicts instilled in both American and Soviet citizens a justified feeling of mistrust of their governments. The wrong position of the US government, in not condemning the attack of Iraq on Iran, was the subject of letters I wrote to the editors of several newspapers, as well as talks with criticism of this policy, all of which did not endear me to the State Department. Nonetheless, hope remained that relations between the two governments would improve. Unfortunately this did not happen.

At the university, money and endowments came to the Near Eastern Department, and the Jewish Studies section greatly expanded, while Iran receded into the background since students could not go there, and interest in the country diminished considerably. Attention shifted to Central Asia, and because of the course on Buddhism, even to China, especially what formerly had been called Uighuristan, which, since the Chinese conquest in the eighteenth century, had received the name Xinjiang, or new domain. As chairman of the Committee on Inner Asian and Altaic Studies, it was necessary to turn attention to China, which had been neglected since 1941. New vistas beckoned, and now I regretted my neglect of Chinese. A trip to western China was needed to bring field experience to book learning.

CHAPTER 30

Two Trips to Western China

OBTAINING a visa and travelling to China in 1985 was more complicated than to the Soviet Union thirty years ago. At the beginning of June I received an invitation to participate in a conference in Urumqi of the Dunhuang and Turfan Research Group of Beijing, from August 3 through 10, from the Academy of Social Sciences of Xinjiang. It was not clear whether the Academy or the Research Group in Beijing was sponsoring the conference. The letter said that living expenses would be borne by the Academy, unless the invitation came from the Research Group in Beijing. This was the first confusion but not the last. Eden also wanted to go to China, so her visa was requested as well as mine.

A telephone call to the embassy of the PRC in Washington for visas brought the response that the foreign affairs section of the Academy had to issue an 'official' invitation. A telegram sent to Urumqi elicited a reply that the foreign affairs section had no authority to issue an 'official' invitation, and the Research Group in Beijing had to be contacted. No reply came from them in Beijing, so a decision was made to fly to Hongkong to obtain visas there for the PRC. On Friday 26 July, five days before departure for Hongkong, a telephone call to the Consulate of the PRC in New York revealed that authorization for a visa had been received. A trip to New York was necessary to pick up the visas and return to Boston the same day to catch a Pan American plane to Hongkong. The hectic last day at least secured unusual tickets from Boston to Hongkong, then from Canton to Shanghai and to

Urumqi, all on one continuous ticket. Such tickets would not be possible in future times, when direct flights to mainland China became routine but internal tickets had to be purchased separately.

There was no problem in obtaining tickets on the train from Hongkong to Canton, but on arriving at the airport in Canton we were told that the reservation to Shanghai was wrong, but we could go on a later flight. In Shanghai, however, we found that all Saturday flights to Urumqi in the month of August had been cancelled, and it was the first day of August. A taxi trip from the airport to the Pan American office in the city brought results, for a kind lady, after much arguing, changed our tickets from Shanghai to Beijing to Urumqi, and we were able to board the next plane to the capital. At the Beijing airport we were told that the next seats available to Urumqi were on the 24th of August, so again I had to take a taxi to the city to argue with the officials of the CAAC (Chinese Airlines), that it was imperative to be in Urumqi the following day, August 3, for the start of the conference. Exhausted from arguing, Eden took over, and in good Near Eastern fashion persuaded the officials to find two seats on the plane the following day. It had been a strenuous day but successful. I thought to myself never underestimate the power of a woman.

On the plane we met Victor Mair, a Sinologist from the University of Pennsylvania, who was going to the same conference. He was completely astonished at our story of obtaining seats on the plane, since it was so difficult. At the Kunlun hotel in Urumqi, where the conference was being held, we were put in a room with three beds and told the three of us would have to pay tourist prices for the room. The Chinese had many special rates, for overseas Chinese, for students, government officials, etc., and we were placed in the most expensive category for tourists. All three of us protested at being placed in one room and paying top rates, with a threat to leave the conference if it were not changed. A compromise was made, that as experts we would pay reduced rates for that category but full tourist rates for meals, which, however, would be reimbursed by the congress. We had to purchase special coupons for foreign tourists for payments not only of meals but anything else we wished to purchase. The various bureaucracies were pacified and we could relax. I concluded that the bureaucracy was worse than in the Soviet Union but could be circumvented easier here.

The conference was divided into five sections, history, archaeology, art, literature, and nationality questions in the PRC. For the most part I attended the history sessions where all papers were in Chinese, but fortunately my former Harvard roommate, Beijing University Professor Chou I-liang translated most talks into English for me. Thirteen minority scholars attended the conference, eleven Uighurs, one Tibetan and one Mongol. Discussion on papers presented by Uighurs was lively, and I was able to participate using Turkish, to the annoyance of some Chinese present. In addition to we three Americans, several overseas Chinese and Japanese scholars participated in the conference, and in spite of language difficulties, Eden and I were able to establish good contacts with several Uighurs, Kahar Barat and Dolkun Kamberi, as well as with a Kazakh, Jiger Janabel, but not with the Han Chinese. Eden was able to attend sessions on nationality questions, one of her specialties.

At the end of the conference Eden and I went on a four day bus trip over dirt roads to Kashgar, 1465 km. from Urumqi, a trip more reminiscent of Afghanistan or Iran than of China. Every night we stopped in a primitive roadside tea house rather than a hotel in a town, but fortunately no bed bugs or other vermin were encountered. The beds were similar to Afghan *charpoys*. On the fifth day, after tire blowouts, and similar experiences, we were glad to reach Kashgar, a Uighur cultural center, with a large statue of Mao in the town square. The only means of travel in town at that time was by simple two wheeled carts, which were more uncomfortable than those of Afghanistan or Pakistan. Most of the time in the city was spent buying journals and books in the Uighur language for the Harvard library. All publications had to be packed, carried to the post office, unpacked and controlled by both a Chinese and a Uighur customs (censor) officer, and then repacked. The officials were astonished that we were sending Uighur language books abroad, some of them forbidden, so those we had to take in our luggage. The Uighur officer could read them but not the Chinese, but nothing was said between the two. The post office was similar to those in Tehran and Kabul in the past, with scribes sitting outside to write letters in various languages for illiterate people. I was asked to write a letter in Russian by a Kazakh for a relative in Alma Ata of the USSR. At that time we were a curiosity in the bazaar as the only foreigners in the city. The bazaar reminded us of Kabul more than of Isfahan or Istanbul. There were a few handicrafts for sale, but the heavy hand of Beijing had produced the same apathy about hand working as in Soviet Central Asia. The influx of Japanese and other foreign wares had not yet reached Kashgar.

Kashgar had a native pharmacy and hospital where herbs and local medicine were to be found, and many Uighurs preferred the homemade cures to imported items. Some of the clerics knew Arabic or Persian and inscriptions in both languages were written on several shrines in the city. The atmosphere in the town took me back to over forty years previously in Afghanistan with the same green tea in small bowls and similar food. The Afghan clothes of turbans and robes, however, were rare in Kashgar which on the whole had adopted Chinese communist garb.

There was one daily plane to Urumqi, and naturally our booking had not been received by the tourist agency in Kashgar, so a battle ensued over seats, which we were able to obtain a day later than our reservations. The short trip by air again was reminiscent of terrain in Afghanistan and the Iranian central deserts, all mountains and sand. From Urumqi we went with a young Uighur teacher in the university, Kahar Barat, to Turfan where we spent two pleasant but very hot days investigating ruins, the caves at Bezeklik, and manuscripts found in the area, at that time in the home of the director of the Turfan museum, a rather forlorn one room building.

As an afternote, both Barat and Janabel were given scholarships by the Harvard-Yenching Institute to come to Harvard and study for the PhD, while Kamberi came to the Metropolitan Museum on a special grant. Kahar and Jiger both obtained their degrees, and the former ended in the USA with a post at Yale, while Jiger went to Kazakhstan for the United Nations. Both married women of their own nationality. Dolkun brought his family to the USA and worked in the Uighur section of Radio Asia in Washington.

The trip home was not without difficulty, finding a hotel room in Beijing and seats on a flight to Hongkong. Large hotels were full, for foreign businessmen were beginning to pour into the capital. Somehow we managed to secure a room with one single bed in a small Chinese hotel in the capital, and seats on a plane, again with considerable argument. I had enough pidgin Chinese to function in such cases which actually surprised me. Afterwards I made a short report for the American Council of Learned Societies about travel to China, in which it was observed that all foreigners, tourists, students and specialists, were supposed to stay in tourist hotels and eat in restaurants which only accepted FEC (foreign exhange certificates), and they had to be purchased from a tourist bureau. Like my first trip to the USSR exceptions were possible, but knowledge of Chinese was highly desirable, as well as previous experience in the Orient. Both would aid in adjusting to Chinese practices and customs. The last certainly aided us.

The following year in April I was able to make an approach to western China through Pakistan, on the other side of the Karakorum highway built by the Chinese. Ahmed Dani, an old friend in Islamabad, convinced me that the best way to study the inscriptions and rock carvings in the north was to fly to Gilgit and hire a local jeep with driver who knew the region.

Air travel to the northern regions was subsidized by the government, and only slightly more expensive than bus fares, but the small 30 passenger prop planes only flew in clear weather, and seats were in high demand. After two days of persistence a seat became available, and the hour long trip was similar to old flights in Afghanistan, flying between two mountain ranges up the gorge of the Indus River. After a spectacular trip between snow covered mountains and glaciers, landing on a small strip almost in the middle of Gilgit town was a relief. Since an airplane crash happened after my flight I decided to return by land.

My mission was to photograph Sogdian inscriptions and rock carvings, and to learn about the people who lived on the other side of the Chinese border. It was a surprise to find that the villages north of Gulmit, beyond Hunza, were occupied by Wakhi speakers, followers of the Aga Khan. Were these Ismaili speakers of an Iranian tongue migrants from northern Afghanistan, or

Soviet Central Asia, and were the Hunza people refugee remnants of a formerly larger population which once extended into Yarkand and Kashgar in western China? Intriguing questions about the past of this mountainous area occupied my thoughts more than the inscriptions which proved to be primarily names, and, as I discovered, were being studied and then published by others.

I have maintained that for years a *jinn* or evil spirit always has sat on my shoulder when taking photos, ruining them. This trip proved no exception, with rolls of film falling from the camera, and other problems. Several times avalanches of snow from melting glaciers blocked the road, but the Pakistan army with bulldozers quickly cleared the path, a yearly task for the experienced crews. The small, terraced plots of intensely cultivated land on both sides of the river, carved out of the mountain slopes, were marvels of ingenuity, and apparently quite productive of fruit trees, especially apricots.

As an Aga Khan professor I was obliged to visit a school and the A.K. Rural Support Programme offices in Gilgit, and to deliver talks in both. The Hunzakuts, who speak Burushaski, a language related to no other, just as the Basque language in Spain, were friendly and informative, and several suggested that their ancestral homeland really was to the north in China. This made another trip to western China intriguing, and so it was later planned.

The return trip from Gilgit to Rawalpindi by bus was a nightmare in pouring rain, through waterfalls over the roads and mud slides which required removing stones and mud to continue. As a result this primary road to the north was much worse than those previously travelled in Afghanistan or Iran. A visit to Peshawar to the *mujahideen* fighters of two parties—Jamiat Islami of Rabbani, and the *hizb-e Islami*—to deliver written propaganda in Russian for the foreign troops in Afghanistan, revealed serious divisions between the parties, which were to intensify after the retreat of the Soviets from Afghanistan. New excavations at Swat by Peshawar University archaeologists, Abdur Rehman and Durrani had uncovered many Buddhist remains, which promised to reveal changes in our ideas about Gandharan art. I reflected that the 19th century division between European scholars of the

Orient and local savants was vanishing fast and soon would disappear.

A surprise invitation from the Academy of Social Science of the PRC paved the way for another trip to China. On 13 June 1987 a four hour delay in a flight to New York because of weather caused a missed connection with a Pakistani Airlines flight, but after spending the night in the airport lounge, another flight to Karachi was arranged. After a second night in the stifling heat of Karachi, the onward flight to Beijing over the Himalaya and Tian Shan mountains was spectacular in scenery, and I had no words to describe the thrill of this flight. At Beijing the following morning was spent at the Academy, talking about Inner Asian Studies in the USA, and proposing several ideas about the ancient populations of western China.

In the evening an art historian, Wu Zhuo, came to the Ritan hotel, where I was staying and we, through his English speaking wife, discussed many matters of common interest in art and archeology. The next day at Beijing University Professor Yeh-I liang, head of a new section on Oriental Cultures, spoke fluent Persian, having spent years in Afghanistan and Iran. We became friends and corresponded for years afterwards. On June 23 Eden arrived in Beijing by air from San Francisco, and we spent much time together at the Institute for the Study of Nationalities, where Uighurs, Kazakhs and others were studying. In the evening we had dinner with Duan Qing, a charming young lady who had obtained her PhD in Hamburg with a thesis on a Khotanese Saka text. At the apartment was her father, a retired air force general who knew much about western China, and gave us information about the land and inhabitants of the Pamirs.

On June 30 we flew to Lanzhou where a representative of the foreign affairs bureau of the Gansu Academy of sciences met us, but was dismayed that we spoke little Chinese, since he knew no other tongue. At a meeting at the university fortunately a young lady spoke Russian, and acted as interpreter during three hours of talks. One of the tourist attractions was the Buddhist Labran monastery in the mountains southwest of the city, where we spent the night, after turning the Tibetan Buddhist religious wheels in a temple to insure prosperity. On the return trip our car could not proceed because of extensive road repairs, so we walked several miles around the obstacles, and in so doing encountered many Hui Muslims (Dungans), one of whom spoke Arabic well. On inquiry if he had been to an Arabic speaking country, he replied that he had studied the language in Lin Shao, a Muslim town with a high school. That the students learned to speak Arabic, instead of just memorizing the Quran, spoke to the quality of education in that language. The intense attention to religion of these Chinese Muslims was surprising, compared to the Uigurs and Kazakhs, who were much more lax in observances. We returned to Lanzhou in a large pipe-carrying truck on the other side of the impassable area, down a long, winding pass to the city, for our car could not proceed along the road and remained behind.

Shortly after World War II a colleague at Berkeley, Otto Maenchen-Helfen, had sent me a photo and cast of a strange coin or weight which had been found in China. It was about 2 inches in diameter and a quarter of an inch thick. But around the edge were corrupt Greek letters and other signs. He had declared it to be a copy of a Parthian coin legend, but I suspected it was only a forgery. At the Lanzhou museum, however, in a glass case were over a hundred of these objects which had been excavated from tombs in the vicinity, dating to the fourth century of our era. Needless to say I was surprised and found it fascinating, for the purpose of these objects is still an enigma.

Our trip continued by air to the caves of Dunhuang, and by car and train to Urumqi. The train was slow because of former floods which caused delays. A tourist trip to the 'Heavenly Lake' in the mountains was tempered by the large quantity of plastic, bottles and cans on the ground, as in Saudi Arabia, symbols of modernization. I hope we embarrassed the Chinese by picking up the debris and bringing it to a large container. Dinners were sumptuous with Janabel's father, second secretary of the Communist party in the province, and with Uighur poets and writers at the home of Kahar Barat's parents. We were able to buy books, and in general meet many more people than on our previous voyage. While the atmosphere was much more relaxed, for China was proceeding in the same direction as the USSR, the tension between Han Chinese and Uighurs was apparent.

A flight in a small turbo-prop plane to Kulja was uneventful, but the Ili valley was surprisingly large and green. It must have been fertile also in antiquity, and probably on many occasions provided a base for Turkic nomadic dynasties to secure support from the settled population and expand. A short car trip to Sairam lake, found it clear, cold and deep. Over night in a Kazakh yurt with local food was an experience to be remembered. The weather was quite cold, even in summer, but the morning sun over the shimmering blue lake was a splendid sight.

On the return trip to Kulja we passed close to the Soviet frontier and the ruins of Almalik, with the lovely mausoleum of Tughluk Timur, the Chagatay ruler who had been converted to Islam. Shades of Timur's Samarkand came to mind, and a belief that this site needed to be investigated. At night at the local state theater we laughed at a Uighur farce translated from Uzbek, some of which Eden was able to understand because of the closeness of the two languages, but which was too different from Turkish for me to follow.

On July 18 we visited the village of Chapchal, one of several where the Shibo live. These local people are descendants of Manchu 'Banner Men' sent to guard the frontiers of the Ching empire in the eighteenth century. Not only did they still speak Manchu, but signs on the streets were written in the vertical Manchu alphabet, and books and newspapers were published in that language. This must be the last remnants of Manchu speakers in the world. At night watching TV in Kulja, we saw an exciting film about Nurhachi the first ruler or founder of the Manchu (Ching) dynasty. Although in Chinese, it had sub-titles in Uighur in modified Arabic script, and it was exciting and well done.

In Urumqi we had a Uighur guide, Taher Jan, and a pleasant driver Tuyghun, who took us in a Toyota Land Cruiser to Turfan. Breakfast en route was garlic bread, soup and tea, but by the time we reached Turfan at 10 AM the temperature had reached 43° C or 120 F. Without air-conditioning in the hotel it would have been difficult to survive, but we were able to photograph sites in the evening and early morning, with a night of Uighur music and dancing. As in Iran and Afghanistan, our usual fare in summer consisted of melons and tea, the former even sweeter and juicier than their Near Eastern counterparts. Near the ancient town of Yarghul people suffering from arthritis and rheumatism buried themselves in hot, grey sand to help their ailments, an example of folk remedies which we also were to find in a local pharmacy in Kashgar.

The trip from Turfan to Kucha was not as difficult as two years previously for the road had been paved in several stretches, and our Land Cruiser navigated the rough parts well. In Kucha we had to negotiate with the Chinese representative of the foreign ministry to secure permission to go to the caves of Kyzyl some 70 km distant. Since the driver was not feeling well, I substituted for him for several hours on this trip, again shades of the past. Kyzyl had over 130 caves in the cliffs, some on top of each other, resembling Bamiyan in Afghanistan. Inside were wall paintings, but some of the faces of the Buddhas had been destroyed by zealous Muslims.

Continuing through well watered fields with many streams, we stopped for lunch in Bai, where only Uighurs and no Han Chinese were to be seen. Swollen streams before and after Aksu made driving difficult, and after two days we were happy but tired to reach Kashgar. The large statue of Mao was still in the main square, but more foreign goods were obvious in the bazaar. Kashgar was changing, and soon would have a railroad and many automobiles instead of the two wheeled carts, which had become few in number.

On July 30 we set out for Tashkurghan but stopped at the village of Opal, where there was a small mausoleum of Mahmud al-Kashgari, an eleventh century author of a Turkish dictionary in Arabic. In a kind of museum at the site we found pre-Islamic potsherds and paintings, evidence of a settlement here from ancient times. The road to Tashkurgan repeated the Pakistani side of the border, with avalanches and delays, and the need for the army to clear the way. In Tashkurghan we went to sleep at once, completely exhausted by the strenuous voyage. My hopes to stay several days in Tashkurghan to record the local Sarikoli dialect were thwarted by the Uighurs with us, for they wanted to return to their homes. Only a smattering of the dialect was recorded before we continued to the frontier post on the Khunderab Pass, where we were deposited, and they departed. It was a three hour wait for a scheduled Pakistani bus at an altitude of 15,000 feet. I felt sick with difficulty in breathing, so the Chinese authorities allowed us to board a special Pakistani mini-bus to take us to the customs office at Sust in Pakistan. The driver stopped at a cave on the way, and fetched several bottles of liquor which a Uighur border guard had planted for him to smuggle into Pakistan. At Sust, after spending a miserable night with others snoring in a small room, we were able to squeeze into a broken down bus, with people standing in the aisle, and reach Gilgit. Here we were stranded because of landslides on the road to Rawalpindi. We had to catch a plane from Islamabad in two days to return home, and after much searching finally hired a car with a driver willing to take a risk, after a bribe of $200. It was a long and most difficult journey, but fortunately the Pakistani army had cleared enough of the road, so we were able to get through the places where the road had been washed away. Busses, however, were unable to pass. We reached Islamabad and visited an ailing Dr. Dani before boarding our plane for home.

We recorded several impressions gained from our trips, especially about minorities. Although the nationalities' policy of the PRC is similar to that of the Soviet Union, yet the minorities in China are treated almost as museum pieces, although they are given funds by Beijing to build mosques, temples and print publications. Nonetheless Han Chinese are everywhere, not just as rulers and directors, but also as peasants, road builders and performing menial tasks. Only Han came to tourist sites such as Turfan and Kyzyl, and the Uighurs should follow suit to study their own past, for that will aid in preserving their identity, as we advised them. But in the long run the Han Chinese believe they will absorb everyone, and perhaps they are correct.

CHAPTER 31

Retirement

> *The theologian to the philosopher: "You are like a blind man in a dark room looking for a black cat which isn't there. Philosopher: "But you would find that black cat."*
> —Julian Huxley

THE AGE for retirement had been advanced from 66 to 70, so several years remained for trips and conferences to which I had become addicted. Much effort was spent on meetings in Paris for UNESCO, to advise on several many-volumed projects—a History of Humanity and a History of Central Asia. Writing chapters, and editing relevant sections of these works, kept me busy for several years. Conferences too were the means to keep in touch with colleagues and friends; a conference on Islam in China at Harvard in April, and one on Manichaeism in Bonn in August1989, kept both Near and Far Eastern interests alive. Many talks and conferences at NAASR also maintained interest in Armenian matters. Already candidates for my position were being invited to talk at the university and future plans were uncertain. Then came an invitation by the Tajik Academy of Sciences to a commemorative meeting in memory of Bobojan Gafurov, who had died in 1977. Both respect for him as the developer of Oriental Studies in the USSR, and close friendship, led me to undertake a long and arduous journey just before Christmas 1989.

At the outset baggage was lost somewhere between Boston, New York or Moscow, and it was not recovered until leaving the

Soviet Union. At Sheremetyevo airport I telephoned my friend Boris Litvinsky who, after a wait of three hours at the airport, came with a car which, however, on the way broke down in the sub-zero cold. After work on the motor by the driver, finally we were able to reach the Tajik 'hotel' in the center of town, a miserable, decrepit building, but at least warm and a place to sleep on a cot. The next day, because of fog at Domodyedyevo airport southeast of Moscow, passengers to Dushanbe had to wait twenty hours, not knowing when the plane would depart. The only positive feature of the delay was an opportunity to talk to fellow passengers, to whom I observed that Raisa Gorbachev, was a lovely example of the new mood of a *perestroika* of Soviet women. This remark, however, made no impression on others. While world peace and friendship were still two items of conversations, it was clear that domestic concerns were top priority for Russians now. The fate of the ruble and inflation, and what the future would hold for the Soviet economy, were everyone's concern. It was shortly after the funeral of the dissident Andrei Sakharov, and people spoke with great emotion and respect for the late scientist, who had broken silence and so openly echoed the sentiments of his people. Finally the plane departed, and the flight was non-stop and much quicker than the first trip to Central Asia.

In Dushanbe many armored helicopters were visible at the airport, even though the Soviets had evacuated Afghanistan. No one defended the invasion, but instead asked if the United States really wanted to support a fanatic, fundamentalist government in such a country. In view of later developments in Afghanistan, the Tajiks had a premonition of the tragedy in that land.

The city had grown greatly since my last visit twelve years previously, and new construction of apartment buildings was visible on all sides, primarily the result of the Afghan war. The bazaar seemed well-stocked with food and goods, with little sign of poverty. At the memorial meeting in the overflowing opera house I was the only Westerner present, and the audience was appreciative of a florid talk in both Russian and Tajiki. A suggestion that an international center of Iranian Studies should be created in Dushanbe met with applause, but another recommendation that a section on Turkic Studies might be created at the university or in the Academy of Sciences, elicited boos. Nonetheless, the warm reception persuaded me to try to come here after retirement, especially since it was impossible to go to Iran, which was trying to recover from the war with Iraq, ended the previous year.

It was with regret that I left the warm land of the Tajiks to fly back to the ice and snow of Moscow. As the Aeroflot plane nosed down after only two and a half hours flight, passengers knew something was wrong. It was not the plane, however, but the airport in Moscow was covered with fog, so we landed at Orenburg in the foothills of the Urals. In the bitter cold, and on the ice-covered field around the airport, it seemed on this evening of December 23 that there was little chance of reaching home for Christmas. All hotels were jammed full, so the passengers had to stay in the airport. After watching on a public television set a fascinating denunciation of the Stalin-Hitler pact of 1939, with a strong criticism of the former ruler, I jumped over the counter of a closed souvenir booth to the astonishment of bystanders, and slept on the carpeted floor. Early in the morning the flight was announced and Christmas was after all held at home.

My successor at Harvard, a Norwegian scholar Prods Oktor Skjaervø, was confirmed by the department, and in April I returned to Moscow to arrange the trip of our family to Dushanbe. A Fulbright grant had been received, but the Russians tried to persuade me to go to Tashkent, saying there were no foreigners living in Dushanbe, and there was no proper place to stay. Fortunately my friend Kamol Aini agreed to put us up in his house until we could find lodging, so finally permission was secured, but only at the end of September. A May symposium in Louvain on Middle Iranian topics, and an international Orientalist congress in Toronto in August, brought an end to such activities, with retirement from the university and a new life, or so I thought.

Bureaucracy, and a need to put our house in order before a long stay in Tajikistan, postponed the trip of our family. While waiting, an unexpected invitation by UNESCO to come to Samarkand, as the American delegate, for a 'Silk Road' conference from September 27 to October 14, brought a chance to make sure everything was in order for a family stay in Dushanbe. As a Russian friend exclaimed, "You spend more time in the USSR than at home." My reply was that since I could not go to Iran, Central Asia was a substitute. I flew to Göteborg Sweden and, after visiting relatives, continued on to Stockholm and Helsinki on a faster flight than earlier.

This time a train trip from Helsinki to Moscow proved most comfortable, and at the Leningradskii station in Moscow an Uzbek guide, Abdallaev, escorted me to the Uzbek 'hotel' far from the center of the city, but much nicer than its Tajik counterpart, which really was not a hotel but considered as a kind of embassy for Tajiks. The flight to Samarkand was uneventful, but the main hotel was full, so a camping ground outside the city served as a hotel. The director of the Uzbek Institute of Archaeology in Samarkand, Ahmed Ali Askarov, was our host, and the first event on the program was a bus trip to Panjikant. Unfortunately the bus broke down at Dzar tepa (Uzbek for tepe) on the way, so we did not reach our goal, but had to wait for a rescue bus from the city. Askarov was quite annoyed when the guide on our bus said that the majority population of Samarkand spoke Tajiki, an indication of later hostility between the two groups after the fall of the Soviet Union.

Uzbek banquets were sumptuous, and the vodka and cognac consumed even exceeded Russian practices. During the conference the Turkish UNESCO representative, Nejat Diyarbekrli, wanted to go to Bukhara, my favorite Central Asian city, so I accompanied him as a guide. It was a surprise to see 150 students at the Islamic *medraseh* in Bukhara, all dressed smartly in turbans and robes, evidence of a change in the air. Their Arabic was fully as good as the Chinese Muslims.

After the conference the delegates left on a bus trip, first to Urgut where large centuries old trees were held in reverence by the local population, and then on to Panjikant to view the extensive excavations, which had uncovered many ancient wall paintings in merchant houses. We had lunch in a *kolhoz* (collective farm), and as the oldest in our group I was nominated to be the spokesman or 'white beard' (*aksakgal*). I protested that I had no white beard but was nominated against my wishes. It was necessary to prepare brief talks in Russian and Uzbek at each stop we made for tea or lunch. Also it fell to me to eat the bread and salt which villagers invariably presented, and usually music and dancing girls accompanied the offering. The hospitality was overwhelming, even with an excess of salt and bread.

At Karshi (ancient Nasaf) where we spent the night, a play in Uzbek by Fitrat, called 'Abul Faiz Khan' was followed by the usual greetings for the audience. Needless to say the local people were happy to find an American as *aksakgal*, who could address them in their own tongue as well as Russian. The ruined Timurid monuments in Shahrisabz (ancient Kesh) were unexpectedly impressive, and in the past they rivaled those of Samarkand. By the seventh of October we left the Kashka Darya valley over the 'Iron Gate,' where ruins of an ancient wall were still visible, to the prehistoric site of Djargutan Tepa. After an early dinner at a *kolhoz* we hoped to spend the night at the excavation house at the Buddhist site of Dalverzin Tepa, but no one was there and we had to continue to Dushanbe, arriving at the hotel at midnight.

The conference continued at the Hall of Writers, and it was a relief to speak only Tajiki and Russian, which did not require preparation as did the Uzbek tongue. Now it became clear why I had been urged to attend this conference, which was to act as chairman of the sessions. Afterwards our Odyssey continued. The bus trip continued over the spectacular pass of the Vakhsh Darya to Kulyab and the Islamic excavations of Khulbuk. Since the bus had developed trouble we were delayed in our itinerary and had to skip the sites of Adjina Tepe and Kafyr Kaleh to return to Dushanbe in another bus. Back to Moscow, where the temperature was slightly above freezing, brought a delay, since it was impossible to book a flight or train out of the country. Two days of telephoning in the Uzbek hotel, with visits to Intourist and the railroad station brought no results, so in desperation a small bribe of $5 at the railroad station secured a berth on the night train to Leningrad and Helsinki. At the Finnish frontier the Soviet guards asked why I had overstayed my visa, but they accepted reasonable excuses, so unlike previous occasions.

In Helsinki no hotel room was found, so the night was spent in the airport before the return flight to the USA. The next day, however, I had to fly to Los Angeles for Becky's wedding to Michael Shanley, both of them at that time American Sikhs.

Needless to say, exhaustion from travel dampened my spirits. But there was little rest, for the time of our family trip to Dushanbe was approaching.

This would be a new experience in a new land, and I always had welcomed variety and novelty in many aspects of living, whether food, clothing or thought, anything unknown. Now that I was free of administration and teaching I assumed that relaxation would follow, but it was not to be.

CHAPTER 32

A Tajik Interlude

THE YEAR 1990 was an interesting time to be in Russia, but in Central Asia the Soviet past continued with little change. It had proven much more difficult to make arrangements than expected, but at last we took Nels out of his small, private Academy Hill School and arrived in Moscow with more luggage than was appropriate for a plane to Dushanbe, so we went by train. We left the capital in the late afternoon in a compartment with one other passenger going to Volgograd, which we reached the following morning, and the huge statue to heroes of the war was impressive even from a distance. The second day and night we passed through Astrakhan and Guryev to the north of the Caspian, and over the empty steppes of western Kazakhstan. By this time the train had run out of food and there were no peasants to sell their wares when the train stopped, which it frequently did. Fortunately we had brought some food supplies with us, which we shared with our new companion, an Uzbek returning home.

While at first an exciting new adventure for Nels, the endless desert bored the nine year old. By the third day we had no more water for tea, which annoyed all passengers. Finally we reached Urgench on the Amu Darya, and I consoled Nels and Eden that our trip would soon end; but we turned towards Kagan or new Bukhara, before heading south through Karshi, which took a fourth day and night. Early on the fifth day we arrived in Dushanbe, but, asleep in our bunks, our wagon was shunted onto rails in a yard some distance from the station. We awoke to find a difficult task of moving the baggage to the station and then finding a taxi.

It had been a tiresome trip, but we finally reached Aini's house and were warmly received. His son was away on military service, so we unpacked in his small room, thankful that we had arrived. Aini's house was a large one storied brick structure with a wall around it, and a garden with apricot and quince trees. Heat was supplied by hot air through large pipes from central heating furnaces in town, and hot water was continually running from a broken spigot in the bathtub. Since the state supplied the heat there was no incentive to repair the faucet, typical of attitudes in the Soviet Union. It reminded us more of Kabul than of Shiraz. Stores were still well-stocked when we arrived , but shortly they began to run out of many items.

Nels was enrolled in a nearby Russian language school, to which he was taken every day by his neighboring playmate Zafar Umarov. Almost all of the pupils were Tajiks, but they were a rowdy lot and began to assault Nels, so I had to go to school to calm the situation, which was accomplished. But Nels disliked the school, or rather, for the most part, his fellow students. If it had not been for Zafar he would have refused to go to classes.

My job was to lecture at the university on the history of Iran and the Middle East. It became clear that the students were well acquainted with Russian history but not with that of their neighbors. It was quite a novelty to have an American, the first anyone had seen, to lecture in their own language, and I was glad to have questions and interest in the subject. By the recommendation of Berna Umarova, who spoke English well, Eden obtained a position teaching English at the teachers' training college, and she was asked to assist the preparation of textbooks. With all of us busy, time passed quickly. Our best friends were the Umarovs, Shahzadeh, an Uzbek, his wife Berna, their three children, and Berna's mother Sakina Khanum. Bakhtiyar was the brother of Berna, and also spoke English. He lived in a nearby apartment, while Bahadur, another brother had an energetic spouse who was head of the main textile firm in the country. The family, as many others, had been moved to Dushanbe, then called Stalinabad, by order of Stalin, after he created Tajikistan out of Uzbekistan. Since that time relations between Uzbeks and Tajiks remained strained, but under Soviet control such enmities were not allowed to surface. The common language of the family, as with many others, was Russian rather than Uzbek or Tajik.

As the only foreigners officially living in Dushanbe at that time, or so we were told, interaction with the local population was close and constant. In February my friend Boris Anatolovich Litvinsky, an academician of the Tajik Academy of Sciences, arrived in Dushanbe and convinced the Academy authorities that we should not be living in one room, but have proper quarters. Fortunately a bungalow was available in the compound of seismological research, located near the center of town, and we moved there. There were several buildings in the compound, which had a wall around it, but the main structure contained equipment for detecting earthquakes, frequent in that part of the world. The bungalow was modestly but comfortably furnished, and we were glad to have more space.

The new school for Nels was also Russian speaking, and most of the pupils were Tajiks, but he had now become better acclimatized and made new friends. He also acted as an informant for English, and every day I walked with him to school several blocks distant, picking him up in the afternoon. Whenever soft drinks, such as orange or a cola, appeared in a local food store we were sure to hasten to buy as much as we could carry, for Nels was not happy to drink tea, either the local green tea, or imported black tea. We were able to arrange for him to take piano lessons at a music school not too far away, but he never practiced much with his Russian teacher.

Living in Dushanbe we adapted to local customs, shopping in the fruit and vegetable bazaar, buying dairy products from local Koreans who seemed to have a monopoly of them. The large department store had little to offer, but bookstores were regularly visited for new publications. The libraries were well stocked with Russian and Tajik publications, but few foreign language books could be found. Especially valuable for my research, however, was the small library of the late Orientalist Semenov who had left his collection to the Academy. Relations with various librarians were cordial and there was no difficulty in reading manuscripts or rare books, but these were few.

In town were Volga Germans, Tatars, Baltic folk and, of course many Russians. The Germans had a local club, and told me they had come to Dushanbe because of jobs which paid more than in Russia. It had been a policy to induce professional people from all over the Soviet Union to come to this poorest republic, and many had heeded the invitation. The war in Afghanistan also had attracted many, but the tree lined streets and pleasant living conditions also attracted migrants. Dushanbe was a pleasant place to live at that time, and it was still living off of the benefits of the Afghan war.

Doudou Diène, a Senegalese in a high position at UNESCO, had initiated a program called the Silk Road, and in April he came to Ashkabad with a group of archaeologists, including an old friend Georgina Hermann. I went to Ashkabad to inaugurate the trip with lectures, but it was impossible to accompany the group throughout Central Asia, so it was back to Dushanbe to classes. But this was the beginning of archaeological excavations by foreigners in Central Asia, for Georgina returned with a group to excavate old Merv, and others followed. Old restrictions were vanishing and people were much more open now.

Since school was ending early, we left Dushanbe in May with the promise that we would return in the fall. An invitation from Omeljan Pritsak, now a Ukrainian academician, brought us to Kiev to lecture. In Kiev I spoke at the new Oriental Institute of the Ukranian Academy of Sciences, headed by Omeljan, retired from Harvard. At the main cathedral in town a *faux pas*, of walking with our backs to the altar, brought a reprimand to leave facing the elaborate rear of the church which proved a bit difficult. As in Central Asia, it was clear that religion had returned to Ukraine. The flat plain stretching east from the city reminded one that we were on the edge of lands occupied in the past by various nomads and then by the Cossacks. After several days of sightseeing we continued on our voyage.

First we flew to Germany, for both of us were scheduled to lecture in Berlin, but only one seat was available on the plane. We concluded that Eden, with current events, was more in demand, so she went to Berlin while Nels and I came to Frankfurt on a later plane. We reunited for talks at Bonn University, and then in a whirlwind on to Bombay for more talks for the Parsis.

Afterwards we flew to Bangkok and spent a time share week at the beach of Pataya, resting from the year. This proved a welcome rest after a strenuous time in Dushanbe. The first of June we were in hot Hongkong and then in Seoul for more lectures at the National University. More at Tokyo and Kyoto, where Nels played with the sons of Professor Eiji Manu, in a Western style house, most unlike a typical Japanese home.

Kyoto had changed, with many of the small bars and eating places now gone, and globalization in full swing. I reflected that only tourist attractions from the old culture would be preserved almost as museum pieces, not only in Japan but perhaps everywhere. The pessimism of old age had taken over, even though the benefits of globalization for most people were obvious.

Tired, but happy that we had gone around the world, life was resumed in Brimfield. Mostly time was spent working in the garden, although Eden did almost all of the work.

Since we had only spent half a year in Dushanbe it was incumbent on us to return to finish another half. This time, however, the changes in Russia finally had reached Central Asia. The spirit of *glasnost* or openness was now evident in Tajikistan, although at first people were fearful that their way of life would be threatened. Then they realized that they could speak their minds, and even criticize the Russians, so they embraced their new freedom with alacrity. Soon with *perestroika* (reorganization) more exciting changes were in store.

Since we had left much of our baggage in Dushanbe, it was no problem to return by air. Already Moscow was showing signs of an influx of foreign enterprises, such as McDonald and Pizza Hut for food, but also foreign clothing and household objects appeared in the large shops. Hotel rooms were very difficult to find, so Litvinsky put us up in his small apartment. But a conference in Vladikavkaz, the revived old name for Ordzhonikidze, beckoned us. Another world of the north Caucasus, with the Iranian region of Ossetia, gave new perspectives on a part of Eurasia which had been neglected. This requires a new chapter, even though the conference lasted only six days.

After that session, our trip to Dushanbe took us by land over steppes to Grozny, where we could catch a plane to the east. As soon as we landed it was clear that we had returned to a different land. In the city there were no living quarters available, and Aini's son had returned from military service, so his house was full. Fortunately, we were invited to occupy a room in the apartment of Bakhtiyar Umarov, who was a high official in the local textile factory. His wife was an Uzbek from Andijan and he had a teen age daughter Sorayya, but the apartment was much smaller than Aini's house. The room in which we stayed, however, was larger than the one in Aini's house. I brought a computer which was much appreciated, although others were to soon appear.

When Nels appeared at his previous school his friends were happy to see him, and they made so much noise the teacher had difficulty to quiet them. The same routine as before continued, only the food was bought and prepared in cooperation with the Umarovs. Changes, however, were in evidence everywhere, for many non-Tajiks were leaving the country. The small stalls on every other street corner, where shoemakers or watch repairers had been busy, were closing, for most of the craftsmen were Bukharan Jews, and they were leaving for Israel or the USA. Russians too were seeking positions in their homeland, since many did not feel welcomed in Tajikistan. As we spoke Tajiki the local people were more friendly towards us than towards Russians, who rarely learned local languages. Many Tajiks felt that they had been relegated to minor positions, while Russians and other nationalities were in the driver's seat.

Elections were to be held this fall, and already several candidates were busy campaigning for the new post of president. The new mood of *perestroika* meant privatization, which again at first dismayed many, until the *nomenklatura* (top officials) realized that they themselves could acquire the land and property formerly held by the state at ridiculously low prices. For example, the last shipment of Volga cars arrived in town, and the officials quarreled among themselves as to who would be those lucky to buy them, at less than a thousand dollars each, the old legal price. There were not enough resources in Tajikistan to make real oligarchs as in Russia, but the loot was enough to make a few people reasonably wealthy by local standards. People in the University and Academy, however, continued to live much the same as previously. Their lot was soon to greatly deteriorate, when greed ruled the land.

In October 1991 an international congress in memory of Borbad, a musician of Sasanian Iran, was organized, and ethnomusicologists and Orientalists from all over the world came to Dushanbe. Ellen Hickmann, an old friend from Hamburg, was one of the prominent musicologists who attended. After the sessions the participants flew to Samarkand to view the monuments. Nels had his first experience with an outdoor, repulsive toilet which made a great negative impression on him. Restoration on the Registan and the Bibi Khanum mosque indicated a hope of local officials for many tourists, but several old master craftsmen in tile work complained of the poor quality of the work by younger colleagues. Now time meant money, and no one was willing to spend the time and effort to do reconstruction work in the old slow but careful manner.

An invitation to lecture in Khojent (Leninabad), revealed that the Red Army had evacuated the citadel where their barracks had been, and the mayor was considering turning the area into a museum. At that suggestion I protested, saying that it was too difficult to build a museum from nothing in a few years, and furthermore tourists would come to Tashkent and make the usual rounds to Samarkand, Bukhara and Khiva, for Khojent had nothing comparable to offer. "Why not turn the barracks into a bazaar", I ventured. "We have a bazaar," was the answer. "You have a Soviet fruit and vegetable bazaar, but I mean a crafts bazaar, as in Isfahan or Istanbul, where silver smiths, carpet weavers, wood carvers, and the like, could ply their wares. Then tourists would come here to shop rather than to view monuments." This could revive private enterprise, and the crafts which had atrophied under the Soviet regime. However I suspect this suggestion was not followed.

Another trip to Andijan in the Ferghana valley, and by car to Osh and Namangan opened my eyes to the fertility of the area, as well as the Muslim revival in the last city. From the crowds around the mosques, and by conversation, Islamic fervor among the populace, released after events in Russia, was evident. As time has shown, Namangan has become the center for Islamic activities for all of Central Asia. Why this city, in Uzbekistan, more than others should exhibit such zeal in championing Islam, is difficult to determine.

As elections approached in Tajikistan a genuine democratic style prevailed, with speeches on radio and television and even debates. Soon rhetoric became shrill, and when the old guard were re-elected to various positions, including president, street demonstrations and riots between the various groups erupted. Many, including most women, fearful of the future, had voted for the old guard, so the election was not rigged, as the opposition claimed. I cannot detail those events which brought a civil war to the country, but essentially there were three crowds, or one might almost say clans, which contested power. The capital was an artificial Soviet creation from a former village, and composed of inhabitants from all over the USSR, as well as Tajikistan. The old local centers of power, however, were three, the people of Khojent in the north, Kulyab in the south, and the smallest number from Hissar, near Dushanbe, which had been the seat of a local khan before Soviet times. The Pamiris, from 'the roof of the world', like the people of Garm and other mountain villages, had their own interests, and could exert influence only by alliances with one of the larger three groups. In effect Tajikistan was reverting to a land of local war lords, each using religion or local chauvinism to stir up the people and maintain control over their followers.

I began to muse about strange coincidences, which attended my visits. After visiting Afghanistan the war with the Soviets began, in Iran it was the revolution followed by the Iraqi invasion, and now Tajikistan was headed for civil war. It was time to leave. We left just as the civil war was beginning in the winter of 1991. I felt sad to leave many friends whom we had made in Dushanbe, but the future was uncertain and we were uncertain of ever returning again.

We decided to stop in England for shopping and rest. In London we stayed with Gillian, an English girl who had been a recent reporter in Tajikistan, and an English Christmas was celebrated on the seventeenth of December. Now that our three Iranian countries were in turmoil, our travels to that part of the world were over. So real retirement from affairs in those three lands came at age seventy-two. Now, I thought, retirement meant devotion to farm work and pleasure.

CHAPTER 33

Land of the *Zhigitovka*

AS NIGHT fell in the Caucasus mountains, the people of Tskhinvali, capital of Southern Ossetia, glanced apprehensively towards the darkening skies. Since 1989 the citizens of this city in the mountainous northern region of the former Soviet republic of Georgia had been victims of a grim ethnic conflict. Each night Georgian guerillas stationed in surrounding villages bombarded Tskhinvali with shells and rockets. The population, originally about 80,000 had shrunk to a quarter of that size, as more people were either killed or fled north or south. The Georgians were trying to evict Ossetes from southern Ossetia, forcing them to evacuate to northern Ossetia, across the new border with Russia. The Ossetes did not want to move, but rather join their area to northern Ossetia, even though a large proportion of the southern Ossetes were Sunni Muslims, while their northern brethren, like the Georgians, primarily were Christians. How did we come to Tskhinvali?

An international conference on Ossetic Studies, history, language, folklore, etc. was held in Vladikavkaz from the 14th to the 19th of October 1991, and we interrupted our return to Dushanbe to attend the conference. Vladikavkaz is intersected by the Terek River, on the west side of which live Ossetes, while on the eastern side are Ingush, a Caucasian people who are Muslims. Even though we were warned by some Ossetes not to go across the river because of tensions between the two people, we did go and talked to the Ingush, Nels even finding two playmates. When they told him they were Ingush, he replied, "no you are not English," and we had to set him straight.

The first evening we were invited to watch a *zhigitovka,* a specialty of the north Caucasus. It was a kind of rodeo with historical and folkloric allusions in the sketches presented. The horse riding, however, was spectacular, with riders standing on their horses, going under the bellies of the horses at full gallop, and other feats. Costumes were traditional Caucasian, with long black coats, held tightly by a decorated belt with jeweled dagger, and tall sheepskin hats. Pretty girls, also in native costumes, danced in the middle of the enclosure as the horsemen raced around the rim. Ossetic folklore is very rich, and in the costumes and plays presented, with long Alpine horns as background music, the pageantry of the epic tales impressed everyone. Though not as belligerent as the Chechens, the Ossetes, in the sketches we saw, appeared fierce and warlike.

The conference was most interesting since Ossetia had been an isolated area of the Soviet Union and this was the first time the Ossetes had an opportunity to meet in their homeland even a few foreigners who were interested in them. Unfortunately my old friend Vasilii Abaev from Moscow was unable to attend the conference, but other local scholars went out of the way to host the participants.

At the end of the conference the four foreign participants were asked to go over the mountains to Tskhinvali, and return to report what had been observed. Only I volunteered, in spite of the protests of Eden and Nels, who feared such a trip to a war zone. With several Ossetes I drove through high passes, past snow covered Mount Kazbek, and through a long tunnel to the other side of the mountain range. On the way we noticed several artillery positions in high places above the road, evidence of the seriousness of the conflict. In a village on the other side we waited until a helicopter gunship, manned by Soviet troops, came from the town to pick us up.

This small ethnic war was just as terrible as other better publicized conflicts. The mayor of the town escorted our small group to the hospitals, and to view the damaged buildings. Patients in the hospitals, who had been wounded, pleaded, "Please tell the world that we are suffering and need medicines and bandages." Many Georgians lived in the town, and of course, rockets could not tell the difference between a Georgian and an Ossete, so both were in hospitals, or buried in a common cemetery. This appeared to be a reprimand to lawless elements, causing bloodshed by pursuing their own ends against both inhabitants of the town.

At that time Zviad Gamsakgurdia, a former college professor, was president of Georgia, and on the radio he said many times that Georgia should only belong to Georgians, and all others should leave the country. He supported the actions of the Georgian guerillas in south Ossetia, but many Georgians were unhappy with their president, and shortly afterward he was deposed and then later killed. At the time, however, he seemed to be riding a wave of nationalism, and he was exploiting it to the full.

On return to Vladikavkaz, the same way we came, I was invited to speak before a session of the parliament of North Ossetia to recount what had been seen. After describing impressions, I made a suggestion, "You northern Ossetes maintain that southern Ossetia is part of your land, while the Georgians say it is their land. It is really the land of the people who live there, and they happen to be both Georgian and Ossetes. If the dispute leads to war, it is better to create a new republic and call it Digoria, because the southern Ossetes speak a different dialect, and are known as Digors. But don't kill people over such a stupid matter as a name." Their bitter reply was, "eight or nine people recently were killed in Lithuania by the Red Army, and the whole world screamed, but we have hundreds being killed, and no one cares." At the parliament we tried to get in touch with Gamsakgurdia by telephone, to organize a meeting in which the problem of south Ossetia could be solved by negotiation and compromise, but that effort failed. Later in Tajikistan I tried to speak to the government people there about the conflict, but the reply was that they had their own problems and were not interested in the Ossetes.

Eventually the fighting died down, but the area remains a tinderbox, since a compromise was not found. As usual the common folk suffer from hunger and disease, while the politicians maneuver to stay in power and to increase their authority. No wonder that people wistfully look back to Soviet days when at least there was peace and cooperation between nationalities in the Soviet Union. Of course, underneath were many suppressed hostilities, which were quick to surface as soon as the authority and tyranny of the Soviet government vanished. Little did we realize that the prosperous city of Grozny, where we took a plane to Dushanbe, would soon become a battleground.

If anything, the Ossetes appeared more friendly and hospitable than Central Asians, and it may have been that they saw in the Westerners fellow Christians who would understand their plight in an area surrounded by Muslims. There was no movement to secede from Russia since the Ossetes felt a common bond with the Slavs. My connection with the Ossetes was not ended, for ten years later cooperation in a project to obtain DNA samples of the local people revived interest in the region. It was with a heavy heart that we left friends in the Caucasus, with ethnic divisions clouding the future. We hoped that the new global order eventually would end the attempts of local war lords to secure their own ends by inciting the varied inhabitants of the area against each other. Only then could the people say their future would be much better than the past.

CHAPTER 34

Conferences Galore

CONFERENCES provided an opportunity to meet friends and colleagues, and to learn about new discoveries or changes in one's field. But they required much time and effort in preparation, both for organizers and participants. Formerly in the USA academic conferences were held at colleges at vacation times, when dormitory rooms and lecture halls would be open to students and anyone interested in the field of study. Today they are held in hotels, with sizable registration fees and other expenses, as well as being 'restricted to members of the sponsoring organization'. Only designated, subsidized students can afford such conferences. Slowly this model is being adopted throughout the world, and the past intimate and friendly meetings have become large, almost mercenary bazaars. But globalization and commercialism go hand in hand, and nostalgia for the past is only for dinosaurs. One reason in the years after Tajikistan I preferred to participate in conferences abroad was that the new American model had not yet reached them. At least it was a personal perception, or even a fancy, perhaps not entirely true, but change was also coming over there.

In the year 1992 I tried to find father's relatives in Sweden, and also learned that I had prostate cancer. Father had never revealed that he had any relatives, and furthermore he wanted to have nothing to do with Sweden. But mother said he had a half sister and maybe a brother too, so a letter was sent to the center for emigrants in southern Sweden asking for information. A reply came saying no clues had been found, so the matter was forgotten until 1999, when a letter arrived to Bill from a Kaj Freij in a suburb of Malmö. Through the internet it had been possible for him to track Bill, and contact was established. It became clear why our name had been changed to Frye, since pronunciation in the American manner of Freij would have sounded ludicrous, especially at the time of father's arrival in the USA.

Eden was invited to a conference in Tehran in February 1992, where she spoke about Tajikistan and Afghanistan, and in June another conference for both of us, about Iran today, to Castel' Gondolfo near Rome, sponsored by the Italian Oil Company. In September an archaeological symposium was held in Mary (old Merv) in Turkmenistan, with a side expedition to Bukhara. Central Asia was beginning to replace Iran for me as a second home. But in October of the same year an invitation came from the Ministry of Foreign Affairs to visit Iran and lecture on Central Asia. It was the first trip after the revolution and I was curious to see any changes.

On October 12 I arrived back in Tehran and was taken to the guest house of the Ministry in Niavaran, in the foothills of the mountains north of Tehran, where a comfortable suite was put at my disposal. Eden had prepared me for the changes, but the new names of the streets were confusing, and the many signs of 'Death to America,' boded ill for American visitors. But I met only hospitality and friendship, even when joking that the Iranians now had to learn Arabic, which few had done after the first Arab invasion. Even my criticism of the TV programs, with recitations from the Quran and an overdose of religious admonitions, met with quiet understanding among educated Persians but ill concealed outbursts from people in the bazaars.

At the same time, in speaking to the Faculty of Law of Tehran University, and in an interview for TV, I honestly gave approval to some actions of the present regime. For example, as remarked on TV, meeting a German woman in the Museum of Antiquities, I asked her how she liked wearing the *hejab* or woman's costume. Her answer was surprising, "I have been all over this country alone, sometimes on the streets late at night, and never had any fear. This would not be the case in my home town of Munich." For the TV audience I added advice, "Iran has to choose the road to follow, either the order of Singapore or Miami vice." This was not said to please the present regime, but in contrast to the dissolute life of the upper classes during the last years of the Shah's time. Again the historical parallels with the French court and that of the Tsar before their revolutions had been striking.

A trip to Qum to talk to several ayatallahs, and to view the library of the late distinguished Mar'ashi in the bazaar, showed a split in the ranks of the religious leaders, between those who were scholars in the old sense, and those in Tehran, who had tasted secular power and were unwilling to relinquish it. The trip brought back memories of the earlier visit to Ayatallah Borudjerdi, and I wondered if that venerable scholar would have approved of the course of affairs in Iran today. The cult of martyrs was spreading throughout the land, and there were plenty, both from the revolution and the war with Iraq. It was a different Iran from what I had known.

Even though conferences continued I was able to finish the manuscript of a small book *The Heritage of Central Asia*, which was published in 1995. In January 1993 there were two, a fascinating meeting at the Hsi Lai Buddhist Taiwanese center in Pasadena on religions in Central Asia, and at the end of the month in Turin, Italy on sealings in the ancient world. In May I went back to Paris to work on the general history of the world for UNESCO, and in September again to Ashkabad, Merv and Bukhara, where I acted as an interpreter and guide for three New Yorkers who also were attending the conference, Judith Lerner, a former art history student at Harvard, and Bo Lawrengren a physical scientist but also an ethno-musicologist and Stefano Carbone of the Metropolitan Museum. Since this trip was different from others it merits some detail.

Going into Istanbul city from the airport was a shock, since I had not been back since 1945. The changes, with excessive traffic, and bridges over the Bosphorus, had transformed the quiet conservative city to a buzzing metropolis. Most of my old friends were dead or gone, as well as the coffee houses and trams, which had made life slow and pleasant in the past. Istanbul had joined the rush and chaos of modern living. My accent and vocabulary had become 'Uzbekized', so it was with some difficulty that I resurrected the smooth Istanbul speech I had learned.

In Ashkabad, the visas the New Yorkers had obtained from the Russian Consulate in New York were not accepted by the airport control, so much to their chagrin, they had to stand in line with the rest of passengers who had no visas. This process took almost three hours, but we finally were met by Towfiq, an archaeologist from the Academy of Sciences, who only spoke Turkmen and Russian. In the small car was only room for two passengers, so Judith and Stefano went to the city to arrange for hotel rooms. They returned saying that the rooms were $90 a night and they refused to pay this amount, so finally in relays we went to the Institute of Archaeology, and slept on the floor of the offices in sleeping bags provided by Towfiq. Early in the morning he collected the bags so people could come to work, and we met the director who informed us that we should fly to Mary (new Merv) the same day. The New Yorkers refused, however, saying they wanted to stay in Ashkabad to visit the museums and to see Nisa, some 20 miles from the city, where excavations had revealed a Parthian town. I had to explain to Atamamedov, head of the Institute, that we would go by train after two days, and we would be on our own until that time. But it was difficult to find reasonable hotel rooms in the city at that time.

A Turkmen lady reporter came from the TV station to interview us, but I only agreed if she would find us hotel rooms at the Kolhozchi hotel which had empty rooms, and where the director was her friend. We accepted from an assistant of the director a suite with three beds and a cot for $60, which we paid and received a receipt. Then the director came and declared it was a mistake, saying the room cost $120. Because of the receipt an uproar ensued, and finally I agreed to stay with Towfiq while the others moved into a smaller room with only three beds. There was a constant quarrel about the rate of exchange, and as a translator and middleman, the burden of calming stormy waters fell on me, an unenviable position.

What were the quarters of a Turkmen archaeologist like? He had a one room apartment with a small porch alcove, on the third floor of a cooperative with fourteen similar apartments. In the alcove was a TV set, a small refrigerator, a small round washing machine, and a hot plate on a shelf with dishes and cutlery. An air conditioner in the window, and rolled-up bedding in the corner completed the furnishings. On the same floor there was a common toilet, shower room, and wash and cook room, with one sink and one gas burner for cooking. Privacy was difficult, if not impossible, and everyone had to cooperate to avoid clashes over space and time. In the one room was a crib with a ten months old baby, and we all slept on the floor.

Since the train for Mary left at 5:00 AM, Towfiq said it would be impossible to find a taxi from the hotel at that time, and his apartment was within walking distance of the station. So we all agreed to stay there for the night, even though the floor space was limited. I tried unsuccessfully to telephone a Turkmen woman Eden had met, for she lived on the outskirts of town, and it was explained that it would be easier to make the phone connection via the USA or Russia than locally. Our object in remaining in town was unobtainable, since the car to take us to Nisa developed a broken axle. Instead we went to a large department store to buy some local objects, including cherry seeders, but they were only for sale to local inhabitants. This required soliciting local people with proper passports to buy the seeders for the Manhattanites, who thought such objects exotic.

Sleeping bags were provided by Towfiq's neighbors, as well as an ample breakfast, at 4 AM, of fried eggs, potatoes, cakes, coffee, pomegranates, with vodka as a farewell toast. At the train a conductor declared that foreigners had no authority to travel to Mary by train , but I convinced him that we were invited guests of the government and had permission. Through desert terrain and over the great Turkmen canal, which brought irrigation water from the east, the slow but not uncomfortable train brought us to Mary and a welcome hotel Sanjar with warm water. Lunch was with an Iranian delegation of film stars, after which our host, and director of the conference, Vadim Mikhailovich Masson, from St. Petersburg, appeared and explained the program of the conference, beginning the following day.

Strolling in the evening we passed a noisy celebration in a yard, and learned that a family with five daughters finally had a son. We were invited to partake of food, dancing and music, especially when several Turkmen recognized me from the television interview of several nights ago in the capital.

In the bazaar many wanted to change rubles into dollars, but we explained that only local people with passports could use the rubles. Everyone feared that the rubles would be changed into new Turkmen currency the *manat*, which happened the following year, when exchanges were closely regulated. Plans were being made for a celebration of 2,500 years of Merv in 1995, and everywhere were large photos and signs extolling the virtues of the president Niyazov, who had taken the nickname Turkmenistanbashi in imitation of Atatürk. One sign, in Latin instead of Cyrillic characters, promised that the president would insure that every Turkmen would be happy and never want for a place to live, and complete contentment.

As the eldest foreign guest, again the *aksakgal*, I chaired the conference and translated the talks of the New Yorkers into Russian, and at a banquet the recitation of a poem by Makhtumkuli, Turkmen national poet, and another by Pushkin, was greatly appreciated by all. One always must be prepared for such occasions. The excavations at Bairam Ali, old Merv, were visited and a Turkmen feast, with native musicians and poets, was especially fascinating, since the Turkmen probably had preserved more of their ancient heritage than other Central Asians. Having lived in Afghanistan, the surroundings in Turkmenistan brought back nostalgic memories.

A bus trip to Charjui on the Amu Darya through saksaul brush, then sandy desert, revealed the ancient transition from Iran to Central Asia, for this desert had been the border between the two areas from ancient times. I understood how Merv had been the eastern outpost of ancient Iranian states, for a new land lay across the river. At the entrance to the province of Charjui the bus was met by pretty Turkmen girls in native costumes bearing bread and salt. Also musicians greeted us, as did the mayor of the city. The specialty of a banquet at Charjui was the head of a cow, the meat of which was given first to foreign guests, and the conference was continued here at the pedagogical institute. A statue of Lenin pointing east remained in a square, but his head had been replaced by one of Niyazov.

In the bazaar shopping proved difficult since local merchants had not seen dollars and were suspicious of unknown banknotes until several young Turkmen acted as intermediaries in arranging transfer of money. There was little of high artistic quality sought by the New Yorkers, for years of Soviet rule had not been propitious for individual initiative in arts and crafts.

On the map, the western bank of the Amu Darya had appeared to be a desert, but a short trip to several archeological sites south of Charjui revealed that in antiquity the banks of the river had supported a large population. The river was crossed by foot on a pontoon bridge, since the bus had to make the trip empty. The river was wide but not very deep at this site. In the past there had been no controls, but now visas and new customs regulated the border between Uzbekistan and Turkmenistan, and relations between the two new states were not happy. At night we arrived in Bukhara where another conference was prepared.

Old friends from Dushanbe, Samarkand and Tashkent were present and I felt at home. Aini asked me to speak in Tajiki, but that would have been rude to the local hosts, so Russian and Turkish were the languages of talks. At the end, the New Yorkers had enough of conferences, and instead went sightseeing. The aim of this conference was to garner signatures on a petition to Karimov, president of Uzbekistan, to name 1995 the 2500th year of Bukhara. Everyone now wanted to copy the Shah's former elaborate pageantry.

The park of Lenin, where the tomb of the Samanids was located, had been renamed the park of the Samanids, and many other name changes were in evidence. Also craftsmen were returning to the bazaar, and it seemed that Bukhara might return to its cultural past. After this conference the New Yorkers went to Tashkent and I returned to Charjui with the Turkmen delegates, but I found that the price of an air ticket on Turkmen Airways to Ashkabad had risen from $15 to $75, which is why no Turkmen returned this way. In Ashkabad the father of a Turkmen acquaintance, who was a distinguished artist, Aikhan Khadzhiev, took me into his home until I left for Istanbul and onward. His house was opulent by Turkmen standards with a separate bathhouse with hot water. I wondered whether we had seen the last vestiges of Central Asian hospitality and friendship, before everyone entered the commercialized frenzy of the new global economy.

CHAPTER 35

My Heart Returns to Iran

IT HAS been said that with age one's memory frequently is better for events in the distant past than more contemporary times. In my case some childhood experiences are vivid, while those of the 1990s are difficult to reconstruct. Perhaps a desire to forget recent particulars and problems played a role in veiling the sequence of events.

On October 31, 1994 Samantha was born to Bob and his wife Jan, and a year and a half later Zoe was born. In January 1996 Becky and her husband Michael Shanley, living in Los Angeles, had a boy called Isaac. Jeff, now called Satpurkha Khalsa, and Navjivan had two children, Abnashi and his younger sister Gur Parkash. Those two children, for their secondary studies, went to a special Sikh school near Amritsar, India. It is neither my place, nor my desire, to go into any trials and tribulations of the children, but Bob's wife died of cancer only a year after giving birth to a boy Calvin. A tremendous burden fell on Bob to raise the three young children, but he responded wonderfully, cooking and caring for them while holding a full time job in a public school of Holyoke, Mass. Naturally I spent more time with Bob and his children than with the others, but it was a blessing that all were well raised. My attention shifted from children to grandchildren, for youngsters always had been my forte.

None of the children had shown an interest to pursue studies related to Iran, even though they had enjoyed living and traveling in the country. Nels had developed a great interest in China as a result of playing a Nintendo game about the *Romance of the*

Three Kingdoms. Consequently, when he began high school he studied Chinese, and in the first summer he went to Beijing with others in his class. When he returned he was speaking enough Chinese to get along in markets.

About the same time Eden gave up her interest in Central Asia, both as an academic pursuit, and any attempt to market the silks of Tajikistan, or to attend conferences. Instead she resolved to devote her time to modern Assyrians. As a last task in the former realm, however, she finished a book with Ralph Magnus called *Afghanistan, Mullah, Marx and Mujahid.* The sorry state of Afghanistan after the evacuation of Soviet troops did not entice one to devote time and energy to such a thankless pursuit. Ralph died, and with the new events in Afganistan, Eden had to update the book alone.

Conferences did not end, including one in Cambridge, England on Iranian Studies, and several organized by Parsis in various cities of the USA on the Avesta and Zoroastrianism. A lecture trip to the University of Indiana in Bloomington, and to Illinois in Urbana, gave me a chance to visit Danville and the graves of my parents. I planted flowers in the weeds around the tombstones, and resolved then to seek a final resting place in Iran where my life had been dedicated, and many friends, such as Iraj Afshar, lived. There was still much to do, but time was fleeting and decisions had to be made. My office in the Semitic Museum was much in demand, and hints were made that it would be better to move to Widener Library where elevators would ease the climbing of stairs. My declining powers were unable to keep up with Eden's activities, especially with prostate cancer and the loss of cartilage in both knees. These maladies, and the moving of my office, persuaded me to sell my library, and with the money received to establish a fellowship in pre-Islamic Iranian and Central Asian Studies at Harvard. This was a slow process and not by any means ended at the new millennium.

Editorial work continued at UNESCO in Paris, and one result of connections there was the establishment of an international institute of Central Asian Studies in Samarkand under the auspices of UNESCO. This had been initiated by Ahmedali Askarov and myself already in 1992, but he retired from the project and left me as the sole founder. In spite of misgivings of colleagues, especially the French, I argued that in the new millenium such studies would be prompted more by local scholars than by Westerners.

Conferences again dominated 1997, beginning in January with the Getty Center in Los Angeles, followed in February at UNESCO in Paris, April in Tehran, June at a meeting on Turfan at Yale University, July in Budapest for the International Congress on Oriental and African Studies, followed by a symposium on Sasanian Iran at the British Museum, where I had to buy a tuxedo for a reception for Princess Margaret. Finally in October came the 2500 years of Bukhara and Khiva, which merits a few details.

Karimov, president of Uzbekistan, wanted to copy the late Shah's 2500 years of monarchy in Iran, and since Samarkand already had held a miniature celebration of 2500 years, Bukhara and Khiva were nominated for a much grander affair. Reporters and various foreign dignitaries were invited, as well as scholars, to attend a symposium in both cities. On arrival in Tashkent early in the morning, guests were placed in rooms of the new hotel, to rest until late afternoon when we were flown to Bukhara, leaving our luggage in the hotel to follow us. Only it did not; because of a mix-up in instructions the hotel personnel thought the luggage would be held until we returned. In Bukhara, after sightseeing, we eagerly awaited the suitcases at our hotel. They did not arrive, and a minor panic ensued, since the meeting was scheduled to begin at 9AM the following day, and no plane from Tashkent was expected until the afternoon. I only had a shirt and trousers, and the text of my talk was in the luggage. Furthermore, I was the first, keynote speaker with no jacket or tie, but there was nothing to be done. A former student from Hamburg, now professor at Tübingen, Heinz Gaube, admonished me, *"Du bist ein alter Herr und musz Jacke und Krawatte tragen!"* The tie I borrowed from Pierre Leriche, a French archaeologist, and the jacket from Boris Stavisky. But half the night was spent in reconstructing my talk, with remarks in Uzbek, Tajik and Russian. The message of advice for the Central Asian countries to cooperate and eventually establish a union was well received, and made up for a reconstructed scholarly text on the origin of the name Bukhara, meaning something like 'praiseworthy'. At night the singers and dancers from various parts of Uzbekistan presented a colorful array of sketches. The next day we saw a repetition of the celebration in Khiva.

Time was divided between conferences with lectures, and the writing of articles for *Festschrifts*, for my eyes and general health did not allow intense work on inscriptions. Most papers, photos and copies of inscriptions were turned over to my successor P. Oktor Skjaervø, for him and younger students. Also efforts to bring Iran and the USA to dialogue or discussions occupied much time, but unfortunately little was accomplished. So passed the last few years of the twentieth century.

CHAPTER 36

Incident in Isfahan

THE ENGLISH speaking Iranian tourist guide approached with an admonition,"Are you flirting with danger on purpose?" Of course not," I replied, "but this official is causing me trouble." It was in the police station of southern Isfahan where foreigners had to register or conduct business, and I had come to extend my visa by five days.

The American tourists, for whom I was a lecturer and interpreter, were visiting the magnificent buildings on the historic square of the city, and I had taken the opportunity early in the morning to attend to the visa before joining them. The papers were correctly filled out and my photos were acceptable, but then the burly official in charge said it was necessary to make a copy of the first page of my passport."Where?" I asked, and was curtly told that he did not know. Obviously he disliked Americans. The guide, who was attending to a visa problem of another foreigner, directed me to a nearby street and pointed to a photography shop. It was closed, but a nearby bank seemed a possible alternative, and sure enough the clerks were happy to make a copy of the first page of the passport. On returning to the station I was informed that also a copy of the receipt for the visa fee was required, and the original would not do. That was too much and I began to upbraid him, without cursing, however, since the only good curses are in Turkish rather than Persian, and Isfahanis generally would not understand. It was then that the guide anxiously warned me. "It doesn't matter if you have friends high in the government. The police, the army and the *pasdaran*, (guardians of the revolution) are all under the religious authorities not the government." The guide was uneasy, but he had to leave, wishing me luck. I insisted that the official could take the original receipt which I did not need. Since he continued to object I walked over to the office of his superior, a major in the police force, and complained about the behavior of his underling. The major quickly ended the shouting match by ordering my adversary to stamp the passport, but it did not end the other's invectives against Americans.

Fortunately the major had a sense of humor, when I explained that I was really more Iranian than they were, since they had been born in Iran and had no choice, whereas I had spent more than half a century studying Iran, writing about it, and living there.

It was a long distance to the square, and a change of busses was needed. Since there were many bus stops at the end of the first line I asked a policeman where one could catch a bus to the square. He not only stopped the traffic, but halted a moving bus so I could get on it. Everyone to whom I spoke was friendly, especially when they learned I was an American. I was told where to get off the bus and where to go to rejoin my group.

This trip was more interesting than previous visits when I had attended conferences, but had not had time to speak to bazaar people or villagers. It was in October 1998, the month before elections to the high council of leaders of the revolution, and everywhere were posters with portraits of the candidates. On TV and radio only speeches were heard, and all the paraphernalia of elections seemed in place. There was a catch, however, for all of the candidates had to be selected by the existing council, and they all had to be religious leaders. It was as though the justices of the supreme court of the US were elected, but the incumbents would decide who could run for office, as their successors, and they all had to belong to one persuasion or one party.

When I mentioned to several rug merchants that foreigners were bored with Iranian TV and radio, listening to the ayatallahs, who all looked alike with their turbans and white beards, and furthermore all said the same things, they exploded. "You are bored; we are fed up to our ears; we must listen to it all the time." A sore spot had been touched, but similar sentiments were repeated even by villagers. A constant dose of religion can be deadening everywhere, but in the theocracy of Iran it has exceeded normal bounds.

Although the absence of the multinational McDonalds, Burger Kings and Pizza Huts was refreshing, with the fascinating multitude and variety of old-fashioned local small shops, yet there were some jarring echoes of the commercialized West. The religious shrine of Imam Reza in Mashhad, and the mall-like surroundings of the mausoleum of Khomeini in the south of Tehran, reminded one of a mixture of Disneyland and the Vatican. The villages, however, on the whole had retained their former character, with the welcome addition of electricity and proper drinking water, usually from deep wells. Since the villages supply many of the devoted supporters of the religious leaders, they have been favored by the present government. What is this government?

The ancient pre-Islamic traditions of Iran, found in many writings, even after the Arab conquests and the establishment of Islam in the seventh century, emphasized the two institutions of power and authority-the church and state. They were brothers or sisters, and as long as they cooperated the nation and the people would flourish. Islam, however, proclaimed the union of the two, and in effect instituted a theocracy under one leader - the caliph. By the tenth century old Iranian traditions had reasserted themselves and soon a sultan became the real authority, while the caliph took a back seat as a religious leader. Occasionally secular authority would weaken and religious leaders would assume power, but it did not last long and usually was local in extent.

After the revolution in Iran in 1979 the religious leaders harked back to the early days of Islam and instituted a theocracy. They would be both *de jure* and *de facto* rulers of Iran. On the other hand a parallel might be made with the Soviet Union, where there had been a duality of party and government, with the former the real power. In Iran a government exists, headed by a liberal cleric president Khatami, but supremacy is wielded by the religious establishment in Tehran, the Islamic party. One might call them the political clerics, whereas the religious scholars and theologians are centered in Qum to the south of Tehran. Many of the latter view the political machinations of their colleagues in the capital with distaste if not alarm. Responsibility for governance should rest with secular authorities in their view, and religious leaders should concern themselves with matters proper to religion. Control could be exercised behind the scenes, and criticism of government should be directed against politicians, not against religious leaders. Such was the opinion voiced by a prominent theologian in Qum.

In Iran it is important to distinguish between the government and the religious establishment, and if the former denies knowledge of acts of terrorism abroad it is likely that is true. Politicized clerics, rather than the government, offered a bounty for the execution of the author Salman Rushdie. One might ask why Iran is unique in the Islamic world, where elsewhere religious leaders are not outright politicians. The hierarchical nature of Shi'ite Islam, the official religion of Iran, lends itself to an intrusion of religion into political affairs. Under Khomeini the intrusion has become a usurpation, and the sheer number of clerics in government offices is excessive. It is a real theocracy, not seen since the Middle Ages. The question is how long can it last in the modern world?

On a main street in Qum a large sign, in English as well as Persian, proclaimed: "Faith, *jihad* (struggle for the faith) and martyrdom is the only road to salvation." The last dominates the scene everywhere in the country, for each town has its cemetery of young martyrs who died in the revolution or in the war against Iraq. No longer need one make a pilgrimage to the tomb of a long departed martyr, for they are now plentiful close at hand. Everywhere one saw boxes asking for donations for families of martyrs or for the poor. In Yazd, however, surprisingly a sign in English expressed the feelings of most of the population; it read "God Bless America." I hope no one was punished for such audacity.

"It is George Orwell's Animal Farm, with the overall philosophy of sacrifice and martyrdom for the leader and his cohorts," so said an Iranian intellectual in Shemiran, the fashionable northern suburb of Tehran. So Iran, like many other lands, wrestles with the problem of preserving local traditions and culture while seeking to participate in the globalization of the twenty-first century. Japan was the first country in Asia to show a way to this end, but even there only the future will reveal if in the long run it has been successful.

In April 2001 I joined six tourists, including brother Bill, on another trip to Iran, longer than the first. This time we spent more time in the countryside, visiting villages and archaeological sites all over the country from Maku and Urmiya in the north to Ahvaz and Firuzabad in the south, Bam and Kashan in the east, and Gurgan and Meshhed the north. Changes had occurred in the country, the most obvious being the expansion of the cult of martyrs, where almost every town and village had portraits of young men killed in the Iraq war painted large on walls and buildings. The enormous increase in traffic on newly paved roads everywhere, not only in Tehran, matched the explosion of population in large cities. Many new controls on the roads had been established, for the safety of everyone, we were told. This applied especially to busses, which also had to have special insurance and were required to register when leaving any large town. At the entrance to every town the record of the bus had to be checked for speeding, and it was clear that traffic regulations had greatly increased, and were being enforced. High towers for cellular phones also dominated the landscape.

Iran had entered the stage of packaging, and plastic bags, bottles and cans were seen beside the roads in deserts, as well as through cultivated fields. The latter had expanded, and many new food processing and canning factories had sprung up since two years ago. Green kiwi fruit had been introduced and was popular among the people. Tourism was booming and not only foreigners, but bus loads of students were found at every historical or archaeological site in the country. Tickets were sold for entry at every site, where previously no care had been taken in most such places. The Iranians were taking great interest in the past of their country. It appeared that the trade sanctions imposed on Iran by the USA had promoted a new self-sufficiency in the country, and banks and mosques appeared like mushrooms in their ubiquitousness, for even in villages one or two banks had been opened. The people we met were even more friendly than previously, and I suspected this warmth was engendered by opposition to the ruling clerics, as much as any great affection for America.

The second trip brought new reflections about the country and its future. In spite of the material progress, and the green fields, where formerly there had been desert, problems remained the same, with the most pressing that of too many people crowding into the cities, where demands for water and electricity exceed capacities. The usual answer that technology will solve those problems may not apply so readily to Iran and other lands of the Middle East. Wells in villages are sunk deeper as the water tables drop. Unemployment soars, especially among the mass of college graduates who finish studies every year. Universities are being established in all large towns, possibly to occupy unemployed youngsters, but this would only be a temporary solution to joblessness. Will solutions be found before an explosion takes place? On the positive side, once having tasted free elections the people are unlikely to tolerate a return to dictatorship, even though in spite of elections the religious leaders in Tehran, with their control of police, army and many followers, can negate the results of elections. The elements of conflict are building and it is difficult to predict the future. In any case the world cannot ignore the fate of a country of over sixty million, and still growing.

So trips and conferences continued, but at the age of 84 it was time to prepare for departure from this world, even though it might not come for some time. Hopes to be interred in the mausoleum of the late Arthur Upham Pope on the banks of the Zayendeh River in Isfahan were discussed with the Iranian President Mohammad Khatami, and the suggestion was favorably received. I felt my tasks were done and only additions to past work, and tying up loose ends, beckoned.

Postscript

In June 2004 I returned to Iran to receive an award from the Mahmud Afshar Foundation for services to Iranian culture and scholarship. It was a moving climax to my sixty odd years spent both in promoting the continuity of Iranian history and in urging the cultural union of those lands and peoples who partook of Iranian culture and who are also its heirs as well as the Persian speakers. A four day trip through western Iran with Iraj Afshar, visiting Sasanian remains near Golpayagan, Khorramabad, Elam, and Kermanshah brought back memories of earlier journeys, but now on wide asphalt roads with supplies everywhere available. A visit to Isfahan secured the approval of city and provincial officials to be buried in an existing mausoleum on the banks of the Zayandeh Rud river. But I shall continue writing and speaking about "Greater Iran" until my time comes.

1- Family picture 1925, myself, mother, father, and Bill.

2- Lab-e Darya, Kabul (1943).

3- Shevaki stupa south of Kabul (Photo A. Engler, 1942)

4- Buddha of Bamiyan (1943); destroyed by the Taliban.

5- Saqao delivering water (1943).

6- Minarets of Musalla, Herat (1943).

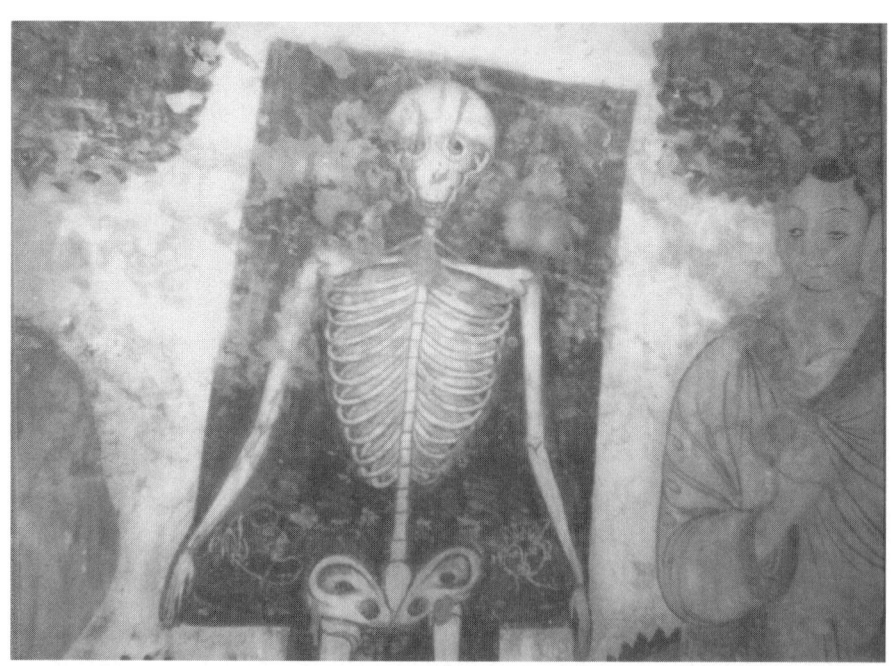
7- Wall mural at Hadda, Afghanistan, now destroyed (1978).

8- Teahouse near Charikar (1942)

9- Kabul bazaar, photo A. Engler (1942).

10- The Kushan conference in Kabul with President Taraki (1979).

11- With British troops of Baalbeck (1944).

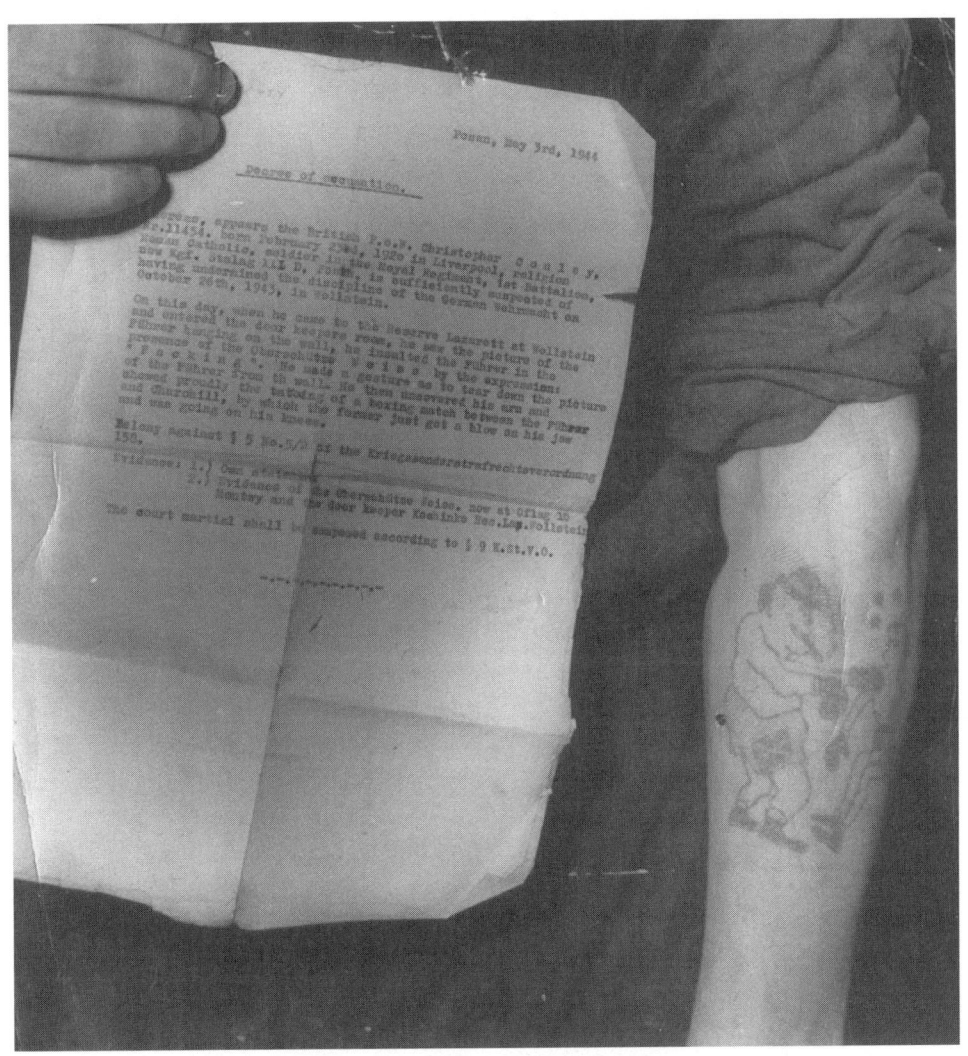

12- Released British war prisoner in Istanbul (1945).

13- With the mayor of Chisht by the Hari Rud (1953).

14- Building the road near Chisht (1953).

15- Street in Bukhara (1955).

16- Honorary award at Dushanbe, Kamol Aini at left (1991)

17- Entrance to bazaar of Bukhara (1955)

18- At Dalverzin Tepe with Uzbeks (1991).

19- Volodya Lukonin in the Hermitage (1974).

20- Sarikoli informants, Tashkurghan (1987).

21- Arg of Bukhara with Eden and Nels (1992).

22- In front of Kirkland House (1964).

23- Entrance to Shiraz (1951).

24- Inundated Road Near Meshed {Mashhad] (1953)

25- With Roman Ghirshman at Susa (1966).

26- Ancient quarries for Persepolis (1976).

27- The Narenjestan, Shiraz which served as the home of Asia Institute(1976).

28- Making bricks for Narenjestan (1970).

29- Narenjestan, Shiraz with Rahim at left (1998).

30- Tomb of Reza Shah Pahlavi (1977); demolished by the Islamic clerics after 1979 revolution.

31- Remains of statue of Mohammad Reza Shah Pahlavi (1995).

32- At Shiraz madraseh (2001).

33- Entrance to the mausoleum of
Arthur Upham Pope in Isfahan (2001).

34- Presentation of Volume 4 of Cambridge History of Iran to the Shah of Iran with British art historian, Basil Grey (1976).

35- Arthur Upham Pope and Phyllis Ackerman in Connecticut (1967).
Source: A.K. Jabbari photo archives.

36- Two pages from the fake manuscript, *Andarz Nameh*.
Source: Mazda Publishers photo archives.

37- Prime Minister Mohammad Mossadegh in his bedroom.

38- Prime Minister Mossadegh with US Ambassador Loy Hendrson who played a major part in the 1953 CIA-engineered coup d'état.

39- A rare photograph showing Ayatollah Abolqasem Kashani having lunch with a few associates in Qom, among them a young cleric (far right), who later became Ayatollah Imam Khomeini (1952).
Source: A.K. Jabbari photo archives.

40- After the CIA coup d'état, from right: Mr. Warren director of Point-4 in Tehran, new Prime Minister, General Fazlallah Zahedi, and Loy Henderson, U.S. ambassador to Tehran. The man on the left is not identified (1953).
Source: A.K. Jabbari photo archives.

41- Archaeologists at symposium in Dushanbe (1990).

42- Iranists at conference in Cambridge, England (1993).

43. Karim Aga Khan (1985).   44. Sadruddin Aga Khan (n.d.)

45- Nathan Pusey at Harvard (1969)   46- Henry Corbin (n.d.)

47- Roman Ghirshman (1974)

48- Ali Akbar Dehkhoda.

49- Arthur Upham Pope and Hassan Taqizadeh at New York harbor (1926).
Source: A.K. Jabbari photo archives.

50- Mojtaba Minovi (1973)
Source: M. Zandi.

51- Bozorg Alavai (1980)
Source: M. Zandi.

52- Iraj Afshar (1991)
Source: M. Zandi.

53- Sadeq Chubak (1972)
Source: M. Zandi.

54- Delivering speech during the award ceremony,
Theran (2004)

55- With Iraj Afshar at presentation of award in Tehran (2004).

56- With Manuchehr Sotudeh in his home (2004)

57- With Badri Gharib and her student-successor, Zahra Zarshenas (2004)

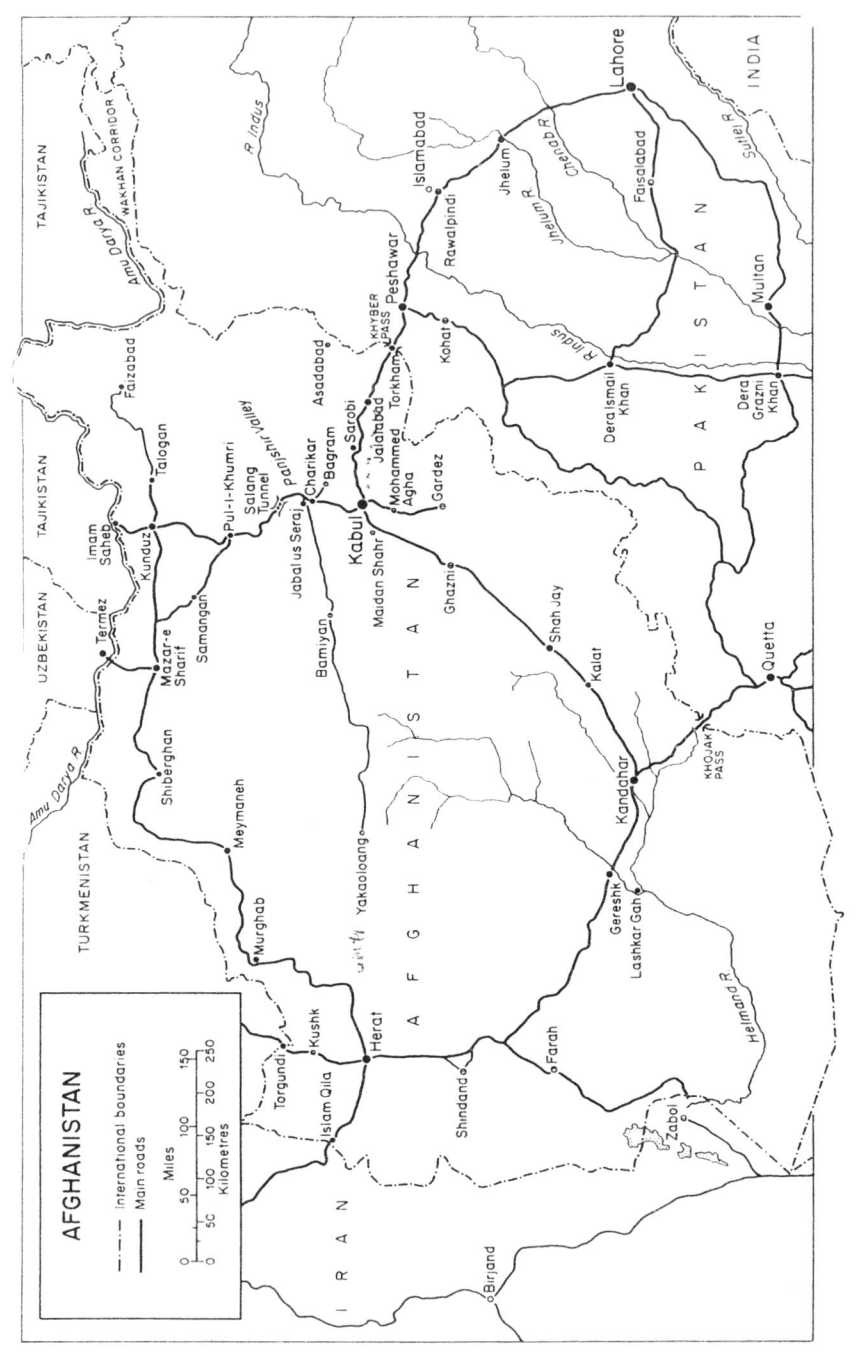

Appendix

It remains unclear exactly when a request for the memories of early life was made perhaps by a psychiatrist in 1994, or earlier. Here is what was recorded at that time, trying to distinguish between memory, and what was told when a child had become a mature person. A person's memory of events in childhood are always colored by the talk of parents or older persons, who later in life remind the grown adult of happenings which they observed, or in which they participated. But if a person, having heard of early escapades then in later life returns to the scene, perhaps his memory is refreshed or activated. In any case, my first memory, or recovered sensation, was of falling into a small pond near our house in Champaign, Illinois, and unable to get out, I cried until someone, probably my older brother and mother found me. I was four years old at the time.

I was born on January 10, 1920 in Birmingham, Alabama, where my father had moved in 1918 as an accountant in the construction of barracks for soldiers in World War I. This was a temporary stay and we returned to the north when I was less than a year old. There followed another short stay, this time on a farm near Sioux City, Iowa, where apparently I almost lost my foot by sticking it into a pen of hogs. Then we moved to Champaign, home of the state university where my father began work related to cinemas.

This was the time of the campus football hero Red Grange, and many fraternities, with their rough hazings, were in full swing at the university. It was at a manmade hollow pond in the creek, called the Bone Yard, that a tug of war took place between initiates of two fraternities, after a riotous football game. The sides were slick with mud, rotten eggs, and such items, and the losing side would be pulled into the muddy pool. After the fraternity boys were gone, somehow I wandered over to the pond and promptly fell in. Unable to climb the sides, my cries continued until rescued, followed by a scolding by my parents.

My father arrived in his adopted country from Sweden in 1903, and came to his uncle (mother's brother) Harry Nelson, a farmer who had migrated to Old Saybrook Connecticut. Nelson, unhappy with the stone-filled New England soil, was attracted by the black earth of Iowa and soon moved to a farm in the west. Nels, however, was sent to North Park College, a Swedish institution in Chicago, where he wholeheartedly adopted his new homeland, and became a citizen in February 1910. Later he attended Northwestern University where he studied economics and business, and then held several positions in accounting before entering the theater business.

At that time in the States everyone tried to conceal his ethnic origin, and as soon a s possible adopt American customs, and of course the English language. My father so much resented his earlier treatment in Malmö that he never again spoke Swedish, even when afterwards in Chicago he married Lillie Hagman from Motala, Sweden. He refused to talk about his early life, such that the sparse information about him had to be wrung from others, who only had a modicum of information. Even his wife was unable to discover why he so completely rejected his origin.

My mother, however, always spoke Swedish when we visited her aunt Josie and uncle Oscar Johnson, who lived on Dearborn St. on the south side of Chicago, but with us only English. A trip on the train from Danville, where we moved after a short stay in Champaign, to Chicago in pre-depression days was a memorable experience, for trains then held an allure similar to later jet airplanes. Vague memories remain of the train stopping at LaSalle St. Station, where we took the elevated train to Cottage Grove and then walked to Aunt Josie and uncle Oscar's apartment The area has changed since that time, when the city was not so populous as after World War II. My brother Bill, two and a half years older than I, always took the lead and was my mentor in many matters. In Chicago I dreamed of being a streetcar conductor when grown up, and turning the handle on top of the wooden coffee bean box in Aunt Josie's home evoked the turning handle of the street car conductor.

The English had their afternoon tea time, while Swedes held a coffee ritual. The s election of beans to be ground and the fastidiousness in preparation of coffee was like a festival, and if the coffee did not taste properly criticism was quick to be heard. Alma Johnson, a Swedish spinster friend of mother, was especially particular about coffee. She worked as a maid for the wealthy Balaban family in Chicago's north side. Balaban & Katz were two movie moguls who owned a chain of cinemas in the Midwest, and later were viewed as unfair competitors by father after he acquired two cinemas in Danville.

Since my father in effect had no close relatives, and never went on vacations with his wife and children, we were raised by her. As long as I can remember he never returned from the cinemas until midnight, and then sat up until two or three in the morning, which was the only time my brother and I had with him. But they were rewarding times, for he was a homespun philosopher, an admirer of Ralph Waldo Emerson, so much that he wanted to give my older brother the three names, but mother refused. William and Richard were American names, and simply taken from the general repertoire, with no connection to ancestors or family. I usually fell asleep at these sessions but Bill stayed awake.

So I grew up in the cinema, with an uneventful life in a small Illinois town 120 miles south of Chicago. We always lived in rented houses, since father could not be bothered with any house work. One memory was the ice man, for a square card with numbers 25, 50, 75 and 100 lbs. had to be placed in the kitchen window, with the amount of ice wanted for the ice-box on top. When he came with a wagon pulled by two horses I would run outside to watch him cut large blocs of ice into smaller pieces. Two of my favorite toys were an eight inch tall wooden doll of Felix the cat, on whom was placed a miniature pair of overalls, union made, given to me by Walter Stuebe, a coal miner neighbor and an avid union organizer, when we lived on Main Street.

The other was a metal model of the Spirit of St. Louis, which came as a Christmas present after the memorable flight across the Atlantic. When five years old Bill and I had our first airplane ride in a World War vintage twin cockpit biplane. We sat together in front but I kept my eyes closed, and only once opened them to see the earth slanting which was frightening. Our mother was incensed that we went up in such a plane, but father wanted to please Bill and the pilot, but afterwards the latter charged quite a large sum for the ride.

Father, who had been engaged as an accountant in Champaign, in 1924 received an offer to manage the three largest theaters in Danville, the Fischer and next to it the Palace, and the largest, the Terrace, where regularly vaudeville was performed. The last we enjoyed most, and do remember the first talking film, the Jazz Singer with Al Jolson, which made a great impression on all of us. Also the three dimension effects of wearing cardboard glasses, with one eye red and the other green, were a source of wonder for children. Charlie Chaplin, Buster Keaton, Karl Dane and George K. Arthur, and even Rudolf Valentino, were household names in the family.

Vaudeville then, whether comedians, magicians, dancers or singers, was always accompanied by music which necessitated hiring musicians who played in the pit below the stage. They were the hippies of that era and frequently were drunk or rowdy, and usually gave father a headache. Consequently he had a low view of anything musical and did not allow musical instruments in our house. As a result we grew up without the pleasure of playing musical instruments, but we did collect 78 RPM records and the first one I acquired was Borodin's on the Steppes of Central Asia. Incidentally, with the coming of sound motion pictures vaudeville and musicians lost their important positions in theaters, and gradually both disappeared. Also many actors lost their jobs because of heavy accents or poor articulation, among them Dane and Arthur. Later the advent of television was to wreak havoc upon cinemas many of which had to close for lack of interest among people. This had a bad effect on father and contributed to his decline and illness.

In 1930 father lost his job as manager of the three cinemas and for a time life was difficult, but he had saved enough money to invest in two smaller cinemas on Main Street—the Tivoli and a very small Colonial theater. No one used the term cinema, a British term, but only theater, and in a town of some 35,000 people there were six of them. Where else could one find entertainment, since only the radio was available? At that time in small Mid-Western towns discrimination existed towards blacks who were not allowed in theaters. Father was in a dilemma since he was liberal and even had a black dentist, unheard of for white people. If the theater was not full he told us to sell tickets to blacks and tell them to sit in the rear. If the seats were all occupied he would bring the black patrons up to the projection room where they could sit and see the film through small windows. Even though the projectionist had little to do except change reels of film, the union demanded that two people be present in the projection room, which also was a source of annoyance to father. I was put to work in the Colonial while Bill worked in the Tivoli, as ticket takers or ushers. He was now thirteen and I was eleven, just having entered Danville High School. How did this loss of almost three school years happen?

Our grade school was Cannon School on Main St. named after Uncle Joe Cannon speaker of the US House of Representatives. When five or six years old father took me to Cannon's large house on Vermillion St. and I sat on his lap, but that is only a hazy memory. My mother said later that when she took me to enter the first grade, that I refused to sit at a desk but several times returned to her, standing at the back wall, saying, I don't want to go to school. But then the teacher began to read a story aloud, Uncle Wiggley and the Cabbage Patch, which was fascinating and I never demanded to leave school again. I wanted to learn to read myself and soon became a book worm. This did not mean giving up everything else, for I played with other boys and did not neglect sports, although because of skipping grades I found myself out of my age group and thus isolated from peers. When six years old, another brother, Kenneth was born providing someone to comfort, but later to molest.

In grade school progressing faster than other kids, I skipped grades, which was a mistake, but in those days considered admirable. Classes 4 B (A= first semester and B = second), and both 6 and 7 B were skipped. So graduation from the eighth grade was at the age of eleven and a half, having entered the first grade at five and a half. This age disparity with peers separated me from classmates and left my connections primarily with neighborhood children, rather than schoolmates.

When we left the flat on Main St., after a short stay at a new bungalow on Virginia Ave., the family moved to 1310 Seminary St., still in the same school district, and there the happiest years of my youth were spent. There were eight or nine boys in the neighborhood and the noise we made together, playing soldiers or cowboys and Indians, was deafening. Making trails in the high grass, and passages with bales of hay in a nearby barn, sometimes frightened us, when other boys tried to block the tunnels with hay. On our porch was an old fashioned swing which was soon broken by pulling out the hooks in the ceiling holding the chains.

At Halloween we were very mischievous, for there are memories of pushing over out-houses, including once when someone was inside. Placing 22 caliber bullets on streetcar tracks to hear them explode, soaping windows, filling cans with water or urine and connecting them with string so a person would trip on them and spill; these were ideas of fun. There was no trick-or-treat, only tricks, and for the fourth of July firecrackers were many and varied, including carbide put in a large can with water, with a small hole in the side, ignited by match, with resulting flight of the can sky-high.

Being fascinated with wars, I constantly played with small iron soldiers. After learning to read, at first it was about Greece and Rome, but since the toy soldiers carried guns rather than spears, it was necessary to turn to American history as a model. Confederate general Stonewall Jackson became a hero, after reading a biography about him, and I tried to duplicate events in the book with toys.

We always had walked to school, but when moved again to the German part of town on 1423 Fairchild St., high school was over two miles away, and sometimes we rode by street car. Across the street was a German Lutheran church, and to practice high school German language classes I began to attend Sunday school, and was even confirmed there. None of the others in the family, however, attended church. Father professed to be a Unitarian, while there was no Swedish Lutheran church in town for mother. Bill had joined the Boy Scouts, and became a Life Scout, while I only attained first class, not acquiring enough merit badges to even make Star scout. Camping in tents was exciting for us and we acted together. Both of us went swimming in the YMCA and, like our father, were interested in football, although we were never on a team.

The first year in High School I slipped in the swimming pool and had to have stitches on the back of my head. Later I used this as an excuse for any stupid action or statement I made. Also a bully called Mike, who persisted in snapping his towel at the bottoms of boys in the locker room, became an enemy. Once I became angry and threw him to the floor, after which he swore he would get even with his gang. For several years I lived in fear of being attacked by his gang. Such gangs did exist in small US towns in the 1930s.

In High School extra curricular activities included a debating club, the school newspaper called Maroon and White, and also the year book, both of which required much writing. Also both Bill and I continued to work at the theaters after school, now usually selling tickets in the box office. Since there was no ticket-taker the tickets were simply torn up, and the entrance had to be guarded from kids trying to sneak into the theater without paying. It was quite a responsibility, which was annoying since reading instead of watching was what I wanted to do. In my Junior year in High School Bill, who had graduated, attended the Danville Junior College, which only lasted the two years he was there. After high school it was fun to go to the college to read books, most of which had been donated, but it could not survive financially because of lack of support. In 1935 Bill and I went to the University of Illinois in Champaign-Urbana , some 35 miles away. We hitchhiked rides or went by interurban, and every week-end we both returned to work in the theaters. We lived together in one room in the house of Mrs. Wright, next to where we had formerly lived in Champaign. Other boys resident in the house were tough Physical Education majors who looked down on the softies until they had to learn fencing. We took our meals at home and Mrs. Wright was a good cook. My chosen sport was fencing which brought a varsity letter for épée or dueling sword in the senior year.

In our family only Bill drove, and he was our chauffeur with a second-hand black Dodge, which we bought in 1934 for about $200, followed by a 34 Nash car in 1936. Then as now used cars were much cheaper than new cars, but they lasted little more than a few years or low mileage.

Since German language classes continued in college, readings of Hitler's Mein Kampf were countered by opposition books, such as Edith Lorand's Sein Kampf. So at fifteen years of age the impending tragedy of war in Europe was foreseen by our refugee teacher and imparted to his students. It was also obvious that the Republican side of the Spanish Civil War should be supported. This applied only to the university, for at that time in the Mid-West the spirit of isolationism was dominant, as well as a scorn for the affairs and people of Europe. In a small town one hardly dared to speak a foreign language in public, and pejoratives for such persons were rife. The French were Frogs, Italians were Dagoes or Wops, Czechs were Bohunks, Germans Krauts, Jews Kykes, Chinese Chinks, Dumb Swedes, while other nationalities were virtually nonexistent. The now forbidden n-word was common for Afro-Americans, while Jews were blamed for the economic depression of the thirties. All in all it was not a pleasant atmosphere for foreigners, or even outsiders to the closed society of small towns. College towns, however, seemed to be small oases of reason in this part of the country.

Summer camp Custer was near Battle Creek, Michigan in 1939, and the routine of peeling potatoes, washing dishes and picking up trash did not endear one to the army, although night maneuvers and climbing telephone poles to string wire for the Signal Corps were intended to toughen the ROTC students.

Because of interest in Oriental history, which had started in High School with the book Tamerlane, the Earth Shaker, in the summer of 1938 1 went to the unique Near Eastern Summer School at Princeton University, and there began my life's career. Arabic was studied with Philip Hitti, Turkish with Walter L. Wright, president of Robert College in Istanbul, and Islamic art with Aga Oglu. Hitti, a Maronite from Lebanon had us memorize verses of the Quran and stand up to recite them, which helped me on numerous occasions in the Orient. Thus passed my years before leaving my home town for graduate study at Harvard.

Index

A

Abadan, 12, 54, 65, 75, 109
Ackerman, Phyllis, 221
Afshar, Iraj, 114, 314
Aga Khan, Karim, 149
Aga Khan, Sadruddin, 149
Aini, Kamol ad-Din, 233, 288, 293, 297, 311
Al-Ahmad, Jalal, 103
Alborz College, 53
Alexander the Great, 126
Andarz Nameh, 113, 146, 148
Andropov, 269
ARAMCO, 13
Arberry, Arthur, 95, 207, 228
Armenian, 91, 130, 132, 146, 156, 157, 158, 180, 182, 183, 208, 219, 234, 257, 267, 286
Asia Institute, 217, 219, 221, 222, 225, 226, 236, 239, 253, 255
Avery, Peter, 188
Avestan, 185
Azores, 77

B

Badakhshi, 34
Bahai, 101
Balkh, 44, 45, 50
Baluchistan, 14, 37, 122, 125, 126, 133, 238, 260
Bani-Sadr, A., 267
Basra, 12
Batavia, 6
Begin, Menachim, 11
Beheshti, Ayatallah, 217
Beijing, 87, 275, 276, 277, 278, 279, 281, 285, 314

Bliss, Robert, 81, 189
Bodh Raj Marjwah, 19
Borujerdi, Ayatallah, 129
Boyce, Mary, 95, 96
Buddha, 19, 42, 50, 212, 232, 251, 272
Bukhara, 5, 72, 91, 102, 151, 153, 158, 161, 163, 164, 165, 166, 167, 168, 289, 292, 298, 306, 307, 311, 315
Byzantine, 70, 71, 74, 81, 84, 189, 210

C

Capetown, 8, 9
Casablanca, 77
Caucasus, 5, 21, 27, 53, 55, 152, 165, 204, 243, 257, 258, 259, 296, 301, 302, 304
Central Asia, 2, 3, 19, 21, 33, *passim*
Chang Kai-Shek, 17
Chishti, Maudud, 136
Choksy, Jamsheed, 272
Chubak, Sadeq, 104, 109, 131
CIA, 100, 183
Corbin, Henry, 68, 93, 178
Ctesiphon, 12

D

DeGaulle, C., 47
Dehkhuda, Ali Akbar, 131, 143
Dhahran, 13, 179

Dugin, Lucien, 33
Dulles, John Foster, 143
Dushanbe, 202, 203, 204, 205, 220, *passim*

E

Eisenhower, President, 143
Enver Pasha, 72

F

Forester, 2

G

Gailani, Rashid al-, 12, 264
Gandharan, 18, 280
Gandhi, M., 32, 37
Ghirshman, Roman, 34, 35, 41, 47, 55, 132, 134, 135, 137, 138, 163, 210, 220
Gluck, Jay, 221, 224, 241, 251
Grabar, Oleg, 150
Grozny, 296, 304

H

Habibiya, 2, 6, 26, 27, 46, 58, 61, 63
Hackin, Josef, 33
Hartog, Jan der, 7
Hashim Khan, 26, 32
Hedayat, Sadeq, 109
Henning, Walter B., 90, 94, 95, 112, 147, 148, 178, 209
Hikmatyar, Gulbedin, 264, 267
Hindko, 18
Hitti, Philip, 3
Hitler, Adolf, 16, 60, 178, 288

I

Imam Reza, 33, 51, 319
Indonesia, 7
Ingush, 40, 301, 302
Iranzamin, 239

Isfahan, 106, 109, 116, 117, 127, 128, 129, 141, 143, 224, 234, 238, 241, 244, 278, 298, 317, 322
Istiqlal, 26, 31

J

Jerusalem, 10, 11, 190, 269
Judeo-Persian, 137

K

Kabul, 2, 5, 6, 8, 12, 15, 17, 18, 19, 20, *passim*
Karabagh, 49
Karim Aga Khan, 149, 150
Karim Khan Zand, 106
Karnak, 75
Kashani, Ayatallah, 120, 144, 145
Kazakhs, 19, 36, 211, 281, 282
Kevorkian, Hagop, 138, 139, 140, 141, 142, 146, 147, 148
Khanlari, Parviz, 108, 130
Khatami, Mohammad, 319, 322
Khiva, 298, 315
Khomeini, Ayatollah, 128, 265, 267, 268, 270, 271, 319, 320
Khyber Pass, 18, 20, 21, 31, 58, 59
King David Hotel, 11
King Farouq, 56, 139
Kipling, 2, 254
Kissinger, Henry, 102, 103, 190
Köprülü, Faud, 68, 71, 73, 74
Kyrgyz, 18, 257

L

Lahore, 2, 14, 31, 36, 37, 57, 64, 192, 252
Landi Khana, 21
Landi Kotal, 21
Lentz, Wolfgang, 189, 213, 216, 217
Luxor, 75

M

Malalay, 27
Malyan Tepe, 240
Manichaeism, 286
Marv Dasht, 240
Mazar-e Sharif, 43, 44
Meshhed, 12, 33, 50, 51, 52, 57, 104, 106, 107, 120, 133, 141, 162, 207, 232, 260, 261, 321
Metropolitan Museum, 57, 139, 278, 307
Minovi, Mojtaba, 141, 147, 148
Mitra Film, 72
Mo'in, Mohammad, 130
Moayyad, Heshmat, 188
Montazeri, Ayatallah, 270
Mossadegh, Mohammad, 130, 138, 143, 144, 145, 148, 178
Mount Kazbek, 302
Muhammad Zaman Khan, 135

N

NAASR, 183, 208, 286
Nader Shah, 38
Nafisi, Sa'id, 108, 130, 205
Nahavandi, Houchang, 221, 224, 231, 241, 243, 251
Naqsh-e Rustam, 106
Naranjestan, 222, 224, 226, 240, 255
Nasr, Seyyed Hosein, 129
Nazis, 26, 47, 53, 57, 180
Nejat, 25, 289
New Delhi, 2, 37
noruz, 40, 259, 261
Nur Mohammed Taraqi, 263

O

Old Persian, 95, 185

P

Pahlbod, 265
Palestine, 54, 55, 66, 75, 88
Parthian, 121, 124, 132, 137, 163, 282, 308
Pasargadae, 76, 241
Pathans, 19, 38, 264
Peabody Museum, 87, 102
Pearl Harbor, 5, 17, 80
Persepolis, 76, 106, 128, 198, 236, 243
Persian Gulf, 13, 95, 107, 237, 241
Peshawar, 1, 2, 3, 14, 15, 19, 20, 21, 22, 31, 35, 39, 47, 57, 59, 63, 64, 145, 212, 264, 266, 267, 280
Pope, Arthur Upham, 146, 219, 221, 232, 239, 322
Pusey, Nathan, 172, 181, 182, 192
Pushtuns, 18, 32, 63, 211, 212, 269
Pushtunwali, 18

Q

Qabus Nameh, 113, 146
Qashghai, 107, 240
Qotbi, 236, 243

R

Rather, Dan, 266
Rescher, Osman, 67
Reza Shah, 2, 107, 115, 120, 132, 134, 144, 145, 244
Ritter, Helmut, 67, 72, 75, 177
Rockefeller Foundation, 100, 192
Romanoff, 46
Roosevelt, Franklin D., 4, 16, 68, 100
Roosevelt, Kermit, 99

S

Saddam Husain, 271
Samarkand, 162, 164, 165, 166, 167, 168, 169, 203, 205, 212, 283, 288, 289, 290, 298, 311, 314, 315

SAVAK, 241, 243
Schimmel, Annemarie, 193, 213
Shafa, Shoja ed-Din, 217, 230, 255, 265
Shahbazi, Shapur, A., 225, 243
Shi'ite, 186, 241, 320
Shiraz, 106, 107, 108, 121, 128, 129, 141, 143, 204, 205, 217, 219, *passim*
Signal Corps, 4, 23, 79
Sinai, 10
Skjaervø, Prods Oktor, 288
SOAS, 99
Society of Fellows, 91, 92
Soviet Union, 19, 29, 81, 142, 152, 154, 156, 158, 161, 162, 168, *passim*
Spuler, Berthold, 213, 218
St. Petersburg, 84, 155, 187, 309
Stalin, 62, 69, 82, 93, 112, 145, 152, 154, 158, 169, 175, 176, 177, 199, 235, 258, 268, 288, 293
Stalingrad, 5
Stronach, David, 241
Suez, 5, 6, 8, 10, 54, 271
Sülemaniye, 68
Sultan ben Saqir al-Qasim, 13

T

Taj Mahal, 64
Tajiks, 19, 169, 199, 200, 243, 257, 263, 269, 287, 288, 289, 293, 294, 297
Taliban, 19, 42, 74
Taqizadeh, Hasan, 109, 148
Tehran, 2, 12, 17, 25, 33, 46, 50, 51, 52, 53, 54, 55, 56, 57, 68, 72, 75, 101, *passim*
Tel Aviv, 11, 54
Tiflis, 84, 258, 259, 261
Tilla Tepe, 263
Top Kapï Saray, 71
Topkapï Saray, 68
Tskhinvali, 301, 302
Tudeh, 105, 127, 131, 248

U

Uzbeks, 19, 53, 163, 165, 166, 167, 168, 169, 170, 191, 257, 263, 269, 293

W

Washington, 2, 4, 14, 17, 23, 65, 75, 78, 79, 80, 81, 82, 88, 90, 93, *passim*
Wilber, Donald, 6

Y

Yalta, 69
Yarshater, Ehsan, 148

Z

Zahir Shah, 21, 25, 261
Zoroastrian, 106, 115, 142, 174, 209, 240, 244, 253, 255